BENCHMARK SERIES
Microsoft®
EXCEL
CORE CERTIFICATION

2002

W9-CEI-824

EMCParadigm
PUBLISHING

Pierce College at Puyallup
Puyallup, Washington

NITA RUTKOSKY

Senior Developmental Editor	Sonja M. Brown
Developmental Editor	Tom Modl
Special Projects Coordinator	Joan D'Onofrio
Senior Designer	Jennifer Wreisner
Editorial Assistant	Susan Capecchi
Copy Editor	Sharon O'Donnell
Proofreader	Lynn Reichel
Indexer	Donald Glassman

Publishing Team—George Provol, Publisher; Janice Johnson, Director of Product Development; Tony Galvin, Acquisitions Editor; Lori Landwer, Marketing Manager; Shelley Clubb, Electronic Design and Production Manager

Acknowledgments—The author and publisher wish to thank the following reviewers for their technical and academic assistance in testing exercises and assessing instruction:

- Christie Jahn, Lincoln Land Community College, Springfield, Illinois
- David Parker, St. Charles Community College, St. Charles, Missouri
- Nora Ryan, Montgomery College, Rockville, Maryland

Special thanks to Christie Jahn for preparing Internet Projects and Job Study scenarios as part of the Unit Performance Assessment sections.

Library of Congress Cataloging-in-Publication Data
Rutkosky, Nita Hewitt.
Microsoft Excel 2002: core certification / Nita Rutkosky.
p.cm. – (Benchmark series)
ISBN 0-7638-1445-8 (Text & CD-ROM)
1. Microsoft Excel for Windows. 2. Business—Computer Programs. 3. Electronic spreadsheets. I. Title. II. Benchmark series (Saint Paul, Minn.)

HF5548.4.M523 R882 2002
005.369-dc21
2001040697

Text: ISBN 0-7638-1445-8
Order Number: 05545

© 2002 by Paradigm Publishing Inc.
Published by **EMC**Paradigm
875 Montreal Way
St. Paul, MN 55102

(800) 535-6865
E-mail: educate@emcp.com
Web site: www.emcp.com

CONTENTS

Welcome	vi
Microsoft Office Specialist Certification	viii
Getting Started	GS1
Using Windows 2000	W1
Browsing the Internet Using Internet Explorer	IE1

Core Level Unit 1: Preparing and Formatting a Worksheet — C1

Unit 1 Microsoft Office Specialist Skills	C2

Chapter 1
Preparing an Excel Worksheet — C3

Creating a Worksheet	C3
Entering Data in a Cell	C6
Saving a Workbook	C7
Opening a Workbook	C7
Printing a Workbook	C8
Closing a Workbook and Exiting Excel	C8
Expanding Drop-Down Menus	C8
Completing Computer Exercises	C8
Copying Data Workbooks	C9
Changing the Default Folder	C9
Editing Data in a Cell	C10
Using Automatic Entering Features	C12
Turning On/Off and Maneuvering in the Task Pane	C15
Selecting Cells	C16
Selecting Cells Using the Mouse	C16
Selecting Cells Using the Keyboard	C17
Selecting Data within Cells	C17
Formatting with AutoFormat	C17
Using Help	C19
Getting Help Using the Ask a Question Button	C19
Displaying the Microsoft Excel Help Window	C19
Using Buttons at the Help Window	C19
Using Options at the Expanded Help Window	C20
Getting Help from the Office Assistant	C22
Chapter Summary	*C23*
Commands Review	*C25*
Concepts Check	*C25*
Skills Check	*C26*

Chapter 2
Formatting an Excel Worksheet — C29

Previewing a Worksheet	C29
Changing the Zoom Setting	C30
Applying Formatting with Buttons on the Formatting Toolbar	C30
Changing Column Width	C33

Changing Column Width Using Column Boundaries	C33
Changing Column Width at the Column Width Dialog Box	C35
Changing Row Height	C37
Changing Row Height Using Row Boundaries	C37
Changing Row Height at the Row Height Dialog Box	C38
Formatting Data in Cells	C39
Formatting Numbers	C39
Aligning, Indenting, and Rotating Data in Cells	C43
Changing the Font at the Format Cells Dialog Box	C46
Inserting/Deleting Cells, Rows, and Columns	C48
Inserting Rows	C48
Inserting Columns	C49
Deleting Cells, Rows, or Columns	C50
Clearing Data in Cells	C50
Adding Borders and Shading to Cells	C51
Adding Shading and a Pattern to Cells	C54
Repeating the Last Action	C55
Formatting with Format Painter	C56
Chapter Summary	*C58*
Commands Review	*C59*
Concepts Check	*C59*
Skills Check	*C60*

Chapter 3
Inserting Formulas in a Worksheet — C63

Using the AutoSum Button	C63
Writing Formulas with Mathematical Operators	C65
Copying a Formula with Relative Cell References	C65
Copying Formulas with the Fill Handle	C66
Writing a Formula by Pointing	C67
Using the Trace Error Button	C68
Inserting a Formula with the Insert Function Button	C70
Writing Formulas with Functions	C72
Writing Formulas with Statistical Functions	C72
Writing Formulas with Financial Functions	C76
Writing Formulas with Date and Time Functions	C78
Writing a Formula with the IF Logical Function	C80
Using Absolute and Mixed Cell References in Formulas	C82
Using an Absolute Cell Reference in a Formula	C83
Using a Mixed Cell Reference in a Formula	C84

Chapter Summary	C85
Commands Review	C86
Concepts Check	C86
Skills Check	C87

Chapter 4
Enhancing a Worksheet — C91

Formatting a Worksheet Page	C91
Controlling the Page Layout	C92
Inserting Headers/Footers	C95
Changing Worksheet Margins	C96
Centering a Worksheet Horizontally and/or Vertically	C97
Inserting and Removing Page Breaks	C98
Printing Column and Row Titles on Multiple Pages	C100
Printing Gridlines and Row and Column Headings	C102
Hiding and Unhiding Workbook Elements	C103
Printing a Specific Area of a Worksheet	C103
Changing Print Quality	C103
Customizing Print Jobs	C104
Completing a Spelling Check	C106
Using Undo and Redo	C106
Finding and Replacing Data in a Worksheet	C108
Finding and Replacing Cell Formatting	C110
Sorting Data	C112
Sorting Data Using Buttons on the Standard Toolbar	C112
Sorting Data at the Sort Dialog Box	C113
Sorting More than One Column	C114
Filtering Lists	C115
Planning a Worksheet	C118
Chapter Summary	C119
Commands Review	C120
Concepts Check	C121
Skills Check	C122

Core Level Unit 1
Performance Assessment — C125

Assessing Proficiency	C125
Writing Activities	C129
Internet Project	C130
Job Study	C130

Core Level Unit 2: Maintaining and Enhancing Workbooks — C131

Unit 2 Microsoft Office Specialist Skills	C132

Chapter 5
Moving Data within and between Workbooks — C133

Moving, Copying, and Pasting Cells	C133
Moving Selected Cells	C134
Copying Selected Cells	C135
Using the Office Clipboard	C136
Creating a Workbook with Multiple Worksheets	C137
Printing a Workbook Containing Multiple Worksheets	C138
Managing Worksheets	C139
Splitting a Worksheet into Windows and Freezing and Unfreezing Panes	C140
Working with Ranges	C143
Working with Windows	C144
Opening Multiple Workbooks	C144
Closing Multiple Workbooks	C145
Arranging Workbooks	C145
Sizing and Moving Workbooks	C147
Moving, Copying, and Pasting Data	C148
Linking Data between Worksheets	C149
Linking Worksheets with a 3-D Reference	C151
Copying and Pasting a Worksheet between Programs	C152
Chapter Summary	C153
Commands Review	C155
Concepts Check	C155
Skills Check	C156

Chapter 6
Maintaining Workbooks — C161

Maintaining Workbooks	C161
Creating a Folder	C162
Selecting Workbooks	C163
Deleting Workbooks and Folders	C164
Deleting to the Recycle Bin	C165
Copying Files	C165
Sending Workbooks to a Different Drive or Folder	C167
Cutting and Pasting a Workbook	C167
Renaming Workbooks	C168
Deleting a Folder and Its Contents	C169
Opening and Closing Workbooks	C169
Printing Workbooks	C170
Managing Worksheets	C170
Copying a Worksheet to Another Workbook	C170
Moving a Worksheet to Another Workbook	C171
Renaming a Worksheet	C172
Saving a Workbook in a Different Format	C173
Searching for Specific Workbooks	C174
Formatting with Styles	C175
Defining a Style	C176
Applying a Style	C177
Copying Styles to Another Workbook	C179
Removing a Style	C179
Deleting a Style	C180

Inserting Comments   C181
   Inserting a Comment   C181
   Displaying a Comment   C181
   Printing a Comment   C182
   Editing and Deleting a Comment   C183
Creating and Responding to Web
   Discussion Comments   C184
Using Excel Templates   C185
   Entering Data in a Template   C185
Chapter Summary   *C187*
Commands Review   *C189*
Concepts Check   *C189*
Skills Check   *C190*

Chapter 7
Creating a Chart in Excel   C193

Creating a Chart   C193
   Printing Only the Chart   C197
   Previewing a Chart   C197
   Creating a Chart in a Separate
    Worksheet   C198
Deleting a Chart   C199
Sizing and Moving a Chart   C199
Changing the Chart Type   C200
   Choosing a Custom Chart Type   C202
Changing Data in Cells   C203
Changing the Data Series   C204
Adding Chart Elements   C206
   Moving/Sizing Chart Elements   C208
   Deleting/Removing Chart Elements   C208
   Adding Gridlines   C209
Formatting Chart Elements   C210
   Changing Element Colors   C213
Chapter Summary   *C214*
Commands Review   *C215*
Concepts Check   *C216*
Skills Check   *C216*

Chapter 8
Enhancing the Display of Workbooks   C219

Creating a Web Page   C219
   Saving a Workbook as a Web Page   C219
   Previewing a Workbook in Web
    Page Preview   C220
   Creating Hyperlinks   C220
Inserting Images in a Workbook   C223
   Narrowing a Search   C224
   Sizing an Image   C225
   Moving and Deleting an Image   C225
   Formatting Images with Buttons
    on the Picture Toolbar   C226
   Downloading Images from the
    Microsoft Design Gallery Live
    Web Site   C228
Creating WordArt   C228
   Entering Text   C229
   Sizing and Moving WordArt   C230
   Customizing WordArt   C232
Drawing Shapes, Lines, and Autoshapes   C235
   Drawing Shapes   C235
   Adding Fill Color   C236
   Changing Line Color   C236
   Aligning Objects   C236
   Drawing Lines   C238
   Creating Autoshapes   C239
   Flipping and Rotating an Object   C239
Chapter Summary   *C241*
Commands Review   *C242*
Concepts Check   *C242*
Skills Check   *C243*

Core Unit 2
Performance Assessment   C247

Assessing Proficiency   C247
Writing Activities   C251
Internet Project   C253
Job Study   C253

Index   C254

WELCOME

You are about to begin working with a textbook that is part of the Benchmark Office XP Series. The word *Benchmark* in the title holds a special significance in terms of *what* you will learn and *how* you will learn. *Benchmark*, according to *Webster's Dictionary*, means "something that serves as a standard by which others may be measured or judged." In this text, you will learn the Microsoft Office Specialist skills required for certification on the Core and/or Expert level of one or more major applications within the Office XP suite. These skills are benchmarks by which you will be evaluated, should you choose to take one or more certification exams.

The design and teaching approach of this textbook also serve as a benchmark for instructional materials on software programs. Features and commands are presented in a clear, straightforward way, and each short section of instruction is followed by an exercise that lets you practice using the new feature. Gradually, as you move through each chapter, you will build your skills to the point of mastery. At the end of a chapter, you are offered the opportunity to demonstrate your newly acquired competencies—to prove you have met the benchmarks for using the Office suite or an individual program. At the completion of the text, you are well on your way to becoming a successful computer user.

EMCParadigm's Office XP Benchmark Series includes textbooks on Office XP, Word 2002, Excel 2002, Access 2002, PowerPoint 2002, Publisher 2002, Outlook 2002, and FrontPage 2002. Note that the programs include the year 2002 in their name, while the suite itself is called Office XP (for "experience"). Each book includes a Student CD, which contains prekeyed documents and files required for completing the exercises. A CD icon and folder name displayed on the opening page of each chapter indicates that you need to copy a folder of files from the CD before beginning the chapter exercises. *(See the inside back cover for instructions on copying a folder.)*

Introducing Microsoft Office XP

Microsoft Office XP, released in May 2001, is a suite of programs designed to improve productivity and efficiency in workplace, school, and home settings. A suite is a group of programs that are sold as a package and are designed to be used together, making it possible to exchange files among the programs. The major applications included in Office are Word, a word processing program; Excel, a spreadsheet program; Access, a database management program; PowerPoint, a slide presentation program; and Outlook, a desktop information management program.

Using the Office suite offers significant advantages over working with individual programs developed by different software vendors. The programs in the Office suite use similar toolbars, buttons, icons, and menus, which means that once you learn the basic features of one program, you can use those same features in the other programs. This easy transfer of knowledge decreases the learning time and allows you to concentrate on the unique commands and options within each program. The compatibility of the programs creates seamless integration of data within and between programs and lets the operator use the program most appropriate for the required tasks.

The number of programs in the Office XP suite varies by the package, or edition. Four editions are available:

- **Standard:** Word, Excel, Outlook, PowerPoint
- **Professional:** Word, Excel, Outlook, PowerPoint, and Access
- **Professional Special Edition:** All Professional package programs plus FrontPage, Publisher, and SharePoint. This edition is available only for a limited time and only to current Office users.
- **Developer:** All Professional package programs (except SharePoint) plus Developer tools

New Features in Office XP

Users of previous editions of Office will find that the essential features that have made Office popular still form the heart of the suite. New enhancements focus on collaboration, or the ability for multiple users to work together on the same document from different locations over the Internet. Another highlight is the Smart Tag feature, which is an icon that when clicked offers a list of commands that are especially useful for the particular job being done. In Excel, for example, a Smart Tag might offer the ability to update a formula or edit an error. A more comprehensive kind of targeted assistance is offered in a new Task Pane, which is a narrow window that appears at the right of the screen to display commands relevant to the current task. Speech recognition technology is available with this edition, offering users the ability to dictate text into any Office program. This feature must be installed separately.

Structure of the Benchmark Textbooks

Users of the Core Certification texts and the complete application textbooks may begin their course with an overview of computer hardware and software, offered in the *Getting Started* section at the beginning of the book. Your instructor may also ask you to complete the *Windows 2000* and the *Internet Explorer* sections so you become familiar with the computer's operating system and the essential tools for using the Internet.

Instruction on the major programs within the Office suite is presented in units of four chapters each. Both the Core and Expert levels contain two units, which culminate with performance assessments to check your knowledge and skills. Each chapter contains the following sections:

- performance objectives that identify specifically what you are expected to learn
- instructional text that introduces and explains new concepts and features
- step-by-step, hands-on exercises following each section of instruction
- a chapter summary
- a knowledge self-check called Concepts Check
- skill assessment exercises called Skills Check

Exercises offered at the end of units provide writing and research opportunities that will strengthen your performance in other college courses as well as on the job. The final activities simulate interesting projects you could encounter in the workplace.

Benchmark Series Ancillaries

The Benchmark Series includes some important resources that will help you succeed in your computer applications courses:

Online Resource Center

Internet Resource Centers hosted by EMC/Paradigm provide additional material for students and teachers using the Benchmark books. Online you will find Web links, updates to textbooks, study tips, quizzes and assignments, and supplementary projects.

Class Connection

Available for both the WebCT and Blackboard e-learning platforms, EMC/Paradigm's Class Connection is a course management tool for traditional and distance learning. The Class Connection allows students to access the course syllabus and assignment schedule online, provides self-quizzes and study aids, and facilitates communication among students and instructors via e-mail and e-discussions.

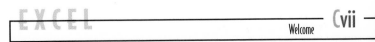

MICROSOFT OFFICE SPECIALIST CERTIFICATION

**Approved
Courseware**

What Does This Logo Mean?

It means this courseware has been approved by the Microsoft® Office Specialist Program to be among the finest available for learning Microsoft Excel 2002. It also means that upon completion of this courseware, you may be prepared to become a Microsoft Office Specialist.

What Is a Microsoft Office Specialist?

A Microsoft Office Specialist is an individual who has certified his or her skills in one or more of the Microsoft Office desktop applications of Microsoft Word, Microsoft Excel, Microsoft PowerPoint®, Microsoft Outlook® or Microsoft Access, or in Microsoft Project. The Microsoft Office Specialist Program typically offers certification exams at the "Core" and "Expert" skill levels.* The Microsoft Office Specialist Program is the only Microsoft approved program in the world for certifying proficiency in Microsoft Office desktop applications and Microsoft Project. This certification can be a valuable asset in any job search or career advancement.

More Information

- To learn more about becoming a Microsoft Office Specialist, visit www.mous.net.
- To purchase a Microsoft Office Specialist certification exam, visit www.DesktopIQ.com.
- To learn about other Microsoft Office Specialist approved courseware from EMC/Paradigm, visit www.emcp.com/college_division/office_specialist_ready.php.

EMC/Paradigm Publishing is independent from Microsoft Corporation, and not affiliated with Microsoft in any manner. This textbook may be used in assisting students to prepare for a Microsoft Office Specialist Exam. Neither Microsoft, its designated program administrator or courseware reviewer, nor EMC/Paradigm Publishing warrants that use of this textbook will ensure passing the relevant exam.

---

* The availability of Microsoft Office Specialist certification exams varies by application, application version and language. Visit www.mous.net for exam availability.

Microsoft and the Microsoft Office Logo are trademarks or registered trademarks of Microsoft Corporation in the United States and/or other countries and the Microsoft Office Specialist Logo is used under license from owner.

 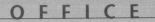

GETTING STARTED IN OFFICE XP

In this textbook, you will learn to operate several microcomputer application programs that combine to make an application "suite." This suite of programs is called Microsoft Office XP. The programs you will learn to operate are the *software*, which include instructions telling the computer what to do. Some of the software programs in the suite include a word processing program called *Word*, a spreadsheet program called *Excel*, a presentation program called *PowerPoint*, and a database program called *Access*.

Identifying Computer Hardware

The computer equipment you will use to operate the suite of programs is referred to as *hardware*. You will need access to a microcomputer system that should consist of the CPU, monitor, keyboard, printer, disk drives, and mouse. If you are not sure what equipment you will be operating, check with your instructor. The computer system displayed in figure G.1 consists of six components. Each component is discussed separately in the material that follows.

FIGURE

G.1 *Microcomputer System*

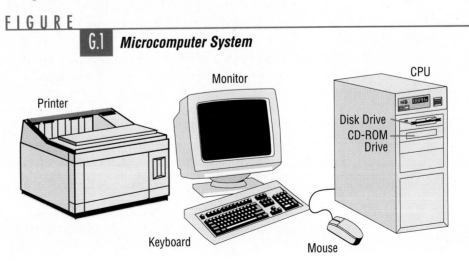

CPU

CPU stands for Central Processing Unit and is the intelligence of the computer. All the processing occurs in the CPU. Silicon chips, which contain miniaturized circuitry, are placed on boards that are plugged into slots within the CPU. Whenever an instruction is given to the computer, that instruction is processed through circuitry in the CPU.

Monitor

The monitor is a piece of equipment that looks like a television screen. It displays the information of a program and the text being input at the keyboard. The quality of display for monitors varies depending on the type of monitor and the type of resolution. Monitors can also vary in size—generally from 14-inch size up to 21-inch size or larger.

Keyboard

The keyboard is used to input information into the computer. Keyboards for microcomputers vary in the number and location of the keys. Microcomputers have the alphabetic and numeric keys in the same location as the keys on a typewriter. The symbol keys, however, may be placed in a variety of locations, depending on the manufacturer. In addition to letters, numbers, and symbols, most microcomputer keyboards contain function keys, arrow keys, and a numeric keypad. Figure G.2 shows an enhanced keyboard.

F I G U R E

G.2 *Microcomputer Enhanced Keyboard*

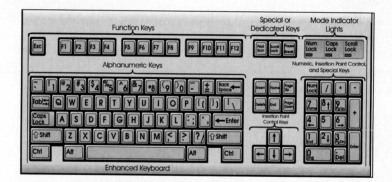

The 12 keys at the top of the enhanced keyboard, labeled with the letter F followed by a number, are called *function keys*. These keys can be used to perform functions within each of the suite programs. To the right of the regular keys is a group of *special* or *dedicated keys*. These keys are labeled with specific functions that will be performed when you press the key. Below the special keys are arrow keys. These keys are used to move the insertion point in the document screen.

In the upper right corner of the keyboard are three mode indicator lights. When certain modes have been selected, a light appears on the keyboard. For example, if you press the Caps Lock key, which disables the lowercase alphabet, a light appears next to Caps Lock. Similarly, pressing the Num Lock key will disable the special functions on the numeric keypad, which is located at the right side of the keyboard.

Disk Drives

Depending on the computer system you are using, Microsoft Office XP is installed on a hard drive or as part of a network system. Whether you are using

Office on a hard drive or network system, you will need to have available a CD drive and a floppy disk drive. You will insert the CD (Compact Disk) that accompanies this textbook in the CD drive and then copy folders from the CD to a disk in the floppy disk drive. You will also save documents you complete at the computer to folders on your disk in the floppy drive.

Printer

When you create a document in Word, it is considered *soft copy*. If you want a *hard copy* of a document, you need to print it. To print documents you will need to access a printer, which will probably be either a laser printer or an ink-jet printer. A laser printer uses a laser beam combined with heat and pressure to print documents while an ink-jet printer prints a document by spraying a fine mist of ink on the page.

Mouse

Many functions in the suite of programs are designed to operate more efficiently with a *mouse*. A mouse is an input device that sits on a flat surface next to the computer. A mouse can be operated with the left or the right hand. Moving the mouse on the flat surface causes a corresponding mouse pointer to move on the screen. Figure G.1 shows an illustration of a mouse.

Using the Mouse

The programs in the Microsoft Office suite can be operated using a keyboard or they can be operated with the keyboard and a mouse. The mouse may have two or three buttons on top, which are tapped to execute specific functions and commands. To use the mouse, rest it on a flat surface or a mouse pad. Put your hand over it with your palm resting on top of the mouse and your wrist resting on the table surface. As you move the mouse on the flat surface, a corresponding pointer moves on the screen.

When using the mouse, there are four terms you should understand—point, click, double-click, and drag. When operating the mouse, you may need to *point* to a specific command, button, or icon. Point means to position the mouse pointer on the desired item. With the mouse pointer positioned on the desired item, you may need to *click* a button on the mouse. Click means quickly tapping a button on the mouse once. To complete two steps at one time, such as choosing and then executing a function, *double-click* a mouse button. Double-click means to tap the left mouse button twice in quick succession. The term *drag* means to press and hold the left mouse button, move the mouse pointer to a specific location, and then release the button.

Using the Mouse Pointer

The mouse pointer will change appearance depending on the function being performed or where the pointer is positioned. The mouse pointer may appear as one of the following images:

The mouse pointer appears as an I-beam (called the *I-beam pointer*) in the document screen and can be used to move the insertion point or select text.

The mouse pointer appears as an arrow pointing up and to the left (called the *arrow pointer*) when it is moved to the Title bar, Menu bar, or one of the toolbars at the top of the screen or when a dialog box is displayed. For example, to open a new document with the mouse, you would move the I-beam pointer to the File option on the Menu bar. When the I-beam pointer is moved to the Menu bar, it turns into an arrow pointer. To make a selection, position the tip of the arrow pointer on the File option, and then click the left mouse button. At the drop-down menu that displays, make selections by positioning the arrow pointer on the desired option, and then clicking the left mouse button.

The mouse pointer becomes a double-headed arrow (either pointing left and right, pointing up and down, or pointing diagonally) when performing certain functions such as changing the size of an object.

In certain situations, such as moving an object or image, the mouse pointer becomes a four-headed arrow. The four-headed arrow means that you can move the object left, right, up, or down.

When a request is being processed or when a program is being loaded, the mouse pointer may appear with an hourglass beside it. The hourglass image means "please wait." When the process is completed, the hourglass image is removed.

The mouse pointer displays as a hand with a pointing index finger in certain functions such as Help and indicates that more information is available about the item.

Choosing Commands

Once a program is open, several methods can be used in the program to choose commands. A command is an instruction that tells the program to do something. You can choose a command with one of the following methods:

- Click a toolbar button with the mouse
- Choose a command from a menu
- Use shortcut keys
- Use a shortcut menu

Choosing Commands on Toolbars

When a program such as Word or PowerPoint is open, several toolbars containing buttons for common tasks are available. In many of the suite programs, two toolbars are visible on the screen. One toolbar is called the Standard toolbar; the other is referred to as the Formatting toolbar. To choose a command from a toolbar, position the tip of the arrow pointer on a button, and then click the left mouse button. For example, to print the file currently displayed in the screen, position the tip of the arrow pointer on the Print button on the Standard toolbar, and then click the left mouse button.

Choosing Commands on the Menu Bar

Each of the suite programs contains a Menu bar that displays toward the top of the screen. This Menu bar contains a variety of options you can use to perform functions and commands on data. Functions are grouped logically into options, which display on the Menu bar. For example, features to work with files are grouped in the File option. Either the mouse or the keyboard can be used to make choices from the Menu bar or make a choice at a dialog box.

To use the mouse to make a choice from the Menu bar, move the I-beam pointer to the Menu bar. This causes the I-beam pointer to display as an arrow pointer. Position the tip of the arrow pointer on the desired option, and then click the left mouse button.

To use the keyboard, press the Alt key to make the Menu bar active. Options on the Menu bar display with an underline below one of the letters. To choose an option from the Menu bar, key the underlined letter of the desired option, or move the insertion point with the left or right arrow keys to the option desired, and then press Enter. This causes a drop-down menu to display.

For example, to display the File drop-down menu in Word as shown in figure G.3 using the mouse, position the arrow pointer on File on the Menu bar, and then click the left mouse button. To display the File drop-down menu with the keyboard, press the Alt key, and then key the letter F for File.

FIGURE

G.3 Word File Drop-Down Menu

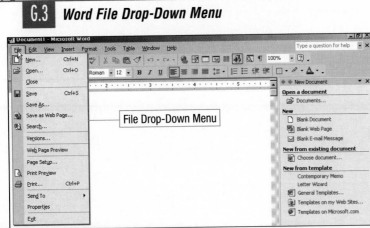

Choosing Commands from Drop-Down Menus

To choose a command from a drop-down menu with the mouse, position the arrow pointer on the desired option, and then click the left mouse button. At the drop-down menu that displays, move the arrow pointer down the menu to the desired option, and then click the left mouse button.

To make a selection from the drop-down menu with the keyboard, key the underlined letter of the desired option. Once the drop-down menu displays, you do not need to hold down the Alt key with the underlined letter. If you want to close a drop-down menu without making a choice, click in the screen outside the drop-down menu; or, press the Esc key twice.

If an option can be accessed by clicking a button on a toolbar, the button is displayed preceding the option in the drop-down menu. For example, buttons display before the New, Open Save, Save as Web Page, Search, Print Preview, and Print options at the File drop-down menu (see figure G.3).

Some menu options may be gray shaded (dimmed). When an option is dimmed, that option is currently not available. For example, if you choose the Table option on the Menu bar, the Table drop-down menu displays with dimmed options including Merge Cells, Split Cells, and Split Table.

Some menu options are preceded by a check mark. The check mark indicates that the option is currently active. To make an option inactive (turn it off) using the mouse, position the arrow pointer on the option, and then click the left mouse button. To make an option inactive (turn it off) with the keyboard, key the underlined letter of the option.

If an option from a drop-down menu displays followed by an ellipsis (...), a dialog box will display when that option is chosen. A dialog box provides a variety of options to let you specify how a command is to be carried out. For example, if you choose File and then Print from the PowerPoint Menu bar, the Print dialog box displays as shown in figure G.4.

FIGURE

G.4 **PowerPoint Print Dialog Box**

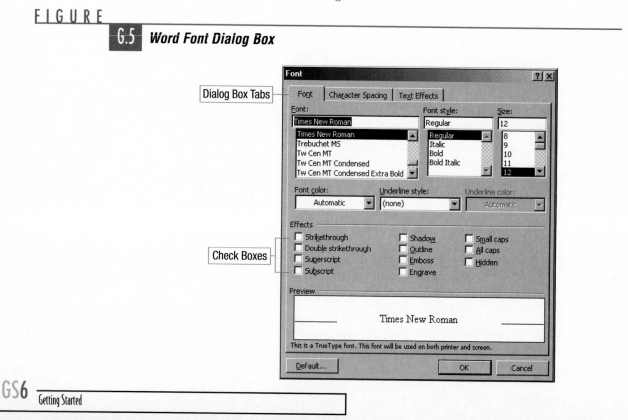

Or, if you choose Format and then Font from the Word Menu bar, the Font dialog box displays as shown in figure G.5.

FIGURE

G.5 **Word Font Dialog Box**

Some dialog boxes provide a set of options. These options are contained on separate tabs. For example, the Font dialog box shown in figure G.5 contains a tab at the top of the dialog box with the word Font on it. Two other tabs display to the right of the Font tab. The tab that displays in the front is the active tab. To make a tab active using the mouse, position the arrow pointer on the desired tab, and then click the left mouse button. If you are using the keyboard, press Ctrl + Tab or press Alt + the underlined letter on the desired tab. For example, to change the tab to Character Spacing in the Font dialog box, click Character Spacing, or press Ctrl + Tab, or press Alt + R.

To choose options from a dialog box with the mouse, position the arrow pointer on the desired option, and then click the left mouse button. If you are using the keyboard, press the Tab key to move the insertion point forward from option to option. Press Shift + Tab to move the insertion point backward from option to option. You can also hold down the Alt key and then press the underlined letter of the desired option. When an option is selected, it displays either in reverse video (white letters on a dark background) or surrounded by a dashed box called a *marquee*.

A dialog box contains one or more of the following elements: text boxes, list boxes, check boxes, option buttons, spin boxes, and command buttons.

Text Boxes

Some options in a dialog box require text to be entered. For example, the boxes below the Find what and Replace with options at the Excel Find and Replace dialog box shown in figure G.6 are text boxes. In a text box, you key text or edit existing text. Edit text in a text box in the same manner as normal text. Use the left and right arrow keys on the keyboard to move the insertion point without deleting text and use the Delete key or Backspace key to delete text.

FIGURE

G.6 *Excel Find and Replace Dialog Box*

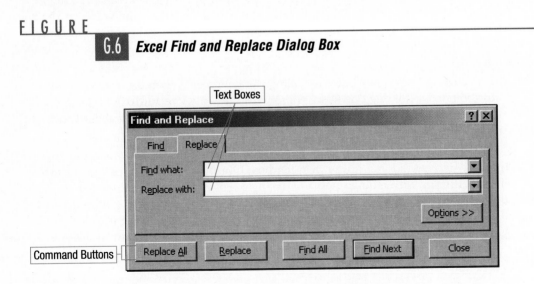

List Boxes

Some dialog boxes such as the Access Open dialog box shown in figure G.7 may contain a list box. The list of files below the Look in: option is contained in a list box. To make a selection from a list box with the mouse, move the arrow pointer to the desired option, and then click the left mouse button.

G.7 *Access Open Dialog Box*

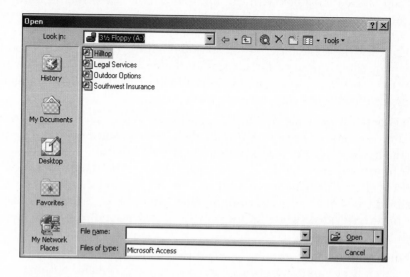

Some list boxes may contain a scroll bar. This scroll bar will display at the right side of the list box (a vertical scroll bar) or at the bottom of the list box (a horizontal scroll bar). Either a vertical scroll bar or a horizontal scroll bar can be used to move through the list if the list is longer than the box. To move down through a list on a vertical scroll bar, position the arrow pointer on the down scroll triangle and hold down the left mouse button. To scroll up through the list in a vertical scroll bar, position the arrow pointer on the up scroll triangle and hold down the left mouse button. You can also move the arrow pointer above the scroll box and click the left mouse button to scroll up the list or move the arrow pointer below the scroll box and click the left mouse button to move down the list. To move through a list with a horizontal scroll bar, click the left scroll triangle to scroll to the left of the list or click the right scroll triangle to scroll to the right of the list.

To make a selection from a list using the keyboard, move the insertion point into the box by holding down the Alt key and pressing the underlined letter of the desired option. Press the up and/or down arrow keys on the keyboard to move through the list.

In some dialog boxes where enough room is not available for a list box, lists of options are inserted in a drop-down list box. Options that contain a drop-down list box display with a down-pointing triangle. For example, the Underline style option at the Word Font dialog box shown in figure G.5 contains a drop-down list. To display the list, click the down-pointing triangle to the right of the Underline style option box. If you are using the keyboard, press Alt + U.

Check Boxes

Some dialog boxes contain options preceded by a box. A check mark may or may not appear in the box. The Word Font dialog box shown in figure G.5 displays a variety of check boxes within the Effects section. If a check mark appears in the box, the option is active (turned on). If there is no check mark in the check box, the option is inactive (turned off).

Any number of check boxes can be active. For example, in the Word Font dialog box, you can insert a check mark in any or all of the boxes in the Effects section and these options will be active.

To make a check box active or inactive with the mouse, position the tip of the arrow pointer in the check box, and then click the left mouse button. If you are using the keyboard, press Alt + the underlined letter of the desired option.

Option Buttons

In the PowerPoint Print dialog box shown in figure G.4, the options in the Print range section are preceded by option buttons. Only one option button can be selected at any time. When an option button is selected, a dark circle displays in the button.

To select an option button with the mouse, position the tip of the arrow pointer inside the option button, and then click the left mouse button. To make a selection with the keyboard, hold down the Alt key, and then press the underlined letter of the desired option.

Spin Boxes

Some options in a dialog box contain measurements or numbers that can be increased or decreased. These options are generally located in a spin box. For example, the Word Paragraph dialog box shown in figure G.8 contains spin boxes located after the Left, Right, Before, and After options. To increase a number in a spin box, position the tip of the arrow pointer on the up-pointing triangle to the right of the desired option, and then click the left mouse button. To decrease the number, click the down-pointing triangle. If you are using the keyboard, press Alt + the underlined letter of the desired option, and then press the up arrow key to increase the number or the down arrow key to decrease the number.

FIGURE

G.8 **Word Paragraph Dialog Box**

Command Buttons

In the Excel Find and Replace dialog box shown in figure G.6, the boxes along the bottom of the dialog box are called *command buttons*. A command button is used to execute or cancel a command. Some command buttons display with an ellipsis (...). A command button that displays with an ellipsis will open another dialog box. To choose a command button with the mouse, position the arrow pointer on the desired button, and then click the left mouse button. To choose a command button with the keyboard, press the Tab key until the desired command button contains the marquee, and then press the Enter key.

Choosing Commands with Shortcut Keys

At the left side of a drop-down menu is a list of options. At the right side, shortcut keys for specific options may display. For example, the shortcut keys to save a document are Ctrl + S and are displayed to the right of the Save option at the File drop-down menu shown in figure G.3. To use shortcut keys to choose a command, hold down the Ctrl key, key the letter for the command, and then release the Ctrl key.

Choosing Commands with Shortcut Menus

The software programs in the suite include menus that contain commands related to the item with which you are working. A shortcut menu appears right where you are working in the document. To display a shortcut menu, click the *right* mouse button or press Shift + F10.

For example, if the insertion point is positioned in a paragraph of text in a Word document, clicking the *right* mouse button or pressing Shift + F10 will cause the shortcut menu shown in figure G.9 to display in the document screen.

FIGURE

G.9 *Word Shortcut Menu*

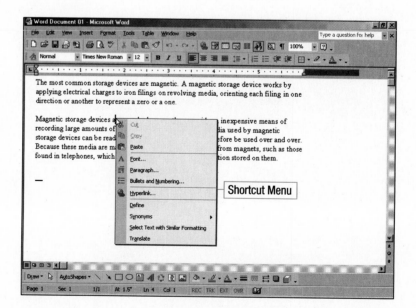

To select an option from a shortcut menu with the mouse, click the desired option. If you are using the keyboard, press the up or down arrow key until the desired option is selected, and then press the Enter key. To close a shortcut menu without choosing an option, click anywhere outside the shortcut menu or press the Esc key.

Working with Multiple Programs

As you learn the various programs in the Microsoft Office suite, you will notice how executing commands in each is very similar. For example, the steps to save, close, and print are virtually the same whether you are working in Word, Excel, or PowerPoint. This consistency between programs greatly enhances a user's ability to easily transfer knowledge learned in one program to another within the suite.

Another appeal of Microsoft Office is the ability to have more than one program open at the same time. For example, you can open Word, create a document, and then open Excel, create a spreadsheet, and copy the spreadsheet into Word.

When a program is open, the name of the program, followed by the file name, displays in a button on the Taskbar. When another program is opened, the program name and file name display in a button that is positioned to the right of the first program button. Figure G.10 shows the Taskbar with Word, Excel, and PowerPoint open. To move from one program to another, all you need to do is click the button on the Taskbar representing the desired program file.

FIGURE

G.10 *Taskbar with Word, Excel, and PowerPoint Open*

| Start | Word Document 01 - Micr... | Microsoft Excel - Excel Wo... | Microsoft PowerPoint... | | | 10:41 AM |

Setting Clicking Options

You can set clicking options for the Windows environment and specify either a double-click or single-click to open a program or file. Steps in this textbook assume that you will double-click to open a file or program. To change from single-click to open (point to select) to double-click to open (single-click to select), complete these steps:

1. At the Windows desktop, click the My Computer icon.
2. At the My Computer window, click Tools on the Menu bar, and then click Folder Options at the drop-down menu.
3. At the Folder Options dialog box with the General tab selected, click the Double-click to open an item (single-click to select) option located in the Click items as follows section.
4. Click the Apply button and then click OK.

Completing Computer Exercises

Some computer exercises in this textbook require that you open an existing file. Exercise files are saved on the CD that accompanies this textbook. The files you need for each chapter are saved in individual folders. Before beginning a chapter, copy the necessary folder from the CD to a preformatted data disk. After completing exercises in a chapter, delete the chapter folder before copying the next chapter folder. (Check with your instructor before deleting a folder.)

Copying a Folder

The CD that accompanies this textbook contains numerous files you use to complete some exercises and assessments in chapters. As you begin working in a chapter, copy the chapter folder from the CD to your disk. (Not every chapter contains a folder on the CD. For example, when completing exercises in the Access chapters, you will copy database files from the Database folder rather than individual chapter folders. This is to ensure that there is adequate space on your disk for saving files.) Copy the chapter folder from the CD to your disk using Windows Explorer by completing the following steps:

1. Insert the CD that accompanies this textbook in the CD drive.
2. Insert a formatted 3.5-inch disk in the disk drive.
3. At the Windows desktop, open Windows Explorer by clicking the Start button, pointing to Programs, pointing to Accessories, and then clicking Windows Explorer.
4. Double-click My Computer in the Folders pane.
5. Double-click the CD drive in the Folders pane (probably displays as OFFICEXP_BENCH followed by the drive letter).
6. Double-click the desired program folder name in the Contents pane. (For example, if you are copying a folder for a core Word chapter, double-click the *Word 2002 Core* folder in the Contents pane.)
7. Click once on the desired chapter subfolder name to select it.
8. Click the Copy To button on the toolbar.
9. At the Browse For Folder dialog box, click *3^1/$_2$ Floppy (A:)* in the list box and then click OK. (If *3^1/$_2$ Floppy (A:)* is not visible, click the plus symbol preceding *My Computer.*)
10. After the folder is copied to your disk, close Windows Explorer by clicking the Close button (contains an X) located in the upper right corner of Windows Explorer.

Deleting a Folder

Before copying a chapter folder onto your disk, delete any previous chapter folders. Do this in Windows Explorer by completing the following steps:

1. Insert your disk in the disk drive.
2. At the Windows desktop, click the Start button on the Taskbar, point to Programs, point to Accessories, and then click Windows Explorer.
3. In Windows Explorer, click the down-pointing triangle at the right side of the Address list box.
4. At the drop-down list that displays, click the drive where your disk is located.
5. Click the chapter folder in the list box.
6. Click the Delete button on the Windows Explorer toolbar.
7. At the message asking if you want to remove the folder and all its contents, click the Yes button.
8. At the message asking if you want to delete a read-only file, click the Yes to All button.
9. Close Windows Explorer by clicking the Close button located in the upper right corner of Windows Explorer.

USING WINDOWS 2000

A computer requires an operating system to provide necessary instructions on a multitude of processes including loading programs, managing data, directing the flow of information to peripheral equipment, and displaying information. Windows 2000 Professional is an operating system that provides functions of this type (along with much more) in a graphical environment. Windows is referred to as a *graphical user interface* (GUI—pronounced *gooey*) that provides a visual display of information with features such as icons (pictures) and buttons. In this introduction you will learn basic features of Windows 2000 Professional.

Before using one of the software programs in the Microsoft Office suite, you will need to start the operating system. To do this, turn on the computer. Depending on your computer equipment configuration, you may also need to turn on the monitor and printer. When the computer is turned on, the Windows 2000 operating system is automatically started and, after a few moments, the desktop will display as shown in figure W.1. (Your desktop may vary from what you see in figure W.1.)

FIGURE

W.1 **Windows 2000 Desktop**

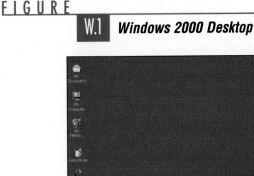

Taskbar

Exploring the Desktop

When Windows 2000 is loaded, the main portion of the screen is called the *desktop*. Think of the desktop in Windows as the top of a desk in an office. A business person places necessary tools—such as pencils, pens, paper, files, calculator—on his or her desktop to perform functions. Like the tools that are located on a desk, the desktop contains tools for operating the computer. These tools are logically grouped and placed in dialog boxes or panels that can be displayed using one of the icons at the left side of the desktop.

The desktop contains a variety of icons and features for using your computer and software programs installed on the computer. The features available on the desktop are described in the following text.

Using Icons

Icons are visual symbols that represent programs, files, or folders. In figure W.2, the figure on the left shows an icon for the Microsoft program Internet Explorer and the figure on the right shows the Windows folder icon. To open a folder or start a program, you double-click the icon.

FIGURE

W.2   *Internet Explorer Icon and Windows Folder*

Using the Taskbar

The bar that displays at the bottom of the desktop (see figure W.1) is called the Taskbar. The Taskbar, shown in figure W.3, is divided into four areas: the Start button, the Quick Launch toolbar, the program button area, and the System tray.

FIGURE

W.3   *Windows 2000 Taskbar*

Start Button | Quick Launch Toolbar | Program Button Area | System Tray

The Start button is located at the left side of the Taskbar. Use this button to start a program, use the Help feature, change settings, and open files. To display the options available with the Start button, position the arrow pointer on the Start button, and then click the left mouse button. This causes a pop-up menu to display, as shown in figure W.4.

FIGURE

W.4 *Start Button Pop-up Menu*

To choose an option from this pop-up menu, move the arrow pointer to the desired option (referred to as *pointing*), and then click the left mouse button. Pointing to options at the Start pop-up menu followed by a right-pointing triangle will cause a side menu to display with additional options.

When a program is open, a program button appears in the Taskbar. In the Taskbar shown in figure W.5, the Microsoft Word 2002 program is open. An icon representing Word displays in the program button area of the Taskbar.

FIGURE

W.5 *Windows Taskbar with Microsoft Word Open*

| Start | Document1 - Mic... | | 7:03 PM |

Switching between Open Programs

To switch between open programs, click the program's button on the Taskbar. In figure W.6, three programs are open—Microsoft Word, Excel, and Publisher. Microsoft Excel is the active button. Clicking either the Microsoft Word or Microsoft Publisher button will activate that program.

FIGURE

W.6 *Taskbar with the Microsoft Excel Program Active*

| Start | Document1 - Micro... | Microsoft Excel - ... | Unsaved Publicati... | | 7:08 PM |

Almost every program you open will appear on the Taskbar. (A few specialized tools may not.) Each button on the Taskbar gets a little smaller each time you open a program.

exercise

OPENING PROGRAMS AND SWITCHING BETWEEN PROGRAMS

1. Open Windows 2000. (To do this, turn on the computer and, if necessary, turn on the monitor and/or printer. Check with your instructor to determine if you need to complete additional steps.)
2. When the desktop displays, open Microsoft Word by completing the following steps:
    a. Position the arrow pointer on the Start button on the Taskbar and then click the left mouse button.
    b. At the Start pop-up menu, point to *Programs*. (This causes a side menu to display.)
    c. Drag the arrow pointer to *Microsoft Word* in the side menu and then click the left mouse button.
    d. When the Microsoft Word program is opened, notice that a button representing Word displays in the program button area of the Taskbar.
3. Open Microsoft Excel by completing the following steps:
    a. Position the arrow pointer on the Start button on the Taskbar and then click the left mouse button.
    b. At the Start pop-up menu, point to *Programs*.
    c. Drag the arrow pointer to *Microsoft Excel* in the side menu and then click the left mouse button.
    d. When the Microsoft Excel program is opened, notice that a button representing Excel displays in the program button area of the Taskbar to the right of the button representing Word.
4. Switch to the Word program by clicking the button on the Taskbar representing Word.
5. Switch to the Excel program by clicking the button on the Taskbar representing Excel.
6. Exit Excel by clicking File on the Excel Menu bar and then clicking Exit at the drop-down menu.
7. Click the button on the Taskbar representing Word.
8. Exit Word by clicking File on the Word Menu bar and then clicking Exit at the drop-down menu.

Exploring the System Tray

The System tray is the recessed area on the far right side of the Taskbar. The System tray contains a digital clock and specialized programs that run in the background. Position the arrow pointer over the current time on the Taskbar and today's date displays in a small yellow box as shown in figure W.7. (Your date will vary.)

FIGURE

W.7 *Current Time and Date in System Tray*

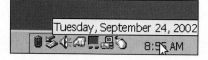

Double-click the current time displayed on the Taskbar and the Date/Time Properties dialog box displays as shown in figure W.8.

W.8 *Date/Time Properties Dialog Box*

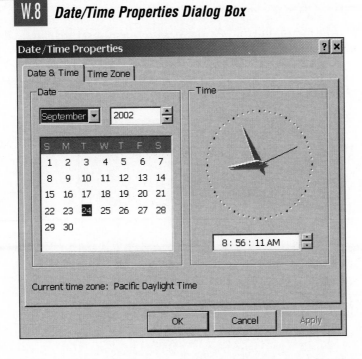

Change the date with options in the Date section of the dialog box. For example, to change the month, click the down-pointing triangle at the right side of the list box containing the current month, and then click the desired month at the drop-down list. Change the year by clicking the up- or down-pointing triangle at the right side of the list box containing the current year until the desired year displays. To change the day, click the desired day in the monthly calendar that displays in the dialog box. To change the time, double-click either the hour, minute, or seconds and use the up and down arrows to adjust the time.

Using the Quick Launch Toolbar

The Quick Launch toolbar is positioned between the Start button and the program button area on the Taskbar. It contains icons for programs that can be launched with a single click, such as Internet Explorer. The appearance of the Quick Launch toolbar can vary considerably depending on your installation of Windows 2000. A typical installation is shown in figure W.9.

W.9 *Windows 2000 Taskbar Quick Launch Toolbar*

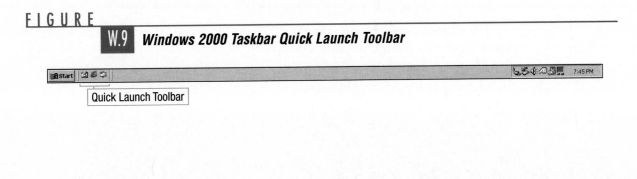

Quick Launch Toolbar

Setting Taskbar Properties

The default settings for the Taskbar display it at the bottom of the desktop with the time displayed. These default settings can be changed with options at the Taskbar and Start Menu Properties dialog box, shown in figure W.10. To display this dialog box, position the arrow pointer on any empty spot on the Taskbar, and then click the *right* mouse button. At the pop-up menu that displays, click *Properties*.

FIGURE

W.10   Taskbar and Start Menu Properties Dialog Box

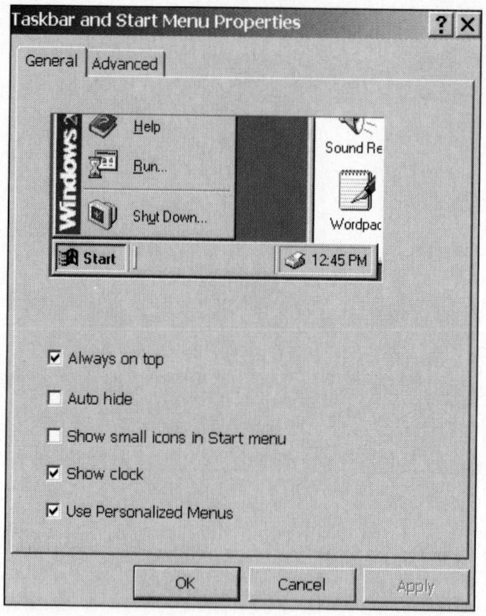

Each property is controlled by a check box. Property options containing a check mark are active. Click the option to remove the check mark and make the option inactive. If an option is inactive, clicking the option will insert a check mark in the check box and turn on the option (make it active). The Taskbar and Start Menu Properties dialog box contains these options:

Always on top: Keeps the Taskbar visible at all times. Check this if you want to see the Taskbar even when you are running programs.

Auto hide: Collapses the Taskbar into a thin line at the bottom of the screen. When you move the insertion point to the bottom of the screen, the Taskbar will display.

Show small icons in Start menu: Displays small icons in the Start menu. If unchecked, large icons are used (see figure W.11).

Show clock: Shows or hides the clock.

Use Personalized Menus: Keeps the Programs menu clean by hiding items you have not used recently. Access hidden programs by clicking the down-pointing triangle at the bottom of the Programs menu.

W.11 *Start Menu Showing Large and Small Icons*

Large Icons   Small Icons

exercise 2

CHANGING TASKBAR PROPERTIES

1. Make sure Windows 2000 is open and the desktop is displayed.
2. Change the size of the icons in the Start pop-up menu and remove the display of the clock by completing the following steps:
   a. Position the arrow pointer on any empty area on the Taskbar and then click the *right* mouse button.
   b. At the pop-up menu that displays, click *Properties*.
   c. At the Taskbar and Start Menu Properties dialog box, click *Show small icons in Start menu*. (This inserts a check mark in the check box.)
   d. Click *Show clock*. (This removes the check mark from the check box.)
   e. Click the Apply button.
   f. Click OK to close the dialog box.
3. Notice that the time no longer displays at the right side of the Taskbar. Click the Start button at the left side of the Taskbar and notice that the icons in the pop-up menu are smaller. Click on any empty spot on the desktop to remove the pop-up menu.
4. Return to the default settings for the Taskbar by completing the following steps:
   a. Position the arrow pointer on any empty area on the Taskbar and then click the *right* mouse button.
   b. At the pop-up menu that displays, click *Properties*.
   c. At the Taskbar and Start Menu Properties dialog box, click *Show small icons in Start menu*. (This removes the check mark from the check box.)
   d. Click *Show clock*. (This inserts a check mark in the check box.)
   e. Click the Apply button.
   f. Click OK to close the dialog box.

Setting Clicking Options

You can set clicking options for the Windows environment and specify either a double-click or single-click to open a program or file. Steps in this textbook assume that you will double-click to open a file or program. To change from single-click to open (point to select) to double-click to open (single-click to select), complete these steps:

1. At the Windows desktop, click the My Computer icon.
2. At the My Computer window, click Tools on the Menu bar, and then click Folder Options at the drop-down menu.
3. At the Folder Options dialog box with the General tab selected, click the <u>D</u>ouble-click to open an item (single-click to select) option located in the Click items as follows section.
4. Click the Apply button and then click OK.

Using Windows Explorer

Windows Explorer in Windows 2000 is a file management program. Use Windows Explorer to see the contents of every drive and folder attached to your computer. You can even look into drives and folders on a network.

Looking at the Windows Explorer Window

To open Windows Explorer, click the Start button on the Taskbar, point to *Programs*, point to *Accessories*, and then click *Windows Explorer*. This displays the Windows Explorer window similar to the one shown in figure W.12. (Your Windows Explorer window will vary from what you see in figure W.12.)

FIGURE

W.12 *Windows Explorer Window*

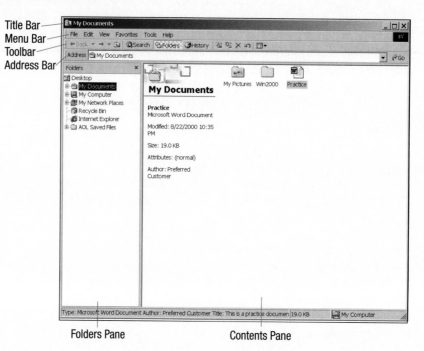

The left side of the Windows Explorer window is referred to as the Folders pane. (You can turn off the display of the Folders pane by clicking the Folders button on the toolbar.) The Folders pane shows special system folders and gives you a large view of your computer system. The right side of the Windows Explorer window is referred to as the Contents pane and displays the contents of the folder as well as related hyperlinks. (The related hyperlinks display as underlined blue text. Click a hyperlink and the hyperlinked folder displays in the Contents pane.)

Open Windows Explorer and the My Documents folder opens by default as shown in figure W.12. The Folders pane is based on a *hierarchy* with Desktop displayed at the top. As you can see from figure W.12, all the other icons are shown below the Desktop icon.

A folder may display preceded by a plus symbol. This plus symbol indicates that the folder contains additional folders (or drives). Double-click the folder name in the Folders pane and the contents of the folder display in the Folders pane as well as the Contents pane. You can also click the plus symbol and the contents of the folder display in the Folders pane but not the Contents pane. When the contents of a folder display, the plus symbol changes to a minus symbol. Click the minus symbol and the contents of the folder are hidden in the Folders pane. Double-click the My Computer folder name in the Folders pane and the Windows Explorer window displays as shown in figure W.13 (your window may vary slightly).

F I G U R E

W.13 *Contents of My Computer*

Clicking the *Up* button on the toolbar moves Windows Explorer up the hierarchy. You can also click the Back button on the toolbar to move back to the previously displayed folder or drive. Figure W.14 identifies the buttons on the Windows Explorer toolbar.

F I G U R E

W.14 *Windows Explorer Toolbar Buttons*

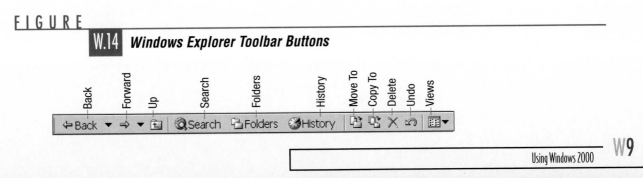

Copying, Moving, and Deleting Files/Folders in Windows Explorer

File and folder management activities can be performed in Windows Explorer. These activities include copying and moving files or folders from a folder or drive to another or deleting files or folders. Windows Explorer offers a variety of methods for copy, moving, and deleting files/folders. You can use buttons on the toolbar, drop-down menu options, or shortcut menu options. This section will provide you with the steps for copying, moving, and deleting files/folders using buttons on the toolbar.

To copy a file/folder to another folder or drive, select the file or folder by clicking it in the Contents pane and then clicking the Copy To button on the toolbar. At the Browse For Folder dialog box shown in figure W.15, click the desired folder or drive (you may need to click a plus symbol to display hidden folders) and then click OK. To move a file or folder to another folder or drive, select the file or folder and then click the Move To button on the toolbar. At the Browse For Folder dialog box, specify the location, and then click OK. Copying a file or folder leaves the file or folder in the original location and saves a copy at the new location while moving removes the file or folder from the original location and moves it to the new location.

FIGURE

W.15 **Browse For Folder Dialog Box**

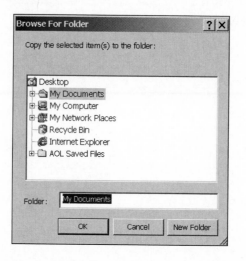

A file or folder can be easily removed (deleted) from Windows Explorer. To delete a file or folder, click the file or folder and then click the Delete button on the toolbar. At the dialog box asking you to confirm the deletion, click the Yes button. A deleted file or folder is sent to the Recycle Bin. You will learn more about the Recycle Bin in the next section.

1. At the Windows 2000 desktop, open Windows Explorer by completing the following steps:
   a. Click the Start button located at the left side of the Taskbar.
   b. At the pop-up menu that displays, point to *Programs*, point to *Accessories*, and then click *Windows Explorer*.
2. Copy a file from the CD that accompanies this textbook to a disk in drive A by completing the following steps:
   a. Insert the CD that accompanies this textbook into the CD drive.
   b. Insert a formatted 3.5-inch disk in drive A.
   c. Double-click the My Computer folder name in the Folders pane.
   d. Double-click the name of the drive containing the CD in the Folders pane (probably displays as OFFICEXP_BENCH followed by a drive letter). (Make sure you double-click because you want the contents of the CD to display in the Folders pane as well as the Contents pane.)
   e. Double-click the *Windows* folder in the Contents pane.
   f. Click *Word Document 01* in the Contents pane to select it.
   g. Click the Copy To button on the toolbar.
   h. At the Browse For Folder dialog box, display the drives and folders in My Computer by double-clicking My Computer in the dialog box list box. (Skip this step if the drives and folders are already displayed.)
   i. Click *3¹/₂ Floppy (A:)* in the dialog box list box.
   j. Click OK.
3. Delete *Word Document 01* from drive A by completing the following steps:
   a. Scroll up the display in the Folders pane until *3¹/₂ Floppy (A:)* is visible and then double-click *3¹/₂ Floppy (A:)*.
   b. Click *Word Document 01* (all of the document name may not be visible) in the Contents pane to select it.
   c. Click the Delete button on the toolbar.
   d. At the message asking you to confirm the deletion, click the Yes button.
4. Copy the *Windows* folder from the CD drive to the disk in drive A by completing the following steps:
   a. Scroll down the display in the Folders pane until the drive containing the CD displays (this will probably display as OFFICEXP_BENCH followed by the letter of the CD drive) and then double-click the drive.
   b. Click the *Windows* folder in the Contents pane to select it.
   c. Click the Copy To button on the toolbar.
   d. At the Browse For Folder dialog box, click *3¹/₂ Floppy (A:)* in the list box.
   e. Click OK.
5. Close Windows Explorer by clicking File on the Menu bar and then clicking Close at the drop-down menu. (You can also close Windows Explorer by clicking the Close button [contains an X] located in the upper right corner of Windows Explorer.)

Selecting Files/Folders

More than one file or folder can be moved, copied, or deleted at one time. Before moving, copying, or deleting files/folders, select the desired files or folders. Selecting files/folders in Windows Explorer is easier when the display of the Files pane is changed to List or Details. To change the display, open Windows Explorer and then click View on the Menu bar. At the drop-down menu, click the List option or the Details option.

To move adjacent files/folders, click the first file or folder and then hold down the Shift key and click the last file or folder. This selects and highlights all files/folders from the first file/folder you clicked to the last file/folder you clicked. With the adjacent files/folders selected, click the Move To button on the toolbar and then specify the desired location at the Browse For Folder dialog box. To select nonadjacent files/folders, click the first file/folder to select it, hold down the Ctrl key and then click any other files/folders to be moved or copied.

COPYING AND DELETING FILES

1. At the Windows 2000 desktop, open Windows Explorer by clicking the Start button, pointing to *Programs*, pointing to *Accessories*, and then clicking *Windows Explorer*.
2. Copy files from the CD that accompanies this textbook to a disk in drive A by completing the following steps:
   a. Insert the CD that accompanies this textbook into the CD drive.
   b. Insert your disk in drive A.
   c. Double-click My Computer in the Folders pane.
   d. Double-click the CD drive in the Folders pane (probably displays as OFFICEXP_BENCH followed by the drive letter).
   e. Double-click the *Windows* folder in the Contents pane.
   f. Change the display to Details by clicking View on the Menu bar and then clicking Details.
   g. Position the arrow pointer on *Word Document 01* in the Contents pane and then click the left mouse button.
   h. Hold down the Shift key, click *Word Document 05*, and then release the Shift key. (This selects *Word Document 01, Word Document 02, Word Document 03, Word Document 04,* and *Word Document 05.*)
   i. Click the Copy To button on the toolbar.
   j. At the Browse For Folder dialog box, click *3¹/₂ Floppy (A:)* in the list box and then click OK.
3. Double-click *3¹/₂ Floppy (A:)* in the Folders pane to display the files saved on the disk in drive A. (You may need to scroll up the Folders pane to display *3¹/₂ Floppy (A:)*.)
4. Delete the files from drive A that you just copied by completing the following steps:
   a. Change the view by clicking View on the Menu bar and then clicking List.
   b. Position the arrow pointer on *Word Document 01* in the Contents pane and then click the left mouse button.
   c. Hold down the Shift key, click *Word Document 05*, and then release the Shift key. (This selects *Word Document 01, Word Document 02, Word Document 03, Word Document 04,* and *Word Document 05.*)
   d. Click the Delete button on the toolbar.
   e. At the message asking you to confirm the deletion, click the Yes button.
   f. At the message telling you that the document is a read-only file and asking if you want to delete it, click the Yes to All button.
5. Close Windows Explorer by clicking File and then Close, or clicking the Close button (contains an X) located in the upper right corner of Windows Explorer.

Manipulating and Creating Folders in Windows Explorer

Organize and group files in folders. To help you organize files, you can create folders in Windows Explorer. To do this, double-click in the Folders pane the drive or folder in which you want to create the new folder. Click File on the Menu bar, point to New, and then click <u>F</u>older. This inserts a folder icon in the Contents pane and names the folder *New Folder* as shown in figure W.16. Key the desired name for the new folder and then press Enter.

FIGURE

W.16 *New Folder Icon in Windows Explorer*

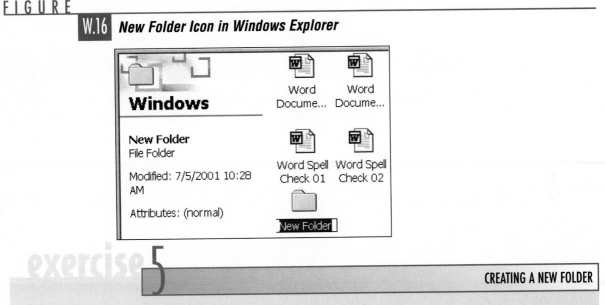

exercise 5

CREATING A NEW FOLDER

1. At the Windows 2000 desktop, open Windows Explorer.
2. Create a new folder by completing the following steps:
   a. Insert your disk in drive A (this disk contains the *Windows* folder you copied in exercise 3).
   b. Double-click *3¹/₂ Floppy (A:)* in the Folders pane.
   c. Double-click the *Windows* folder in the Contents pane. (This opens the folder.)
   d. Click File on the Menu bar, point to New, and then click <u>F</u>older.
   e. Key **Spell Check Files** and then press Enter. (This changes the name from *New Folder* to *Spell Check Files*.)
3. Copy *Word Spell Check 01, Word Spell Check 02, Word Spell Check 03,* and *Word Spell Check 04* into the Spell Check Files folder you just created by completing the following steps:
   a. Click View on the Menu bar and then click List.
   b. Click once on the file named *Word Spell Check 01* located in the Contents pane.
   c. Hold down the Shift key, click once on the file named *Word Spell Check 04,* and then release the Shift key. (This selects *Word Spell Check 01, Word Spell Check 02, Word Spell Check 03,* and *Word Spell Check 04.*)
   d. Click the Copy To button on the toolbar.
   e. At the Browse For Folder dialog box, double-click *3¹/₂ Floppy (A:)* in the list box.
   f. Double-click *Windows* (below *3¹/₂ Floppy (A:)*) in the list box.
   g. Click once on *Spell Check Files* in the list box (below *Windows*) and then click OK.
4. Display the files you just copied by double-clicking the Spell Check Files folder in the Contents pane.
5. Double-click *3¹/₂ Floppy (A:)* in the Folders pane. (This displays in the Contents pane the contents of the your disk.)

6. Delete the Spell Check Files folder and its contents by completing the following steps:
   a. Double-click the *Windows* folder in the Contents pane.
   b. Click the Spell Check Files folder in the Contents pane to select it.
   c. Click the Delete button on the toolbar.
   d. At the message asking you to confirm the deletion, click the Yes button.
   e. At the message telling you that the document is a read-only file and asking if you want to delete it, click the Yes to All button.
7. Close Windows Explorer by clicking File and then Close, or clicking the Close button (contains an X) located in the upper right corner of Windows Explorer.

Using the Recycle Bin

Deleting the wrong file can be a disaster but Windows 2000 helps protect your work with the Recycle Bin (see figure W.17). The Recycle Bin acts just like an office wastepaper basket; you can throw away unwanted files, but you can reach in and take paper out if you threw it away by accident.

FIGURE

W.17 *Recycle Bin Icon*

Deleting Files to the Recycle Bin

A file/folder or selected files/folders deleted from the hard drive are automatically sent to the Recycle Bin. Files/folders deleted from a disk are deleted permanently. (Recovery programs are available, however, that will help you recover deleted text. If you accidentally delete a file/folder from a disk, do not do anything more with the disk until you can run a recovery program.)

Another method for deleting a file is to drag the file to the Recycle Bin icon on the desktop. Drag a file icon to the Recycle Bin until the Recycle Bin icon is selected (displays with a blue background) and then release the mouse button. This drops the file you are dragging into the Recycle Bin.

Recovering Files from the Recycle Bin

If you accidentally delete a file to the Recycle Bin, it can be easily restored. To restore a file, double-click the Recycle Bin icon on the desktop. This opens the Recycle Bin window shown in figure W.18. (The contents of the Recycle Bin will vary.)

W.18 Recycle Bin Window

To restore a file, click the file you want restored, click File on the Menu bar, and then click Restore at the drop-down menu. The file is removed from the Recycle Bin and returned to its original location. You can also restore a file by positioning the arrow pointer on the file, clicking the *right* mouse button, and then clicking *Restore* at the pop-up menu.

exercise 6

DELETING FILES TO AND RECOVERING FILES FROM THE RECYCLE BIN

(Before completing this exercise, check with your instructor to determine if you can copy files to the hard drive.)

1. At the Windows 2000 desktop, open Windows Explorer.
2. Copy files from your disk in drive A to the My Documents folder on your hard drive by completing the following steps:
   a. Insert your disk in drive A (this disk contains the *Windows* folder).
   b. Double-click My Computer in the Folders pane.
   c. Double-click *3¹/₂ Floppy (A:)* in the Folders pane.
   d. Double-click the *Windows* folder in the Contents pane.
   e. Position the arrow pointer on *Word Spell Check 01* and then click the left mouse button.
   f. Hold down the Shift key, click *Word Spell Check 04,* and then release the Shift key.
   g. Click the Copy To button on the toolbar.
   h. At the Browse For Folder dialog box, click *My Documents* in the list box.
   i. Click OK.
3. Double-click My Documents in the Folders pane to display the files located in the folder. (The files you copied, *Word Spell Check 01* through *Word Spell Check 04,* will display in the Contents pane in alphabetical order.)
4. Delete *Word Spell Check 01* through *Word Spell Check 04* from the My Documents folder and send them to the Recycle Bin by completing the following steps:

a. Select *Word Spell Check 01* through *Word Spell Check 04* in the Contents pane. (If these files are not visible, you will need to scroll down the list of files.)

b. Click the Delete button on the toolbar.

c. At the message asking you to confirm the deletion, click the Yes button.

d. At the message telling you that the document is a read-only file and asking if you want to delete it, click the Yes to All button.

5. Close Windows Explorer.

6. At the desktop, display the contents of the Recycle Bin by double-clicking the Recycle Bin icon.

7. At the Recycle Bin window, restore *Word Spell Check 01* through *Word Spell Check 04* to the My Documents folder by completing the following steps:

a. Scroll to the end of the list of files.

b. When *Word Spell Check 01* through *Word Spell Check 04* display in the list box, select all four files.

c. With the files selected, click File on the Menu bar and then click Restore at the drop-down menu.

d. At the message asking you to confirm that you want to move the read-only file, click the Yes to All button.

8. Close the Recycle Bin window by clicking File on the Menu bar and then clicking Close at the drop-down menu.

9. Open Windows Explorer.

10. Make sure the My Documents folder is selected. (If it is not, select it by double-clicking My Documents in the Folders pane.)

11. Delete the files you restored by completing the following steps:

a. Select *Word Spell Check 01* through *Word Spell Check 04* in the Contents pane. (If these files are not visible, you will need to scroll down the list of files. These are the files you recovered from the Recycle Bin.)

b. Click the Delete button on the toolbar.

c. At the message asking you to confirm the deletion, click the Yes button.

d. At the message telling you that the document is a read-only file and asking if you want to delete it, click the Yes to All button.

12. Close Windows Explorer.

Emptying the Recycle Bin

Just like a wastepaper basket, the Recycle Bin can get full. To empty the Recycle Bin, position the arrow pointer on the Recycle Bin icon on the desktop and then click the *right* mouse button. At the pop-up menu that displays, click *Empty Recycle Bin*. At the message asking you to confirm the deletion, click the Yes button. You can also empty the Recycle Bin by double-clicking the Recycle Bin icon. At the Recycle Bin window that displays, click the Empty Recycle Bin button that displays at the left side of the window. At the message asking you to confirm the deletion, click the Yes button. (You can also empty the Recycle Bin by clicking File on the Menu bar and then clicking Empty Recycle Bin at the drop-down menu.)

Emptying the Recycle Bin deletes all files/folders. You can delete a specific file/folder from the Recycle Bin (rather than all files/folders). To do this, double-click the Recycle Bin icon on the desktop. At the Recycle Bin window, select the file/folder or files/folders to be deleted, and then click the Delete button on the toolbar. At the message asking you to confirm the deletion, click the Yes button.

(Before completing this exercise, check with your instructor to determine if you can delete files/folders from the Recycle Bin.)

1. At the Windows 2000 desktop, double-click the Recycle Bin icon.
2. At the Recycle Bin window, empty the contents of the Recycle Bin by completing the following steps:
    a. Click the Empty Recycle Bin button that displays at the left side of the window.
    b. At the message asking you to confirm the deletion, click the Yes button.
3. Close the Recycle Bin window by clicking File and then Close.

When the Recycle Bin is emptied the files cannot be recovered by the Recycle Bin or by Windows 2000. If you have to recover a file, you will need to use a file recovery program such as Norton Utilities. These utilities are separate programs, but might be worth their cost if you ever need them.

Customizing the Recycle Bin

The Recycle Bin settings can be customized at the Recycle Bin Properties dialog box. To display this dialog box, position the arrow pointer on the Recycle Bin icon on the desktop and then click the *right* mouse button. At the pop-up menu that displays, click *Properties*.

Using My Computer

Use the My Computer folder to display the contents of the floppy disk and hard disk, CD-ROM drive, mapped network drives and to open the Control Panel. To display the My Computer window shown in figure W.19, double-click the My Computer icon on the desktop.

FIGURE

W.19 *My Computer Window*

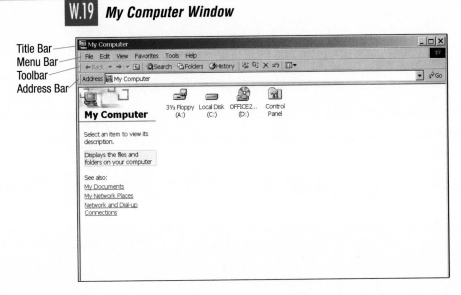

Using the My Computer window, you can navigate to the various drives and folders on your computer. You can also double-click on a file in the My Computer window and the program in which the file was created is opened (provided the program is located on your computer) as well as the file. You can copy, move, and delete folders and files in My Computer following the same steps you learned earlier in the *Using Windows Explorer* section. For example, to copy a file/folder, click the file or folder, and then click the Copy To button on the My Computer window toolbar. At the Browse For Folder dialog box, click the desired location in the list box, and then click OK.

Changing the My Computer Window Display

By default, the My Computer window displays objects in the window as large icons. With the Large Icons option selected at the View drop-down menu, the My Computer window should look something like the window shown in figure W.19.

Click the Small Icons option at the View drop-down menu and the icons in the My Computer window are reduced in size. Clicking the List option displays objects in the My Computer window in a list towards the left side of the window. Click the Details option at the View drop-down menu and a detailed view of each object displays in the My Computer window as shown in figure W.20.

FIGURE

W.20 **My Computer Window in Details View**

exercise 8

(Before completing this exercise, check with your instructor to determine if you can copy files to the My Documents folder on the hard drive.)

1. At the Windows 2000 desktop, double-click the My Computer icon.
2. At the My Computer window, display folders and files in a list (rather than large icons) by clicking View and then List.
3. Insert your disk in drive A.
4. Copy a document from the *Windows* folder on the disk in drive A to the My Documents folder on the hard drive by completing the following steps:
   a. Double-click *3¹/₂ Floppy (A:)* in the My Computer list box.
   b. Double-click the *Windows* folder (this displays the documents in the folder).
   c. Change the display of the files in the *Windows* folder by clicking View on the Menu bar and then clicking Details.
   d. Click once on the document named *Word Document 01*.
   e. Click the Copy To button on the toolbar.
   f. At the Browse For Folder dialog box, click My Documents in the list box.
   g. Click OK.
5. Delete *Word Document 01* from the My Documents folder by completing the following steps:
   a. Click the down-pointing triangle at the right side of the Address bar located towards the top of the My Computer window (just below the toolbar).
   b. At the drop-down list that displays, click *My Documents*.
   c. Click *Word Document 01* to select it.
   d. Click the Delete button on the toolbar.
   e. At the message asking you to confirm the deletion, click the Yes button.
6. Close the My Computer window by clicking File on the Menu bar and then clicking Close or by clicking the Close button (displays with an X) located at the right side of the My Computer Title bar.

Creating a Shortcut

Shortcuts are specialized icons. They are very small files that point the operating system to the actual item, whether it is a file, a folder, or an application. For example, in figure W.21, the *Shortcut to Practice Document* icon represents a path to a specific file in the Word 2002 program. The icon is not the actual file but a path to the file. Double-click the shortcut icon and Windows opens the Word 2002 program and also opens the file named Practice Document.

FIGURE

W.21 *Practice Document Shortcut Icon*

Shortcuts provide quick and easy access to files or programs used every day without having to remember where the file is stored. One method for creating a shortcut is to display the My Computer window and then display the drive or folder where the file is located. Position the arrow pointer on the file, hold down the *right* mouse button, drag the outline of the file to the desktop, and then release the mouse button. At the pop-up menu that displays, click *Create Shortcut(s) Here*. This creates a shortcut icon on the desktop like the one shown in figure W.21.

A shortcut icon can be easily deleted from the desktop by dragging the shortcut icon to the Recycle Bin icon. This deletes the shortcut icon but does not delete the file to which the shortcut pointed.

exercise 9

CREATING A SHORTCUT

1. At the Windows 2000 desktop, double-click the My Computer icon.
2. Insert your disk in drive A.
3. At the My Computer window, double-click *3¹/₂ Floppy (A:)*.
4. Double-click the *Windows* folder.
5. Change the display of files to a list by clicking View on the Menu bar and then clicking List at the drop-down menu.
6. Create a shortcut to the file named *Word Letter 01* by completing the following steps:
   a. Position the arrow pointer on *Word Letter 01*.
   b. Hold down the *right* mouse button, drag the outline of the file to the desktop window, and then release the mouse button.
   c. At the pop-up menu that displays, click *Create Shortcut(s) Here*.
7. Close the My Computer window by clicking the Close button located in the upper right corner of the window.
8. Open Word 2002 and the file named *Word Letter 01* by double-clicking the Word Letter 01 shortcut icon on the desktop.
9. After viewing the file in Word, exit Word by clicking <u>F</u>ile on the Menu bar and then clicking E<u>x</u>it at the drop-down menu.
10. Delete the Word Letter 01 shortcut icon by completing the following steps:
    a. At the desktop, position the arrow pointer on the Word Letter 01 shortcut icon.
    b. Hold down the left mouse button, drag the icon on top of the Recycle Bin icon, and then release the mouse button.

Customizing the Desktop

The Windows 2000 operating environment is very customizable. You can change background patterns and colors and set screen savers directly from the desktop. To change display properties, position the arrow pointer on any empty location on the desktop and then click the *right* mouse button. At the pop-up menu that displays, click *Properties*. This displays the Display Properties dialog box with the Background tab selected as shown in figure W.22.

W.22 *Display Properties Dialog Box with Background Tab Selected*

Changing the Desktop Background

The desktop background is customized at the Display Properties dialog box with the Background tab selected. Add a wallpaper background to the Windows desktop with options in the dialog box list box. Click any wallpaper option in the list box and preview the results in the preview screen. Wallpaper can be centered, tiled or stretched. Choose the display by clicking the down-pointing triangle at the right side of the Picture Display list box and then clicking the desired display. Choose the Tile option and the wallpaper covers the entire screen with a repeated series of images. Choose Center and the wallpaper is one image set in the middle of the screen or choose the Stretch option and the image is stretched across the entire screen. You can use the Browse button to select an HTML document from the network for your desktop background.

Add a pattern to the desktop with options from the Pattern dialog box. Display this dialog box by clicking the Pattern button located towards the bottom right corner of the Display Properties dialog box. The Pattern button is available only when the Picture Display option is set for Center.

If you want, you can choose (None) for both the wallpaper and pattern. This leaves the desktop one solid color. When you are satisfied with the pattern and wallpaper choices, click OK to set the changes and close the Display Properties dialog box.

Adding a Screen Saver

If your computer sits idle for periods of time, consider adding a screen saver. If a screen sits idle for a long period of time, you run the risk of burning any images onto the screen. (Fortunately, monitor technology has improved and burning images on the screen is becoming less of a problem.) A screen saver is a pattern that changes constantly, thus eliminating the problem of an image staying on the screen too long.

To add a screen saver, display the Display Properties dialog box and then click the Screen Saver tab. This displays the dialog box as shown in figure W.23.

 Display Properties Dialog Box with Screen Saver Tab Selected

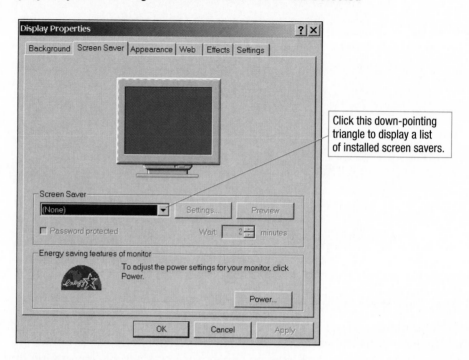

Click the down-pointing triangle at the right side of the Screen Saver list box to display a list of installed screen savers. Click a screen saver and a preview displays in the monitor located toward the top of the dialog box. Click the Preview button and the dialog box is hidden and the screen saver displays on your monitor. Move the mouse or click a button on the mouse and the dialog box will reappear.

Click the Settings button to display additional options for customizing a screen saver. Protect the screen saver with a password by clicking the Password protected check box. If a check mark appears in this check box, you must enter the correct password to clear the screen saver and return to the desktop.

If your computer's hardware is Energy Star compatible, the *Energy saving features of monitor* section is enabled. Click the Power button and a dialog box displays with options for choosing a power scheme appropriate to the way you use your computer. The dialog box also includes options for specifying how long the computer can be left unused before the monitor and hard disk are turned off and the system goes to standby or hibernate mode.

Changing Colors

Click the Appearance tab at the Display Properties dialog box and the dialog box displays as shown in figure W.24. At this dialog box, you can change the desktop scheme. Schemes are predefined collections of colors that are used in windows, menus, title bars, and system fonts. Windows 2000 loads with the Windows Standard scheme. Click the down-pointing triangle at the right side of the Scheme list box to display a list of available schemes. When you choose a scheme, the results are previewed in the sample dialog boxes.

W.24 *Display Properties Dialog Box with Appearance Tab Selected*

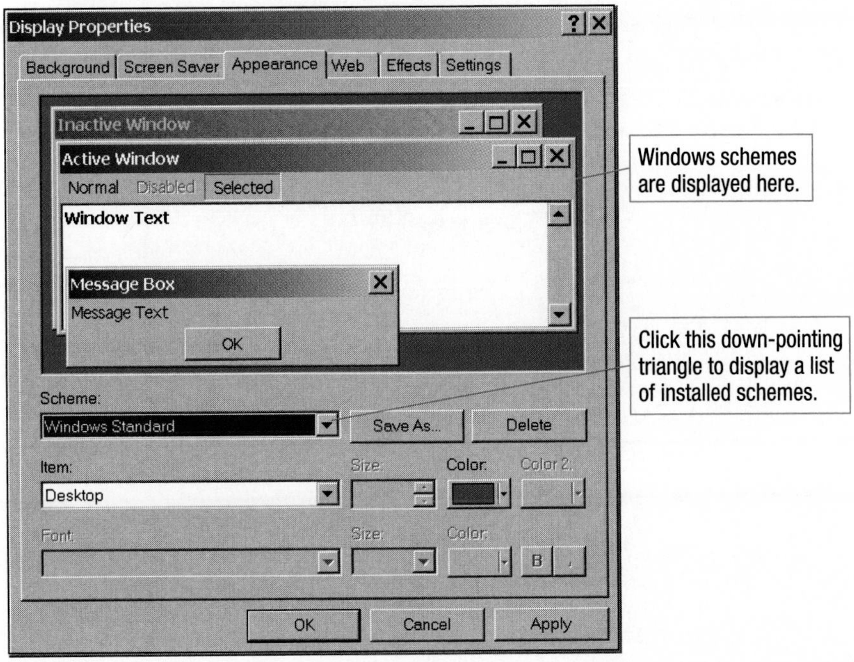

Windows schemes are displayed here.

Click this down-pointing triangle to display a list of installed schemes.

Schemes set the appearance of the entire operating system. If you want to set the desktop to a unique color, but leave the rest of the scheme intact, specify options at the Item drop-down list. Click the down-pointing triangle at the right side of the Item list box and then click the specific object to which you want the scheme applied.

Displaying Web Pages on the Desktop

Click the Web tab and the Display Properties dialog box displays. Windows uses your Internet browser to display Web pages and other Internet files on your desktop. Using the tab requires a working Internet connection.

Changing Desktop Icons

Click the Effects tab and the Display Properties dialog box displays. Use options from this dialog box to change desktop icons from the default icons used by Windows. Select the icon you want to change, click the Change Icon button, and select a new icon from the Current icon list box in the Change Icon dialog box. Use the Browse button to select an icon of your own design.

Changing Settings

Click the Settings tab at the Display Properties dialog box and the dialog box displays as shown in figure W.25. At this dialog box, you can set color and screen resolution.

W.25 *Display Properties Dialog Box with Settings Tab Selected*

The Colors option determines how many colors are displayed on your monitor. The more colors that are shown, the more realistic the images will appear. However, a lot of computer memory is required to show thousands of colors. Your exact choice is determined by the specific hardware you are using. The Screen area slide bar sets the screen's resolution. The higher the number, the more you can fit onto your screen. Again, your actual values depend on your particular hardware. Clicking the Advanced button displays a dialog box with advanced display settings for changing font size.

exercise **10**

CUSTOMIZING THE DESKTOP

(Before completing this exercise, check with your instructor to determine if you can customize the desktop.)

1. At the Windows 2000 desktop, display the Display Properties dialog box by positioning the arrow pointer on an empty location on the desktop, clicking the *right* mouse button, and then clicking *Properties* at the pop-up menu.
2. At the Display Properties dialog box, add wallpaper to the desktop by completing the following steps:
   a. Make sure the Background tab is selected. (If it is not, click the Background tab.)
   b. Click *Blue Lace 16* in the Wallpaper list box. (If this option is not available, choose another wallpaper.)
   c. Make sure Center is selected in the Picture Display list box.
   d. Click OK to close the dialog box.
3. After viewing the desktop with the Blue Lace 16 wallpaper, add a pattern to fill in the space around the wallpaper by completing the following steps:
   a. Display the Display Properties dialog box.

b. At the Display Properties dialog box with the Background tab selected, click the Pattern button. (This displays the Pattern dialog box.)

c. Click *Paisley* in the Pattern list box. (If *Paisley* is not visible, click the down-pointing triangle in the Pattern list box until *Paisley* displays.)

d. Click OK to close the Pattern dialog box, and then click OK to close the Display Properties dialog box.

4. After viewing the desktop with the Blue Lace 16 wallpaper and the Paisley pattern applied, add a screen saver by completing the following steps:

a. Display the Display Properties dialog box.

b. At the Display Properties dialog box, click the Screen Saver tab. (If a screen saver is already selected in the Screen Saver list box, make a note of this screen saver name.)

c. Click the down-pointing triangle at the right side of the Screen Saver list box.

d. At the drop-down list that displays, click a screen saver that interests you. (A preview of the screen saver displays in the screen located toward the top of the dialog box.)

e. Click a few other screen savers to see how they will display on the monitor.

f. With a screen saver selected, click OK. (This closes the dialog box.)

g. At the desktop the screen saver will display, by default, after the monitor has sat idle for 15 minutes.

5. Return all settings back to the default by completing the following steps:

a. Display the Display Properties dialog box.

b. Make sure the Background tab is selected.

c. Click *(None)* in the Wallpaper list box.

d. Click the Pattern button.

e. At the Pattern dialog box, click *(None)* in the Pattern list box.

f. Click OK to close the Pattern dialog box.

g. Click the Screen Saver tab.

h. At the Display Properties dialog box with the Screen Saver tab selected, click the down-pointing triangle at the right side of the Screen Saver list box, and then click *(None)*. (If a screen saver was selected before completing this exercise, return to that screen saver.)

i. Click OK to close the Display Properties dialog box.

Exploring Windows 2000 Help Files

Windows 2000 includes an on-screen reference guide providing information, explanations, and interactive help on learning Windows features. The on-screen reference guide, referred to as "Help," contains complex files with hypertext used to access additional information by clicking a word or phrase. The Help feature can interact with open programs to help guide you through difficult tasks.

Using Windows Help Files

Display the Help window by clicking the Start button on the Taskbar and then click Help at the pop-up menu. The pane at the left side of the window contains four tabs—Contents, Index, Search, and Favorites. Click the Contents tab and help topics display in the list box below the tabs with each option preceded by a book icon as shown in figure W.26. Click a book icon and a list of subtopics appears. Click a subtopic that interests you and information about the topic displays in the pane at the right side of the window.

W.26 *Help Window with Contents Tab Selected*

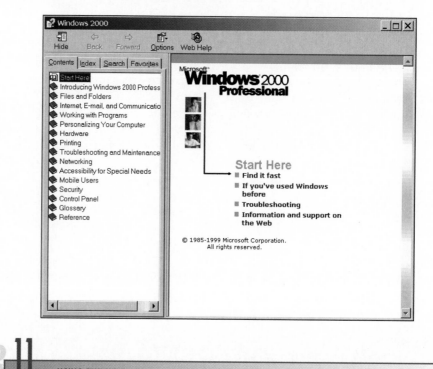

exercise 11

USING THE HELP TOPICS OR WINDOWS HELP DIALOG BOX WITH THE CONTENTS TAB SELECTED

(Depending on the type of installation completed on Windows, some of the Help categories may not be available. If some of the Help categories in exercise 11 do not display, experiment with other categories that interest you.)

1. At the Windows 2000 desktop, use the Help feature to learn about new Windows 2000 features by completing the following steps:
   a. Click the Start button located at the left side of the Taskbar.
   b. At the pop-up menu that displays, click *Help*.
   c. At the Help window, click the Contents tab. (Skip this step if the Contents tab is already selected.)
   d. Click *Introducing Windows 2000 Professional* located in the list box in the pane at the left side of the window. (This causes the book icon preceding *Introducing Windows 2000 Professional* to display as an open book and a list of subtopics to display below *Introducing Windows 2000 Professional*.)
   e. Click *What's new?* and information about new Windows 2000 features displays in the pane at the right side of the window.
   f. Click *Easier to use* (located in the pane at the right side of the window) and then read the information that displays below the topic.
   g. Click the other topics in the pane at the right side of the window and read the information supplied.
2. Close the Help window by clicking the Close button (displays with an X) that displays in the upper right corner of the window.

Click the Index tab and the Help window displays as shown in figure W.27. Key the desired feature, keyword, term, etc., in the *Type in the keyword to find* text box. Help displays a list of topics matching or related to the keyed text. Using the Help window with the I<u>n</u>dex tab selected is often easier than looking through the window with the <u>C</u>ontents tab selected.

F I G U R E

W.27   *Help Window with I<u>n</u>dex Tab Selected*

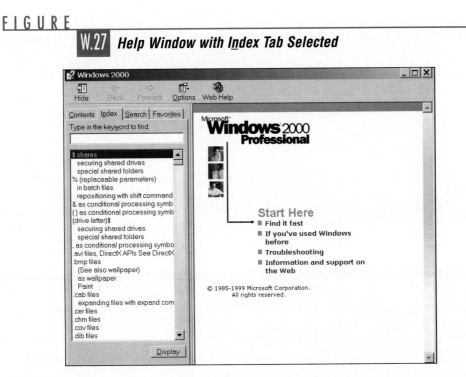

Use the Help window with the <u>S</u>earch tab selected to search for a specific word, term, or phrase. At the Help window with the <u>S</u>earch tab selected, as shown in figure W.28, key the desired word or phrase in the *Type in the key<u>w</u>ord to find* list box and then press Enter or click the <u>L</u>ist Topics button.

F I G U R E

W.28   *Help Window with <u>S</u>earch Tab Selected*

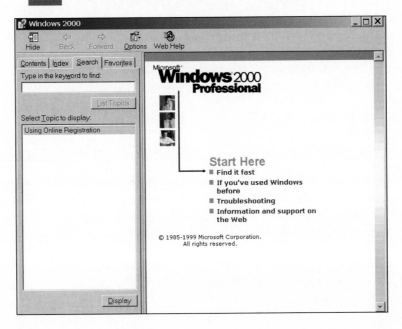

You can enter a word or phrase in the *Type in the keyword to find* list box. If you want to find help topics that contain a specific phrase, enclose the phrase in quotation marks. This tells Help to display only those topics that contain all the words in the phrase in the specific order.

If you repeatedly use a Help topic, you can add it to the Favorites tab. To do this, display the Help window and then display the desired topic. With the topic displayed in the pane at the right side of the window, click the Favorites tab. Click the Add button and the topic name is added to the list box located in the pane at the left side of the window. The next time you want to display the Help topic, display the Help window, click the Favorites tab, and then double-click the desired topic.

exercise 12

USING THE HELP WINDOW WITH THE INDEX TAB AND THE SEARCH TAB SELECTED

1. At the Windows 2000 desktop, use the Help feature to learn about deleting files and folders to the Recycle Bin by completing the following steps:
   a. Click the Start button and then click *Help* at the pop-up menu.
   b. At the Help window, click the Index tab.
   c. With the insertion point positioned in the *Type in the keyword to find* text box, key **deleting files**.
   d. At the list of topics that displays in the list box in the pane at the left side of the window, double-click the subtopic *Recycle Bin* that displays below the *deleting files* topic.
   e. At the Topics Found dialog box with the *Delete or restore files in the Recycle Bin* topic selected, click the Display button.
   f. Read the information that displays in the pane at the right side of the window.
   g. Click Related Topics that displays at the bottom of the pane at the right side of the window.
   h. At the pop-up list box that displays, click the *Remove items permanently when you delete them* topic.
   i. Read the information that displays in the pane at the right side of the window.
   j. Click the Close button (contains an X) that displays in the upper right corner of the Help window.
2. Use the Help feature to search for information on the Display Properties dialog box by completing the following steps:
   a. Click the Start button and then click *Help* at the pop-up menu.
   b. At the Help window, click the Search tab.
   c. Key "**Display Properties dialog box**" in the *Type in the keyword to find* text box. (Make sure you key the quotation marks.)
   d. Click the List Topics button.
   e. When a list of topics displays, double-click *Display overview*. (This displays the topic in the pane at the right side of the window with the phrase *Display Properties dialog box* selected.)
   f. Read the information that displays in the pane at the right side of the window.
   g. Select the text currently displayed in the *Type in the keyword to find* text box and then key **Display Properties dialog box** (without the quotation marks).
   h. Press Enter or click the List Topics button.
   i. Notice the list of topics that displays is different than the list that displayed for the previous search. Double-click one of the topics in the list and notice that the topic displays with one or more of the words in the phrase selected.
   j. Close the Help window.

OFFICE XP

BROWSING THE INTERNET USING INTERNET EXPLORER

Microsoft Internet Explorer is a Web browser program with options and features for displaying sites as well as navigating and searching for information on the Internet. The *Internet* is a network of computers connected around the world. Users access the Internet for several purposes: to communicate using e-mail, to subscribe to news groups, to transfer files, to socialize with other users around the globe in "chat" rooms, and largely to access virtually any kind of information imaginable.

Using the Internet, people can access a phenomenal amount of information for private or public use. To use the Internet, three things are generally required—an Internet Service Provider (ISP), a program to browse the Web (called a *Web browser*), and a *search engine*. In this section, you will learn how to use the Internet Explorer Web browser to browse web sites, search for specific sites, and download a web page and image.

Browsing the Internet

You will use the Microsoft Internet Explorer Web browser to locate information on the Internet. Uniform Resource Locators, referred to as URLs, are the method used to identify locations on the Internet. The steps for browsing the Internet vary but generally include: opening Internet Explorer, keying the URL for the desired site, navigating the various pages of the site, printing web pages, and then closing Internet Explorer.

To launch Internet Explorer, double-click the Internet Explorer icon on the Windows desktop. Figure IE.1 identifies the elements of the Internet Explorer, version 5.5, window. The web page that displays in your Internet Explorer window may vary from what you see in Figure IE.1.

FIGURE

IE.1 *Internet Explorer Window*

Title Bar
Menu Bar
Toolbar
Address Bar

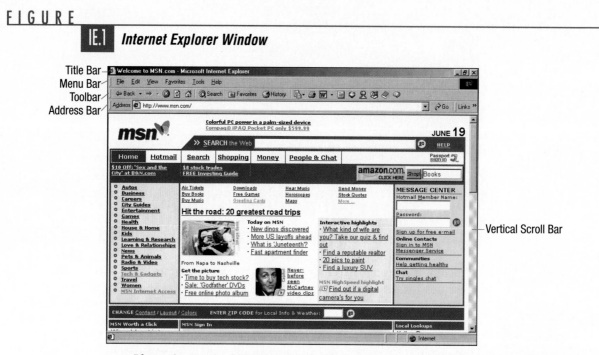

Vertical Scroll Bar

If you know the URL for the desired web site, click in the Address bar, key the URL, and then press Enter. In a few moments, the web site opening page displays in the Internet Explorer window. URLs (Uniform Resource Locators) are the method used to identify locations on the Internet. The format of a URL is *http://server-name.path*. The first part of the URL, *http* stands for HyperText Transfer Protocol, which is the protocol or language used to transfer data within the World Wide Web. The colon and slashes separate the protocol from the server name. The server name is the second component of the URL. For example, in the URL http://www.microsoft.com, the server name is *microsoft*. The last part of the URL specifies the domain to which the server belongs. For example, *.com* refers to "commercial" and establishes that the URL is a commercial company. Other examples of domains include *.edu* for "educational," *.gov* for "government," and *.mil* for "military."

exercise 1

BROWSING THE INTERNET WITH INTERNET EXPLORER

1. Make sure you are connected to the Internet through an Internet Service Provider and that the Windows desktop displays. (Check with your instructor to determine if you need to complete steps for accessing the Internet.)
2. Launch Microsoft Internet Explorer by double-clicking the Internet Explorer icon located on the Windows desktop.
3. At the Internet Explorer window, explore the web site for Yosemite National Park by completing the following steps:
    a. Click in the Address bar, key **www.nps.gov/yose** and then press Enter.

Step 3a

b. Scroll down the web site home page for Yosemite National Park by clicking the down-pointing triangle on the vertical scroll bar located at the right side of the Internet Explorer window.

c. Print the web site home page by clicking the Print button located on the Internet Explorer toolbar.

4. Explore the web site for Glacier National Park by completing the following steps:

a. Click in the Address bar, key **www.nps.gov/glac** and then press Enter.

b. Print the web site home page by clicking the Print button located on the Internet Explorer toolbar.

5. Close Internet Explorer by clicking the Close button (contains an X) located in the upper right corner of the Internet Explorer window. (You can also close Internet Explorer by clicking <u>F</u>ile on the Internet Explorer Menu bar and then clicking <u>C</u>lose at the drop-down menu.)

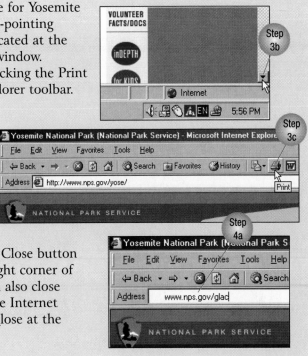

Navigating Using Hyperlinks

Most web pages contain "hyperlinks" that you click to connect to another page within the web site or to another site on the Internet. Hyperlinks may display in a web page as underlined text in a specific color or as images or icons. To use a hyperlink, position the mouse pointer on the desired hyperlink until the mouse pointer turns into a hand, and then click the left mouse button. Use hyperlinks to navigate within and between sites on the Internet. The Internet Explorer toolbar contains a Back button that, when clicked, will take you back to the previous web page. If you click the Back button and then want to go back to the previous page, click the Forward button. By clicking the Back button, you can back your way out of hyperlinks and return to the web site home page.

exercise **2**

VISITING WEB SITES AND NAVIGATING USING HYPERLINKS

1. Make sure you are connected to the Internet and then double-click the Internet Explorer icon on the Windows desktop.

2. At the Internet Explorer window, display the White House web page and navigate in the page by completing the following steps:

a. Click in the Address bar, key **whitehouse.gov** and then press Enter.

b. At the White House home web page, position the mouse pointer on the *History* hyperlink located towards the left side of the window until the pointer turns into a hand, and then click the left mouse button. (If this hyperlink is not available, click another hyperlink that interests you.)

c. At the History web page, click the Back button.

d. At the White House home web page, click the Forward button to return to the History page.

e. Print the History page by clicking the Print button on the Internet Explorer toolbar.

3. Display the Amazon.com web site and navigate in the site by completing the following steps:

a. Click in the Address bar, key **www.amazon.com** and then press Enter.

b. At the Amazon.com home page, click a hyperlink related to books.

c. When a book web page displays, click the Print button on the Internet Explorer toolbar.

4. Close Internet Explorer by clicking the Close button (contains an X) located in the upper right corner of the Internet Explorer window.

Searching for Specific Sites

If you do not know the URL for a specific site or you want to find information on the Internet but do not know what site to visit, complete a search with a search engine. A search engine is a software program created to search quickly and easily for desired information. A variety of search engines are available on the Internet, each offering the opportunity to search for specific information. One method for searching for information is to click the Search button on the Internet Explorer toolbar. This displays a Search pane, as shown in figure IE.2 with options for completing a search. Another method for completing a search is to visit the web site home page for a search engine and use options at the site.

FIGURE

IE.2 *Internet Explorer Search Pane*

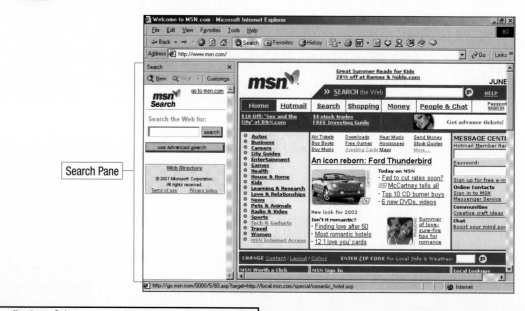

Search Pane

1. Make sure you are connected to the Internet and then double-click the Internet Explorer icon on the Windows desktop.
2. At the Internet Explorer window, search for sites on Bluegrass music by completing the following steps:

    a. Click the Search button on the Internet Explorer toolbar. (This displays the Search pane at the left side of the window.)
    b. Click in the search text box, key **Bluegrass music** and then click the search button.
    c. When a list of sites displays in the Search pane, click a site that interests you.
    d. When the web site home page displays, click the Print button.
3. Click the Search button on the Internet Explorer toolbar to remove the Search pane.
4. Use the Yahoo search engine to find sites on Bluegrass music by completing the following steps:

    a. Click in the Address bar, key **www.yahoo.com** and then press Enter.
    b. At the Yahoo web site, click in the Search text box, key **Bluegrass music** and then click the Search button (or press Enter). (Notice that the sites displayed vary from the sites displayed in the earlier search.)
    c. Click hyperlinks until a Web site displays that interests you.
    d. When the site displays, click the Print button on the Internet Explorer toolbar.
5. Use the Excite search engine to find sites on Jazz music by completing the following steps:

    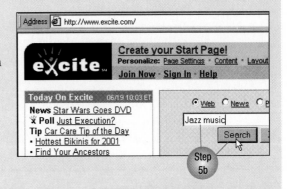

    a. Click in the Address bar, key **www.excite.com** and then press Enter.
    b. When the Excite web site home page displays, click in the Search text box, key **Jazz music** and then click the Search button.
    c. Click a site that interests you.
    d. When the web site home page displays, click the Print button on the Internet Explorer toolbar.
6. Close Internet Explorer.

Completing Advanced Searches for Specific Sites

The Internet contains a phenomenal amount of information. Depending on what you are searching for on the Internet and the search engine you use, some searches can result in several thousand "hits" (sites). Wading through a large number of sites can be very time consuming and counterproductive. Narrowing a search to very specific criteria can greatly reduce the number of hits for a search. To narrow a search, use the advanced search options offered by the search engine.

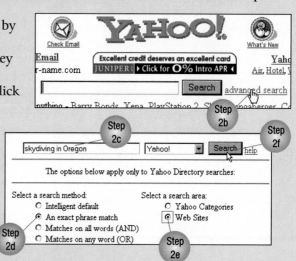

NARROWING A SEARCH

1. Make sure you are connected to the Internet and then double-click the Internet Explorer icon on the Windows desktop.
2. Search for sites on skydiving in Oregon by completing the following steps:
   a. Click in the Address bar and then key **www.yahoo.com**.
   b. At the Yahoo web site home page, click the *advanced search* hyperlink.
   c. At the Search Options page, click in the search text box and then key **skydiving in Oregon**.
   d. Click the *An exact phrase match* option in the *Select a search method* section. (This limits the search to any web sites that contain the exact phrase "skydiving in Oregon.")
   e. Click the *Web Sites* option in the *Select a search area* section. (Clicking this option tells Yahoo to display only web sites that contain the exact phrase and not Yahoo categories.)
   f. Click the Search button.
   g. When the list of web sites displays, click a hyperlink that interests you.
   h. Click the Print button on the Internet Explorer toolbar to print the web page.
   i. Click the Back button on the Internet Explorer toolbar until the Yahoo Search Options page displays.
3. Search for specific sites on tandem skydiving and static line skydiving in Oregon by completing the following steps:
   a. Select the text currently displayed in the search text box and then key **skydiving Oregon tandem static line**.
   b. Click the *Matches on all words (AND)* option in the *Select a search method* section. (Clicking this option tells Yahoo to find web sites that contain all of the words keyed in the Search text box.)
   c. Make sure *Web Sites* is selected in the *Select a search area* section.
   d. Click the Search button.
   e. When the list of web sites displays, click a hyperlink that interests you, and then print the web page.
4. Close Internet Explorer.

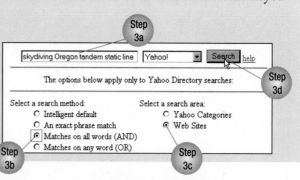

Downloading Images, Text, and Web Pages from the Internet

The image(s) and/or text that display when you open a web page as well as the web page itself can be saved as a separate file. This separate file can be viewed, printed, or inserted in another file. The information you want to save in a separate file is downloaded from the Internet by Internet Explorer and saved in a folder of your choosing with the name you specify. Copyright laws protect much of the information on the Internet. Before using information downloaded from the Internet, check the site for restrictions. If you do use information, make sure you properly cite the source.

exercise 5

DOWNLOADING IMAGES AND WEB PAGES

1. Make sure you are connected to the Internet and then double-click the Internet Explorer icon on the Windows desktop.
2. Download a Web page and image from the Banff National Park by completing the following steps:
   a. Use a search engine of your choosing to search for the Banff National Park web site.
   b. From the list of sites that displays, choose a site that contains information about Banff National Park and at least one image of the park.
   c. Insert a formatted disk in drive A. (Check with your instructor to determine if you should save the web page on a disk or save it into a folder on the hard drive or network.)
   d. Save the web page as a separate file by clicking File on the Internet Explorer Menu bar and then clicking Save As at the drop-down menu.
   e. At the Save Web Page dialog box, click the down-pointing triangle at the right side of the Save in option and then click *3¹/₂ Floppy (A:)* at the drop-down list. (This step may vary depending on where your instructor wants you to save the web page.)
   f. Click in the File name text box (this selects the text inside the box), key **Banff Web Page** and then press Enter.
3. Save the image as a separate file by completing the following steps:
   a. Right-click the image of the park. (The image that displays will vary from what you see to the right.)
   b. At the shortcut menu that displays, click Save Picture As.
   c. At the Save Picture dialog box, change the location to drive A (or the location specified by your instructor).

Step 2d

Step 2f

Step 3b

d. Click in the File name text box, key **Banff Image** and then press Enter.
4. Close Internet Explorer.

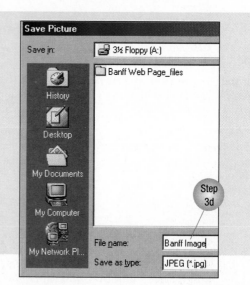

Step 3d

exercise

OPENING THE SAVED WEB PAGE AND IMAGE IN A WORD DOCUMENT

1. Open Microsoft Word by clicking the Start button on the Taskbar, pointing to Programs, and then clicking Microsoft Word.
2. With Microsoft Word open, insert the Banff image in a document by completing the following steps:
   a. Click Insert on the Menu bar, point to Picture, and then click From File.
   b. At the Insert Picture dialog box, change the Look in option to drive A (or the location where you saved the Banff image) and then double-click *Banff Image*.

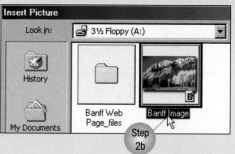

   c. When the image displays in the Word document, print the document by clicking the Print button on the Word Standard toolbar.
   d. Close the document by clicking File on the Menu bar and then clicking Close at the drop-down menu. At the message asking if you want to save the changes, click No.
3. Open the Banff Web Page file by completing the following steps:
   a. Click File on the Menu bar and then click Open at the drop-down menu.
   b. At the Open dialog box, change the Look in option to drive A (or the location where you saved the Banff Web page), and then double-click *Banff Web Page*.
   c. Print the web page by clicking the Print button on the Word Standard toolbar.
   d. Close the *Banff Web Page* file by clicking File and then Close.
4. Close Word by clicking the Close button (contains an X) that displays in the upper right corner of the screen.

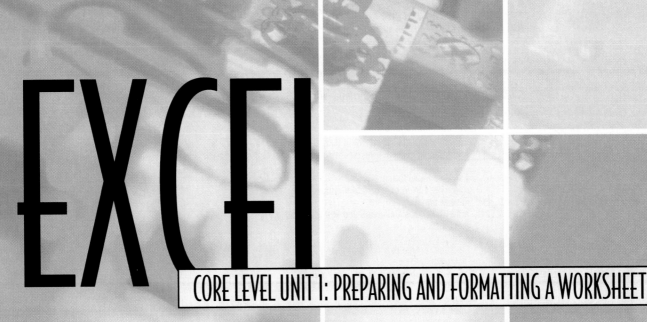

EXCEL

CORE LEVEL UNIT 1: PREPARING AND FORMATTING A WORKSHEET

Preparing an Excel Worksheet

Formatting an Excel Worksheet

Inserting Formulas in a Worksheet

Enhancing a Worksheet

MICROSOFT® EXCEL 2002

CORE BENCHMARK MICROSOFT OFFICE SPECIALIST SKILLS-UNIT 1

Reference No.	Skill	Pages
Ex2002-1 Working with Cells and Cell Data		
Ex2002-1-1	Insert, delete and move cells	
	Insert/delete cells, rows, and columns; merge and split cells	C48-C50; C43, C45-C46
Ex2002-1-2	Enter and edit cell data including text, numbers and formulas	
	Enter data in cells; automatic entering features; clear cell content	C6-C7; C12-C15; C50-C51
	Edit data in cells; select cells	C10-C12; C16-C17
	Apply cell formatting; format numbers	C30-C47, C51-C57
	Format numbers	C39-C43
	Insert functions and create and edit formulas	C63-C85
Ex2002-1-3	Check spelling	C106-C107
Ex2002-1-4	Find and replace cell data and formats	
	Find and replace data and formatting; move to a specific cell	C108-C112; C6, C12
Ex2002-1-5	Work with a subset of data by filtering lists	C115-C117
Ex2002-2	**Managing Workbooks**	
Ex2002-2-1	Manage workbook files and folders	
	Open a workbook	C7, C18
Ex2002-2-3	Save workbooks using different names and file formats	
	Save a workbook	C7, C11
	Save a workbook with a different name	C18
Ex2002-3	**Formatting and Printing Worksheets**	
Ex2002-3-1	Apply and modify cell formats	C30-C47
Ex2002-3-2	Modify row and column settings	
	Insert/delete row and columns; hide/unhide rows and columns	C48-C51; C103-C104
Ex2002-3-3	Modify row and column formats	
	Change column width and row height	C33-C39
	Modify cell alignment	C43-C46
Ex2002-3-5	Use automated tools to format worksheets	C17-C18
Ex2002-3-6	Modify Page Setup options for worksheets	
	Format with Page Setup options	C91-C101
	Change worksheet orientation; insert header/footer; set print options	C92-C96
	Insert header and footer	C95-C96
	Set print options	C96-C105
Ex2002-3-7	Preview and print worksheets and workbooks	
	Set and print specific area of worksheet; print nonadjacent selections	C103-C104
	Preview worksheet; display Page Break Preview	C29-C30; C99-C100
Ex2002-5	**Creating and Revising Formulas**	
Ex2002-5-1	Create and revise formulas	
	Use AutoSum	C63-C65
	Write formulas; copy formulas	C65-C67
	Write formulas by pointing/dragging	C67-C70
	Write formulas with functions	C70-C82
	Use absolute and mixed cell references	C82-C85
Ex2002-5-2	Use statistical, date and time, financial, and logical functions in formulas	C72-C82

CHAPTER 1

PREPARING AN EXCEL WORKSHEET

PERFORMANCE OBJECTIVES

Upon successful completion of chapter 1, you will be able to:
- **Identify the various elements of an Excel worksheet**
- **Create, save, and print a worksheet**
- **Enter data in a worksheet**
- **Edit data in a worksheet**
- **Use the Help feature**

Excel Chapter 01C

Many companies use a spreadsheet for numerical and financial data and to analyze and evaluate information. An Excel spreadsheet can be used for such activities as creating financial statements, preparing budgets, managing inventory, and analyzing cash flow. In addition, numbers and values can be easily manipulated to create "what if" situations. For example, using a spreadsheet, a person in a company can ask questions such as "What if the value in this category is decreased? How would that change affect the department budget?" Questions like these can be easily answered in an Excel spreadsheet. Change the value in a category and Excel will recalculate formulas for the other values. In this way, a spreadsheet can be used not only for creating financial statements or budgets, but also as a planning tool.

Creating a Worksheet

Open Excel by clicking the Start button at the left side of the Taskbar, pointing to *Programs*, and then clicking *Microsoft Excel*. When Excel is opened, you are presented with a blank worksheet like the one shown in figure 1.1. The elements of a blank Excel worksheet are described in figure 1.2.

Start

On your screen, the Standard and Formatting toolbars may display side by side with only a portion of the buttons visible. If this is the case, move the Formatting toolbar below the Standard toolbar by completing the following steps:
1. Click <u>T</u>ools and then <u>C</u>ustomize.
2. At the Customize dialog box, click the <u>O</u>ptions tab.
3. Click the <u>S</u>how Standard and Formatting toolbars on two rows option to insert a check mark in the check box.
4. Click the Close button to close the dialog box.

The display of the Standard and Formatting toolbars (as well as other toolbars) can be turned on or off. To do this, position the mouse pointer anywhere on a toolbar, and then click the *right* mouse button. At the drop-down menu that displays, click the toolbar name you want turned on or off. You can also turn on or off the display of a toolbar by clicking <u>V</u>iew on the Menu bar, pointing to <u>T</u>oolbars, and then clicking the toolbar name.

FIGURE

1.1 *Blank Excel Worksheet*

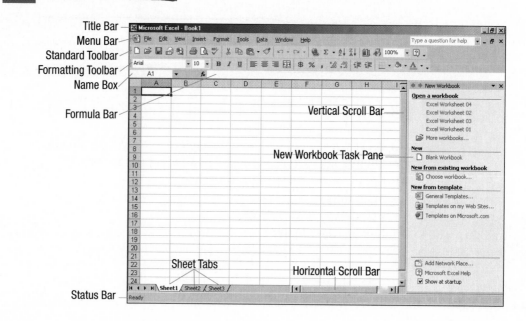

FIGURE

1.2 *Elements of an Excel Worksheet*

Title bar	The Title bar displays the name of the program along with the name of a workbook. The buttons at the far right side of the Title bar can be used to minimize, maximize, restore, or close Excel.
Menu bar	Excel commands are grouped into related functions and placed on the Menu bar. For example, options for formatting cells, rows, or columns are grouped in the F<u>o</u>rmat option on the Menu bar.
Standard toolbar	Icons for the most common commands in Excel are placed on the Standard toolbar.
Formatting toolbar	Options that are used to format elements of a worksheet are placed on buttons on the Formatting toolbar.
<u>**Name box**</u>	The cell address, also called the cell reference, displays in the Name box and includes the column letter and row number.
<u>**Formula bar**</u>	The Formula bar provides information about the active cell. Formulas can be entered and edited in the Formula bar.

EXCEL

Scroll bars	A vertical scroll bar displays toward the right side of the worksheet (immediately left of the task pane) and a horizontal scroll bar displays at the bottom of the worksheet. These scroll bars are used to navigate within a worksheet.
Task pane	The task pane presents features to help the user easily identify and use more of the program. The name of the task pane and the features contained in the task pane change depending on the actions being performed by the user.
Sheet tabs	Sheet tabs identify the current worksheet. The tab for the active worksheet displays with a white background while the inactive worksheets display with a gray background (the background color may vary depending on the Windows color scheme).
Status bar	The Status bar is located below the horizontal scroll bar and displays information about the worksheet and the currently active cell.
Worksheet area	The worksheet area is a collection of cells where information such as labels, values, or formulas is entered. (A cell is an intersection between a row and a column.)

A document created in Excel is referred to as a *workbook*. An Excel workbook consists of individual worksheets (or *sheets*) like the sheets of paper in a notebook. Notice the tabs located toward the bottom of the Excel window that are named *Sheet1*, *Sheet2*, and so on. The area containing the gridlines in the Excel window is called the *worksheet area*. Figure 1.3 identifies the elements of the worksheet area. Create a worksheet in the worksheet area that will be saved as part of a workbook. Columns in a worksheet are labeled with letters of the alphabet and rows are numbered.

FIGURE

1.3 *Elements of a Worksheet Area*

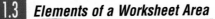

The gray horizontal and vertical lines that define the cells in the worksheet area are called *gridlines*. When the insertion point (which displays as a thick white plus sign) is positioned in a cell, the *cell address*, also called the *cell reference*, displays at the left side of the Formula bar in what is called the *Name box*. The cell reference includes the column letter and row number. For example, if the insertion point is positioned in the first cell of the worksheet, the cell reference *A1* displays in the Name box located at the left side of the Formula bar. In a worksheet, the cell containing the insertion point is considered the *active cell* and a thick black border surrounds the active cell.

Entering Data in a Cell

Enter data such as a heading, number, or value in a cell. To enter data in a cell, make the desired cell active, and then key the data. To move the insertion point to the next cell in the worksheet, press the Tab key. Other commands for moving the insertion point within a worksheet are displayed in figure 1.4.

FIGURE

1.4 *Commands for Moving Insertion Point in a Worksheet*

To move the insertion point here	Press
Down to the next cell	Enter
Up to the next cell	Shift + Enter
Next cell	Tab
Previous cell	Shift + Tab
Cell at beginning of row	Home
Next cell in the direction of the arrow	Up, down, left, or right arrow keys
Last cell in worksheet	Ctrl + End
First cell in worksheet	Ctrl + Home
Cell in next window (approximately 16-24 rows)	Page Down
Cell in previous window (approximately 16-24 rows)	Page Up
Cell in window to right (approximately 8-11 columns)	Alt + Page Down
Cell in window to left (approximately 8-11 columns)	Alt + Page Up

Another method for moving the insertion point to a specific cell is to use the Go To feature. To use this feature, click Edit and then Go To. At the Go To dialog box, key the cell reference in the Reference text box, and then click OK.

When you are ready to key data into the active cell, check the Status bar. The word *Ready* should display at the left side. As data is being keyed in the cell, the word *Ready* changes to *Enter*. Data being keyed in a cell displays in the cell as well as in the Formula bar. If the data being keyed is longer than the cell can accommodate, the data overlaps the next cell to the right (it does not become a part of the next cell—it simply overlaps it). You will learn how to change column widths to accommodate data later in this chapter.

If the data you enter in a cell consists of text and the text does not fit into the cell, it overlaps the next cell. If, however, you enter a number in a cell, specify it as a number (rather than text) and the number is too long to fit in the cell, Excel changes the display of the number to number symbols (###). This is because Excel does not want you to be misled by a number when you see only a portion of it in the cell.

In addition to moving the insertion point with the keyboard, you can also move it using the mouse. To make a specific cell active with the mouse, position the mouse pointer, which displays as a white plus sign (called the *cell pointer*), on the desired cell, and then click the left mouse button. The cell pointer displays as a white plus sign when positioned in a cell in the worksheet and displays as an arrow pointer when positioned on other elements of the Excel window such as toolbars or scroll bars.

Scroll through a worksheet using the horizontal and/or vertical scroll bars. Scrolling shifts the display of cells in the worksheet area, but does not change the active cell. Scroll through a worksheet until the desired cell is visible and then click the desired cell.

Saving a Workbook

Save

Save an Excel workbook, which may consist of a worksheet or several worksheets, by clicking the Save button on the Standard toolbar or clicking File and then Save. At the Save As dialog box, key a name for the workbook in the File name text box, and then press Enter or click Save. A workbook file name can contain up to 255 characters, including drive letter and any folder names, and can include spaces. Some symbols cannot be used in a file name such as:

forward slash (/)	question mark (?)
backslash (\)	quotation mark (")
greater than sign (>)	colon (:)
less than sign (<)	semicolon (;)
asterisk (*)	pipe symbol (|)

HINT

Ctrl + S is the keyboard command to display the Save As dialog box.

HINT

You cannot give a workbook the same name in first uppercase and then lowercase letters.

To save an Excel workbook in the *Excel Chapter 01C* folder on your disk, display the Save As dialog box and then click the down-pointing triangle at the right side of the Save in option box. Click *3½ Floppy (A:)* that displays in the drop-down list and then double-click *Excel Chapter 01C* in the list box.

Opening a Workbook

Open

Open an Excel workbook by displaying the Open dialog box and then double-clicking the desired workbook name. Display the Open dialog box by clicking the Open button on the Standard toolbar or by clicking File and then Open.

HINT

Ctrl + O is the keyboard command to display the Open dialog box.

Print

Printing a Workbook

Click the Print button on the Standard toolbar to print the active worksheet. You can also print a worksheet by clicking File and then Print. At the Print dialog box that displays, click the OK button.

Close

Closing a Workbook and Exiting Excel

To close an Excel workbook, click the Close button that displays at the right side of the Menu bar (the second Close button from the top) or click File and then Close. To exit Excel, click the Close button that displays at the right side of the Title bar (the first Close button from the top) or click File and then Exit. You can also exit Excel by double-clicking the *Excel* icon that displays at the left side of the Menu bar.

Expanding Drop-Down Menus

Microsoft Excel personalizes menus and toolbars as you work. When you click an option on the Menu bar, only the most popular options display (considered first-rank options). A drop-down menu that displays first-rank options is referred to as an *adaptive menu*. To expand a drop-down menu and display the full set of options (first-rank options as well as second-rank options), click the down-pointing arrows that display at the bottom of the drop-down menu. A drop-down menu will also expand if you click an option on the Menu bar and then pause on the menu for a few seconds. Second-rank options on the expanded drop-down menu display with a lighter gray background. If you choose a second-rank option, it is promoted and becomes a first-rank option the next time the drop-down menu is displayed.

If you want all menu options displayed when you click an option, you would complete the following steps:

1. Click Tools, expand the drop-down menu by clicking the down-pointing arrows that display at the bottom of the menu, and then click Customize.
2. At the Customize dialog box, click the Options tab.
3. At the Customize dialog box with the Options tab selected, click in the Always show full menus check box to insert a check mark.
4. Click the Close button to close the dialog box.

In this textbook, you will not be instructed to expand the drop-down menu. If you do not see a specified option, click the down-pointing arrows that display at the bottom of the menu to expand it. Or, consider following the steps above to show full menus.

Completing Computer Exercises

At the end of sections within chapters and at the end of chapters, you will be completing hands-on exercises at the computer. These exercises will provide you with the opportunity to practice the presented functions and commands. The skill assessment exercises at the end of each chapter include general directions. If you do not remember how to perform a particular function, refer to the text in the chapter.

Copying Data Workbooks

In several exercises in each chapter, you will be opening workbooks provided with this textbook. Before beginning each chapter, copy the chapter folder from the CD that accompanies this textbook to a floppy disk (or other folder). For this chapter, copy to your disk or directory the *Excel Chapter 01C* subfolder from the *Excel 2002 Core* folder on the CD that accompanies this textbook. Steps on how to copy a folder from the CD to your floppy disk are printed on the inside of the back cover of this textbook.

Changing the Default Folder

At the end of this and the remaining chapters in the textbook, you will be saving workbooks. More than likely, you will want to save workbooks onto a disk. You will also be opening workbooks that have been saved on your disk. To save workbooks in and open workbooks from the chapter folder on your disk, you will need to specify the drive where your disk is located as the default folder. Once you specify the chapter folder on your disk, Excel uses this as the default folder until you exit the Excel program. The next time you open Excel, you will again need to specify the drive where your disk is located.

Change the default folder at the Open dialog box or the Save As dialog box. To change the folder to the *Excel Chapter 01C* folder on the disk in drive A at the Open dialog box, you would complete the following steps:

1. Click the Open button on the Standard toolbar (the second button from the left); or click File and then Open.
2. At the Open dialog box, click the down-pointing triangle at the right side of the Look in option box.
3. From the drop-down list that displays, click *3½ Floppy (A:)*.
4. Double-click *Excel Chapter 01C* that displays in the list box.
5. Click the Cancel button in the lower right corner of the dialog box.

If you want to change the default folder permanently, make the change at the Options dialog box with the General tab selected as shown in figure 1.5. To permanently change the default folder to drive A, you would complete these steps:

1. Click Tools and then Options.
2. At the Options dialog box, click the General tab.
3. Select the text that displays in the Default file location text box and then key **A:**.
4. Click the OK button.

FIGURE

1.5 **Options Dialog Box with General Tab Selected**

Key in this text box the drive
letter where your disk is located.

Editing Data in a Cell

Edit data being keyed in a cell by pressing the Backspace key to delete the
character left of the insertion point or pressing the Delete key to delete the
character to the right of the insertion point. To change the data in a cell, click the
cell once to make it active, and then key the new data. When a cell containing
data is active, anything keyed will take the place of the existing data. If you want
to edit only a portion of the data in a cell, double-click the cell. This makes the
cell active, moves the insertion point inside the cell, and displays the word *Edit* at
the left side of the Status bar. Move the insertion point using the arrow keys or
the mouse and then make the needed corrections. If you are using the keyboard,
you can press the Home key to move the insertion point to the first character in
the cell or Formula bar, or press the End key to move the insertion point to the
last character.

When you are done editing the data in the cell, be sure to change out of the
Edit mode. To do this, make another cell active. You can do this by pressing Enter,
Tab, or Shift + Tab. You can also change out of the *Edit* mode and return to the
Ready mode by clicking another cell or clicking the Enter button on the Formula
bar.

If the active cell does not contain data, the Formula bar displays only the cell
reference (by column letter and row number). As data is being keyed in a cell, the
two buttons shown in figure 1.6 display on the Formula bar to the right of the
Name box. Click the Cancel button to delete the current cell entry. You can also
delete the cell entry by pressing the Esc key. Click the Enter button to indicate
that you are done keying or editing the cell entry. When you click the Enter
button on the Formula bar, the word *Enter* (or *Edit*) located at the left side of the
Status bar changes to *Ready*.

Cancel

Enter

1.6 Buttons on the Formula Bar

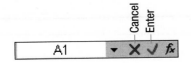

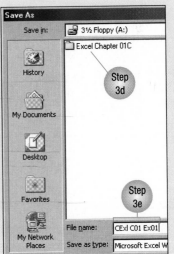

✓ exercise 1

CREATING AND EDITING A WORKSHEET

1. Open Excel by completing the following steps:
   a. At the Windows desktop, click the Start button that displays at the left side of the Taskbar.
   b. At the pop-up menu that displays, point to *Programs*.
   c. At the side menu that displays, click *Microsoft Excel*.
2. At the Excel worksheet that displays, create the worksheet shown in figure 1.7 by completing the following steps:
   a. With cell A1 the active cell (displays with a thick black border), key **Name**.
   b. Press the Tab key. (This makes cell B1 the active cell.)
   c. Key **Hours** and then press the Tab key. (This makes cell C1 the active cell.)
   d. Key **Rate** and then press Enter to move the insertion point to cell A2.
   e. With A2 the active cell, key the name **Avery**.
   f. Continue keying the data shown in figure 1.7. Key the dollar signs as shown in the figure. Use the Tab key to move to the next cell in the row, press Shift + Tab to move to the previous cell in the row, or press the Enter key to move down a row to the cell at the left margin. (For other commands for moving the insertion point, refer to figure 1.4.)
3. After keying the data shown in the cells in figure 1.7, save the worksheet by completing the following steps:
   a. Click the Save button on the Standard toolbar.
   b. At the Save As dialog box, click the down-pointing triangle to the right of the Save in option.
   c. From the drop-down list that displays, click *3½ Floppy (A:)* (this may vary depending on your system).
   d. Double-click the *Excel Chapter 01C* folder that displays in the list box.
   e. Select the text in the File name text box and then key **CExl C01 Ex01**.
   f. Press Enter or click the Save button.
4. Print CExl C01 Ex01 by clicking the Print button on the Standard toolbar. (The gridlines will not print.)
5. With the worksheet still open, make the following edits:
   a. Double-click cell A6 (contains *Mikulich*).
   b. Move the insertion point immediately left of the *k* and then key a **c**. (This changes the spelling to *Mickulich*.)
   c. Click once in cell A3 (contains *Connors*) and then key **Bryant**. (Clicking only once allows you to key over the existing data.)

d. Click once in cell B4 (contains *24*), key **30**, and then press Enter.

e. Edit cell C7 by completing the following steps:
   1) Click <u>E</u>dit and then <u>G</u>o To.
   2) At the Go To dialog box, key **C7** in the <u>R</u>eference text box, and then click OK.
   3) Key **$14.25** (over *$10.00*).

f. Click once in any other cell.

6. Click the Save button on the Standard toolbar to save the worksheet again.

7. Click the Print button on the Standard toolbar to print the worksheet again.

8. Close the worksheet by clicking <u>F</u>ile on the Menu bar and then clicking <u>C</u>lose at the drop-down menu.

Go To

Go to:

Reference:
C7

Special...   OK

Step 5e2

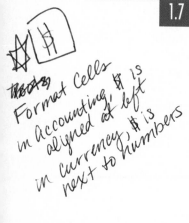

FIGURE

1.7 *Exercise 1*

Format Cells
in Accounting # is
aligned at left
in currency, # is
next to numbers

	A	B	C	D
1	Name	Hours	Rate	
2	Avery	45	$19.50	
3	Connors	35	$18.75	
4	Estrada	24	$15.00	
5	Juergens	24	$17.50	
6	Mikulich	20	$15.25	
7	Talbot	15	$10.00	
8				

Using Automatic Entering Features

Excel contains several features that help you enter data into cells quickly and efficiently. These features include *AutoComplete*, which automatically inserts data in a cell that begins the same as a previous entry; *AutoCorrect*, which automatically corrects many common typographical errors; and *AutoFill*, which will automatically insert words, numbers, or formulas in a series.

The AutoComplete feature will automatically insert data in a cell that begins the same as a previous entry. If the data inserted by AutoComplete is the data you want in the cell, press Enter. If it is not the desired data, simply continue keying the correct data. This feature can be very useful in a worksheet that contains repetitive data entries. For example, consider a worksheet that repeats the word *Payroll*. The second and subsequent times this word is to be inserted in a cell, simply keying the letter *P* will cause AutoComplete to insert the entire word.

The AutoCorrect feature automatically corrects many common typing (keying) errors. To see what symbols and words are in the AutoCorrect feature, click <u>T</u>ools and then <u>A</u>utoCorrect Options. This displays the AutoCorrect dialog box with the AutoCorrect tab selected shown in figure 1.8 with a list box containing the replacement data.

Tools - AutoCorrect Options

1.8 *AutoCorrect Dialog Box with AutoCorrect Tab Selected*

When you key the text displayed in the first column in a worksheet and then press the spacebar, the text is replaced by the text in the second column.

At the AutoCorrect dialog box, key the text shown in the first column in the list box in a worksheet and the text in the second column is inserted in the cell. Along with symbols, the AutoCorrect dialog box contains commonly misspelled words and common typographical errors. The AutoCorrect feature is a helpful tool when entering text in cells.

exercise 2

INSERTING DATA IN CELLS WITH AUTOCOMPLETE

1. Create the worksheet shown in figure 1.9 by completing the following steps:
   a. Begin at a clear worksheet window. (If a blank screen displays, click the *Blank Workbook* hyperlink located in the New Workbook Task Pane below the New section; or, click the New button on the Standard toolbar.)
   b. Key the text in cell A1 and insert the ® symbol by keying **(r)**. AutoCorrect will change (r) to ®.
   c. Key the remaining text in the cells. AutoCorrect will correct the spelling of *Benifits*. When you key the **W** in **West** in cell B4, the AutoComplete feature will insert **West**. Accept this by pressing the Enter key. Use the AutoComplete feature to enter *West* in B5 and B7 and *North* in cell B6. Use AutoComplete to enter the second and subsequent occurrences of *No* and *Yes*.
2. Save the worksheet and name it CExl C01 Ex02.
3. Print CExl C01 Ex02.
4. Close CExl C01 Ex02.

FIGURE

1.9 **Exercise 2**

	A	B	C	D
1	Team Net®			
2	Employee	Location	Benifits	
3	Abbot	West	No	
4	Blalock	North	No	
5	Calhoun	West	Yes	
6	Davis	West	Yes	
7	Hogan	North	Yes	
8	Mikelson	West	No	
9				

When a cell is active, a thick black border surrounds it and a small black square displays in the bottom right side of the border. This black square is called the AutoFill *fill handle* (see figure 1.3). With the fill handle, you can quickly fill a range of cells with the same data or with consecutive data. For example, suppose you need to insert the year 2002 in consecutive cells. To do this quickly, key **2002** in the first cell, position the mouse pointer on the fill handle, hold down the left mouse button, drag across the cells where you want the year inserted, and then release the mouse button.

You can also use the AutoFill fill handle to insert a series in consecutive cells. For example, suppose you are creating a worksheet with data for all of the months in the year. Key **January** in the first cell, position the mouse pointer on the fill handle, hold down the left mouse button, drag down or across to 11 more cells, and then release the mouse button. Excel automatically inserts the other 11 months in the year in the proper order. When using the fill handle, the cells must be adjacent. Figure 1.10 identifies the sequence inserted in cells by Excel when specific data is entered.

FIGURE

1.10 **AutoFill Fill Handle Series**   *examples*

Enter this data	And the AutoFill fill handle will insert this sequence in adjacent cells
(Commas represent data in separate cells.)	
January	February, March, April, etc....
Jan	Feb, Mar, Apr, etc....
Jan 98, Jan 99	Jan-98, Jan-99, Jan-00, Jan-01, etc....
Monday	Tuesday, Wednesday, Thursday, etc....
Product 1	Product 2, Product 3, Product 4, etc....
Qtr 1	Qtr 2, Qtr 3, Qtr 4
2, 4	6, 8, 10, etc....

Certain sequences, such as *2, 4* and *Jan 98, Jan 99,* require that both cells be selected before using the fill handle. If only the cell containing *2* is active, the fill handle will insert 2s in the selected cells. The list in figure 1.10 is only a sampling of what the fill handle can do. You may find a variety of other sequences that can be inserted in a worksheet using the fill handle.

An Auto Fill Options button displays when you fill cells with the fill handle. Click this button and a list of options display for filling the cells. By default, data and formatting are filled in each cell. You can choose to fill only the formatting in the cells or fill only the data without the formatting.

HINT

If you do not want a series to increment, hold down the Ctrl key while dragging the fill handle.

Auto Fill
Options

Turning On/Off and Maneuvering in the Task Pane

The New Workbook Task Pane displays at the right side of the screen when you first open Microsoft Excel. Depending on the actions you are performing, the task pane may be removed from the screen. For example, if you click the *Blank Workbook* hyperlink in the New Workbook Task Pane, a blank worksheet displays and the task pane is removed. You can control whether the display of the task pane is on or off by clicking View and then Task Pane. You can also close the task pane by clicking the Close button (contains an *X*) located in the upper right corner of the task pane.

As you learn more features in Excel, the options in the task pane as well as the task pane name may change. Maneuver within various task panes by clicking the Back button (contains a left-pointing arrow) and/or the Forward button (contains a right-pointing arrow) that display at the top of the task pane. You can also maneuver within various task panes by clicking the Other Task Panes button (contains a down-pointing triangle) and then clicking the desired task pane at the drop-down list.

The task pane can be docked and undocked. By default, the task pane is docked at the right side of the screen. Move (undock) the task bar by positioning the mouse pointer on the task pane Title bar, holding down the left mouse button, and then dragging the task pane to the desired location. If you move the task pane (undock it), you can dock it back at the right side of the screen by double-clicking the task pane Title bar.

✓ exercise 3

INSERTING DATA IN CELLS WITH THE FILL HANDLE

1. Create the worksheet shown in figure 1.11 by completing the following steps:
   a. Begin at a clear worksheet window. (If a blank screen displays, click the *Blank Workbook* hyperlink located in the New Workbook Task Pane below the New section; or, click the New button on the Standard toolbar.)
   b. Key **January** in cell B1.
   c. Position the mouse pointer on the fill handle for cell B1, hold down the left mouse button, drag across to cell G1, and then release the mouse button.

	A	B	C	D	E	F	G
1		January	February	March	April	May	June
2							
3							

Step
1c

d. Key the years (1999, 2000, etc.) in cells A2 through A5.
e. Make cell B2 active and then key **100**.
f. Drag the fill handle for cell B2 to cell E2. (This inserts *100* in cells C2, D2, and E2.)

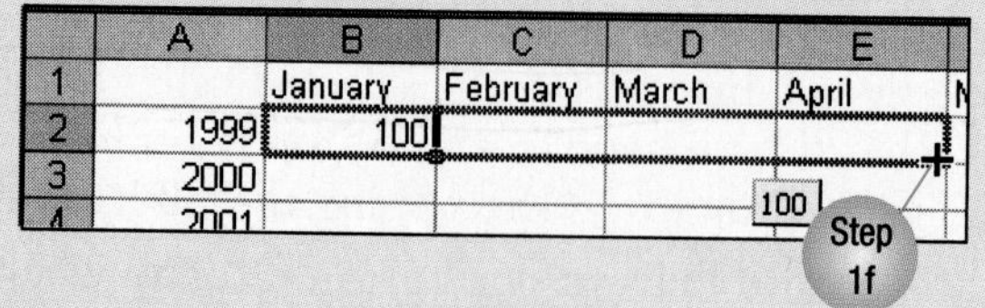

Step 1f

g. Key the text in the remaining cells as shown in figure 1.11. Use the fill handle to fill adjacent cells.
2. Save the worksheet and name it CExl C01 Ex03.
3. Print and then close CExl C01 Ex03.

FIGURE

1.11 *Exercise 3*

	A	B	C	D	E	F	G	H
1		January	February	March	April	May	June	
2	1999	100	100	100	100	125	125	
3	2000	150	150	150	150	175	175	
4	2001	200	200	200	150	150	150	
5	2002	250	250	250	250	250	250	
6								

Selecting Cells

Cells within a worksheet can be formatted in a variety of ways. For example, the alignment of data in cells or rows can be changed or character formatting can be added. To identify the cells that are to be affected by the formatting, the specific cells need to be selected.

Selecting Cells Using the Mouse

Select specific cells in a worksheet using the mouse or select columns or rows. Methods for selecting cells using the mouse display in figure 1.12.

FIGURE

1.12 *Selecting with the Mouse*

To select this	Do this
Column	Position the cell pointer on the column header (a letter) and then click the left mouse button.
Row	Position the cell pointer on the row header (a number) and then click the left mouse button.
Adjacent cells	Drag with mouse to select specific cells.

EXCEL

| Nonadjacent cells | Hold down the Ctrl key while clicking column header, row header, or specific cells. |
| All cells in worksheet | Click Select All button (refer to figure 1.3). |

Selected cells, except the active cell, display with a light blue background (this may vary) rather than a white background. The active cell is the first cell in the selection block and displays in the normal manner (white background with black data). Selected cells remain selected until you click a cell with the mouse or press an arrow key on the keyboard.

HINT

Select nonadjacent columns or rows by holding down the Ctrl key while selecting cells.

Selecting Cells Using the Keyboard

The keyboard can be used to select specific cells within a worksheet. Figure 1.13 displays the commands for selecting specific cells.

HINT

The first cell in a range displays with a white background and is the active cell.

FIGURE

1.13 *Selecting Cells Using the Keyboard*

To select	*Press*
Cells in direction of arrow key	Shift + arrow key
To beginning of row	Shift + Home
To beginning of worksheet	Shift + Ctrl + Home
To last cell in worksheet containing data	Shift + Ctrl + End
An entire column	Ctrl + spacebar
An entire row	Shift + spacebar
An entire worksheet	Ctrl + A or Ctrl + Shift + spacebar

Selecting Data within Cells

The selection commands presented select the entire cell. You can also select specific characters within a cell. To do this with the mouse, position the cell pointer in the desired cell, and then double-click the left mouse button. Drag with the I-beam pointer through the data you want selected. If you are using the keyboard, hold down the Shift key, and then press the arrow key that moves the insertion point in the desired direction. Data the insertion point passes through will be selected. You can also press F8 to turn on the *Extend* mode, move the insertion point in the desired direction to select the data, and then press F8 to turn off the *Extend* mode.

Formatting with AutoFormat

An Excel worksheet contains default formatting. For example, letters and words are aligned at the left of a cell, numbers are aligned at the right, and data is set in 10-point sans serif typeface (usually Arial). Excel contains the AutoFormat feature you can use to apply a variety of predesigned formats to cells in a worksheet. Choose formatting at the AutoFormat dialog box shown in figure 1.14. Display this dialog box by clicking Format and then AutoFormat.

FIGURE

1.14 *AutoFormat Dialog Box*

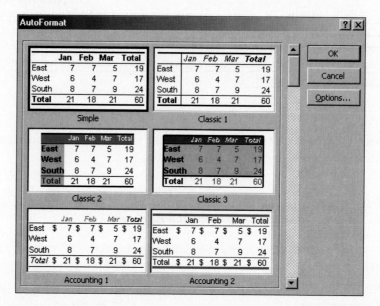

To automatically format a worksheet, select the cells that make up the worksheet, click Format and then click AutoFormat. (Do not click the Select All button—this selects the entire worksheet, even the empty cells. If you apply an autoformat to all cells, it may lock up your computer.) At the AutoFormat dialog box, double-click the desired worksheet format.

✓*exercise* 4

FORMATTING A WORKSHEET WITH AUTOFORMAT

1. Open Excel Worksheet 01. (This worksheet is located in the *Excel Chapter 01C* folder on your disk.)
2. Click File and then Save As. At the Save As dialog box, key **CEx1 C01 Ex04** in the File name text box, and then press Enter.
3. Apply autoformatting to the worksheet by completing the following steps:
   a. Select cells A1 through D10.
   b. Click Format and then AutoFormat.
   c. At the AutoFormat dialog box, click the down scroll arrow on the vertical scroll bar until the *Colorful 1* sample worksheet displays.
   d. Double-click *Colorful 1*.
4. Save, print, and then close CExl C01 Ex04.

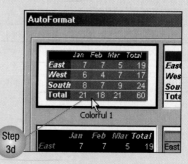

Step 3d

EXCEL

Using Help

Excel's Help feature is an on-screen reference manual containing information about all Excel features and commands. Excel's Help feature is similar to the Windows Help and the Help features in Word, PowerPoint, and Access. Get help using the Ask a Question button on the Menu bar, the Office Assistant, or from the Help Topics window.

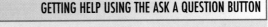

Ask a Question

Getting Help Using the Ask a Question Button

Click the text inside the Ask a Question button located at the right side of the Menu bar (this removes the text), key a help question, and then press Enter. A list of topics matching key words in your question displays below the Ask a Question button. Click the desired topic and a Help window displays with information about the topic.

exercise 5

GETTING HELP USING THE ASK A QUESTION BUTTON

1. At a clear Excel worksheet, click the text inside the Ask a Question button located at the right side of the Menu bar.
2. Key **How do I change column width?**
3. Press the Enter key.
4. From the list of topics that displays below the Ask a Question button, click the Change column width and row height option.
5. When the Help window displays, click the *Show All* hyperlink that displays in the upper right corner of the window. (This expands the Help window so all information displays.)
6. Read the information contained in the window, and then click the Close button (contains an *X*) located in the upper right corner of the Help window.

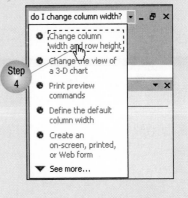

Step 4

Displaying the Microsoft Excel Help Window

Keying a question in the Ask a Question button and then pressing Enter displays the Microsoft Excel Help window. You can also display this Help window by clicking the Microsoft Excel Help button on the Standard toolbar, clicking Help and then Microsoft Excel Help, or clicking the *Microsoft Excel Help* hyperlink in the New Workbook Task Pane.

Microsoft Excel
Help Button

HINT

Press F1 to display the Microsoft Excel Help window.

Auto Tile

Using Buttons at the Help Window

The Help window contains a toolbar with buttons. Click the Auto Tile button and all open windows are tiled so each window displays next to each other. Click the Auto Tile button and it changes to the Untile button. Click the Show button to expand the window and display three tabs—Contents, Answer Wizard, and Index. If you move to various help items, click the Back button to return to the

Show

Print

Options

previous window. Click the Forward button to move forward to a help item. Click the Print button to send the Help information to the printer. Click the Options button and a drop-down menu displays with many of the same features as the buttons. For example, a Show Tabs option is available that will expand the window and Back and Forward options that do the same thing as the Back and Forward buttons. Additional options include Home, Stop, Refresh, Internet Options, and Print.

Using Options at the Expanded Help Window

The Help window toolbar contains a Show button. Click the Show button and the window expands as shown in figure 1.15. Three tabs display in the expanded dialog box—Contents, Answer Wizard, and Index.

FIGURE

1.15 Expanded Microsoft Excel Help Window

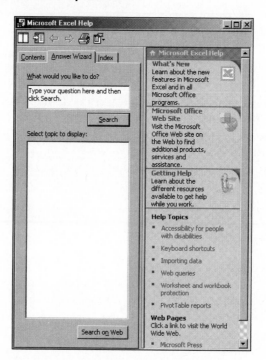

Select the Contents tab at the expanded Microsoft Excel Help window and a variety of categories display preceded by an icon of a closed book. Most of these categories contain additional categories. To display these additional categories, double-click a category. This causes the closed book icon to change to an open book icon and the additional categories to display below the selected category.

Click the Answer Wizard tab and a text box displays preceded by the question *What would you like to do?* Key your question in the text box and then click the Search button. This displays a list of categories in the Select topic to display list box. Click a topic in the list box, and information about the topic displays at the right side of the window.

With the Index tab selected, enter a keyword in the Type keywords list box, and then click the Search button. Topics related to the keyword display in the Choose a topic list box. Click a topic in this list box and information about that

HINT

Click Help, About Microsoft Excel, and then click the System Info button to display information about your computer such as your processor type, operating system, memory, and hard disk space.

topic displays at the right side of the window. You can also scroll through the Or choose <u>k</u>eywords list box to display the desired topic. The topics in this list box are alphabetized.

In some situations, the Help window will display a list of topics. If you want to expand the topics and display all of the information related to each topic, click the *Show All* hyperlink located in the upper right corner of the Help window. (The *Show All* hyperlink changes to the *Hide All* hyperlink.)

exercise 6

GETTING HELP FROM THE EXPANDED HELP WINDOW

1. Use the Help feature with the <u>C</u>ontents tab selected to find information on entering data in a worksheet by completing the following steps:
    a. Click the Microsoft Excel Help button on the Standard toolbar.
    b. At the Help window, click the Show button to expand the window. (Skip this step if the window is already expanded.)
    c. Click the <u>C</u>ontents tab. (Skip this step if the <u>C</u>ontents tab is already selected.)
    d. Click the plus symbol that displays before the *Microsoft Excel Help* option in the list box. (Skip this step if a minus symbol displays before the option.)
    e. Click the plus symbol that precedes the *Data in Worksheets* option.
    f. Click the plus symbol that precedes the *Entering and Selecting Data* option.
    g. Click the plus symbol that precedes the *Entering Data* option.
    h. Click a subcategory topic that interests you and then read the information about the subcategory that displays at the right side of the window.

    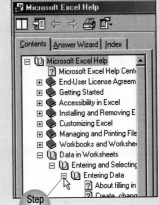

    Step 1g

    i. Click several other subcategories that interest you and read the information about the subcategory.
2. Use the Help feature with the Answer Wizard tab selected to search for information on applying borders to a cell by completing the following steps:
    a. Click the Answer Wizard tab.
    b. Key **How do I apply a border to a cell?** in the <u>W</u>hat would you like to do? text box and then click the <u>S</u>earch button.

    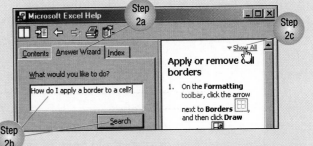

    Step 2a

    Step 2c

    Step 2b

    c. When information displays in the window at the right about applying cell borders, click the *Show All* hyperlink, and then read the information.
3. Use the Help feature with the <u>I</u>ndex tab selected to search for information on selecting cells by completing the following steps:
    a. Click the <u>I</u>ndex tab.
    b. Key **select** in the <u>T</u>ype keywords text box and then click the <u>S</u>earch button.
    c. Click the *Select data or cells* topic that displays in the C<u>h</u>oose a topic list box.

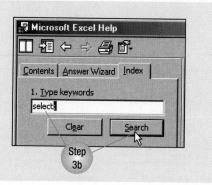

Step
3b

d. Read the information that displays at the right side of the window.

4. Click the Close button (contains an *X*) that displays in the upper right corner of the Help window.

Getting Help from the Office Assistant

The Office Assistant provides information about specific topics. Display the Office Assistant by clicking <u>H</u>elp and then Show the <u>O</u>ffice Assistant. To get help, click the Office Assistant and a help box displays above the assistant as shown in figure 1.16. Key a question about a specific feature in the text box, and then click the <u>S</u>earch button. The Office Assistant displays a list of related topics. At this list, click the desired topic and information displays in the Help window. After reading the information, click the Close button (contains an *X*) located in the upper right corner of the Help window.

FIGURE

1.16 *Office Assistant Help Box*

Key a question in the text box and then click the Search button.

To turn off the display of the Office Assistant, click <u>H</u>elp and then Hide the <u>O</u>ffice Assistant. This only hides the assistant. If you click <u>H</u>elp and then Microsoft Excel <u>H</u>elp, the Office Assistant will display again. To permanently turn off the display of the Office Assistant, click the Office Assistant to display the Help box and then click the <u>O</u>ptions button. At the Office Assistant dialog box, click in the <u>U</u>se the Office Assistant check box to remove the check mark, and then click OK.

USING THE OFFICE ASSISTANT TO LEARN HOW TO PRINT A WORKSHEET

1. At a clear worksheet window, use the Office Assistant to read information about printing a worksheet by completing the following steps:
   a. Click <u>H</u>elp and then Show the <u>O</u>ffice Assistant.
   b. Click the Office Assistant.
   c. Key **How do I print a worksheet?**.
   d. Click the <u>S</u>earch button.
   e. At the list that displays in the yellow box, click *About printing*. (When you position the arrow pointer on the topic, the pointer turns into a hand.)
   f. Click the *Show All* hyperlink that displays in the upper right corner of the Help window and then read the information that displays in the window.
   g. Click the Close button (contains an *X*) located in the upper right corner of the Microsoft Excel Help window.
2. Turn off the display of the Office Assistant permanently by completing the following steps:
   a. Click the Office Assistant. (This displays the Help box above the assistant.)
   b. Click the <u>O</u>ptions button.
   c. At the Office Assistant dialog box, click in the <u>U</u>se the Office Assistant check box to remove the check mark.
   d. Click OK.

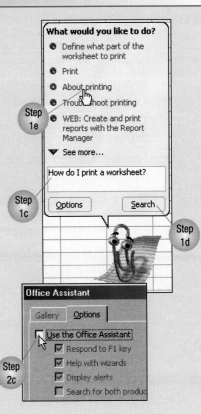

CHAPTER summary

➤ Use an Excel spreadsheet to create financial statements, prepare budgets, manage inventory, and analyze cash flow. Numbers and values can be easily manipulated in an Excel spreadsheet to answer "what if" questions.

➤ A document created in Excel is called a workbook. A workbook consists of individual worksheets. The intersection of columns and rows in a worksheet are referred to as cells.

➤ An Excel window contains the following elements: Title bar, Menu bar, Standard toolbar, Formatting toolbar, Formula bar, worksheet area, task pane, scroll bars, sheet tabs, and Status bar.

➤ The gray horizontal and vertical lines that define cells in the worksheet area are called gridlines.

➤ When the insertion point is positioned in a cell, the cell reference displays in the Name box located at the left side of the Formula bar. The cell reference includes the column letter and row number.

➤ To enter data in a cell, make the cell active, and then key the data. To move the insertion point to the next cell, press the Tab key. To move the insertion point to the previous cell, press Shift + Tab. For other insertion point movement commands, refer to figure 1.4.

➤ Data being entered in a cell display in the cell as well as in the Formula bar.

➤ If data entered in a cell consists of text (letters) and the text does not fit into the cell, it overlaps the cell to the right. However, if the data being entered are numbers and do not fit in the cell, the numbers are changed to number symbols (###).

➤ To replace data in a cell, click the cell once, and then key the new data. To edit data within a cell, double-click the cell, and then make necessary changes.

➤ The AutoComplete feature will automatically insert a previous entry if the character or characters being keyed in a cell match a previous entry.

➤ The AutoCorrect feature corrects many common typographical errors.

➤ Use the AutoFill fill handle to fill a range of cells with the same or consecutive data.

➤ The task pane presents features to help the user easily identify and use more of the program.

➤ Select all cells in a column by clicking the column header. Select all cells in a row by clicking the row header. Select all cells in a worksheet by clicking the Select All button located immediately to the left of the column headers.

➤ To select cells with the mouse, refer to figure 1.12; to select cells using the keyboard, refer to figure 1.13.

➤ Apply automatic formatting to selected cells in a worksheet with autoformats available at the AutoFormat dialog box.

➤ Excel's Help feature is an on-screen reference manual containing information about all Excel features and commands.

➤ Get help by keying a question in the Ask a Question button located at the right side of the Menu bar.

➤ Display the Help window by clicking the Microsoft Excel Help button on the Standard toolbar, clicking Help and then Microsoft Word Help, or by clicking the *Microsoft Excel Help* hyperlink in the New Workbook Task Pane.

➤ Click the Show button to expand the Help window. The expanded Microsoft Excel Help window displays with three tabs—Contents, Answer Wizard, and Index.

➤ Display the Office Assistant by clicking Help and then Show the Office Assistant. Turn off the display of the assistant by clicking Help and then Hide the Office Assistant. Turn off the display of the Office Assistant permanently by clicking the Office Assistant and then clicking the Options button. At the Office Assistant dialog box, click the Use the Office Assistant option to remove the check mark, and then click OK.

COMMANDS review

Command	Mouse/Keyboard
Display Save As dialog box	Click File and then Save As
Display Open dialog box	Click Open button on Standard toolbar; or click File and then Open
Display Print dialog box	Click File and then Print
Close a worksheet	Click File and then Close
Display AutoFormat dialog box	Click Format and then AutoFormat
Display Help window	Click Microsoft Excel Help button on Standard toolbar; or click Help, Microsoft Excel Help; or click *Microsoft Excel Help* hyperlink at New Workbook Task Pane
Display Office Assistant	Click Help, Show the Office Assistant
Display Office Assistant dialog box	Click Office Assistant, click Options button

F1

CONCEPTS check

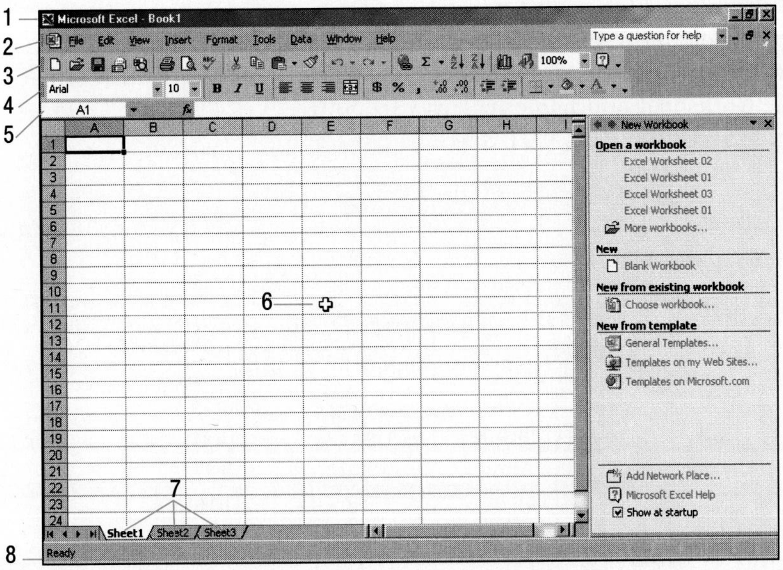

1. title bar
2. menu bar
3. standard toolbar
4. Formatting toolbar
5. Name box
6. ~~insertion point~~ cell pointer
7. Sheet tabs
8. status bar

Identifying: Look at the Excel screen shown above. This screen contains numbers with lines pointing to specific items. On a blank sheet of paper, write the name of the item that corresponds with the number in the Excel screen.

Completion: On a blank sheet of paper, indicate the correct term, symbol, or command for each item.

1. Press this key on the keyboard to move the insertion point to the next cell. *Tab*
2. Press these keys on the keyboard to move the insertion point to the previous cell. *Shift +Tab*
3. Columns in a worksheet are labeled with this. *letters*
4. Rows in a worksheet are labeled with this. *numbers*
5. Click this button in the worksheet area to select all cells in the table. *Select all Button*
6. The gray horizontal and vertical lines that define the cells in a worksheet area are referred to as this. *gridlines*
7. If a number entered in a cell is too long to fit inside the cell, the number is changed to this. *number symbols (###)*
8. Data being keyed in a cell displays in the cell as well as here. *Formula bar*
9. This is the name of the small black square that displays in the bottom right corner of the active cell. *fill ~~cell~~ handle*
10. To select nonadjacent columns using the mouse, hold down this key on the keyboard while clicking the column headers. *Ctrl*
11. Automatically apply formatting to selected cells in a worksheet with formats available at this dialog box. *AutoFormat*
12. Click this tab at the Microsoft Excel Help dialog box to search for information by entering a keyword. *Index*

SKILLS check

✓ Assessment 1

1. Create the worksheet shown in figure 1.17.
2. Select cells A1 through C5 and then apply the Accounting 1 autoformat.
3. Save the worksheet and name it CExl C01 SA01.
4. Print and then close CExl C01 SA01.

FIGURE

1.17 **Assessment 1**

	A	B	C	D
1	Expense	Original	Current	
2	Labor	97000	98500	
3	Material	129000	153000	
4	Permits	1200	1350	
5	Tax	1950	2145	
6				

EXCEL

✓ Assessment 2

1. Create the worksheet shown in figure 1.18. To create the © symbol in cell A1, key (c). Key the misspelled words as shown and let the AutoCorrect feature correct the spelling. Use the AutoComplete feature to insert the second occurrence of *Category*, *Available*, and *Balance*.
2. Select cells A1 through B7 and then apply the Classic 2 autoformat.
3. Save the worksheet and name it CExl C01 SA02.
4. Print and then close CExl C01 SA02.

FIGURE

1.18 *Assessment 2*

	A	B	C
1	Premiere Plan©		
2	Plan A	Catagory	
3		Availalbe	
4		Balence	
5	Plan B	Category	
6		Available	
7		Balance	
8			

✓ Assessment 3

1. Create the worksheet shown in figure 1.19. Key **Monday** in cell B2 and then use the fill handle to fill in the remaining days of the week. Use the fill handle to enter other repetitive data.
2. Select cells A1 through F4 and then apply an autoformat of your choosing.
3. Save the worksheet and name it CExl C01 SA03.
4. Print and then close CExl C01 SA03.

FIGURE

1.19 *Assessment 3*

	A	B	C	D	E	F	G
1	CAPITAL INVESTMENTS						
2		Monday	Tuesday	Wednesday	Thursday	Friday	
3	Budget	350	350	350	350	350	
4	Actual	310	425	290	375	400	
5							
6							

✓ Assessment 4

1. Use the Help feature to learn more about how to scroll within an Excel worksheet.
2. Read and then print the information provided by Help.
3. Create a worksheet containing the information. Set this up as a worksheet with two columns (cells will contain only text—not numbers). Create a title for the worksheet.
4. Apply an autoformat to the cells in the table.
5. Save the completed worksheet and name it CExl C01 SA04.
6. Print and then close CExl C01 SA04.

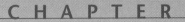

CHAPTER 2

FORMATTING AN EXCEL WORKSHEET

PERFORMANCE OBJECTIVES

Upon successful completion of chapter 2, you will be able to:
- Preview a worksheet
- Apply formatting to data in cells
- Change column widths
- Change row heights
- Format numbers in a worksheet
- Insert rows and columns in a worksheet
- Delete cells, rows, and columns in a worksheet
- Clear data in cells
- Add borders, shading, and patterns to cells in a worksheet
- Repeat the last action
- Automate formatting with Format Painter

Excel Chapter 02C

The appearance of a worksheet on the screen and how it looks when printed is called the *format*. In the previous chapter, you learned how to apply formatting automatically with choices at the AutoFormat dialog box. You can also apply specific formatting to cells in a worksheet. For example, you can change column width and row height; apply character formatting such as bold, italics, and underlining; specify number formatting; insert and delete rows and columns; and apply borders, shading, and patterns to cells.

Previewing a Worksheet

Before printing a worksheet, consider previewing it to see how it will appear when printed. To preview a worksheet, click the Preview button in the Print dialog box; click the Print Preview button on the Standard toolbar; or click File and then Print Preview. This causes the worksheet to display on the screen as it will appear when printed. Figure 2.1 displays the worksheet named Excel Worksheet 01 in Print Preview. Notice that the gridlines in the worksheet will not print.

Print
Preview

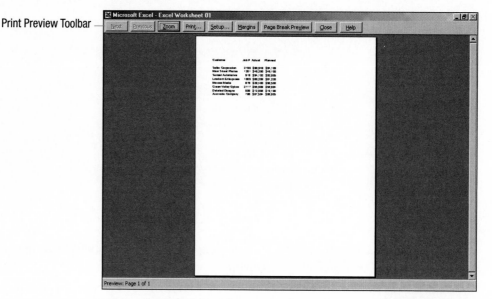

2.1 *Worksheet in Print Preview*

Print Preview Toolbar

To zoom in on the worksheet and make the display bigger, click the Zoom button on the Print Preview toolbar. This toolbar displays at the top of the screen immediately below the Title bar. Click the Print button on the Print Preview toolbar to send the worksheet to the printer. Click the Setup button and the Page Setup dialog box displays where you can specify the orientation of the page and the paper size. Clicking the Margins button causes margin boundary lines to display on the worksheet. Clicking this button again removes the margin boundary lines. After viewing the worksheet, click the Close button to remove Print Preview and return to the worksheet.

Changing the Zoom Setting

In Print Preview, you can zoom in on the worksheet and make the display bigger. You can also change the size of the display at the worksheet (not in Print Preview) with the options on the Zoom button. To change the percentage of display, click the down-pointing triangle at the right side of the Zoom button on the Standard toolbar and then click the desired percentage at the drop-down list. You can also click the Zoom button to select the current percentage measurement, key a new percentage, and then press Enter.

Zoom

Bold

Italic

Underline

Applying Formatting with Buttons on the Formatting Toolbar

A variety of formatting can be applied to cells in a worksheet using buttons on the Formatting toolbar. With buttons on the Formatting toolbar shown in figure 2.2, you can change the font and font size and bold, italicize, and underline data in cells. To apply bold to a cell or selected cells, click the Bold button on the Formatting toolbar; click the Italic button to apply italics; and click the Underline button to apply underlining formatting.

2.2 *Formatting Toolbar*

Font · Font Size · Bold · Italic · Underline · Align Left · Center · Align Right · Merge and Center · Currency · Percent Style · Comma Style · Increase Decimal · Decrease Decimal · Decrease Indent · Increase Indent · Borders · Fill Color · Font Color

Arial ▼ 10 ▼ **B** *I* U ≡ ≡ ≡ ▦ $ % , .0 .00 / .00 .0 ⇥ ⇤ ▭ ▼ ◇ ▼ A ▼ ▼

With other buttons on the Formatting toolbar, you can change the alignment of text within cells, increase or decrease the number of digits after a decimal point, increase or decrease indents, change the cell border, add fill color to a cell, and change text color.

(Note: Before completing computer exercises, delete the Excel Chapter 01C *folder on your disk. Next, copy the* Excel Chapter 02C *subfolder from the* Excel 2002 Core *folder on the CD that accompanies this textbook to your disk and then make* Excel Chapter 02C *the active folder.)* (1,2,3,6,7,8)

✓ exercise

FORMATTING AND PREVIEWING A WORKSHEET

1. Open Excel Worksheet 01.
2. Save the worksheet with Save As and name it CExl C02 Ex01.
3. Apply character formatting to data within cells by completing the following steps:
   a. Select and then bold and italicize the first row by completing the following steps:
      1) Position the cell pointer on the row 1 header and then click the left mouse button. (This is the number 1 that displays at the left side of the screen, immediately left of *Customer*.)
      2) Click the Bold button and then click the Italic button on the Formatting toolbar.
   b. Select and then bold the data in cells A3 through A10 by completing the following steps:
      1) Position the cell pointer in cell A3, hold down the left mouse button, drag the cell pointer to cell A10, and then release the mouse button.
      2) Click the Bold button on the Formatting toolbar.
   c. Select and then italicize the data in cells B3 through D10 by completing the following steps:

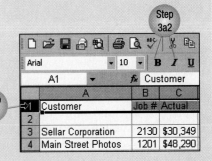

1) Position the cell pointer in cell B3, hold down the left mouse button, drag the cell pointer to cell D10, and then release the mouse button.

2) Click the Italic button on the Formatting toolbar.

d. Click in cell A1. (This deselects the cells.)

4. Preview the worksheet by completing the following steps:
   a. Click the Print Preview button on the Standard toolbar.
   b. At the print preview screen, click the Zoom button. (This increases the display of the worksheet cells.)
   c. After viewing the worksheet, click the Close button.

5. Change the zoom display by completing the following steps:
   a. Click the down-pointing triangle at the right side of the Zoom button on the Standard toolbar and then click *200%* at the drop-down list.
   b. After viewing the worksheet at 200% display, click the Zoom button (this selects *200%*), key **150**, and then press Enter. (This changes the zoom percentage to 150%.)
   c. Change the zoom back to 100% by clicking the down-pointing triangle at the right side of the Zoom button and then clicking *100%* at the drop-down list.

6. Save, print, and then close CExl C02 Ex01. (The gridlines will not print.)

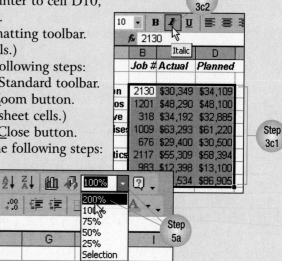

✓ exercise 2

1. Open Excel Worksheet 01.
2. Save the worksheet with Save As and name it CExl C02 Ex02.
3. Make the following changes to the worksheet:
   a. Select the entire worksheet and then change the font and font color by completing the following steps:
      1) Click the Select All button. (This is the gray button that displays immediately left of column header A and immediately above row header 1.)
      2) Click the down-pointing triangle at the right side of the Font button on the Formatting toolbar.
      3) At the drop-down menu that displays, scroll down the list and then click *Garamond*. (If Garamond is not available, choose another serif typeface such as Century Schoolbook.)
      4) Click the down-pointing triangle at the right side of the Font Size button on the Formatting toolbar and then click *11* at the drop-down menu.

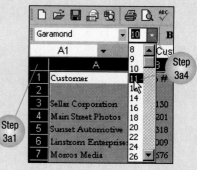

5) Click the down-pointing triangle at the right side of the Font Color button (this is the last button on the Formatting toolbar). At the palette of color choices, click the blue color that is the sixth color from the left in the second row.

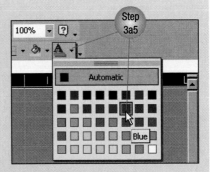

   b. Click once in cell A6 and then change *Linstrom Enterprises* to *Jefferson, Inc.*
   c. Double-click in cell A7 and then change *Morcos Media* to *Morcos Corp.*
   d. Click once in cell C6 and then change *$63,293* to *$59,578.*
   e. Click once in any other cell.
4. Preview the worksheet by completing the following steps:
   a. Click the Print Preview button on the Standard toolbar.
   b. At the print preview screen, increase the size of the display by clicking the <u>Z</u>oom button. (Skip this step if the size is already increased.)
   c. After viewing the worksheet, click the <u>C</u>lose button.
5. Save, print, and then close CExl C02 Ex02. (The gridlines will not print. If you are not printing on a color printer, the data will print in black rather than blue.)

Changing Column Width

Columns in a worksheet are the same width by default. In some worksheets you may want to change column widths to accommodate more or less data. Changes to column widths can be made using the mouse on column boundaries or at a dialog box.

Changing Column Width Using Column Boundaries

The mouse can be used to change the width of a column or selected columns. For example, to change the width of column B, you would position the mouse pointer on the black boundary line between columns B and C in the column header until the mouse pointer turns into a double-headed arrow pointing left and right and then drag the boundary to the right to increase the size or to the left to decrease the size. The width of selected columns that are adjacent can be changed at the same time. To do this select the columns and then drag one of the column boundaries within the selected columns. As the boundary is being dragged, the column width changes for all selected columns.

As a column boundary is being dragged, the column width displays in a yellow box above the mouse pointer. The column width number that displays represents the average number of characters in the standard font that can fit in a cell.

1. At a blank Excel worksheet, create the worksheet shown in figure 2.3 by completing the following steps:
   a. Change the width of column A by completing the following steps:
      1) Position the mouse pointer on the column boundary in the column header between columns A and B until it turns into a double-headed arrow pointing left and right.
      2) Hold down the left mouse button, drag the column boundary to the right until *Width: 17.00 (124 pixels)* displays in the yellow box, and then release the mouse button.

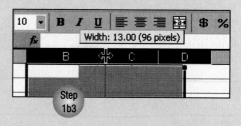

   b. Change the width of columns B, C, and D by completing the following steps:
      1) Select columns B, C, and D. To do this, position the cell pointer on the letter *B* in the column header, hold down the left mouse button, drag the cell pointer to the letter *D* in the column header, and then release the mouse button.
      2) Position the cell pointer on the column boundary between columns B and C until it turns into a double-headed arrow pointing left and right.
      3) Hold down the left mouse button, drag the column boundary to the right until *Width: 13.00 (96 pixels)* displays in the yellow box, and then release the mouse button.

   c. Key the data in the cells as shown in figure 2.3. Key the dollar signs and decimal points as shown. (Consider using the AutoFill fill handle for the months. To do this, key **October** in cell B1, position the mouse pointer on the fill handle, hold down the left mouse button, drag to cell D1, and then release the mouse button.)

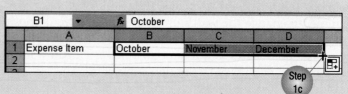

   d. After keying the data in the cells, make the following formatting changes:
      1) Select the entire worksheet and then change the font to 12-point Tahoma (or a similar typeface).
      2) Select row 1 and then apply bold and italic formatting.
   e. Click in cell A1. (This deselects the cells.)
2. Save the worksheet and name it CExl C02 Ex03.
3. Preview the worksheet.
4. Print and then close CExl C02 Ex03.

2.3 *Exercise 3*

	A	B	C	D	E
1	Expense Item	October	November	December	
2	Salaries	$25,450.50	$26,090.65	$26,445.00	
3	Lease	$5,650.00	$5,650.00	$5,650.00	
4	Insurance	$5,209.65	$5,335.55	$5,621.45	
5	Utilities	$2,100.50	$2,249.75	$2,441.35	
6	Maintenance	$1,430.00	$1,119.67	$1,450.50	
7					

A column width in an existing worksheet can be adjusted to fit the longest entry in the column. To automatically adjust a column width to the longest entry, position the cell pointer on the column boundary at the right side of the column, and then double-click the left mouse button.

✓ exercise 4

CHANGING COLUMN WIDTH AUTOMATICALLY IN AN EXISTING WORKSHEET

1. Open Excel Worksheet 01.
2. Save the worksheet with Save As and name it CExl C02 Ex04.
3. Select the entire worksheet and then change the font to 14-point Times New Roman.
4. Adjust the width of the first column to accommodate the longest entry in the column by completing the following steps:
   a. Position the cell pointer on the column boundary between columns A and B until it turns into a double-headed arrow pointing left and right.
   b. Double-click the left mouse button.
5. Select row 1 and then click the Bold button on the Formatting toolbar.
6. Click in cell A1. (This deselects the cells.)
7. Save, preview, print, and then close CExl C02 Ex04.

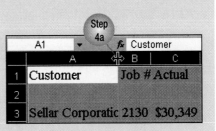

Changing Column Width at the Column Width Dialog Box

At the Column Width dialog box shown in figure 2.4, you can specify a column width number. The column width number represents the average number of characters in the standard font that will fit in a cell. Increase the column width number to make the column wider or decrease the column width number to make the column narrower.

To display the Column Width dialog box, click Format, point to Column, and then click Width. At the Column Width dialog box, key the number representing the average number of characters in the standard font that you want to fit in the column, and then press Enter or click OK.

2.4 *Column Width Dialog Box*

✓*exercise* 5

CHANGING COLUMN WIDTH AT THE COLUMN WIDTH DIALOG BOX

1. At a blank Excel worksheet, create the worksheet shown in figure 2.5 by completing the following steps:
   a. Change the width of column A by completing the following steps:
      1) Make sure any cell in column A is active.
      2) Click Format, point to Column, and then click Width.
      3) At the Column Width dialog box, key **10** in the Column width text box.
      4) Click OK to close the dialog box.
   b. Make any cell in column B active and then change the width of column B to *5* by completing steps similar to those in step 1a.
   c. Make any cell in column C active and then change the width of column C to *10* by completing steps similar to those in step 1a.
   d. Make any cell in column D active and then change the width of column D to *10* by completing steps similar to those in step 1a.
   e. Key the data in the cells as shown in figure 2.5. Use the fill handle to insert the months.
   f. After keying the data in the cells, make the following formatting changes:
      1) Select the entire worksheet and then change the font to 12-point Garamond (or a similar serif typeface).
      2) Select row 1 and then apply bold formatting.
   g. Click in cell A1.
2. Save the worksheet and name it CExl C02 Ex05.
3. Preview, print, and then close CExl C02 Ex05.

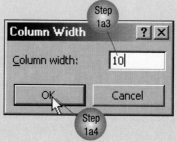

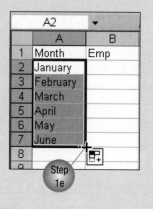

EXCEL

2.5 *Exercise 5*

	A	B	C	D	E
1	Month	Emp	Actual	Budget	
2	January	320	$3,121.50	$3,005.60	
3	February	197	$3,450.78	$3,500.20	
4	March	763	$2,109.45	$2,229.67	
5	April	804	$4,312.50	$4,110.30	
6	May	334	$5,110.40	$4,995.00	
7	June	105	$1,894.35	$1,995.15	
8					

Changing Row Height

Row height can be changed in much the same manner as column width. For example, you can change the row height using the mouse on a row boundary, or at the Row Height dialog box.

Changing Row Height Using Row Boundaries

Change row height using a row boundary in the same manner as you learned to change column width. To do this, position the cell pointer on the boundary between rows in the row header until it turns into a double-headed arrow pointing up and down, hold down the left mouse button, drag up or down until the row is the desired height, and then release the mouse button.

The height of selected rows that are adjacent can be changed at the same time. (The height of nonadjacent rows will not all change at the same time.) To do this, select the rows, and then drag one of the row boundaries within the selected rows. As the boundary is being dragged, the row height changes for all selected rows.

As a row boundary is being dragged, the row height displays in a yellow box above the mouse pointer. The row height number that displays represents a point measurement. There are approximately 72 points in a vertical inch. Increase the point size to increase the row height; decrease the point size to decrease the row height.

✓ *exercise* **6**

CHANGING ROW HEIGHT USING A ROW BOUNDARY

1. Open Excel Worksheet 05.
2. Save the worksheet with Save As and name it CExl C02 Ex06.
3. Make the following changes to the worksheet:
   a. Change the font size of *January* to 14 by completing the following steps:
      1) Make cell A1 the active cell.
      2) Click the down-pointing triangle at the right of the Font Size button on the Formatting toolbar.
      3) From the drop-down menu that displays, click *14*.

b. Change the height of row 1 by completing the
   following steps:
   1) Position the cell pointer in the row header on the
      row boundary between rows 1 and 2 until it turns
      into a double-headed arrow pointing up and down.
   2) Hold down the left mouse button, drag the row
      boundary down until *Height: 27.00 (36 pixels)*
      displays in the yellow box, and then release the
      mouse button.

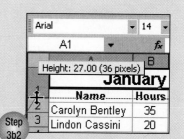

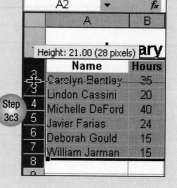

c. Change the height of rows 2 through 8 by completing
   the following steps:
   1) Select rows 2 through 8. To do this, position the cell pointer on the number 2 in
      the row header, hold down the left mouse button,
      drag the cell pointer to the number 8 in the row
      header, and then release the mouse button.
   2) Position the cell pointer on the row boundary
      between rows 2 and 3 until it turns into a double-
      headed arrow pointing up and down.
   3) Hold down the left mouse button, drag the row
      boundary down until *Height: 21.00 (28 pixels)*
      displays in the yellow box, and then release the
      mouse button.
d. Click in cell A1.
4. Save, preview, print, and then close CExl C02 Ex06.

Changing Row Height at the Row Height Dialog Box

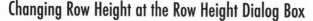

At the Row Height dialog box shown in figure 2.6, you can specify a row height
number. To display the Row Height dialog box, click Format, point to Row, and
then click Height.

FIGURE

2.6 *Row Height Dialog Box*

EXCEL

CHANGING ROW HEIGHT AT THE ROW HEIGHT DIALOG BOX

1. Open Excel Worksheet 07.
2. Save the worksheet with Save As and name it CExl C02 Ex07.
3. Make the following changes to the worksheet:
   a. Change the font size of *REAL PHOTOGRAPHY* to 14 points.
   b. Change the height of row 1 by completing the following steps:
      1) With cell A1 active, click Format, point to Row, and then click Height.
      2) At the Row Height dialog box, key **30** in the Row height text box, and then click OK.

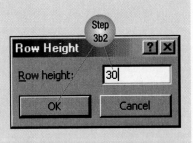

Step 3b2

   c. Change the height of rows 2 through 10 by completing the following steps:
      1) Select rows 2 through 10.
      2) Click Format, point to Row, and then click Height.
      3) At the Row Height dialog box, key **20** in the Row height text box, and then press Enter or click OK.
   d. Click in cell A1.
4. Save, preview, print, and then close CExl C02 Ex07.

Formatting Data in Cells

An Excel worksheet contains default formatting. For example, by default, letters and words are aligned at the left of a cell, numbers are aligned at the right, and data is set in a 10-point sans serif typeface such as Arial. Depending on the data you are entering in cells, you may want to change some of these default settings.

Formatting Numbers

Numbers in a cell, by default, are aligned at the right and decimals and commas are not displayed unless they are keyed in the cell. Also, numbers display in a 10-point sans serif typeface such as Arial. Depending on the type of numbers used in a worksheet, you may want to change these default settings. You can format numbers using a *format symbol*, or change number formatting with buttons on the Formatting toolbar or with options at the Format Cells dialog box.

Format symbols you can use to format numbers include a percent sign (%), a comma (,), and a dollar sign ($). For example, if you key the number *$45.50* in a cell, Excel automatically applies Currency formatting to the number. If you key *45%*, Excel automatically applies the Percent formatting to the number.

Five buttons on the Formatting toolbar can be used to format numbers in cells. The five buttons are shown and described in figure 2.7.

FIGURE

2.7 *Number Formatting Buttons on Formatting Toolbar*

Click this button	Named	To do this
$	Currency Style	Add a dollar sign, any necessary commas, and a decimal point followed by two decimal digits, if none are keyed; right align number in cell
%	Percent Style	Multiply cell value by 100 and display result with a percent symbol; right align number in cell
,	Comma Style	Add any necessary commas and a decimal point followed by two decimal digits, if none are keyed; right align number in cell
.0 .00	Increase Decimal	Increase number of decimal places displayed after decimal point in selected cells
.00 .0	Decrease Decimal	Decrease number of decimal places displayed after decimal point in selected cells

.0 .00

Increase Decimal

.00 .0

Decrease Decimal

Specify the formatting for numbers in cells in a worksheet before keying the numbers, or format existing numbers in a worksheet. The Increase Decimal and Decrease Decimal buttons on the Formatting toolbar will change decimal places for existing numbers only.

✓ exercise 8

FORMATTING NUMBERS WITH BUTTONS ON THE FORMATTING TOOLBAR

1. Open Excel Worksheet 08.
2. Save the worksheet with Save As and name it CExl C02 Ex08.
3. Make the following changes to the worksheet:
   a. Change the width of column A to 13.00.
   b. Select columns B, C, and D, and then change the column width to 10.00.
   c. Change the width of column E to 8.00.
   d. Make the following number formatting changes:
      1) Select cells B3 through D12.
      2) Click the Currency Style button on the Formatting toolbar.
      3) Click twice the Decrease Decimal button on the Formatting toolbar. (There should now be no decimal places in the numbers in the selected cells.)

Step 3d2

Step 3d3

Step 3d1

	10	B I U	≡ ≡ ≡	$ % ,	.0 .00 .00 .0
ƒx	624000				

	B	C	D	E	F
	Sales	Break Even	Safety	Safety %	
	$ 624,000	$ 587,230	$ 36,770	0.0627	
	$ 725,400	$ 634,350	$ 91,050	0.144	
	$ 358,650	$ 315,350	$ 43,300	0.137	
	$ 402,805	$ 399,850	$ 2,955	0.0074	
	$ 768,293	$ 721,420	$ 46,873	0.065	
	$ 734,210	$ 706,780	$ 27,430	0.0389	

EXCEL

4) Select cells E3 through E12.
5) Click the Percent Style button on the Formatting toolbar.
6) Click twice the Increase Decimal button on the Formatting toolbar. (There should now be two decimal places in the percent numbers in the selected cells.)

e. Select and then bold column A.
f. Select cells B1 through E1 and then click the Bold button.
g. Click in cell A1.
4. Save, print, and then close CExl C02 Ex08.

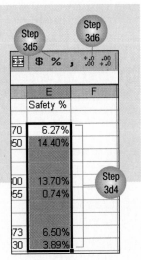

Numbers in cells can also be formatted with options at the Format Cells dialog box with the Number tab selected as shown in figure 2.8. Display this dialog box by clicking Format and then Cells.

FIGURE

2.8 *Format Cells Dialog Box with Number Tab Selected*

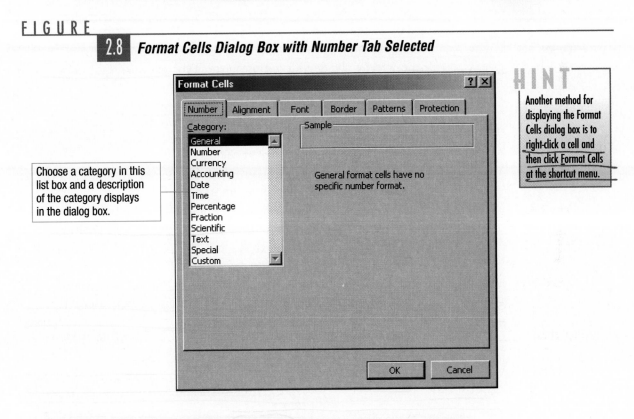

Choose a category in this list box and a description of the category displays in the dialog box.

The left side of the dialog box displays number categories. The default category is *General*. At this setting no specific formatting is applied to numbers except right aligning numbers in cells. The other number categories are described in figure 2.9.

2.9 *Number Categories at the Format Cells Dialog Box*

Click this category	*To apply this number formatting*
Number	Specify number of decimal places and whether or not a thousand separator should be used; choose the display of negative numbers; right align numbers in cell
Currency	Apply general monetary values; dollar sign is added as well as commas and decimal points, if needed; right align numbers in cell
Accounting	Line up the currency symbol and decimal points in a column; add dollar sign and two digits after a decimal point; right align numbers in cell
Date	Display date as date value; specify the type of formatting desired by clicking an option in the Type list box; right align date in cell
Time	Display time as time value; specify the type of formatting desired by clicking an option in the Type list box; right align time in cell
Percentage	Multiply cell value by 100 and display result with a percent symbol; add decimal point followed by two digits by default; number of digits can be changed with the Decimal places option; right align number in cell
Fraction	Specify how fraction displays in cell by clicking an option in the Type list box; right align fraction in cell
Scientific	Use for very large or very small numbers. Use the letter *E* to tell Excel to move a decimal point a specified number of positions
Text	Treat number in cell as text; number is displayed in cell exactly as keyed
Special	Choose a number type, such as Zip Code, Phone Number, or Social Security Number in the Type option list box; useful for tracking list and database values
Custom	Specify a numbering type by choosing an option in the Type list box

exercise 9

FORMATTING NUMBERS AT THE FORMAT CELLS DIALOG BOX

1. Open Excel Worksheet 02.
2. Save the worksheet with Save As and name it CExl C02 Ex09.
3. Make the following changes to the worksheet:
   a. Change the number formatting by completing the following steps:
      1) Select cells B2 through D8.
      2) Click Format and then Cells.

3) At the Format Cells dialog box with the Number tab selected, click *Currency* in the Category section.
4) Click the down-pointing triangle at the right of the Decimal places option until *0* displays in the Decimal places text box.
5) Click OK to close the dialog box.

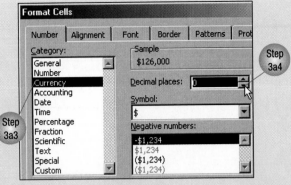

Step 3a3

Step 3a4

b. Select and then bold and italicize row 1.
4. Save and then print CExl C02 Ex09.
5. With CExl C02 Ex09 still open, change the display of negative numbers by completing the following steps:
a. Select cells D2 through D8.
b. Click Format and then Cells.
c. At the Format Cells dialog box, click the fourth option displayed in the Negative numbers list box (displays as *($1,234)*).
d. Click OK to close the dialog box.
e. Click in cell A1.
6. Save, print, and then close CExl C02 Ex09.

Step 5c

Aligning, Indenting, and Rotating Data in Cells

The alignment of data in cells depends on the type of data entered. For example, words or text combined with numbers entered in a cell are aligned at the left edge of the cell while numbers are aligned at the right. Alignment of data can be controlled with buttons on the Formatting toolbar or options at the Format Cells dialog box with the Alignment tab selected.

Four buttons on the Formatting toolbar, shown in figure 2.11, can be used to control the alignment of data in a cell or selected cells. Click the Align Left button to align data at the left side of a cell, click the Center button to align data between the left and right side of a cell, and click Align Right to align data at the right side of a cell. Click the Merge and Center button to merge selected cells and center data within the merged cells. If you have merged cells and want to split them again, select the cells and then click the Merge and Center button.

Indent text within a cell or selected cells by clicking the Increase Indent button or the Decrease Indent button on the Formatting toolbar. These buttons are identified in figure 2.10. The Increase Indent button will move text within the cell or selected cells to the right while the Decrease Indent button will move text to the left.

Align Left

Center

Align Right

Merge and Center

Increase Indent

Decrease Indent

2.10 *Alignment and Indent Buttons on the Formatting Toolbar*

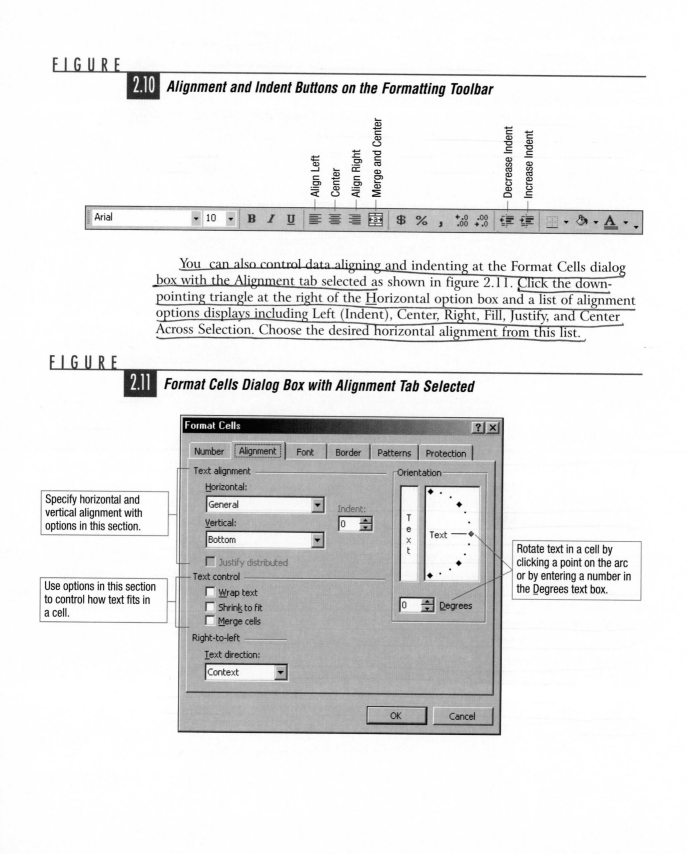

You can also control data aligning and indenting at the Format Cells dialog box with the Alignment tab selected as shown in figure 2.11. Click the down-pointing triangle at the right of the Horizontal option box and a list of alignment options displays including Left (Indent), Center, Right, Fill, Justify, and Center Across Selection. Choose the desired horizontal alignment from this list.

2.11 *Format Cells Dialog Box with Alignment Tab Selected*

EXCEL

By default, data in a cell is aligned at the bottom of the cell. Change this alignment to top, center, or justify with choices from the Vertical drop-down list. To display this list, click the down-pointing triangle at the right side of the Vertical option. Use the Indent box to indent cell contents from the left side of the cell. Each increment entered in the Indent box is equivalent to the width of one character.

In the Orientation section, you can choose to rotate data. A portion of the Orientation section shows points on an arc. Click a point on the arc to rotate the text along that point. You can also key a rotation degree in the Degrees text box. Key a positive number to rotate selected text from the lower left to the upper right of the cell. Key a negative number to rotate selected text from the upper left to the lower right of the cell.

As you learned earlier, if data keyed in a cell is longer than the cell, it overlaps the next cell to the right. If you want data to remain in a cell and wrap to the next line within the same cell, click the Wrap text option in the Text control section of the dialog box. Click the Shrink to fit option to reduce the size of the text font so all selected data fits within the column. Use the Merge cells option to combine two or more selected cells into a single cell.

If you want to enter data on more than one line within a cell, enter the data on the first line and then press Alt + Enter. Pressing Alt + Enter moves the insertion point to the next line within the same cell.

Alt + Enter

exercise 10

ALIGNING AND ROTATING DATA IN CELLS

1. Open Excel Worksheet 01.
2. Save the worksheet with Save As and name it CExl C02 Ex10.
3. Make the following changes to the worksheet:
   a. Select the entire worksheet and then change the font to 12-point Tahoma (or a similar sans serif typeface).
   b. Automatically increase the width of column A by positioning the cell pointer on the boundary between columns A and B and then double-clicking the left mouse button.
   c. Select row 1, click the Bold button, and then click the Center button on the Formatting toolbar.
   d. Select cells B3 through B10 and then click the Center button on the Formatting toolbar.
   e. Change the orientation of data in cells by completing the following steps:
      1) Select cells B1 through D1.
      2) Click Format and then Cells.
      3) At the Format Cells dialog box, click the Alignment tab.
      4) Select 0 in the Degrees text box and then key 45.
      5) Click OK to close the dialog box.
4. Merge and center data in a cell by completing the following steps:
   a. Select cells A12 through D12.

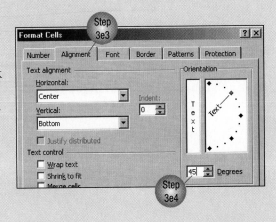

b. Click the Merge and Center button on the Formatting toolbar.
c. Double-click in the newly merged cell.
d. Turn on bold, key **YEARLY JOB REPORT**, and then press Enter.
5. Enter text on a separate line in cell A1 by completing the following steps:
a. Double-click cell A1.
b. Move the insertion point to the end of *Customer*.
c. Press Alt + Enter.
d. Key **Products Dept.**
6. Save, print, and then close CExl C02 Ex10.

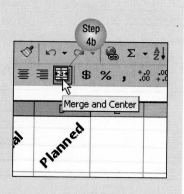

Changing the Font at the Format Cells Dialog Box

As you learned earlier in this chapter, the font for data can be changed with the Font button on the Formatting toolbar and the font size can be changed with the Font Size button. The font for data in selected cells can also be changed at the Format Cells dialog box with the Font tab selected as shown in figure 2.12.

FIGURE

2.12 *Format Cells Dialog Box with Font Tab Selected*

HINT

Use the Format Painter button on the Standard toolbar to copy formatting from one range of cells to another.

At the Format Cells dialog box with the Font tab selected, you can change the font, font style, font size, and font color. You can also change the underlining method and add effects such as superscript and subscript.

exercise 11

1. Open Excel Worksheet 02.
2. Save the worksheet with Save As and name it CExl C02 Ex11.
3. Make the following changes to the worksheet:
   a. Change the font and font color by completing the following steps:
      1) Select the entire worksheet.
      2) Click Format and then Cells.
      3) At the Format Cells dialog box, click the Font tab.
      4) At the Format Cells dialog box with the Font tab selected, click *Garamond* in the Font list box (you will need to scroll down the list to make this font visible).
      5) Click *12* in the Size list box (you will need to scroll down the list to make this size visible).
      6) Click the down-pointing triangle at the right of the Color option box (contains the word *Automatic*).
      7) At the palette of color choices that displays, click the Blue color.
      8) Click OK to close the dialog box.

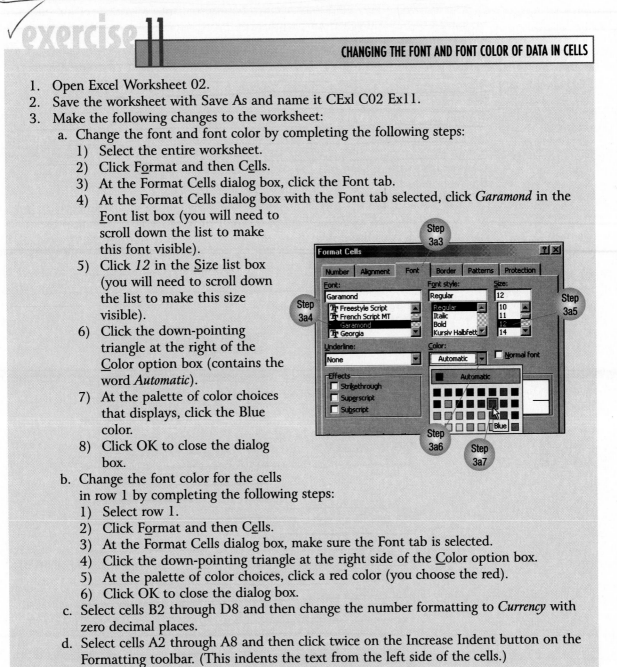

   b. Change the font color for the cells in row 1 by completing the following steps:
      1) Select row 1.
      2) Click Format and then Cells.
      3) At the Format Cells dialog box, make sure the Font tab is selected.
      4) Click the down-pointing triangle at the right side of the Color option box.
      5) At the palette of color choices, click a red color (you choose the red).
      6) Click OK to close the dialog box.
   c. Select cells B2 through D8 and then change the number formatting to *Currency* with zero decimal places.
   d. Select cells A2 through A8 and then click twice on the Increase Indent button on the Formatting toolbar. (This indents the text from the left side of the cells.)
   e. Automatically adjust the width of columns A, B, C, and D.
4. Save, print, and then close CExl C02 Ex11.

Inserting/Deleting Cells, Rows, and Columns

New data may need to be included in an existing worksheet. For example, a row or several rows of new data may need to be inserted into a worksheet; or, data may need to be removed from a worksheet.

Inserting Rows

HINT

At the Insert dialog box, specify the direction in which cells should move.

After a worksheet has been created, rows can be added (inserted) to the worksheet. Insert a row with options from the Insert drop-down menu or with options at the Insert dialog box. By default, a row is inserted above the row containing the active cell. To insert a row in a worksheet, make a cell active in the row below where the row is to be inserted, click Insert and then click Rows. If you want to insert more than one row, select the number of rows in the worksheet that you want inserted, click Insert and then click Rows.

You can also insert a row by making a cell active in the row below where the row is to be inserted, clicking Insert, and then clicking Cells. This causes the Insert dialog box to display as shown in figure 2.13. At the Insert dialog box, click Entire row. This inserts an entire row above the active cell.

FIGURE

2.13 *Insert Dialog Box*

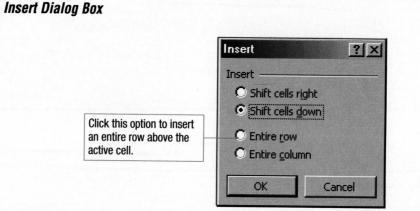

Click this option to insert an entire row above the active cell.

**exercise 12**

INSERTING ROWS IN A WORKSHEET

1. Open Excel Worksheet 01.
2. Save the worksheet with Save As and name it CExl C02 Ex12.
3. Make the following changes to the worksheet:
   a. Add two rows and enter data in the new cells by completing the following steps:
      1) Select rows 7 and 8 in the worksheet.
      2) Click Insert and then Rows.
      3) Key the following data in the specified cells (you do not need to key the dollar sign or the comma in cells containing money amounts):

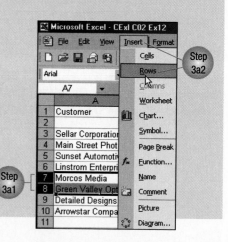

EXCEL

A7	=	Summit Clinic
B7	=	570
C7	=	$33,056
D7	=	$32,500
A8	=	Franklin Center
B8	=	690
C8	=	$19,745
D8	=	$19,250

    b. Select cells A1 through D12 and then apply an autoformat of your choosing. (Make sure the numbers display properly.)

4. Save, print, and then close CExl C02 Ex12.

Inserting Columns

Insert columns in a worksheet in much the same way as rows. Insert a column with options from the Insert drop-down menu or with options at the Insert dialog box. By default, a column is inserted immediately to the left of the column containing the active cell. To insert a column in a worksheet, make a cell active in the column immediately to the right of where the new column is to be inserted, click Insert and then click Columns. If you want to insert more than one column, select the number of columns in the worksheet that you want inserted, click Insert and then click Columns.

You can also insert a column by making a cell active in the column immediately to the right of where the new column is to be inserted, clicking Insert, and then clicking Cells. This causes the Insert dialog box to display. At the Insert dialog box, click Entire column. This inserts an entire column immediately to the left of the active cell.

 **exercise 13**

1. Open Excel Worksheet 03.
2. Save the worksheet with Save As and name it CExl C02 Ex13.
3. Make the following changes to the worksheet:
    a. Add a column to the worksheet and enter data in the new cells by completing the following steps:
       1) Click in any cell in column D.
       2) Click Insert and then Columns.
       3) Key the following data in the specified cell:

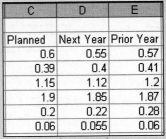

C	D	E
Planned	Next Year	Prior Year
0.6	0.55	0.57
0.39	0.4	0.41
1.15	1.12	1.2
1.9	1.85	1.87
0.2	0.22	0.28
0.06	0.055	0.06

 Step 3a3

D2	=	Next Year
D3	=	0.55
D4	=	0.4
D5	=	1.12
D6	=	1.85
D7	=	0.22
D8	=	0.055

    b. Select cells B3 through E8 and then click the Percent Style button on the Formatting toolbar.
    c. Select cells A1 through E8 and then apply an autoformat of your choosing.
4. Save, print, and then close CExl C02 Ex13.

Deleting Cells, Rows, or Columns

Specific cells in a worksheet or rows or columns in a worksheet can be deleted. To delete a specific cell, make the cell active, and then press the Delete key. You can also select the cells to be deleted and then press the Delete key. If you use the Delete key to delete cell(s), only the cell text is deleted. The empty cell(s) remains in the worksheet.

If you want to delete the cell(s) as well as the cell text, make the specific cell active or select cells, click Edit, and then click Delete. At the Delete dialog box shown in figure 2.14, choose what you wanted deleted, and then click OK.

FIGURE

2.14 *Delete Dialog Box*

The Delete dialog box can also be displayed by positioning the cell pointer in the worksheet, clicking the *right* mouse button, and then clicking Delete on the shortcut menu. To delete several rows of cells, select the rows, click Edit, and then click Delete. To delete several columns of cells, select the columns, click Edit, and then click Delete.

Clearing Data in Cells

HINT

One method for clearing the contents of a cell is to right-click the cell and then click Clear Contents at the shortcut menu.

With the Clear option from the Edit drop-down menu, the contents of selected cells can be cleared. This is useful in a situation where the cells are to remain but the contents need to be changed. To clear cell contents, select the cells, click Edit, point to Clear, and then click All. This deletes the cell contents and the cell formatting. Click Formats to remove formatting from selected cells while leaving the data. Click Contents to remove the contents of the cell, leaving any formatting. You can also click the Delete key to clear the contents of the selected cells.

EXCEL

1. Open Excel Worksheet 02.
2. Save the worksheet with Save As and name it CExl C02 Ex14.
3. Make the following changes to the worksheet:
   a. Delete column D in the worksheet by completing the following steps:
      1) Click in any cell in column D.
      2) Click Edit and then Delete.
      3) At the Delete dialog box, click Entire column.
      4) Click OK or press Enter.
   b. Delete row 5 by completing the following steps:
      1) Select row 5.
      2) Click Edit and then Delete.
   c. Clear row contents by completing the following steps:
      1) Select rows 5 and 6.
      2) Click Edit, point to Clear, and then click Contents.
   d. Key the following data in the specified cell:

A5	=	**Lodging**
B5	=	**4535**
C5	=	**5100**
A6	=	**Entertainment**
B6	=	**3210**
C6	=	**3000**

   e. Select cells A1 through C7 and then apply the Accounting 1 autoformat.
   f. Clear cell formatting and then apply different formatting by completing the following steps:
      1) Select cells A1 through C1.
      2) Click Edit, point to Clear, and then click Formats.
      3) With cells A1 through C1 still selected, click the Bold button on the Formatting toolbar and then click the Center button.
4. Save, print, and then close CExl C02 Ex14.

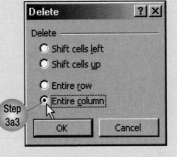

Step 3a3

Step 3d

	A	B	C
1	Expense	Actual	Budget
2	Salaries	126000	126000
3	Commissions	58000	54500
4	Media space	8250	10100
5	Lodging	4535	5100
6	Entertainment	3210	3000
7	Telephone	1450	1500

Adding Borders and Shading to Cells

The gridlines that display in a worksheet do not print. Borders that will print can be added to cells, however. Add borders with options from the Borders button on the Formatting toolbar or with options from the Format Cells dialog box with the Border tab selected.

Borders

To add a border to a cell or selected cells, make the desired cell active or select the desired cells, and then click the Borders button on the Formatting toolbar. By default, a single-line border is added to the bottom of the active cell or the selected cells. To change the style of border, click the down-pointing triangle at the right of the Borders button. This causes a palette of border style choices to display. Click the choice that represents the type of border desired for the cell or selected cells. Clicking the desired border style removes the palette and also applies that border style to the active cell or the selected cells.

HINT

Click the Erase button on the Borders toolbar and the mouse pointer turns into an eraser. Use this pointer to erase borders from cells.

Click the down-pointing triangle at the right side of the Borders button, click the Draw Borders option, and the Borders toolbar displays. Use buttons on this toolbar to draw, customize, and erase border lines.

ADDING BORDERS TO CELLS USING THE BORDERS BUTTON

1. Open Excel Worksheet 01.
2. Save the worksheet with Save As and name it CExl C02 Ex15.
3. Make the following changes to the worksheet:
   a. Select row 1 and then turn on bold and change the alignment to center.
   b. Select cells B3 through B10 and then change the alignment to center.
   c. Add a border to all cells in the worksheet (that contain data) by completing the following steps:

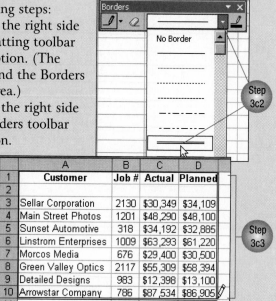

Step 3c2

   1) Click the down-pointing triangle at the right side of the Borders button on the Formatting toolbar and then click the Draw Borders option. (The mouse pointer turns into a pencil and the Borders toolbar displays in the worksheet area.)
   2) Click the down-pointing triangle at the right side of the Line Style button on the Borders toolbar and then click the double-line option.
   3) Using the mouse pointer (pencil), draw a double-line border around the outside of the cells containing data.

	A	B	C	D
1	**Customer**	**Job #**	**Actual**	**Planned**
2				
3	Sellar Corporation	2130	$30,349	$34,109
4	Main Street Photos	1201	$48,290	$48,100
5	Sunset Automotive	318	$34,192	$32,885
6	Linstrom Enterprises	1009	$63,293	$61,220
7	Morcos Media	676	$29,400	$30,500
8	Green Valley Optics	2117	$55,309	$58,394
9	Detailed Designs	983	$12,398	$13,100
10	Arrowstar Company	786	$87,534	$86,905
11				

Step 3c3

   4) Change back to a single line by clicking the down-pointing triangle at the right side of the Line Style button on the Borders toolbar, and then clicking the top single-line option.
   5) Turn off the display of the Borders toolbar by clicking the Close button (contains an X) located in the upper right corner of the toolbar.
   d. Add a single-line border to specific cells by completing the following steps:

Step 3d2

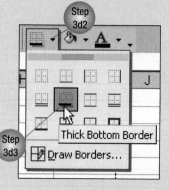

J

Step 3d3

Thick Bottom Border

Draw Borders...

   1) Select cells A1 through D1.
   2) Click the down-pointing triangle at the right of the Borders button on the Formatting toolbar.
   3) At the palette of border style choices that displays, click the Thick Bottom Border option (second option from the left in the middle row).
   e. Click in cell A1.
4. Save, print, and then close CExl C02 Ex15.

You can also add borders to the active cell or selected cells with options at the Format Cells dialog box with the Border tab selected as shown in figure 2.15. With options in the Presets section, you can remove borders with the None option, add only outside borders with the Outline option, or click the Inside option to add borders to the inside of selected cells. In the Border section of the dialog box, specify the side of the cell or selected cells to which you want to apply a border. Choose the style of line desired for the border with the options that display in the Style list box. Add color to border lines with choices from the color palette that displays when you click the down-pointing triangle located at the right side of the Color option box (contains the word *Automatic*).

HINT

Apply shading and patterns to cells at the Format Cells dialog box with the Patterns tab selected.

FIGURE

2.15 **Format Cells Dialog Box with Border Tab Selected**

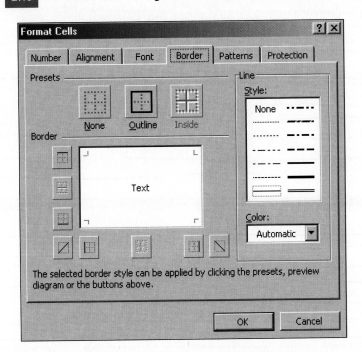

✓ exercise 16

ADDING BORDERS TO CELLS AT THE FORMAT CELLS DIALOG BOX

1. Open Excel Worksheet 02.
2. Save the worksheet with Save As and name it CExl C02 Ex16.
3. Make the following changes to the worksheet:
    a. Select the entire worksheet, display the Format Cells dialog box with the Font tab selected, change the font to 12-point Times New Roman (or a similar typeface), the color to green (you determine the green), and then close the dialog box.
    b. Select row 1 and then turn on bold and change the alignment to center.
    c. Select cells B2 through D8, display the Format Cells dialog box with the Number tab selected, change the Category option to *Currency* with zero decimal places, and then click OK to close the dialog box.
    d. Automatically adjust the width of columns A, B, C, and D.

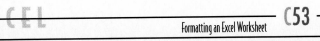

e. Add a green outline border to the worksheet by completing the following steps:
1) Select cells A1 through D8 (all cells containing data).
2) Click Format and then Cells.
3) At the Format Cells dialog box, click the Border tab.
4) Click the sixth option from the top in the second column in the Style list box.
5) Click the down-pointing triangle located at the right side of the Color option box (contains the word *Automatic*).
6) At the palette of color choices, click the same green color that you chose for the font.
7) Click the Outline option in the Presets section of the dialog box.
8) Click OK to close the dialog box.

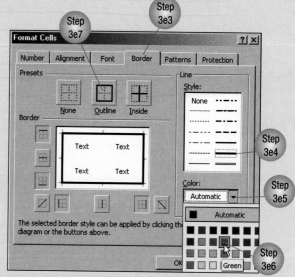

f. Click in cell A1.
4. Save, print, and then close CExl C02 Ex16.

Adding Shading and a Pattern to Cells

Fill Color

To enhance the visual display of cells and data within cells, consider adding shading and/or a pattern to cells. Add color shading to cells in a worksheet by clicking the Fill Color button on the Formatting toolbar. You can also add color shading and/or a pattern to cells in a worksheet with options at the Format Cells dialog box with the Patterns tab selected.

To add color shading using the Fill Color button on the Formatting toolbar, make the desired cell active or select the desired cells, and then click the Fill Color button. By default, the color yellow is added to the cell or selected cells. To add a shading of a different color, click the down-pointing triangle at the right of the Fill Color button, and then click the desired color at the palette that displays.

Add color shading as well as a pattern to the active cell or selected cells with options at the Format Cells dialog box with the Patterns tab selected as shown in figure 2.16. Choose a color shading for a cell or selected cells by clicking a color choice in the Color palette. To add a pattern to a cell or selected cells, click the down-pointing triangle at the right of the Pattern option box, and then click the desired pattern. When you click a pattern, that pattern displays in the Sample box in the dialog box. The Sample box also displays any chosen color shading.

2.16 Format Cells Dialog Box with Patterns Tab Selected

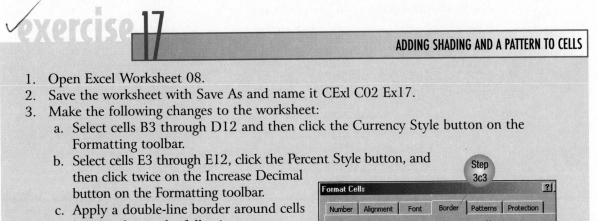

Repeating the Last Action

If you want to apply other types of formatting, such as number, border, or shading formatting to other cells in a worksheet, use the Repeat command by pressing F4 or Ctrl + Y. The repeat command repeats the last action performed.

exercise 17

ADDING SHADING AND A PATTERN TO CELLS

1. Open Excel Worksheet 08.
2. Save the worksheet with Save As and name it CExl C02 Ex17.
3. Make the following changes to the worksheet:
   a. Select cells B3 through D12 and then click the Currency Style button on the Formatting toolbar.
   b. Select cells E3 through E12, click the Percent Style button, and then click twice on the Increase Decimal button on the Formatting toolbar.
   c. Apply a double-line border around cells by completing the following steps:
      1) Select cells A1 through E12.
      2) Click Format and then Cells.
      3) At the Format Cells dialog box, click the Border tab.
      4) Click the double-line option in the Style list box.
      5) Click the Outline button in the Presets section.

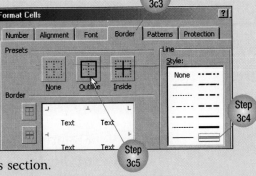

6) Click OK to close the dialog box.

d. Select cells B1 through E1 and then turn on bold and change the alignment to center.

e. With cells B1 through E1 selected, apply shading by clicking the down-pointing triangle at the right of the Fill Color button and then clicking the light green color.

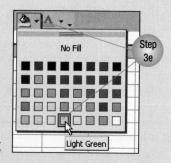

Step 3e

f. Repeat the shading by selecting cells A2 through A12 and then pressing F4 or Ctrl + Y.

g. Apply shading to specific cells by completing the following steps:

1) With cells B3 through E4 selected, click Format and then Cells.

2) At the Format Cells dialog box, click the Patterns tab.

3) Click the light yellow color in the Color section.

4) Click OK.

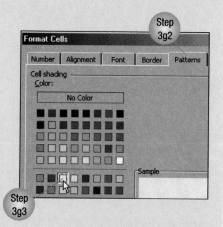

Step 3g2

Step 3g3

h. Use the Repeat command, F4 or Ctrl + Y, to apply the same light yellow shading to cells B7 through E8 and also to cells B11 through E12.

i. Apply a pattern to cells by completing the following steps:

1) Select cells B2 through E2 (these are empty cells).

2) Click Format and then Cells.

3) At the Format Cells dialog box with the Patterns tab selected, click the down-pointing triangle at the right side of the Pattern option box, and then click the Thin Diagonal Stripe option (fourth option from the left in the bottom row).

4) Click OK.

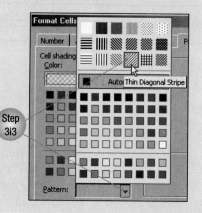

Step 3i3

j. Use the Repeat command, F4 or Ctrl + Y, to apply the same pattern to cells B5 through E6 and also to cells B9 through E10.

k. Click in cell A1.

4. Save, print, and then close CExl C02 Ex17.

Formatting with Format Painter

The Standard toolbar contains a button that can be used to copy formatting to different locations in the worksheet. This button is called the Format Painter and displays on the Standard toolbar as a paintbrush. To use the Format Painter button, make a cell or selected cells active that contain the desired formatting, click the Format Painter button, and then click the cell or selected cells to which you want the formatting applied.

When you click the Format Painter button, the mouse pointer displays with a paintbrush attached. If you want to apply formatting a single time, click the

EXCEL

Format Painter brush once. If, however, you want to apply the character formatting in more than one location in the worksheet, double-click the Format Painter button. If you have double-clicked the Format Painter button, turn off the feature by clicking the Format Painter button once.

exercise 18

FORMATTING WITH FORMAT PAINTER

1. Open Excel Worksheet 06.
2. Save the worksheet with Save As and name it CExl C02 Ex18.
3. Select and then delete columns K through M.
4. Use Format Painter to "paint" formatting to cells by completing the following steps:
   a. Select cells B1 through B20 and then apply pale blue shading to the cells.
   b. Make a cell active that contains a percentage number in column B.
   c. Double-click the Format Painter button on the Standard toolbar.
   d. Select each of the following columns:
      Column D
      Column F
      Column H
      Column J
   e. Select each of the following rows:
      Row 3
      Row 5
      Row 7
      Row 9
      Row 11
      Row 13
      Row 15
      Row 17
      Row 19
   f. Turn off Format Painter by clicking the Format Painter button on the Standard toolbar.
   g. Select row 1 and then click twice on the Bold button on the Formatting toolbar. (The Format Painter removed the bold formatting from the cells you formatted with pale blue shading. Selecting the row and then clicking the Bold button the first time removes bold from all headings. Clicking the Bold button the second time inserts bold formatting for the headings.)
5. Save, print, and then close CExl C02 Ex18.

CHAPTER summary

- Preview a worksheet by clicking the Preview button in the Print dialog box; clicking the Print Preview button on the Standard toolbar; or clicking File and then Print Preview.
- Change the size of the worksheet display with options on the Zoom button on the Standard toolbar.
- Apply character formatting to selected cells with buttons on the Formatting toolbar such as Font, Font Size, Bold, Italic, Underline, and Font Color.
- Change column width using the mouse on column boundaries or with options at the Column Width dialog box.
- To automatically adjust a column to accommodate the longest entry in the column, double-click the column header boundary on the right.
- Change row height using the mouse on row boundaries or with options at the Row Height dialog box.
- Format numbers in cells with the Currency Style, Percent Style, Comma Style, Increase Decimal, and Decrease Decimal buttons on the Formatting toolbar.
- Numbers in cells can also be formatted at the Format Cells dialog box with the Number tab selected.
- Change alignment of data within cells with these buttons on the Formatting toolbar: Align Left, Center, Align Right, and Merge and Center.
- You can also change the alignment of data within cells at the Format Cells dialog box with the Alignment tab selected.
- Indent text in a cell or selected cells by clicking the Increase Indent button on the Formatting toolbar. Decrease the indent of text in a cell or selected cells by clicking the Decrease Indent button.
- Change font type, font size, font style, and font color for data in a cell or selected cells with options at the Format Cells dialog box with the Font tab selected.
- Insert a row in a worksheet by clicking Insert and then Rows. To insert more than one row, select the number of rows you want inserted, click Insert and then click Rows. A row can also be inserted at the Insert dialog box.
- Insert a column in a worksheet by clicking Insert and then Columns. To insert more than one column, select the number of columns you want inserted, click Insert and then click Columns. A column can also be inserted at the Insert dialog box.
- Delete a specific cell by clicking Edit and then Delete. This displays the Delete dialog box where you can specify if you want to delete just the cell or an entire row or column.
- Remove contents of a cell with the Clear option from the Edit drop-down menu or by pressing the Delete key.
- Add borders to a cell or selected cells with the Borders button on the Formatting toolbar or options at the Format Cells dialog box with the Border tab selected.
- Click the down-pointing triangle at the right side of the Borders button, click the Draw Borders option, and the Borders toolbar displays. Use buttons on this toolbar to draw borders.

➤ Add color shading to a cell or selected cells with the Fill Color button on the Formatting toolbar. Shading as well as a pattern can be added to a cell or selected cells with options at the Format Cells dialog box with the Patterns tab selected.

➤ Press F4 or Ctrl + Y to repeat the last action performed.

➤ Use the Format Painter button on the Standard toolbar to copy formatting to different locations in a worksheet.

COMMANDS review

Command	Mouse/Keyboard
Display worksheet in Print Preview	Click Preview button in Print dialog box; click Print Preview button on Standard toolbar; or click File, Print Preview
Change Zoom display	Click the down-pointing triangle at the right side of the Zoom button on the Standard toolbar
Display Column Width dialog box	Click Format, Column, Width
Display Row Height dialog box	Click Format, Row, Height
Display Format Cells dialog box	Click Format, Cells
Display Insert dialog box	Click Insert, Cells
Display Delete dialog box	Click Edit, Delete
Display Borders toolbar	Click down-pointing triangle on Borders button, then click Draw Borders option
Repeat last action	Press F4 or Ctrl + Y

CONCEPTS check

Completion: On a blank sheet of paper, indicate the correct term, symbol, or command for each item.

1. To preview a worksheet, click this button on the Standard toolbar. *Print Preview*
2. This toolbar contains buttons for applying character formatting to data within selected cells. *Formatting*
3. To automatically adjust a column width to accommodate the longest entry in the cell, do this with the mouse on the column header boundary. *double-click*
4. As a column boundary is being dragged, the column width displays in this. *yellow box*
5. Click this button on the Formatting toolbar to multiply the value of numbers in selected cells by 100 and display the result followed by a percent symbol. *Percent Style (%)*
6. Click this button on the Formatting toolbar to add a dollar sign, any necessary commas, and a decimal point followed by two decimal digits to numbers in selected cells. *Currency Style ($)*
7. Click this button on the Formatting toolbar to merge selected cells and center any data within the cells. *Merge and Center*
8. Rotate data in cells with options at the Format Cells dialog box with this tab selected. *Alignment*

9. By default, a row is inserted in this direction from the row containing the active cell. *up*

10. By default, a column is inserted in this direction from the column containing the active cell. *left*

11. Add color shading to selected cells in a worksheet with options at the Format Cells dialog box with this tab selected. *Patterns*

12. Press this key to repeat the last action. *F4*

13. Use this button on the Standard toolbar to copy formatting to different locations in a worksheet. *Format Painter*

SKILLS check

√Assessment 1

1. Create the worksheet shown in figure 2.17 with the following specifications:
   a. Select the entire worksheet and then change the font to 12-point Garamond (or a similar typeface).
   b. Change the width of column A to 14.00 and the width of columns B and C to 9.00.
   c. Key the text in the cells as shown in figure 2.17. (Bold and center the data in row 1 as shown in the figure.)
   d. After keying the data, select cells B2 through C6, and then change the number formatting to *Currency* with zero decimal places.
2. Save the worksheet and name it CExl C02 SA01.
3. Print and then close CExl C02 SA01.

FIGURE

2.17 *Assessment 1*

	A	B	C	D
1	**Expense**	**Original**	**Current**	
2	Labor	97000	98500	
3	Material	129000	153000	
4	Subcontracts	20450	21600	
5	Permits	1200	1350	
6	Tax	1950	2145	
7				

√Assessment 2

1. Open Excel Worksheet 03.
2. Save the worksheet with Save As and name it CExl C02 SA02.
3. Make the following changes to the worksheet:
   a. Select the entire worksheet and then change the font to 11-point Tahoma (or a similar sans serif typeface).
   b. Select row 1 and then turn on bold.
   c. Select row 2 and then turn on bold and italics and change the alignment to center.

d. Select cells A1 through D1 and then click the Merge and Center button on the Formatting toolbar.
　　e. Select cells B3 through D8 and then click the Percent Style button on the Formatting toolbar.
　　f. Select rows 1 through 8 and then change the row height to 18.00.
　　g. Automatically adjust the widths of columns A through D.
4. Save, print, and then close CExl C02 SA02.

Assessment 3

1. Open CExl C02 SA01.
2. Save the worksheet with Save As and name it CExl C02 SA03.
3. Make the following changes to the worksheet:
　　a. Change the font for the entire worksheet to 14-point Arial and change the font color to violet.
　　b. Change the font color to dark blue for the cells in row 1.
　　c. Automatically adjust the widths of columns A, B, and C.
　　d. Add a single-line outside border to cells A1 through C6.
4. Save, print, and then close CExl C02 SA03.

Assessment 4

1. Open CExl C02 SA02.
2. Save the worksheet with Save As and name it CExl C02 SA04.
3. Make the following changes to the worksheet:
　　a. Change the font for the entire worksheet to 12-point Garamond (or a similar serif typeface) and the font color to violet.
　　b. Select row 2, turn off bold and italics, and then change the font color to dark blue.
　　c. Select row 1 and then change the font color to dark blue.
　　d. Select cells A1 through D8 and then add an outside border with a line style of your choosing.
4. Save, print, and then close CExl C02 SA04.

Assessment 5

1. Open CExl C02 SA01.
2. Save the worksheet with Save As and name it CExl C02 SA05.
3. Select rows 5 and 6, insert two new rows, and then insert the following data in the new specified cells:

A5	=	Insurance
B5	=	2000
C5	=	1300
A6	=	Management
B6	=	20000
C6	=	14500

4. Insert a new column between columns B and C and then insert the following data in the specified cells:

C1	=	Budgeted
C2	=	95000
C3	=	130000
C4	=	22000
C5	=	2000
C6	=	18000

C7   =   **1500**
C8   =   **2000**

5. Automatically adjust the widths of columns A, B, C, and D.
6. Add the following formatting to the worksheet:
   a. Select cells A1 through D8 and then add a border around the cells (you choose the border-line style).
   b. With the cells still selected, add light yellow shading to the selected cells.
   c. Select cells A1 through D1 and then add a pattern of your choosing to the cells.
7. Save, print, and then close CExl C02 SA05.

✓Assessment 6

1. Create an Excel worksheet with the information shown in figure 2.18. You determine the following:
   a. Font
   b. Width of columns
   c. Number formatting
2. Add the following enhancements to the worksheet:
   a. Add a border to all cells in the worksheet containing data.
   b. Add a color shading to all cells in the worksheet containing data.
   c. Add a pattern to column headings (the cells containing *Project, Projected,* and *Actual*).
3. Save the completed worksheet and name it CExl C02 SA06.
4. Print and then save CExl C02 SA06.

FIGURE

| 2.18 | *Assessment 6* |

CAPITAL PROJECT SUMMARY

Project	Projected	Actual
Rail siding installation	$43,300	$41,200
Cement slabs	$12,000	$13,980
Silos	$28,420	$29,600
Conveying system	$56,700	$58,200
Modulators	$8,210	$8,100
Winder	$6,400	$7,100

✓Assessment 7

select – Format – cells – alignment – shrink to fit √box

1. Use the Help feature to learn how to shrink the font size to show all data in a cell.
2. Open Excel Worksheet 03.
3. Save the worksheet with Save As and name it CExl C02 SA07.
4. Select cells A1 through D8 and then change the font size to 12.
5. Select cells A1 through D2 and then shrink the font size to show all data in the selected cells.
6. Save, print, and then close CExl C02 SA07.

EXCEL

CHAPTER 3

INSERTING FORMULAS IN A WORKSHEET

PERFORMANCE OBJECTIVES

Upon successful completion of chapter 3, you will be able to:
- **Insert a formula in a cell using the AutoSum button**
- **Write formulas with mathematical operators**
- **Key a formula in the Formula bar**
- **Copy a formula**
- **Use the Insert Function feature to insert a formula in a cell**
- **Write formulas with the AVERAGE, MAX, MIN, COUNT, PMT, FV, DATE, NOW, and IF functions**
- **Create an absolute and mixed cell reference**

Excel Chapter 03C

Excel is a powerful decision-making tool containing data that can be manipulated to answer "what if" situations. Insert a formula in a worksheet and then manipulate the data to make projections, answer specific questions, and use as a planning tool. For example, the manager of a department might use an Excel worksheet to prepare a department budget and then determine the impact on the budget of hiring a new employee or increasing the volume of production.

Insert a formula in a worksheet to perform calculations on values. A formula contains a mathematical operator, value, cell reference, cell range, and a function. Formulas can be written that add, subtract, multiply, and/or divide values. Formulas can also be written that calculate averages, percentages, minimum and maximum values, and much more. Excel includes an AutoSum button on the Standard toolbar that inserts a formula to calculate the total of a range of cells. Insert Function is an Excel feature that offers a variety of functions to create a formula.

Using the AutoSum Button

To perform a calculation in a worksheet, make active the cell in which you want to insert the formula (this cell should be empty). Key the formula in the cell and the formula displays in the cell as well as in the Formula bar. When the formula is completed, and you exit the cell, the result of the formula displays in the active cell while the actual formula displays in the Formula bar.

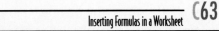

Enter

AutoSum

You can also enter a formula in the Formula bar located below the Formatting toolbar. To do this, click in the Formula bar text box, key the desired formula, and then press Enter or click the Enter button (contains a green check mark) on the Formula bar.

One of the advantages of using formulas in a worksheet is that cell entries can be changed and the formula will automatically recalculate the values and insert the result in the cell containing the formula. This is what makes an Excel worksheet a decision-making tool.

In addition to keying a formula in a cell, you can also use the AutoSum button on the Standard toolbar. The AutoSum button adds numbers automatically with the SUM function. When you click the AutoSum button, Excel looks for a range of cells containing numbers above the active cell. If no cell above contains numbers, then it looks to the left of the active cell. Excel suggests the range of cells to be added. If the suggested range is not correct, drag through the desired range with the mouse, and then press Enter. You can also just double-click the AutoSum button and this will insert the SUM function with the range Excel chooses.

(Note: Before completing computer exercises, delete the Excel Chapter 02C folder on your disk. Next, copy the Excel Chapter 03C subfolder from the Excel 2002 Core folder on the CD that accompanies this textbook to your disk and make Excel Chapter 03C the active folder.)

exercise

ADDING VALUES WITH THE AUTOSUM BUTTON

1. Open Excel Worksheet 02.
2. Save the worksheet with Save As and name it CExl C03 Ex01.
3. Calculate the sum of cells by completing the following steps:
   a. Make B9 the active cell.
   b. Click the AutoSum button on the Standard toolbar.
   c. Excel inserts the formula =SUM(B2:B8) in cell B9. This is the correct range of cells, so press Enter.
   d. Make C9 the active cell.
   e. Click the AutoSum button on the Standard toolbar.
   f. Excel inserts the formula =SUM(C2:C8) in cell C9. This is the correct range of cells, so press Enter.
   g. Make D9 the active cell.
   h. Double-click the AutoSum button on the Standard toolbar. (This inserts the formula =SUM(D2:D8) in cell D9 and inserts the sum -1820.)
4. Select cells A1 through D9 and then apply the Accounting 1 autoformat.
5. Save and then print CExl C03 Ex01.
6. With the worksheet still open, make the following changes to cell entries:
   B4: Change *8,250.00* to *9550*
   D4: Change *1,850.00* to *550*
   B7: Change *2,430.00* to *2050*
   D7: Change *(230.00)* to *150*
7. Save, print, and then close CExl C03 Ex01.

Step 3b

AutoSum

	A	B	C	D	E	F	G
		SUM	▾ ✗ ✓ ƒₓ =SUM(B2:B8)				
1	Expense	Actual	Budget	Variance			
2	Salaries	126000	126000	0			
3	Commissions	58000	54500	-3500			
4	Media space	8250	10100	1850			
5	Travel expenses	6350	6000	-350			
6	Dealer display	4140	4500	360			
7	Payroll taxes	2430	2200	-230			
8	Telephone	1450	1500	50			
9		=SUM(B2:B8)					
10		SUM(**number1**, [number2], ...)					

Step 3c

Writing Formulas with Mathematical Operators

The AutoSum button on the Standard toolbar essentially creates the formula for you. You can also write your own formulas using mathematical operators. Commonly used mathematical formulas and their functions are described in figure 3.1.

When writing your own formula, begin the formula with the equals (=) sign. For example to divide the contents of cell B2 by the content of cell C2 and insert the result in cell D2, you would make D2 the active cell, and then key **=B2/C2**.

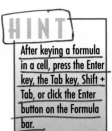

FIGURE

3.1 **Mathematical Operators**

To perform this function	Key this operator
Addition	+
Subtraction	-
Multiplication	*
Division	/
Percent	%
Exponentiation	^

If a formula contains two or more operators, Excel uses the same order of operations used in algebra. From left to right in a formula, this order, called the *order of operations*, is: negations (negative number—a number preceded by -) first, then percents (%), then exponentiations (^), followed by multiplications (*), divisions (/), additions (+), and finally subtractions (-). If you want to change the order of operations, use parentheses around the part of the formula you want calculated first.

ORDER OF OPERATIONS

*neg.#, %, ^, *, /, +, -*

Copying a Formula with Relative Cell References

In many worksheets, the same basic formula is used repetitively. In a situation where a formula is copied to other locations in a worksheet, use a *relative cell reference*. Copy a formula containing relative cell references and the cell references change. For example if you enter the formula *=SUM(A2:C2)* in cell D2 and then copy it relatively to cell D3, the formula in cell D3 displays as *=SUM(A3:C3)*. (Additional information on cell references is discussed later in this chapter in the "Using an Absolute Cell Reference in a Formula section.")

To copy a formula relatively in a worksheet, use the Fill option from the Edit drop-down menu. To do this, select the cell containing the formula as well as the cells to which you want the formula copied, and then click Edit. At the Edit drop-down menu, point to Fill. This causes another drop-down menu to display. The choices active in this drop-down menu will vary depending on the selected cells. For example, if you select cells down a column, options such as Down and Up will be active. If cells in a row are selected, options such as Right and Left will be active. Click the desired direction and the formula is copied relatively to the selected cells.

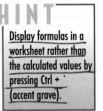

exercise 2

1. Open Excel Worksheet 01.
2. Save the worksheet with Save As and name it CExl C03 Ex02.
3. Make the following changes to the worksheet:
   a. Change the width of column A to 19.00.
   b. Make cell E1 active and then key **Variance**.
4. Insert a formula and then copy it to other cells by completing the following steps:
   a. Make E3 the active cell.
   b. Key the formula **=D3-C3**.
   c. Press Enter.
   d. Copy the formula to cells E4 through E10 by completing the following steps:
      1) Select cells E3 through E10.
      2) Click Edit, point to Fill, and then click Down.

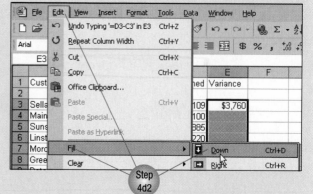

5. Select cells A1 through E10 and then apply the Colorful 1 autoformat.
6. Select cells B3 through B10 and then change the alignment to right.
7. Save and then print CExl C03 Ex02.
8. With the worksheet still open, make the following changes to cell contents:

   C4: Change $48,290 to 46425
   D6: Change $61,220 to 60000
   C8: Change $55,309 to 57415
   C9: Change $12,398 to 14115
9. Save, print, and then close CExl C03 Ex02.

Copying Formulas with the Fill Handle

HINT

Use the AutoFill fill handle to copy a relative version of a formula.

Use the AutoFill fill handle to copy a formula up, down, left, or right within a worksheet. To use the fill handle, insert the desired data in the cell (text, value, formula, etc.). With the cell active, position the mouse pointer (white plus sign) on the fill handle until the mouse pointer turns into a thin black cross. Hold down the left mouse button, drag and select the desired cells, and then release the mouse button. If you are dragging a cell containing a formula, a relative version of the formula is copied to the selected cells.

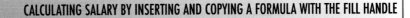

exercise 3   CALCULATING SALARY BY INSERTING AND COPYING A FORMULA WITH THE FILL HANDLE

1. Open Excel Worksheet 05.
2. Save the worksheet with Save As and name it CExl C03 Ex03.
3. Make cell D2 active, turn on bold, change the alignment to center, and then key **Salary**.
4. Insert a formula and then copy it to other cells using the fill handle by completing the following steps:

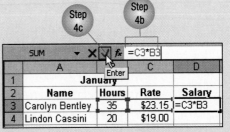

   a. Make D3 the active cell.
   b. Click in the Formula bar text box and then key **=C3*B3**.
   c. Click the Enter button on the Formula bar.
   d. Copy the formula to cells D4 through D8 by completing the following steps:
      1) Make sure cell D3 is the active cell.
      2) Position the mouse pointer (white plus sign) on the fill handle that displays at the lower right corner of cell D3 until the pointer turns into a thin black cross.
      3) Hold down the left mouse button, drag down to cell D8, and then release the mouse button.
5. Save and then print CExl C03 Ex03.
6. With the worksheet still open, make the following changes to cell contents:

   B4: Change *20* to *28*
   C5: Change *$18.75* to *19.10*
   B7: Change *15* to *24*
7. Save, print, and then close CExl C03 Ex03.

Writing a Formula by Pointing

In exercises 2 and 3, you wrote formulas using cell references such as *=C3-B3*. Another method for writing a formula is to "point" to the specific cells that are to be part of the formula. Creating a formula by pointing is more accurate than keying the cell reference since a mistake can happen when entering the cell reference.

To write a formula by pointing, click the cell that will contain the formula, key the equals sign to begin the formula, and then click the cell you want to reference in the formula. This inserts a moving border around the cell and also changes the mode from *Enter* to *Point*. (The word *Point* displays at the left side of the Status bar.) Key the desired mathematical operator and then click the next cell reference. Continue in this manner until all cell references are specified and then press the Enter key. This ends the formula and inserts the result of the calculation of the formula in the active cell. When writing a formula by pointing, you can also select a range of cells you want included in a formula.

WRITING A FORMULA BY POINTING THAT CALCULATES PERCENTAGE OF ACTUAL BUDGET

1. Open Excel Worksheet 02.
2. Save the worksheet with Save As and name it CExl C03 Ex04.
3. Make the following changes to the worksheet:
   a. Delete column D.
   b. Make cell D1 active and then key **% of Actual**.
   c. Enter a formula by pointing that calculates the percentage of actual budget by completing the following steps:
      1) Make cell D2 active.
      2) Key the equals sign.
      3) Click cell C2. (This inserts a moving border around the cell and the mode changes from *Enter* to *Point*.)
      4) Key the forward slash symbol (/).
      5) Click cell B2.
      6) Make sure the formula looks like this **=C2/B2** and then press Enter.
   d. Make cell D2 active and then click the Percent Style button on the Formatting toolbar.
   e. With cell D2 still active, position the mouse pointer on the fill handle, drag down to cell D8, and then release the mouse button.
   f. Select cells B2 through C8 and then click the Currency Style button on the Formatting toolbar.
   g. Automatically increase the width of column D to accommodate the column heading.
   h. Select cells A1 through D8 and then apply the Classic 2 autoformat.
4. Save, print, and then close CExl C03 Ex04.

	A	B	C	D
1	Expense	Actual	Budget	% of Actual
2	Salaries	126000	126000	=C2/B2
3	Commissions	58000	54500	
4	Media space	8250	10100	
5	Travel expenses	6350	6000	
6	Dealer display	4140	4500	
7	Payroll taxes	2430	2200	
8	Telephone	1450	1500	

Step 3c

Using the Trace Error Button

Trace Error

As you are working in a worksheet, you may occasionally notice a button pop up near the active cell. The general term for this button is *smart tag*. The display of the smart tag button varies depending on the action performed. In exercise 5, you will insert a formula that will cause a smart tag button, named the Trace Error button, to appear. When the Trace Error button appears, a small dark green triangle also displays in the upper left corner of the cell. Click the Trace Error button and a drop-down list displays with options for updating the formula to include specific cells, getting help on the error, ignoring the error, editing the error in the Formula bar, and completing an error check. In exercise 5, two of the formulas you insert return the desired results. You will click the Trace Error button, read information on what Excel perceives as the error, and then tell Excel to ignore the error.

WRITING A FORMULA BY POINTING THAT CALCULATES PERCENTAGE OF DOWN TIME

1. Open Excel Worksheet 09.
2. Save the worksheet with Save As and name it CExl C03 Ex05.
3. Make the following changes to the worksheet:
   a. Make cell A11 active, key (in bold) **Percentage of**, press Alt + Enter, and then key (in bold) **Down Time**.
   b. Enter a formula by pointing that computes the percentage of equipment down time by completing the following steps:
      1) Make cell B11 active.
      2) Key the equals sign followed by the left parenthesis: **=(**.
      3) Click cell B3. (This inserts a moving border around the cell and the mode changes from *Enter* to *Point*.)
      4) Key the minus symbol (-).
      5) Click cell B9.
      6) Key the right parenthesis followed by the forward slash: **)/**.
      7) Click cell B3.
      8) Make sure the formula looks like this **=(B3-B9)/B3** and then press Enter.
   c. Make cell B11 active and then click the Percent Style button on the Formatting toolbar.
   d. With cell B11 still active, position the mouse pointer on the fill handle, drag across to cell M11, and then release the mouse button.
   e. Enter a formula by dragging through a range of cells by completing the following steps:
      1) Click in cell A13, key (in bold) **Hours Available**, press Alt + Enter, and then key (in bold) **Jan - June**.
      2) Click in cell B13 and then click the AutoSum button on the Standard toolbar.
      3) Select cells B3 through G3.
      4) Click the Enter button on the Formula bar. (This inserts 14,340 in cell B13.)
   f. Click in cell A14, key (in bold) **Hours Available**, press Alt + Enter, and then key (in bold) **July - Dec**.
   g. Click in cell B14 and then complete steps similar to those in steps 3e2 through 3e4 to create a formula that totals hours available from July through December (cells H3 through M3). (This inserts 14,490 in cell B14.)
4. Click in cell B13 and notice the Trace Error button that displays. Complete the following steps to read about the error and then tell Excel to ignore the error:
   a. Click the Trace Error button.
   b. At the drop-down list that displays, click the <u>H</u>elp on this error option.

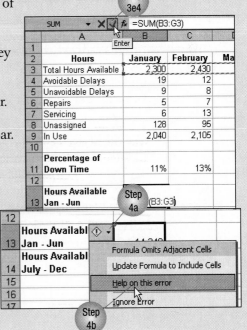

Step 3b8

Step 3e4

Step 4a

Step 4b

c. Read the information on *Formula Omits Cells in Region* that displays in the Microsoft Excel Help window and then close the window.

d. Click the Trace Error button again and then click Ignore Error at the drop-down list.

5. Remove the dark green triangle from cell B14 by completing the following steps:

a. Click in cell B14.

b. Click the Trace Error button and then click Ignore error at the drop-down list.

6. Save, print, and then close CExl C03 Ex05. (The worksheet will print on two pages. In the next chapter, you will learn about features that control how worksheets are printed.)

13	Hours Availabl ① ▾	
	Jan - Jun	Formula Omits Adja
14	Hours Availabl	Update Formula to
	July - Dec	Help on this error
15		
16		Ignore Error
17		
18	Step 4d	Edit in Formula Bar

Inserting a Formula with the Insert Function Button

In exercise 1, the AutoSum button inserted a formula that began with =*SUM*. This part of the formula is called a *function*, which is a built-in formula. Using a function takes less keystrokes when creating a formula. For example, the =*SUM* function saved you from having to key each cell to be included in the formula with the plus (+) symbol between cell entries.

Excel provides other functions for writing formulas. A function operates on what is referred to as an *argument*. An argument may consist of a constant, a cell reference, or another function (referred to as a nested function). In exercise 1, when you made cell B10 active and then clicked the AutoSum button, the formula =*SUM(B3:B9)* was inserted in the cell. The cell range *(B3:B9)* is an example of a cell reference argument. An argument may also contain a *constant*. A constant is a value entered directly into the formula. For example, if you enter the formula =*SUM(B3:B9,100)*, the cell range *B3:B9* is a cell reference argument and *100* is a constant. In this formula, 100 is always added to the sum of the cells. If a function is included in an argument within a function, it is called a *nested function*. (You will learn about nested functions later in this chapter.)

When a value calculated by the formula is inserted in a cell, this process is referred to as *returning the result*. The term *returning* refers to the process of calculating the formula and the term *result* refers to the value inserted in the cell.

Insert Function

You can key a function in a cell in a worksheet or you can use the Insert Function button on the Formula bar to help you write the formula. When you click the Insert Function button, or click Insert and then Function, the Insert Function dialog box displays as shown in figure 3.2.

EXCEL

3.2 **Insert Function Dialog Box**

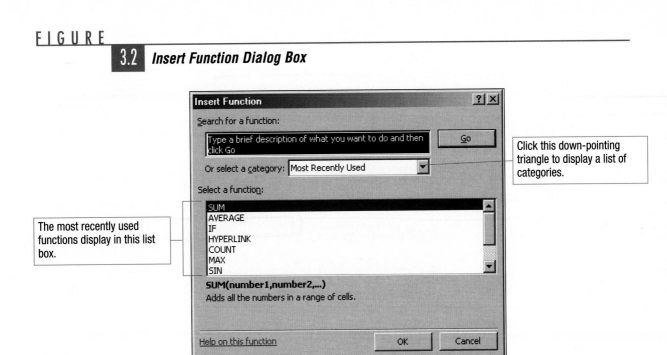

The most recently used functions display in this list box.

Click this down-pointing triangle to display a list of categories.

At the Insert Function dialog box, the most recently used functions display in a list box. You can choose a function category by clicking the down-pointing triangle at the right side of the Or select a category list box, and then clicking the desired category at the drop-down list. Use the Search for a function option to locate a specific function. With the desired function category selected, choose a function in the Select a function list box and then click OK. This displays a Function Arguments palette like the one shown in figure 3.3. At this palette, enter in the Number1 text box the range of cells you want included in the formula, enter any constants that are to be included as part of the formula, or enter another function. After entering a range of cells, a constant, or another function, click the OK button. More than one argument can be included in a function. If the function you are creating contains more than one argument, press the Tab key to move the insertion point to the Number2 text box, and then enter the second argument.

HINT

You can also display the Insert Function dialog box by clicking the down-pointing triangle at the right side of the AutoSum button and then clicking More Functions.

HINT

If you need to display a specific cell or cells behind the formula palette, move the palette by clicking and dragging it.

3.3 *Example Function Arguments Palette*

Enter in this text box the range of cells you want included in the formula.

Information about the AVERAGE function displays here.

Click this hyperlink to display help on the function.

Function Arguments   **? X**

AVERAGE
Number1 B3:M3   = {0.89,0.65,0.76,0.8
Number2   = number

                                            = 0.761666667
Returns the average (arithmetic mean) of its arguments, which can be numbers or names, arrays, or references that contain numbers.

Number1: number1,number2,... are 1 to 30 numeric arguments for which you want the average.

Formula result =   0.761666667

Help on this function   OK   Cancel

Writing Formulas with Functions

HINT

Click the down-pointing triangle at the right side of the AutoSum button and common functions display in a drop-down list.

Excel includes over 200 functions that are divided into 9 different categories including Financial, Date & Time, Math & Trig, Statistical, Lookup & Reference, Database, Text, Logical, and Information. Clicking the AutoSum button on the Standard toolbar automatically adds numbers with the SUM function. The SUM function is included in the Math & Trig category. In some sections in this chapter, you will write formulas with functions in other categories including Statistical, Financial, Date & Time, and Logical.

Writing Formulas with Statistical Functions

In this section, you will learn to write formulas with the statistical functions AVERAGE, MAX, MIN, and COUNT. The AVERAGE function returns the average (arithmetic mean) of the arguments. The MAX function returns the largest value in a set of values and the MIN function returns the smallest number in a set of values. Use the COUNT function to count the number of cells that contain numbers within the list of arguments.

Finding Averages

A common function in a formula is the AVERAGE function. With this function, a range of cells is added together and then divided by the number of cell entries. In exercise 6 you will use the AVERAGE function, which will add all test scores for a student and then divide that number by the total number of tests. You will use the Insert Function feature to simplify the creation of the formula containing an AVERAGE function.

One of the advantages to using formulas in a worksheet is the ability to easily manipulate data to answer certain questions. In exercise 6 you will learn the impact of retaking certain tests on the final average score.

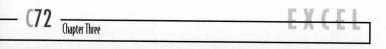

✔ exercise 6

1. Open Excel Worksheet 06.
2. Save the worksheet with Save As and name it CExl C03 Ex06.
3. Make cell N1 the active cell, turn on bold, and then key **Average**.
4. Use the Insert Function feature to find the average of test scores and copy the formula by completing the following steps:
   a. Make N3 the active cell.
   b. Click the Insert Function button on the Formula bar.
   c. At the Insert Function dialog box, click the down-pointing triangle at the right side of the Or select a category list box, and then click *Statistical* at the drop-down list.
   d. Click *AVERAGE* in the Select a function list box.
   e. Click OK.
   f. At the Function Arguments palette, make sure *B3:M3* displays in the Number1 text box. (If not, key **B3:M3** in the Number1 text box.)
   g. Click OK.
   h. Copy the formula by completing the following steps:
      1) Make cell N3 active.
      2) Position the mouse pointer on the fill handle until the pointer turns into a thin black cross.
      3) Hold down the left mouse button, drag down to cell N20, and then release the mouse button.
5. Save and then print CExl C03 Ex06. (The worksheet will print on two pages.)
6. After viewing the averages of test scores, you notice that a couple of people have a low average. You decide to see what happens to the average score if students make up tests where they scored the lowest. You decide that a student can make up to a 70% on a retake of the test. Make the following changes to test scores to see how the changes will affect the test average.

        L5: Change *45* to *70*
        M5: Change *49* to *70*
        C10: Change *45* to *70*
        M10: Change *49* to *70*
        C14: Change *0* to *70*
        I14: Change *0* to *70*
        J14: Change *0* to *70*

7. Save, print, and then close CExl C03 Ex06. (Compare the test averages for Jack Calahan, Stephanie Flanery, and Kathleen Kwieciak to see what the effect of retaking the tests has on their final test averages.)

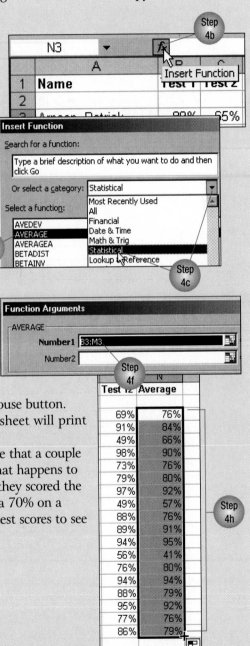

When a formula such as the AVERAGE formula you inserted in a cell in exercise 6 calculates cell entries, it ignores certain cell entries. The AVERAGE function will ignore text in cells and blank cells (not zeros). For example, in the worksheet containing test scores, a couple of cells contained a 0% entry. This entry was included in the averaging of the test scores. If you did not want that particular test to be included in the average, enter text in the cell such as *N/A* (for *not applicable*) or leave the cell blank.

Finding Maximum and Minimum Values

The MAX function in a formula returns the maximum value in a cell range and the MIN function returns the minimum value in a cell range. As an example, you could use the MAX and MIN functions in a worksheet containing employee hours to determine which employee worked the most number of hours and which worked the least. In a worksheet containing sales commissions, you could use the MAX and MIN functions to determine the salesperson who earned the most commission dollars and the one who earned the least.

Insert a MAX and MIN function into a formula in the same manner as an AVERAGE function. In exercise 7, you will use the Insert Function feature to insert MAX and MIN functions in cells to determine the highest test score average and the lowest test score average.

	FINDING MAXIMUM AND MINIMUM VALUES IN A WORKSHEET

1. Open CExl C03 Ex06.
2. Save the worksheet with Save As and name it CExl C03 Ex07.
3. Key the following in the specified cells:
   A22: Turn on bold and then key **Highest Test Average**.
   A23: Turn on bold and then key **Lowest Test Average**.
   A24: Turn on bold and then key **Average of All Tests**.
4. Automatically adjust the width of column A.
5. Insert the following formulas in the worksheet:
   a. Insert a formula to identify the highest test score average by completing the following steps:
      1) Make cell B22 active.
      2) Click the Insert Function button on the Formula bar.
      3) At the Insert Function dialog box, make sure *Statistical* is selected in the Or select a category list box. (If not, click the down-pointing triangle at the right side of the Or select a category list box and then click *Statistical* at the drop-down list.)
      4) Click *MAX* in the Select a function list box. (You will need to scroll down the list to display *MAX*.)
      5) Click OK.
      6) At the Function Arguments palette, key **N3:N20** in the Number1 text box.
      7) Click OK.
   b. Insert a formula to identify the lowest test score average by completing the following steps:

Insert Function

Search for a function:

Type a brief description of what
click Go

Or select a category: Statistical

Select a function:

LOGNORMDIST
MAX
MAXA
MEDIAN
MIN
MINA
MODE

Step 5a4

Function Arguments

MAX

Number1 N3:N20

Number2

Step 5a6

1) Make cell B23 active.
2) Click the Insert Function button on the Formula bar.
3) At the Insert Function dialog box, make sure *Statistical* is selected in the Or select a category list box, and then click *MIN* in the Select a function list box. (You will need to scroll down the list to display *MIN*.)
4) Click OK.
5) At the Function Arguments palette, key **N3:N20** in the Number1 text box, and then click OK.

  c. Insert a formula to determine the average of all test scores by completing the following steps:
1) Make cell B24 active.
2) Click the Insert Function button on the Formula bar.
3) At the Insert Function dialog box, make sure *Statistical* is selected in the Or select a category list box and then click *AVERAGE* in the Select a function list box.
4) Click OK.
5) At the Function Arguments palette, key **N3:N20** in the Number1 text box, and then click OK.

6. Save and then print CExl C03 Ex07. (The worksheet will print on two pages.)
7. Change the 70% values (which were previously 0%) in cells C14, I14, and J14 to *N/A*. (This will cause the average of test scores for Kathy Kwieciak to increase and will change the minimum number and average of all test scores.)
8. Save, print, and then close CExl C03 Ex07.

Counting Numbers in a Range

Use the COUNT function to count the numeric values in a range. For example, in a range of cells containing cells with text and cells with numbers, you can count how many cells in the range contain numbers. In exercise 8, you will use the COUNT function to specify the number of students taking the midterm test and the number taking the final test. In this worksheet, a cell is left blank if a student did not take a test. If a value such as 0% was entered into the cell, the COUNT function would count this as a cell with a number.

✓

exercise 8

COUNTING THE NUMBER OF STUDENTS TAKING TESTS

1. Open Excel Worksheet 19.
2. Save the worksheet and name it CExl C03 Ex08.
3. Count the number of students who have taken the midterm test by completing the following steps:
  a. Make cell A22 active, and turn on Bold.
  b. Key **Number of students**, press Alt + Enter, and then key **completing the midterm**.
  c. Make cell B22 active.
  d. Insert a formula counting the number of students who have taken the midterm test by completing the following steps:
    1) Click the Insert Function button on the Formula bar.

2) At the Insert Function dialog box, make sure *Statistical* is selected in the Or select a category list box. (If not, click the down-pointing triangle at the right side of the Or select a category list box and then click *Statistical* at the drop-down list.)

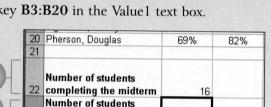

3) Scroll down the list of functions in the Select a function list box until *COUNT* is visible and then double-click *COUNT*.

4) At the Function Arguments palette, key **B3:B20** in the Value1 text box.

5) Click OK.

4. Count the number of students who have taken the final test by completing the following steps:

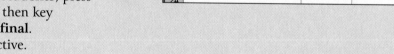

a. Make cell A23 active, and turn on Bold.

b. Key **Number of students**, press Alt + Enter, and then key **completing the final**.

c. Make cell B23 active.

d. Insert a formula counting the number of students who have taken the final test by completing the following steps:

1) Click the Insert Function button on the Formula bar.

2) At the Insert Function dialog box, make sure *Statistical* is selected in the Or select a category list box.

3) Scroll down the list of functions in the Select a function list box until COUNT is visible and then double-click *COUNT*.

4) At the formula palette, key **C3:C20** in the Value1 text box, and then click OK.

5. Save and then print CExl C03 Ex08.

6. Add test scores by completing the following steps:

a. Make cell B14 active and then key **68**.

b. Make cell C14 active and then key **70**.

c. Make cell C19 active and then key **55**.

d. Press Enter.

7. Save, print, and then close CExl C03 Ex08.

Writing Formulas with Financial Functions

In this section, you will learn to write formulas with the financial functions PMT and FV. The PMT function calculates the payment for a loan based on constant payments and a constant interest rate. Use the FV function to return the future value of an investment based on periodic, constant payments and a constant interest rate.

Finding the Periodic Payments for a Loan

The PMT function finds the periodic payment for a loan based on constant payments and a constant interest rate. The PMT function contains the arguments Nper, Pv, Fv, and Type. The Nper argument is the number of payments that will be made to an investment or loan, Pv is the current value of amounts to be received or paid in the future, Fv is the value of a loan or investment at the end of all periods, and Type determines whether calculations will be based on payments made in arrears (at the end of each period) or in advance (at the beginning of each period).

EXCEL

1. Open Excel Worksheet 20.
2. Save the worksheet with Save As and name it CExl C03 Ex09.
3. The owner of Real Photography is interested in purchasing a new developer and needs to determine monthly payments on three different models. Insert a formula that calculates monthly payments and then copy that formula by completing the following steps:
   a. Make cell E7 active.
   b. Click the Insert Function button on the Formula bar.
   c. At the Insert Function dialog box, click the down-pointing triangle at the right side of the Or select a category list box and then click *Financial* at the drop-down list.
   d. Scroll down the Select a function list box until *PMT* is visible and then double-click *PMT*.
   e. At the Function Arguments palette, key **C7/12** in the Rate text box. (This tells Excel to divide the interest rate by 12 months.)
   f. Press the Tab key. (This moves the insertion point to the Nper text box).
   g. Key **D7**. (This is the total number of months in the payment period.)
   h. Press the Tab key. (This moves the insertion point to the Pv text box.)
   i. Key **-B7**. (Excel displays the result of the PMT function as a negative number since the loan represents a negative cash flow to the borrower. Insert a minus sign before *B7* to show the monthly payment as a positive number rather than a negative number.)

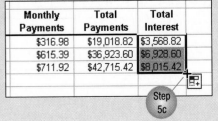

   j. Click OK. (This closes the palette and inserts the monthly payment of *$316.98* in cell E7.)
   k. Copy the formula in cell E7 down to cells E8 and E9.
4. Insert a formula in cell F7 that calculates the total amount of the payments by completing the following steps:
   a. Make cell F7 active.
   b. Key **=E7*D7** and then press Enter.
   c. Make cell F7 active and then copy the formula down to cells F8 and F9.
5. Insert a formula in cell G7 that calculates the total amount of interest paid by completing the following steps:
   a. Make cell G7 active.
   b. Key **=F7-B7** and then press Enter.
   c. Make cell G7 active and then copy the formula down to cells G8 and G9.
6. Save, print, and then close CExl C03 Ex09.

Monthly Payments	Total Payments	Total Interest
$316.98	$19,018.82	$3,568.82
$615.39	$36,923.60	$6,928.60
$711.92	$42,715.42	$8,015.42

Step 5c

Finding the Future Value of a Series of Payments

The FV function calculates the future value of a series of equal payments or an annuity. Use this function to determine information such as how much money can be earned in an investment account with a specific interest rate and over a specific period of time.

exercise 10

FINDING THE FUTURE VALUE OF AN INVESTMENT

1. Open Excel Worksheet 21.
2. Save the worksheet with Save As and name it CExl C03 Ex10.
3. The owner of Real Photography has decided to save money to purchase a new developer and wants to compute how much money can be earned by investing the money in an investment account that returns 9% annual interest. The owner determines that $1,200 per month can be invested in the account for three years. Complete the following steps to determine the future value of the investment account by completing the following steps:
   a. Make cell B6 active.
   b. Click the Insert Function button on the Formula bar.
   c. At the Insert Function dialog box, make sure *Financial* is selected in the Or select a category list box.
   d. Click *FV* in the Select a function list box.
   e. Click OK.
   f. At the Function Arguments palette, key **B3/12** in the Rate text box.
   g. Press the Tab key.
   h. Key **B4** in the Nper text box.
   i. Press the Tab key.
   j. Key **B5** in the Pmt text box.
   k. Click OK. (This closes the palette and also inserts the future value of $49,383.26 in cell B6.)
4. Save and then print CExl C03 Ex10.
5. The owner decides to determine the future return after two years. To do this, change the amount in cell B4 from *36* to *24* and then press Enter. (This recalculates the future investment amount in cell B6.)
6. Save, print, and then close CExl C03 Ex10.

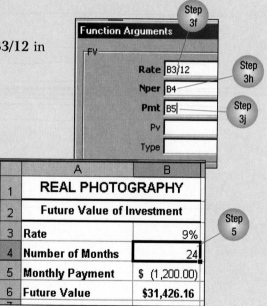

Writing Formulas with Date and Time Functions

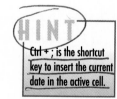

HINT

Ctrl + ; is the shortcut key to insert the current date in the active cell.

In this section, you will learn to write formulas with the date and time functions NOW and DATE. The NOW function returns the serial number of the current date and time. The DATE function returns the serial number that represents a particular date. Excel can make calculations using dates because the dates are represented as serial numbers. To calculate a date's serial number, Excel counts the days since the beginning of the twentieth century. The date serial number for January 1, 1900, is 1. The date serial number for January 1, 2000, is 36,526.

EXCEL

1. Open Excel Worksheet 23.
2. Save the worksheet with Save As and name it CExl C03 Ex11.
3. This worksheet establishes overdue dates for accounts. Enter a formula in cell D5 that returns the serial number for the date March 21, 2002, by completing the following steps:
   a. Make cell D5 active.
   b. Click the Insert Function button on the Formula bar.
   c. At the Insert Function dialog box, click the down-pointing triangle at the right side of the Or select a category list box and then click *Date & Time* at the drop-down list.
   d. Double-click *DATE* in the Select a function list box.
   e. At the Function Arguments palette, key **2002** in the Year text box.
   f. Press the Tab key and then key **03** in the Month text box.
   g. Press the Tab key and then key **21** in the Day text box.
   h. Click OK.

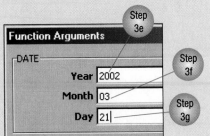

4. Complete steps similar to those in step 3 to enter the following dates as serial numbers in the specified cells:

D6	=	March 27, 2002
D7	=	April 2, 2002
D8	=	April 10, 2002

5. Enter a formula in cell F5 that inserts the due date (the purchase date plus the number of days in the Terms column) by completing the following steps:
   a. Make cell F5 active.
   b. Key **=D5+E5** and then press Enter.
   c. Make cell F5 active and then copy the formula down to cells F6, F7, and F8.

Purchase Date	Terms	Due Date
3/21/2002	30	4/20/2002
3/27/2002	15	4/11/2002
4/2/2002	15	4/17/2002
4/10/2002	30	5/10/2002

   Step 5c

6. Make cell A10 active and then key your name.
7. Insert the current date as a serial number by completing the following steps:
   a. Make cell A11 active.
   b. Click the Insert Function button on the Formula bar.
   c. At the Insert Function dialog box, make sure *Date & Time* is selected in the Or select a category list box.
   d. Scroll down the Select a function list box until *NOW* is visible and then double-click *NOW*.
   e. At the Function Arguments palette telling you that the function takes no argument, click OK.
   f. With cell A11 still active, click the Align Left button on the Formatting toolbar.
8. Save, print, and then close CExl C03 Ex11.

Writing a Formula with the IF Logical Function

The IF function is considered a *conditional function*. With the IF function you can perform conditional tests on values and formulas. A question that can be answered with true or false is considered a *logical test*. The IF function makes a logical test and then performs a particular action if the answer is true and another action if the answer is false.

For example, an IF function can be used to write a formula that calculates a salesperson's bonus as 10% if the quota of $100,000 is met or exceeded, and zero if the quota is less than $100,000. That formula would look like this: =IF(quota=>100000,quota*0.1,0). There are three parts to the formula—the condition or logical test IF(quota=>100000), action taken if the condition or logical test is true (quota*0.1), and the action taken if the condition or logical test is false (0). Commas separate the condition and the actions. In the bonus formula, if the quota is equal to or greater than $100,000, then the quota is multiplied by 10%. If the quota is less than $100,000, then the bonus is zero.

In exercise 12, you will write a formula with cell references rather than cell data. The formula in exercise 12 is =IF(C2>B2,C2*0.15,0). In this formula the condition or logical test is whether or not the number in cell C2 is greater than the number in cell B2. If the condition is true and the number is greater, then the number in cell C2 is multiplied by 0.15 (providing a 15% bonus). If the condition is false and the number in cell C2 is less than the number in cell B2, then nothing happens (no bonus). Notice how commas are used to separate the logical test from the actions.

Revising a Formula

Enter

Revise a formula by making active the cell containing the formula and then editing the formula in the cell or in the Formula bar text box. After revising the formula, press Enter or click the Enter button on the Formula bar and Excel will recalculate the result of the formula.

exercise 12

WRITING A FORMULA WITH AN IF FUNCTION

1. Open Excel Worksheet 10.
2. Save the worksheet with Save As and name it CExl C03 Ex12.
3. Write a formula with the IF function by completing the following steps. (The formula will determine if the quota has been met and, if it has, will insert the bonus [15% of the actual sales]. If the quota has not been met, the formula will insert a zero.)

   a. Make cell D2 active.
   b. Key **=IF(C2>B2,C2*0.15,0)** and then press Enter.
   c. Make cell D2 active and then use the fill handle to copy the formula to cells D3 through D7.
   d. With cells D2 through D7 selected, click the Currency Style button on the Formatting toolbar.

f_x =IF(C2>B2,C2*0.15,0)

B	C	D
Quota	**Actual Sales**	**Bonus**
95,500.00	$ 103,295.00	15494.25
137,000.00	$ 129,890.00	0
124,000.00	$ 133,255.00	19988.25
85,500.00	$ 94,350.00	14152.5
159,000.00	$ 167,410.00	25111.5
110,500.00	$ 109,980.00	0

Step 3c

4. Print the worksheet.
5. Revise the formula so it will insert a 25% bonus
   if the quota has been met by completing the
   following steps:
   a. Make cell D2 active.
   b. Click in the Formula bar, edit the formula
      so it displays as **=IF(C2>B2,C2*0.25,0)**,
      and then click the Enter button on the Formula bar.
   c. Copy the formula down to cells D3 through D7.
6. Save, print, and then close CExl C03 Ex12.

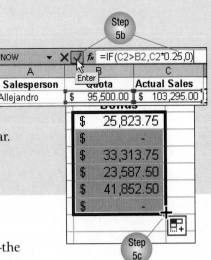

Writing a Nested IF Condition

In exercise 12, the IF function had only two possible actions—the
actual sales times 15% or a zero. In a formula where more than two
actions are required, use nested IF functions. For example, in exercise 13, you will
write a formula with IF conditions that has four possible actions—a letter grade
of A, B, C, or D. When writing nested IF conditions, insert symbols such as
commas, quotation marks, and parentheses in the proper locations. If you want
an IF condition to insert text, insert quotation marks before and after the text.
The formula you will be writing in exercise 13 is shown below.

$$=IF(E2>89,"A",IF(E2>79,"B",IF(E2>69,"C",IF(E2>59,"D"))))$$

This formula begins with the condition *=IF(E2>89,"A",*. If the number in cell
E2 is greater than 89, then the condition is met and the grade of A is returned.
The formula continues with a nested condition, *IF(E2>79,"B",*. If the number in
cell E2 does not meet the first condition (greater than 89), then Excel looks to
the next condition—is the number in cell E2 greater than 79? If it is, then the
grade of B is inserted in cell E2. The formula continues with another nested
condition, *IF(E2>69,"C",*. If the number in cell E2 does not match the first
condition, Excel looks to the second condition, and if that condition is not met,
then Excel looks to the third condition. If the number in cell E2 is greater than
69, then the grade of C is inserted in cell E2. The final nested condition is
IF(E2>59,"D". If the first three conditions are not met but this one is, then the
grade of D is inserted in cell E2. The four parentheses at the end of the formula
end each condition in the formula.

HINT

If you enter a
complicated formula in
a worksheet, consider
protecting the
worksheet. To do this,
click Tools, point to
Protection, and then
click Protect Sheet. At
the Protect Sheet dialog
box, enter a password,
and then click OK.

✓exercise 13

1. Open Excel Worksheet 11.
2. Save the worksheet with Save As and name it CExl C03 Ex13.
3. Insert a formula to average the scores by completing the following steps:
   a. Make cell E2 active.
   b. Key **=AVERAGE(B2:D2)** and then press Enter.
   c. Make cell E2 active and then copy the formula down to cells E3 through E6.
   d. With cells E2 through E6 still selected, click the Decrease Decimal button on the Formatting toolbar five times.
4. Insert a formula with nested IF conditions by completing the following steps:
   a. Make cell F2 active.
   b. Key **=IF(E2>89,"A",IF(E2>79,"B",IF(E2>69,"C",IF(E2>59,"D"))))** and then press Enter.
   c. Make cell F2 active and then use the fill handle to copy the formula down to cells F3 through F6.
   d. With cells F2 through F6 still selected, click the Center button on the Formatting toolbar.
5. Save, print, and then close CExl C03 Ex13.

E	F	G	H	I	J
Average	Grade				
78	=IF(E2>89,"A",IF(E2>79,"B",IF(E2>69,"C",IF(E2>59,"D"))))				
90					
88					
98					
67					

Step 4b

Average	Grade
78	C
90	A
88	B
98	A
67	D

Step 4c

As you keyed the formula with nested IF conditions in step 4b of exercise 13, did you notice that the parentheses were different colors? Each color represents a condition. The four right parentheses at the end of the formula ended each of the conditions and each matched in color a left parenthesis. If an average in column E in CExl C03 Ex13 is 59 or less, the nested formula inserts *FALSE* in the cell. If you want the formula to insert a letter grade, such as *F,* instead of *FALSE*, include another nested IF condition in the formula. A maximum of seven IF functions can be nested in a formula.

Using Absolute and Mixed Cell References in Formulas

A reference identifies a cell or a range of cells in a worksheet and can be relative, absolute, or mixed. Relative cell references refer to cells relative to a position in a formula. Absolute references refer to cells in a specific location. When a formula is copied, a relative cell reference adjusts while an absolute cell reference remains constant. A mixed cell reference does both—either the column remains absolute and the row is relative or the column is relative and the row is absolute. Distinguish between relative, absolute, and mixed cell references using the dollar sign ($). Key a dollar sign before the column and/or row cell reference in a formula to specify that the column or row is an absolute cell reference.

Using an Absolute Cell Reference in a Formula

In this chapter you have learned to copy a relative formula. For example, if the formula =*SUM(A2:C2)* in cell D2 is copied relatively to cell D3, the formula changes to =*SUM(A3:C3)*. In some situations, you may want a formula to contain an absolute cell reference, which always refers to a cell in a specific location. In exercise 14, you will add a column for projected job earnings and then perform "what if" situations using a formula with an absolute cell reference.

To identify an absolute cell reference, insert a $ symbol before the row and also the column. For example, the absolute cell reference C12 would be keyed as $C$12 in a formula.

can hold F4 while clicking on cell reference that you want to be absolute

exercise 14

INSERTING AND COPYING A FORMULA WITH AN ABSOLUTE CELL REFERENCE

1. Open Excel Worksheet 01.
2. Save the worksheet with Save As and name it CExl C03 Ex14.
3. Make the following changes to the worksheet:
   a. Delete columns B and D by completing the following steps:
      1) Click the column B header (the letter *B* at the top of the column).
      2) Hold down the Ctrl key and then click the column D header. (This selects column B and column D.)
      3) Click Edit and then Delete.
   b. Key **Projected** in cell C1.
   c. Center and bold the text in cells A1 through C1.
4. Determine the effect on actual job earnings with a 20% increase by completing the following steps:
   a. Key **% Increase/Decrease** in cell A12.
   b. Key **1.2** in cell B12 and then press Enter. (This number will be used in a formula to determine a 20% increase.)
   c. Make cell B12 active and then change the number formatting to General. (To do this, click Format and then Cells. At the Format Cells dialog box, click the Number tab, click *General* in the Category list box, and then click OK.)
   d. Make cell C3 active, key the formula =B3*$B$12, and then press Enter.
   e. Make cell C3 active and then use the fill handle to copy the formula to cells C4 through C10.
   f. Select cells B3 through C10 and then click the Currency Style button on the Formatting toolbar.
   g. With cells B3 through C10 still selected, click twice on the Decrease Decimal button on the Formatting toolbar.
5. Save and then print the worksheet.
6. With the worksheet still open, determine the effect on actual job earnings with a 10% decrease by completing the following steps:

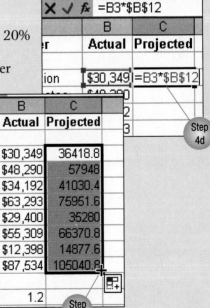

a. Make cell B12 active.
b. Key **0.9** and then press Enter.
7. Save and then print the CExl C03 Ex14.
8. Determine the effects on actual job earnings with a 10% increase. (To do this, key **1.1** in cell B12.)
9. Save, print, and then close CExl C03 Ex14.

	A	B		C	
1	**Customer**	**Actual**		**Projected**	
2					
3	Sellar Corporation	$	30,349	$	27,314
4	Main Street Photos	$	48,290	$	43,461
5	Sunset Automotive	$	34,192	$	30,773
6	Linstrom Enterprises	$	63,293	$	56,964
7	Morcos Media	$	29,400	$	26,460
8	Green Valley Optics	$	55,309	$	49,778
9	Detailed Designs	$	12,398	$	11,158
10	Arrowstar Company	$	87,534	$	78,781
11					
12	% Increase/Decrease		0.9		
13					

Step 6b

Using a Mixed Cell Reference in a Formula

The formula you created in step 4d in exercise 14 contained a relative cell reference (B3) and an absolute cell reference ($B$12). A formula can also contain a mixed cell reference. In a mixed cell reference either the column remains absolute and the row is relative or the column is relative and the row is absolute. In exercise 15, you will create the formula =$A3*B$2. In the first cell reference in the formula, $A3, the column is absolute and the row is relative. In the second cell reference, B$2, the column is relative and the row is absolute. The formula containing the mixed cell references allows you to fill in the column and row data using only one formula.

exercise 15

DETERMINING SIMPLE INTEREST USING A FORMULA WITH MIXED CELL REFERENCES

1. Open Excel Worksheet 12.
2. Save the worksheet with Save As and name it CExl C03 Ex15.
3. Insert a formula containing mixed cell references by completing the following steps:
   a. Make cell B3 the active cell.
   b. Key the formula **=$A3*B$2** and then press Enter.
4. Copy the formula down and to the right by completing the following steps:
   a. Make cell B3 active and then use the fill handle to copy the formula down to cell B13.
   b. Make cell B3 active and then use the fill handle to copy the formula across to cell F3.

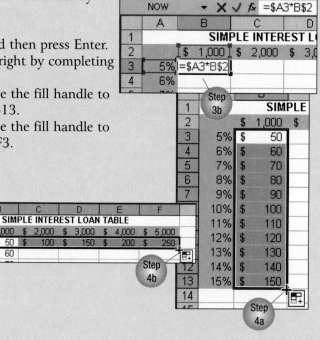

c. Make cell C3 active and then use the fill handle to copy the formula down to cell C13.

d. Make cell D3 active and then use the fill handle to copy the formula down to cell D13.

e. Make cell E3 active and then use the fill handle to copy the formula down to cell E13.

f. Make cell F3 active and then use the fill handle to copy the formula down to cell F13.

5. Save, print, and then close CExl C03 Ex15.

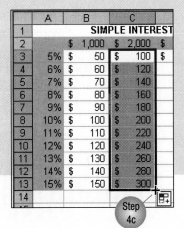

Step 4c

You only had to key one formula in exercise 15 to create the data in the simple interest table. The mixed cell references allowed you to copy the formula down columns and across rows.

CHAPTER summary

➤ Key a formula in a cell and the formula displays in the cell as well as in the Formula bar. If cell entries are changed, a formula will automatically recalculate the values and insert the result in the cell.

➤ Use the AutoSum button on the Standard toolbar to automatically add numbers in rows or columns.

➤ Create your own formula with commonly used operators such as addition (+), subtraction (-), multiplication (*), division (/), percent (%), and exponentiation (^). When writing a formula, begin with the equals (=) sign.

➤ Copy a formula to other cells in a row or column with the Fill option from the Edit drop-down menu or with the fill handle that displays in the bottom right corner of the active cell.

➤ Another method for writing a formula is to point to specific cells that are part of the formula.

➤ If Excel detects an error in a formula, a Trace Error button appears and a dark green triangle displays in the upper left corner of the cell containing the formula.

➤ Excel includes over 200 functions that are divided into nine categories. Use the Insert Function feature to create formulas using built-in functions.

➤ A function operates on an argument, which may consist of a cell reference, a constant, or another function. When a value calculated by a formula is inserted in a cell, this is referred to as returning the result.

➤ The AVERAGE function returns the average (arithmetic mean) of the arguments. The MAX function returns the largest value in a set of values, and the MIN function returns the smallest number in a set of values. The COUNT function counts the number of cells containing numbers within the list of arguments.

➤ The PMT function calculates the payment for a loan based on constant payments and a constant interest rate. The FV function returns the future value of an investment based on periodic, constant payments and a constant interest rate.

➤ The NOW function returns the serial number of the current date and time and the DATE function returns the serial number that represents a particular date.

➤ Use the IF function, considered a conditional function, to perform conditional tests on values and formulas.

➤ Use nested IF functions in a formula where more than two actions are required.

➤ A reference identifies a cell or a range of cells in a worksheet and can be relative, absolute, or mixed. Identify an absolute cell reference by inserting a $ symbol before the column and row.

COMMANDS review

semicolon

Insert Current Date- Ctrl+;

Command	Mouse/Keyboard
Automatically insert sum	Click AutoSum button on Standard toolbar
Display Insert Function dialog box	Click Insert Function button on Formula bar; or click Insert, Function

Copying Formula (select) - Edit - Fill - Down / Right   Ctrl + D
- Fill Handle

CONCEPTS check

Completion: On a blank sheet of paper, indicate the correct term, symbol, or command for each description.

1. When keying a formula, begin the formula with this sign. *=*
2. Click this button on the Standard toolbar to automatically add numbers in cells. *AutoSum*
3. This is the operator for division that is used when writing a formula. */*
4. This is the operator for multiplication that is used when writing a formula. *(asterick) ✱*
5. This is the name of the small black box located at the bottom right corner of a cell that can be used to copy a formula to adjacent cells. *AutoFill fill handle*
6. A function operates on this, which may consist of a constant, a cell reference, or another function. *argument*
7. This function returns the largest value in a set of values. *Max*
8. This function finds the periodic payment for a loan based on constant payments and a constant interest rate. *PMT*
9. This function returns the serial number of the current date and time. *NOW*
10. This function is considered a conditional function. *IF*
11. To identify an absolute cell reference, key this symbol before the column and row. *$*
12. Suppose that cell B2 contains the budgeted amount and cell C2 contains the actual amount. Write the formula (including the IF conditions) that would insert the word *under* if the actual amount was less than the budgeted amount and insert the word *over* if the actual amount was greater than the budgeted amount.

=IF(B2<B2,"under",IF(B2>B2,"over"))

SKILLS check

✓Assessment 1

1. Create a worksheet with the information shown in figure 3.4 with the following specifications:
   a. Key the data shown in figure 3.4 with the appropriate formatting.
   b. Insert the formula to calculate the difference (actual amount minus the budget amount) and then copy the formula down to the other cells.
   c. Use AutoSum to insert the total amounts.
   d. Format the numbers in cells as currency with zero decimal places.
2. Save the worksheet and name it CExl C03 SA01.
3. Print and then close CExl C03 SA01.

FIGURE

3.4 *Assessment 1*

SUMMARY OF PERFORMANCE

	Actual	Budget	Difference
Northeast division	2,505,250	2,250,000	
Southeast division	1,895,200	1,550,000	
Northwest division	2,330,540	2,200,000	
Southwest division	1,850,340	1,950,500	
Total			

✓Assessment 2

1. Open Excel Worksheet 13.
2. Save the worksheet with Save As and name it CExl C03 SA02.
3. Make the following changes to the worksheet:
   a. Determine the average monthly sales using the AVERAGE function.
   b. Format the numbers in cell B3 through H8 as currency with zero decimal places.
   c. Automatically adjust columns B through H.
4. Save, print, and then close CExl C03 SA02.

✓Assessment 3

1. Open CExl C03 SA02.
2. Save the worksheet with Save As and name it CExl C03 SA03.
3. Make the following changes to the worksheet:

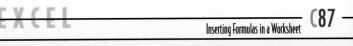

a. Total each monthly column. (Create an appropriate title for the row.)
b. Use the MAX function to determine the highest monthly total (for cells B3 through G8). (You determine where you want this maximum monthly total to appear in the worksheet. Be sure to include a cell title.)
c. Use the MIN function to determine the lowest monthly total (for cells B3 through G8). (You determine where you want this minimum monthly total to appear in the worksheet. Be sure to include a cell title.)
4. Save, print, and then close CExl C03 SA03.

Assessment 4

1. Open Excel Worksheet 24.
2. Save the worksheet with Save As and name it CExl C03 SA04.
3. The manager of Clearline Manufacturing is interested in refinancing a loan for either $125,000 or $300,000 and wants to determine the monthly payments, total payments, and total interest paid. Insert a formula with the following specifications:
   a. Make cell E5 active.
   b. Use the Insert Function button on the Formula bar to insert a formula using the PMT function. At the formula palette, enter the following:
      | Rate | = | C5/12 |
      | Nper | = | D5 |
      | Pv | = | -B5 |
   c. Copy the formula in cell E5 down to cells E6 through E8.
4. Insert a formula in cell F5 that multiplies the amount in E5 by the amount in D5.
5. Copy the formula in cell F5 down to cells F6 through F8.
6. Insert a formula in cell G5 that subtracts the amount in B5 from the amount in F5. (The formula is =F5-B5.)
7. Copy the formula in cell G5 down to cells G6 through G8.
8. Save, print, and then close CExl C03 SA04.

Assessment 5

1. Open Excel Worksheet 21.
2. Save the worksheet with Save As and name it CExl C03 SA05.
3. Make the following changes to the worksheet:
   a. Change the percentage in cell B3 from *9%* to *10%*.
   b. Change the number in cell B4 from *36* to *60*.
   c. Change the amount in cell B5 from *($1,200)* to *-500*.
   d. Use the FV function to insert a formula that calculates the future value of the investment. *(Hint: For help with the formula, refer to exercise 10.)*
4. Save, print, and then close CExl C03 SA05.

Assessment 6

1. Open Excel Worksheet 14.
2. Save the worksheet with Save As and name it CExl C03 SA06.
3. Make the following changes to the worksheet:
   a. Insert a formula using an absolute reference to determine the projected quotas at 10% of the current quotas.
   b. Save and then print CExl C03 SA06.
   c. Determine the projected quotas at 15% of the current quota by changing cell A14 to *15% Increase* and cell B14 to *1.15*.
   d. Save and then print CExl C03 SA06.

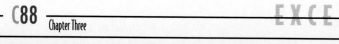

    e. Determine the projected quotas at 20% of the current quota.
4. Save, print, and then close CExl C03 SA06.

Assessment 7

1. Learn about specific options in the Options dialog box by completing the following steps:
   a. Display the Options dialog box by clicking Tools and then Options.
   b. At the Options dialog box, click the View tab.
   c. Read information about each of the options in the Window options section of the dialog box. (To do this, click the Help button [displays with a question mark] that displays in the upper right corner of the dialog box, and then click the desired option.)
2. After reading information about the options in the Window options section, complete the following steps:
   a. Open CExl C03 SA04.
   b. Save the worksheet with Save As and name it CExl C03 SA07.
   c. Display the formulas in the worksheet (rather than the results) using information you learned from the Options dialog box.
3. Save, print, and then close CExl C03 SA07.

ENHANCING A WORKSHEET

PERFORMANCE OBJECTIVES

Upon successful completion of chapter 4, you will be able to:
- Create headers and footers
- Change worksheet margins
- Center a worksheet horizontally and vertically on the page
- Insert a page break in a worksheet
- Print gridlines and row and column headings
- Hide and unhide a worksheet, column, or row
- Set and clear a print area
- Specify more than one print area in Page Break Preview
- Change the print quality
- Complete a spelling check on a worksheet
- Find and replace data in a worksheet
- Find and replace cell formatting
- Sort data in cells in ascending and descending order
- Filter a list using AutoFilter
- Plan and create a worksheet

Excel Chapter 04C

Excel contains features you can use to enhance and control the formatting of a worksheet. In this chapter, you will learn how to create headers and footers, change worksheet margins, print column and row titles, print gridlines, and center a worksheet horizontally and vertically on the page. You will also learn how to complete a spell check on text in a worksheet, find and replace specific data and formatting in a worksheet, sort and filter data, and plan and create a worksheet.

Formatting a Worksheet Page

Worksheets, by default, are printed in *portrait* orientation with default top and bottom margins of 1 inch and left and right margins of 0.75 inch. These settings can be changed with options at the Page Setup dialog box. The Page Setup dialog box contains several tabs for controlling the appearance of the worksheet page.

Controlling the Page Layout

The Page Setup dialog box with the Page tab selected as shown in figure 4.1 provides options for controlling the layout of the worksheet on the page. To display this dialog box, click File and then Page Setup. You can also display the Page Setup dialog box while in Print Preview by clicking the Setup button. At the Page Setup dialog box, make sure the Page tab is selected.

FIGURE

4.1 *Page Setup Dialog Box with Page Tab Selected*

Control how information is printed on the page with choices in the Orientation section of the Page Setup dialog box. The two choices in the Orientation section are represented by sample pages. A sample page that is taller than it is wide shows how the default orientation (Portrait) prints data on the page. The other choice, Landscape, will rotate the data and print it on a page that is wider than it is tall. The Landscape orientation might be useful in a worksheet that contains more columns than rows.

With options in the Scaling section of the Page Setup dialog box, you can adjust the size of the data in the worksheet by percentage. You can also specify on how many pages you want the data to fit. For example, if a worksheet contains too many columns to print on one page, choosing Fit to and leaving *1* as the number of pages will cause the display percentage to be decreased until the columns all fit on one page.

By default, an Excel worksheet is printed on standard paper, which is 8.5 inches wide and 11 inches long. Change this paper size with options from the Paper size drop-down menu. Paper size choices will vary depending on the selected printer. To view the list of paper sizes, click the down-pointing triangle at the right of the Paper size option box.

Depending on the printer you are using, you may or may not have choices for setting the print quality. The data that displays in the Print quality option box will vary depending on the selected printer. To view a list of print quality choices, click the down-pointing triangle at the right side of the Print quality option box. Choose a higher dpi (dots per inch) number to improve the quality of the print.

The worksheets you have printed so far have not been numbered. If you turn on page numbering (discussed in the next section), the first worksheet page is numbered 1 and any additional pages are incrementally numbered. With the First page number option, you can specify a different beginning page number. To do this, select *Auto* in the First page number text box, and then key the new starting number.

Turning On Page Numbering

By default, worksheet pages are not numbered. Apply page numbering to a workbook with options at the Page Setup dialog box with the Header/Footer tab selected as shown in figure 4.2. To display this dialog box, click File and then Page Setup. At the Page Setup dialog box, click the Header/Footer tab.

FIGURE

4.2 *Page Setup Dialog Box with Header/Footer Tab Selected*

To insert page numbering at the top of every page, click the Custom Header button on the Page Setup dialog box. Click the Custom Footer button to insert page numbering at the bottom of every page. If you click the Custom Footer button, the Footer dialog box displays as shown in figure 4.3. (The Header dialog box will display in a similar manner.) At the Footer dialog box, specify whether you want page numbering inserted at the Left section, Center section, or Right section of the page. Click in the text box below the desired location. Insert page numbering by clicking the Page Number button. (The buttons are identified in figure 4.3.) Click OK to close the Footer dialog box and then click OK to close the Page Setup dialog box.

Page Number

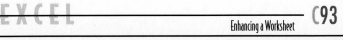

4.3 *Footer Dialog Box*

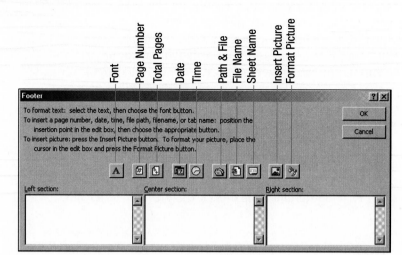

(Note: Before completing computer exercises, delete the Excel Chapter 03C *folder on your disk. Next, copy the* Excel Chapter 04C *subfolder from the* Excel 2002 Core *folder on the CD that accompanies this textbook to your disk and make* Excel Chapter 04C *the active folder.)*

✓ exercise 1

CHANGING PAGE ORIENTATION AND INSERTING PAGE NUMBERING

1. Open Excel Worksheet 06.
2. Save the worksheet with Save As and name it CExl C04 Ex01.
3. Change the orientation of the worksheet and insert page numbering by completing the following steps:
   a. Click File and then Page Setup.
   b. At the Page Setup dialog box, click the Page tab.
   c. Click the Landscape option.
   d. Click twice on the up-pointing triangle at the right side of the Adjust to text box. (This insert *110%* in the text box.)
   e. Click the Header/Footer tab.
   f. At the Page Setup dialog box with the Header/Footer tab selected, click the Custom Footer button.
   g. At the Footer dialog box, click in the text box below Center section.
   h. Click the Page Number button (second button from the left).
   i. Click OK to close the Footer dialog box.
   j. Click OK to close the Page Setup dialog box.

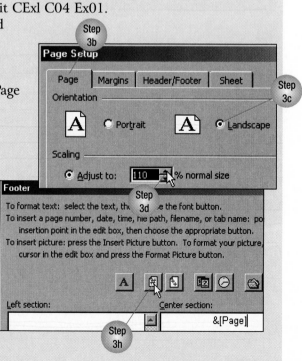

4. Save and then preview CExl C04 EX01.
5. Print CExl C04 Ex01. (Before printing this worksheet, check with your instructor to determine if your printer can print in landscape orientation.)
6. With CExl C04 Ex01 still open, change the page orientation, scale the size of the worksheet so it fits on one page, and change the beginning page number to 3 by completing the following steps:
    a. Click File and then Page Setup.
    b. At the Page Setup dialog box, click the Page tab.
    c. Click the Portrait option.
    d. Click the Fit to option.
    e. Select *Auto* that displays in the First page number text box and then key **3**.
    f. Click OK to close the dialog box.
7. Save, preview, print, and then close CExl C04 Ex01.

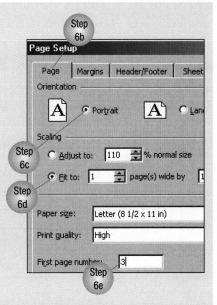

Step 6b

Step 6c

Step 6d

Step 6e

Inserting Headers/Footers

In the previous section, you learned how to insert page numbers in a header or footer. You can also create a header or footer containing text you want to print on every page. At the Page Setup dialog box with the Header/Footer tab selected (see figure 4.2), Excel offers a variety of header and footer text options. Click the down-pointing triangle after the Header option box and a drop-down list displays with options for inserting the user's name, workbook name, current date, and page number. The same list will display if you click the down-pointing triangle at the right of the Footer option box.

HINT

Delete all headers and footers by selecting the (none) option at the Header drop-down list or the Footer drop-down list.

exercise 2

CREATING A HEADER AND FOOTER

1. Open Excel Worksheet 06.
2. Save the worksheet with Save As and name it CExl C04 Ex02.
3. Make the following changes to the worksheet:
    a. Delete row 2.
    b. Insert the text **Average** in cell N1.
    c. Insert a formula in cell N2 that averages the percentages in cells B2 through M2.
    d. Copy the formula in cell N2 relatively to cells N3 through N19.
4. Insert a header and footer in the worksheet by completing the following steps:
    a. Click File and then Page Setup.
    b. At the Page Setup dialog box, click the Header/Footer tab.
    c. At the Page Setup dialog box with the Header/Footer tab selected, click the Custom Header button.
    d. At the Header dialog box, click in the text box below Center section.
    e. Key **Microcomputer Applications**.
    f. Click OK to close the Header dialog box.

g. At the Page Setup dialog box with the Header/Footer tab selected, click the down-pointing triangle at the right side of the Footer option box.

h. At the drop-down list that displays, click *Page 1 of ?*.

i. Click OK to close the Page Setup dialog box.

5. Save, preview, print, and then close CExl C04 Ex02.

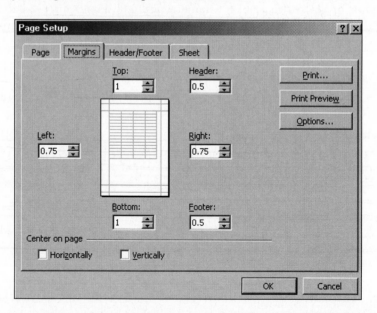

Changing Worksheet Margins

Excel uses 1-inch top and bottom margins for a worksheet and 0.75-inch left and right margins. You can change these default margins at the Page Setup dialog box with the Margins tab selected as shown in figure 4.4.

F I G U R E

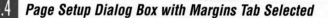

4.4 *Page Setup Dialog Box with Margins Tab Selected*

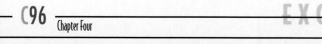

A worksheet page showing the cells and margins displays in the dialog box. As you increase or decrease the Top, Bottom, Left, or Right margin measurements, the sample worksheet page reflects the change. You can also increase or decrease the measurement from the top of the page to the header with the Header option or the measurement from the footer to the bottom of the page with the Footer option.

EXCEL

exercise 3

1. Open Excel Worksheet 02.
2. Save the worksheet with Save As and name it CExl C04 Ex03.
3. Select cells A1 through D8 and then apply the Accounting 2 autoformat.
4. Change the orientation of the worksheet and change the worksheet margins by completing the following steps:
    a. Click File and then Page Setup.
    b. At the Page Setup dialog box, click the Page tab.
    c. Click the Landscape option.
    d. Click the Margins tab.
    e. At the Page Setup dialog box with the Margins tab selected, click the up-pointing triangle at the right of the Top text box until *3.5* displays.
    f. Click the up-pointing triangle at the right of the Left text box until *3.5* displays.
    g. Click OK to close the dialog box.
5. Save, preview, print, and then close CExl C04 Ex03.

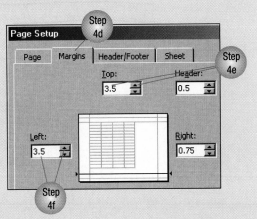

Centering a Worksheet Horizontally and/or Vertically

By default, worksheets print in the upper left corner of the page. You can center a worksheet on the page by changing the margins; however, an easier method for centering a worksheet is to use the Horizontally and/or Vertically options that display at the bottom of the Page Setup dialog box with the Margins tab selected. If you choose one or both of these options, the worksheet page in the Preview section displays how the worksheet will print on the page.

exercise 4

1. Open Excel Worksheet 03.
2. Save the worksheet with Save As and name it CExl C04 Ex04.
3. Select cells B3 through D8 and then click the Percent Style button on the Formatting toolbar.
4. Select cells A1 through D8 and then apply the Colorful 2 autoformat.
5. Horizontally and vertically center the worksheet by completing the following steps:
    a. Click File and then Page Setup.
    b. At the Page Setup dialog box, click the Margins tab.
    c. Click the Horizontally option. (This inserts a check mark.)
    d. Click the Vertically option. (This inserts a check mark.)
    e. Click OK to close the dialog box.
6. Save, preview, print, and then close CExl C04 Ex04.

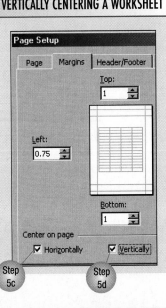

Inserting and Removing Page Breaks

The default left and right margins of 0.75 inch allow a total of 7 inches of cells across the page (8.5 inches minus 1.5 inches equals 7 inches). If a worksheet contains more than 7 inches of cells across the page, a page break is inserted in the worksheet and the remaining columns are moved to the next page. A page break displays as a broken line along cell borders. Figure 4.5 shows the page break in Excel Worksheet 06. (The location of your page break may vary.)

F I G U R E

4.5 *Page Break*

A page break also displays horizontally in a worksheet. By default, a worksheet can contain approximately 9 inches of cells vertically down the page. This is because the paper size is set by default at 11 inches. With the default top and bottom margins of 1 inch, this allows 9 inches of cells to print on one page.

Excel automatically inserts a page break in a worksheet. You can insert your own if you would like more control over what cells print on a page. To insert your own page break, select the column or row, click Insert, and then click Page Break. A page break is inserted immediately left of the selected column or immediately above the selected row. If you want to insert both a horizontal and vertical page break at the same time, make a cell active, click Insert, and then click Page Break. This causes a horizontal page break to be inserted immediately above the active cell, and a vertical page break to be inserted at the left side of the active column. To remove a page break, select the column or row or make the desired cell active, click Insert and then click Remove Page Break.

The page break automatically inserted by Excel may not be visible initially in a worksheet. One way to display the page break is to preview the worksheet. When you close the Print Preview screen, the page break will display in the worksheet. In Print Preview, click the Next button on the Preview bar to display the next page in the worksheet. Click the Previous button to display the previous page in the worksheet.

EXCEL

Excel provides a page break view that will display worksheet pages and page breaks. To display this view, click <u>V</u>iew and then <u>P</u>age Break Preview. This causes the worksheet to display similar to the worksheet shown in figure 4.6. The word *Page* along with the page number is displayed in gray behind the cells in the worksheet. A blue line displays indicating the page break. You can move the page break by positioning the arrow pointer on the blue line, holding down the left mouse button, dragging the line to the desired location, and then releasing the mouse button. To return to the normal view, click <u>V</u>iew and then <u>N</u>ormal.

HINT You can edit a worksheet in Page Break Preview.

FIGURE

4.6 **Worksheet in Page Break Preview**

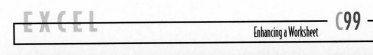

Adjust page break by dragging page break to desired location.

exercise 5

INSERTING A PAGE BREAK IN A WORKSHEET

1. Open Excel Worksheet 06.
2. Save the worksheet with Save As and name it CExl C04 Ex05.
3. View the default page break inserted automatically by Excel by completing the following steps:
    a. Click the Print Preview button on the Standard toolbar.
    b. After previewing the worksheet, click the <u>C</u>lose button.
    c. At the worksheet, click the right scroll triangle at the right side of the horizontal scroll bar until columns L and M are visible. The default page break should display between columns L and M. (The default page break displays as a dashed line. The location of the page break may vary slightly.)
4. Make the following formatting changes:
    a. Select the entire table and then change the font to 12-point Century Schoolbook (or a similar serif typeface such as Garamond).
    b. If necessary, automatically adjust the width of column A.
    c. Select columns B through M and then drag one of the selected column boundaries to the right until the column width displays as *9.00* in the yellow box.

d. Insert a page break between columns F and G by completing the following steps:
   1) Select column G.
   2) Click Insert and then Page Break.
   3) Click once in any cell in column F.

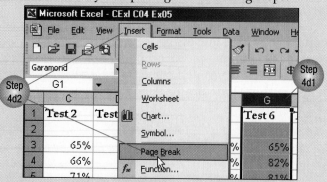

5. View the worksheet in Page Break Preview by completing the following steps:
   a. Click View and then Page Break Preview.
   b. View the pages and page breaks in the worksheet.
   c. Click View and then Normal to return to the normal view.
6. Horizontally and vertically center the worksheet by completing the following steps:
   a. Click File and then Page Setup.
   b. At the Page Setup dialog box, click the Margins tab.
   c. Click the Horizontally option. (This inserts a check mark.)
   d. Click the Vertically option. (This inserts a check mark.)
   e. Click OK to close the dialog box.
7. Save, preview, print, and then close CExl C04 Ex05.

Printing Column and Row Titles on Multiple Pages

Columns and rows in a worksheet are usually titled. For example, in Excel Worksheet 06, column titles include *Name*, *Test 1*, *Test 2*, *Test 3*, and so on. Row titles include the names of the people who have taken the tests. If a worksheet prints on more than one page, having column and/or row titles printing on each page can be useful. For example, when you printed CExl C04 Ex05, the names of the people did not print on the second page. This makes matching test scores with names difficult.

You can print column and/or row titles on each page of a worksheet. To do this, click File and then Page Setup. At the Page Setup dialog box, click the Sheet tab. This displays the dialog box as shown in figure 4.7.

At the Page Setup dialog box with the Sheet tab selected, specify the range of row cells you want to print on every page in the Rows to repeat at top text box. Key a cell range using a colon. For example, if you want cells A1 through J1 to print on every page, you would key **A1:J1** in the Rows to repeat at top text box. Key the range of column cells you want to print on every page in the Columns to repeat at left text box.

4.7 *Page Setup Dialog Box with Sheet Tab Selected*

Key the row range in this text box.

Key the column range in this text box.

✓exercise 6

PRINTING COLUMN TITLES ON EACH PAGE OF A WORKSHEET

1. Open Excel Worksheet 06.
2. Save the worksheet with Save As and name it CExl C04 Ex06.
3. Make the following formatting changes to the worksheet:
   a. Select the entire table and then change the font to 12-point Garamond (or a similar serif typeface).
   b. If necessary, automatically adjust the width of column A.
   c. Select columns B through M and then drag one of the selected column boundaries to the right until the column width displays as *8.00* in the yellow box above the mouse pointer. (This will change the width of columns B through M to *8.00*.)
   d. Select row 1 and then change the alignment to center.
4. Specify that you want column titles to print on each page by completing the following steps:
   a. Click File and then Page Setup.
   b. At the Page Setup dialog box, click the Sheet tab.
   c. At the Page Setup dialog box with the Sheet tab selected, click in the Columns to repeat at left text box.
   d. Key **A1:A20**.
   e. Click OK to close the dialog box.
5. Save, preview, print, and then close CExl C04 Ex06.

Step 4b

Step 4d

Printing Gridlines and Row and Column Headings

The gridlines that create the cells in a worksheet, by default, do not print. If you would like these gridlines to print, display the Page Setup dialog box with the Sheet tab selected, and then click Gridlines in the Print section. This inserts a check mark in the check box. At the Page Setup dialog box with the Sheet tab selected, you can also click Row and column headings and the row numbers and column letters will print with the worksheet.

If you are printing with a color printer, you can print the worksheet in black and white. To do this, display the Page Setup dialog box with the Sheet tab selected, and then click Black and white. This option is located in the Print section of the dialog box.

✓ **exercise 7**

PRINTING GRIDLINES AND ROW AND COLUMN HEADINGS

1. Open Excel Worksheet 05.
2. Save the worksheet with Save As and name it CExl C04 Ex07.
3. Make the following changes to the worksheet:
   a. Insert the text **Total** in cell D2.
   b. Merge and center cells A1 through D1.
   c. Make cell D3 active and then insert a formula that multiplies the contents of cell C3 with B3.
   d. Copy the formula in cell D3 relatively to cells D4 through D8.
   e. Specify that the gridlines and row and column headings are to print by completing the following steps:
      1) Click File and then Page Setup.
      2) At the Page Setup dialog box, click the Sheet tab.
      3) At the Page Setup dialog box with the Sheet tab selected, click the Gridlines check box in the Print section to insert a check mark.
      4) Click the Row and column headings check box in the Print section to insert a check mark.

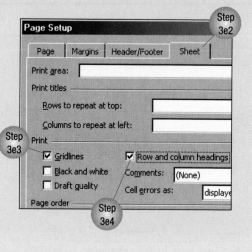

   f. With the Page Setup dialog box still displayed, click the Margins tab.
   g. At the Page Setup dialog box with the Margins tab selected, click the Horizontally option and then click the Vertically option.
   h. Click OK to close the dialog box.
4. Save, preview, print, and then close CExl C04 Ex07.

Hiding and Unhiding Workbook Elements

You can hide various elements in a workbook, such as worksheets, columns, and rows. You may want to hide a worksheet that contains sensitive information, hide rows and/or columns that you are not using or do not want others to view, or hide elements in a workbook in order to use as much of the screen as possible to display specific worksheet data.

To hide a worksheet, click Format, point to Sheet, and then click Hide. To hide columns in a worksheet, select the columns to be hidden, click Format, point to Column, and then click Hide. To hide selected rows, click Format, point to Row, and then click Hide.

To make a hidden worksheet visible, click Format, point to Sheet, and then click Unhide. At the Unhide dialog box that displays, double-click the name of the hidden worksheet you want to display. To make a hidden column visible, select the column to the left and the column to the right of the hidden column, click Format, point to Columns, and then click Unhide. To make a hidden row visible, select the row above and the row below the hidden row, click Format, point to Rows, and then click Unhide.

If the first row or column is hidden, use the Go To feature to make the row or column visible. To do this, click Edit and then Go To. At the Go To dialog box, key **A1** in the Reference text box, and then click OK. At the worksheet, click Format, point to either Column or Row, and then click Unhide.

Printing a Specific Area of a Worksheet

Use the Print Area feature to select and print specific areas in a worksheet. To use this feature, select the cells you want to print, click File, point to Print Area, and then click Set Print Area. This inserts a border around the selected cells. Click the Print button on the Standard toolbar and the cells within the border are printed.

You can specify more than one print area in a worksheet in Page Break Preview. To do this, display the worksheet in Page Break Preview. Select the first group of cells, click File, point to Print Area, and then click Set Print Area. Select the next group of cells, right-click in the selected cells, and then click Add to Print Area at the shortcut menu. Clear a print area by selecting the area, clicking File, pointing to Print Area, and then clicking Clear Print Area.

Each area specified as a print area will print on a separate page. If you want nonadjacent print areas to print on the same page, consider hiding columns and/or rows in the worksheet to bring the areas together.

Changing Print Quality

Most printers have more than one level of print quality. The print quality choices vary with printers and may include options such as *High, Medium, Low,* and *Draft*. Print quality choices are available at the Page Setup dialog box with the Page tab selected. At this dialog box, click the down-pointing triangle at the right side of the Print quality option, and then click the desired print quality at the drop-down list.

1. Open Excel Worksheet 06.
2. Specify a print area by completing the following steps:
    a. Select cells A1 through B20.
    b. Click File, point to Print Area, and then click Set Print Area.
    c. With the border surrounding the cells A1 through B20, click the Print button on the Standard toolbar.
    d. Clear the print area by clicking File, pointing to Print Area, and then clicking Clear Print Area.
3. Suppose you want to print all of the student names and just the percentages for Test 6 and you want the information to print on one page. To do this, hide columns B through F and select the print area by completing the following steps:
    a. Select columns B through F.
    b. Click Format, point to Column, and then click Hide.
    c. Select cells A1 through G20. (Columns A and G are now adjacent.)
    d. Click File, point to Print Area, and then click Set Print Area.
    e. Change the print quality and print the specified print area by completing the following steps:
        1) Click File and then Page Setup.
        2) At the Page Setup dialog box, click the Page tab.
        3) At the Page Setup dialog box with the Page tab selected, click the down-pointing triangle at the right side of the Print quality option, and then click *Draft* (or a similar quality) at the drop-down list.
        4) Click the Print button.
        5) At the Print dialog box, click OK.
    f. Clear the print area by making sure cells A1 through G20 are selected, clicking File, pointing to Print Area, and then clicking Clear Print Area.
    g. With cells A1 through G20 selected, make the hidden columns visible by clicking Format, pointing to Column, and then clicking Unhide.
4. Close Excel Worksheet 06 without saving the changes.

Customizing Print Jobs

The Print dialog box provides options for customizing a print job. Display the Print dialog box shown in figure 4.8 by clicking File and then Print. Use options at the Print dialog box to print a specific range of cells, selected cells, or multiple copies of a workbook.

At the Print dialog box, the currently selected printer name displays in the Name option box. If other printers are installed, click the down-pointing triangle at the right side of the Name option box to display a list of printers.

The Active sheet(s) option in the Print what section is selected by default. At this setting, the currently active worksheet will print. If you want to print an entire workbook that contains several worksheets, click Entire workbook in the Print what section. Click the Selection option in the Print what section to print the currently selected cells.

4.8 *Print Dialog Box*

If you want more than one copy of a worksheet or workbook printed, change to the desired number of copies with the Number of copies option in the Copies section. If you want the copies collated, make sure there is a check mark in the Collate check box in the Copies section.

A worksheet within a workbook can contain more than one page. If you want to print specific pages of a worksheet within a workbook, click Page(s) in the Print range section, and then specify the desired page numbers in the From and To text boxes.

If you want to preview the worksheet before printing, click the Preview button that displays at the bottom left corner of the dialog box. This displays the worksheet as it will appear on the printed page. After viewing the worksheet, click the Close button that displays toward the top of the Preview screen.

exercise 9

PRINTING SPECIFIC CELLS IN A WORKSHEET

1. Open Excel Worksheet 24.
2. Print selected cells by completing the following steps:
   a. Select cells A4 through D8.
   b. Click File and then Print.
   c. At the Print dialog box, click Selection in the Print what section.
   d. Click OK.
3. Close Excel Worksheet 24.

Completing a Spelling Check

Spelling

To spell check text in a worksheet using Excel's spell checking feature, make the first cell in the worksheet active, and then click the Spelling button on the Standard toolbar or click Tools and then Spelling. Figure 4.9 displays the Spelling dialog box. At this dialog box, you can click a button to tell Excel to ignore a word or you can replace a misspelled word with a word from the Suggestions list box.

FIGURE

4.9 *Excel Spelling Dialog Box*

The word in the worksheet not found in the spell check dictionary displays here.

Suggested spellings display in the Suggestions list box.

Spelling: English (U.S.)   ? | X

Not in Dictionary:

| profat | | Ignore Once |

Ignore All

Add to Dictionary

Suggestions:

profit
profits

Change

Change All

AutoCorrect

Dictionary language: English (U.S.)

Options...   Undo Last   Cancel

Using Undo and Redo

Undo

Redo

Ctrl + Z is the keyboard command to Undo a command.

Excel includes an Undo button on the Standard toolbar that will reverse certain commands or delete the last data keyed in a cell. For example, if you apply an autoformat to selected cells in a worksheet and then decide you want the autoformatting removed, click the Undo button on the Standard toolbar. If you decide you want the autoformatting back again, click the Redo button on the Standard toolbar.

In addition to the Undo and Redo buttons on the Standard toolbar, you can use options from the Edit drop-down menu to undo or repeat actions. The first two options at the Edit drop-down menu will vary depending on the last action completed. For example, if you just clicked the Currency Style button on the Formatting toolbar and then displayed the Edit drop-down menu, the first option displays as Undo Style and the second option displays as Repeat Style. If you decide you do not want the currency style applied, click Edit and then Undo Style. You can also just click the Undo button on the Standard toolbar.

EXCEL

1. Open Excel Worksheet 04.
2. Save the worksheet with Save As and name it CExl C04 Ex10.
3. Complete a spelling check on the worksheet by completing the following steps:
   a. Make sure cell A1 is the active cell.
   b. Click the Spelling button on the Standard toolbar.
   c. Click <u>C</u>hange as needed to correct misspelled words in the worksheet.
   d. At the message telling you the spelling check is completed, click OK.

4. Make the following formatting changes to the worksheet:
   a. Select the entire worksheet and then change the font to 11-point Univers (or a similar sans serif typeface such as Tahoma).
   b. Select cells A1 through B12 and then apply the Accounting 4 autoformat.
   c. Select cells B3 through B12 and then click the Currency Style button on the Formatting toolbar.
   d. With cells B3 through B12 still selected, click twice the Decrease Decimal button on the Formatting toolbar.
   e. Make cell B4 active and then add a single-line border at the bottom of the cell. (To do this, click the down-pointing triangle at the right side of the Borders button on the Formatting toolbar and then click the Bottom Border option.)
   f. Make cell B5 active and then add a double-line border at the bottom of the cell. (To do this, click the down-pointing triangle at the right side of the Borders button on the Formatting toolbar and then click the Bottom Double Border option.)
   g. Make cell B10 active and then add a single-line border at the bottom of the cell.
   h. Make cell B12 active and then add a double-line border at the bottom of the cell.
   i. Select row 1 and then turn on bold.
   j. Select cells A1 through B12 and then add a pale blue color shading.
   k. After looking at the worksheet with the light blue color shading, you decide you want to remove it. To do this, click the Undo button on the Standard toolbar.

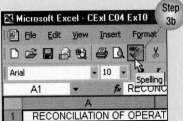

5. Save, print, and then close CExl C04 Ex10.

Finding and Replacing Data in a Worksheet

HINT

Ctrl + F is the keyboard command to display the Find and Replace dialog box with the Find tab selected.

Excel provides a Find feature you can use to look for specific data and either replace it with nothing or replace it with other data. This feature is particularly helpful in a large worksheet with data you want to find quickly. Excel also includes a find and replace feature. Use this to look for specific data in a worksheet and replace it with other data.

To find specific data in a worksheet, click Edit and then Find. This displays the Find and Replace dialog box with the Find tab selected as shown in figure 4.10. Key the data you want to find in the Find what text box and then click the Find Next button. Continue clicking the Find Next button to move to the next occurrence of the data.

FIGURE

4.10 *Find and Replace Dialog Box with Find Tab Selected*

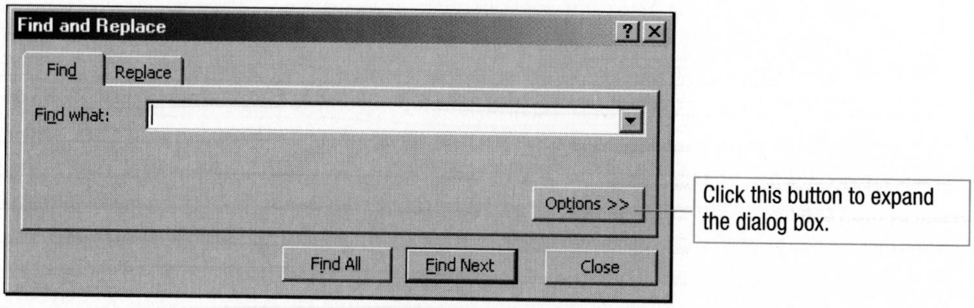

Click this button to expand the dialog box.

HINT

Ctrl + H is the keyboard command to display the Find and Replace dialog box with the Replace tab selected.

To find specific data in a worksheet and replace it with other data, click Edit and then Replace. This displays the Find and Replace dialog box with the Replace tab selected as shown in figure 4.11. Enter the data for which you are looking in the Find what text box. Press the Tab key or click in the Replace with text box and then enter the data that is to replace the data in the Find what text box.

FIGURE

4.11 *Find and Replace Dialog Box with Replace Tab Selected*

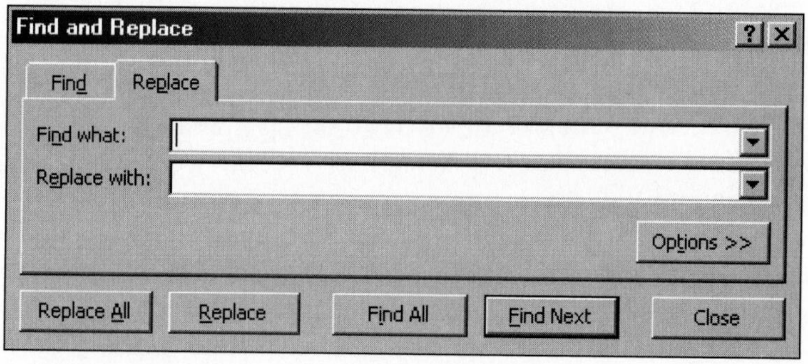

Click the Find Next button to tell Excel to find the next occurrence of the data. Click the Replace button to replace the data and find the next occurrence. If you know that you want all occurrences of the data in the Find what text box replaced with the data in the Replace with text box, click the Replace All button. Click the Close button to close the Replace dialog box.

Display additional find and replace options by clicking the Options button. This expands the dialog box as shown in figure 4.12. By default, Excel will look for any data that contains the same characters as the data in the Find what text box, without concern for the characters before or after the entered data. For example, in exercise 11, you will be looking for test scores of 0%. If you do not specify to Excel that you want to find cells that contain only 0%, Excel will stop at any cell containing 0%. In this example, Excel would stop at a cell containing 90% or a cell containing 100%. To specify that the only data that should be contained in the cell is what is entered in the Find what text box, click the Options button to expand the dialog box, and then insert a check mark in the Match entire cell contents check box.

HINT

If the Find and Replace dialog box obstructs your view of the worksheet, move the box by clicking and dragging the Title bar.

FIGURE

4.12 **Expanded Find and Replace Dialog Box**

Search the active worksheet or the entire workbook with the Within option.

With this option you can search by rows or by columns.

Use these two Format buttons to search for specific cell formatting and replace with other cell formatting.

If the Match case option is active (contains a check mark), Excel will look for only that data that exactly matches the case of the data entered in the Find what text box. Remove the check mark from this check box if you do not want Excel to find exact case matches. Excel will search in the current worksheet. If you want Excel to search an entire workbook, change the Within option to *Workbook*. Excel, by default, searches by rows in a worksheet. This can be changed to *By Columns* with the Search option.

exercise 11

FINDING AND REPLACING DATA

1. Open Excel Worksheet 06.
2. Save the worksheet with Save As and name it CExl C04 Ex11.
3. Find all occurrences of *0%* in the worksheet and replace with *70%* by completing the following steps:
   a. Click Edit and then Replace.
   b. At the Find and Replace dialog box with the Replace tab selected, key **0%** in the Find what text box.
   c. Press the Tab key (this moves the insertion point to the Replace with text box).
   d. Key **70%**.
   e. Click the Options button to display additional options. (If additional options already display, skip this step.)

f. Click the Match entire cell contents option to insert a check mark in the check box.

g. Click the Replace All button.

4. Select the entire worksheet and then change the font to 10-point Times New Roman (or a similar typeface).

5. Automatically adjust the width of columns A through M.

6. Save the worksheet again with the same name (CExl C04 Ex11).

7. Display the Page Setup dialog box with the Page tab selected, click the Landscape option, and then close the dialog box.

8. Print and then close CExl C04 Ex11.

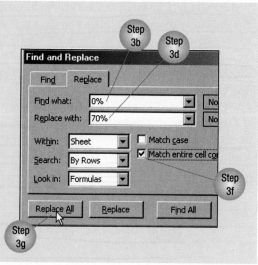

Finding and Replacing Cell Formatting

Use the Format options at the expanded Find and Replace dialog box (see figure 4.12) to search for specific cell formatting and replace with other formatting. Click the down-pointing triangle at the right side of the Format button and a drop-down list displays. Click the *Format* option and the Find Format dialog box displays with the Number, Alignment, Font, Border, Patterns, and Protection tabs. Specify formatting at this dialog box. Click the *Choose Format From Cell* option and the mouse pointer displays with a pointer tool attached. Click in the cell containing the desired formatting and the formatting displays in the Preview box to the left of the Format button. Click the *Clear Find Format* option and any formatting in the Preview box is removed.

FINDING AND REPLACING CELL FORMATTING

1. Open Excel Worksheet 28.

2. Save the worksheet with Save As and name it CExl C04 Ex12.

3. Search for orange shading and replace it with light purple shading by completing the following steps:

   a. Click Edit and then Replace.

   b. At the Find and Replace dialog box with the Replace tab selected, make sure the dialog box is expanded. (If not, click the Options button.) Select and then delete *0%* in the Find what text box and select and then delete *70%* in the Replace with text box.

   c. Make sure the boxes immediately preceding the two Format buttons display with the text *No Format Set*. (If not, click the down-pointing triangle at the right of the Format button, and then click the *Clear Find Format* option at the drop-down list. Do this for each Format button.)

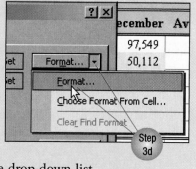

   d. Click the down-pointing triangle at the right side of the top Format button (the one at the far right side of the Find what text box) and then click *Format* at the drop-down list.

Chapter Four

EXCEL

e. At the Find Format dialog box, click the Patterns tab.
f. Click the light orange color (as shown at the right).
g. Click OK to close the dialog box.
h. Click the down-pointing triangle at the right side of the second Format button (the one at the far right side of the Replace with text box and then click *Format* at the drop-down list.
i. At the Find Format dialog box with the Patterns tab selected, click the light purple color (as shown below and to the right).
j. Click OK to close the dialog box.
k. At the Find and Replace dialog box, click the Replace All button.
l. At the message telling you that Excel has completed the search and made replacements, click OK.

4. Complete steps similar to those in 3d through 3l to search for light yellow shading and replace it with light green shading.

5. Search for 11-point Times New Roman formatting and replace with 10-point Arial formatting by completing the following steps:
   a. Clear formatting from the top Format button by clicking the down-pointing triangle and then clicking the *Clear Find Format* option at the drop-down list.
   b. Clear formatting from the bottom Format button by clicking the down-pointing triangle and then clicking *Clear Replace Format.*
   c. Click the down-pointing triangle at the right side of the top Format button and then click *Format* at the drop-down list.
   d. At the Find Format dialog box, click the Font tab.
   e. Click *Times New Roman* in the Font list box (you will need to scroll down the list to display this typeface).
   f. Click *11* in the Size text box.
   g. Click OK to close the dialog box.
   h. Click the down-pointing triangle at the right side of the second Format button and then click *Format* at the drop-down list.
   i. At the Find Format dialog box with the Font tab selected, click *Arial* in the Font list box.
   j. Click *10* in the Size list box.
   k. Click OK to close the dialog box.
   l. At the Find and Replace dialog box, click the Replace All button.
   m. At the message telling you that Excel has completed the search and made replacements, click OK.

6. At the Find and Replace dialog box, remove formatting from both Format buttons.

7. Click the Close button to close the Find and Replace dialog box.

8. Click in cell H3 and then insert a formula that finds the average of cells B3 through G3.

9. Copy the formula in cell H3 down to cells H4 through H8.

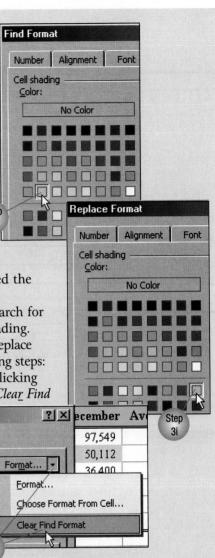

10. Copying the formula removed the double-line border at the bottom of cell H8. Replace the border by selecting the cell, clicking the down-pointing triangle at the right side of the Borders button on the Formatting toolbar and then clicking the Bottom Double Border option at the drop-down palatte.
11. Save, print, and then close CExl C04 Ex12.

Sorting Data

Sort Ascending

Sort Descending

Excel is primarily a spreadsheet program, but it also includes some basic database functions. With a database program, you can alphabetize information or arrange numbers numerically. Data can be sorted by columns in a worksheet. By default, Excel will sort special symbols such as *, @, and # first, numbers second, and letters third. Sort data in a worksheet using the Sort Ascending or Sort Descending buttons on the Standard toolbar or at the Sort dialog box.

Sorting Data Using Buttons on the Standard Toolbar

To sort data in a worksheet using the buttons on the Standard toolbar, open the worksheet, select the cells containing data you want to sort, and then click the Sort Ascending button (sorts text A through Z; sorts numbers lowest to highest) or the Sort Descending button (sorts text Z through A; sorts numbers highest to lowest). If you select more than one column in a worksheet, Excel will sort the data in the first selected column.

exercise 13

SORTING DATA USING THE SORT ASCENDING AND SORT DESCENDING BUTTONS

1. Open Excel Worksheet 03.
2. Save the worksheet with Save As and name it CExl C04 Ex13.
3. Make the following formatting changes to the worksheet:
   a. Select cells A1 through D1, and then merge and center the data in cell A1 across cells A1 through D1.
   b. Bold the data in cell A1.
   c. Bold the data in cells B2 through D2.
   d. Automatically adjust the width of columns A through D.
   e. Select cells B3 through D8 and then click the Percent Style button on the Formatting toolbar.
4. Sort the data in the first column alphabetically in ascending order by completing the following steps:
   a. Select cells A3 through D8.
   b. Click the Sort Ascending button on the Standard toolbar.
5. Save and print CExl C04 Ex13.

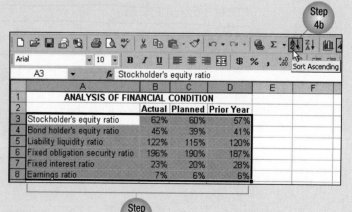

6. Sort the data in the first column alphabetically in descending order by completing steps similar to those in step 4, except click the Sort Descending button on the Standard toolbar.
7. Save, print, and then close CExl C04 Ex13.

Sorting Data at the Sort Dialog Box

If you want to sort data in a column other than the first selected column, use the Sort dialog box. If you select just one column in a worksheet and then click the Sort Ascending or Sort Descending button on the Standard toolbar, only the data in that column is sorted. If this data is related to data to the left or right of the data in the column, that relationship is broken. For example, if you sort cells B3 through B8 in CExl C04 Ex13, the percentages for *Bondholder's equity ratio* are now *23%, 39%,* and *41%*, when they should be *45%, 39%*, and *41%*.

HINT

If you are not satisfied with the results of a sort, immediately click the Undo button.

Use the Sort dialog box to sort data and maintain the relationship of all cells. To sort using the Sort dialog box, select the cells you want sorted, click Data, and then click Sort. This displays the Sort dialog box shown in figure 4.13.

FIGURE 4.13 ***Sort Dialog Box***

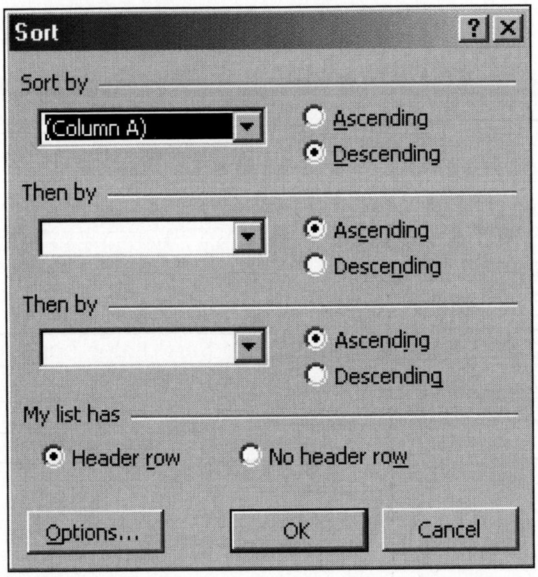

The data displayed in the Sort by option box will vary depending on what you have selected. Generally, the data that displays is the title of the first column of selected cells. If the selected cells do not have a title, the data may display as *Column A*. Use this option to specify what column you want sorted. Using the Sort dialog box to sort data in a column maintains the relationship of the data.

exercise 14

1. Open CExl C04 Ex13.
2. Save the worksheet with Save As and name it CExl C04 Ex14.
3. Sort the percentages in cells B3 through B8 in ascending order and maintain the relationship to the other data by completing the following steps:
   a. Select cells A3 through D8.
   b. Click Data and then Sort.
   c. At the Sort dialog box, click the down-pointing triangle at the right of the Sort by option box, and then click *Actual* from the drop-down list.
   d. Make sure Ascending is selected in the Sort by section of the dialog box. If not, click Ascending.
   e. Click OK to close the dialog box.
4. Save and then print CExl C04 Ex14.
5. Sort the percentages in cells B3 through B8 in *descending* order and maintain the relationship of the data by completing steps similar to those in step 3.
6. Save, print, and then close CExl C04 Ex14.

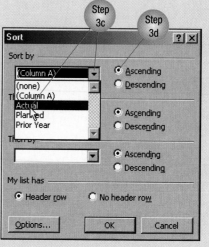

Sorting More than One Column

When sorting data in cells, you can sort in more than one column. For example, in exercise 15, you will be sorting the average test scores in ascending order and then sorting the names of the students alphabetically. In this sort, the test averages are sorted first and then students with the same average are sorted alphabetically within that average. For example, there are several average scores of 76%. Students within that average are sorted alphabetically—not all students.

To sort in more than one column, select all columns in the worksheet that need to remain relative, and then display the Sort dialog box. At the Sort dialog box, specify the first column you want sorted in the Sort by option box, and then specify the second column in the first Then by option box. In Excel, you can sort in up to three columns. If you want to sort the data in a third column, you would specify that in the second Then by option box.

exercise 15

1. Open Excel Worksheet 06.
2. Save the worksheet with Save As and name it CExl C04 Ex15.
3. Select and then delete row 2.
4. Sort the Test 1 percentages in cells B2 through B19 in ascending order and then sort alphabetically by the names in the first column by completing the following steps:
   a. Select cells A2 through M19.
   b. Click Data and then Sort.

c. At the Sort dialog box, click the down-pointing triangle at the right side of the Sort by option box, and then click *Test 1* from the drop-down list.

d. Make sure Ascending is selected in the Sort by section of the dialog box. If not, click Ascending.

e. Click the down-pointing triangle at the right of the first Then by option box and then click *Name* in the drop-down list.

f. Make sure Ascending is selected in the first Then by section.

g. Click OK to close the dialog box.

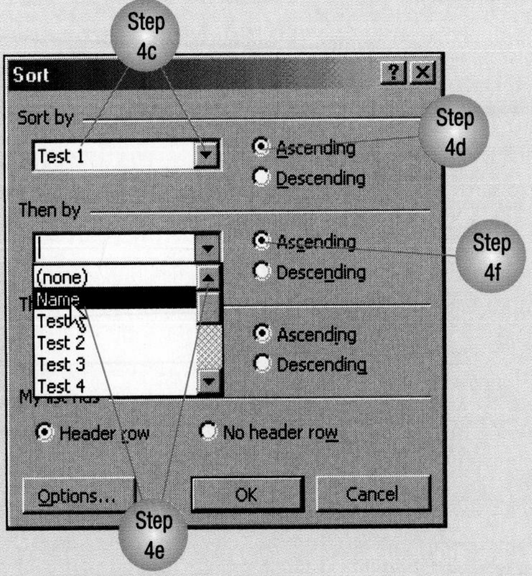

5. Save the worksheet again with the same name (CExl C04 Ex15).

6. Display the Page Setup dialog box with the Page tab selected, click the Landscape option, and then close the dialog box.

7. Print the worksheet. (Notice how the names of the students with the same Test 1 percentages are alphabetized.)

8. Close CExl C04 Ex15.

Filtering Lists

You can place a restriction, called a *filter*, on data in a worksheet to isolate temporarily a specific list. A list is a series of worksheet rows that contain related data, such as a specific customer name, invoice number, product, and so forth. You can apply only one filter to a worksheet at a time. One method for filtering lists is to use the AutoFilter feature. To use this feature, click in a cell in the list you want to filter, click Data, point to Filter, and then click AutoFilter. This causes a down-pointing triangle to appear in each column heading in the worksheet as shown in figure 4.14. Click the down-pointing triangle in the heading you want to filter. This causes a drop-down list to display with options to filter all records in the list, display the top 10 records, create a custom filter, or select an entry that appears in one or more of the cells in the list.

The Top 10 option displays in a list that contains values rather than text. Click *(Top 10...)* and the Top 10 AutoFilter dialog box displays as shown in figure 4.15. With options at this dialog box, you can choose to show the top values, the bottom values, and the number you want filtered.

4.14 *Using AutoFilter*

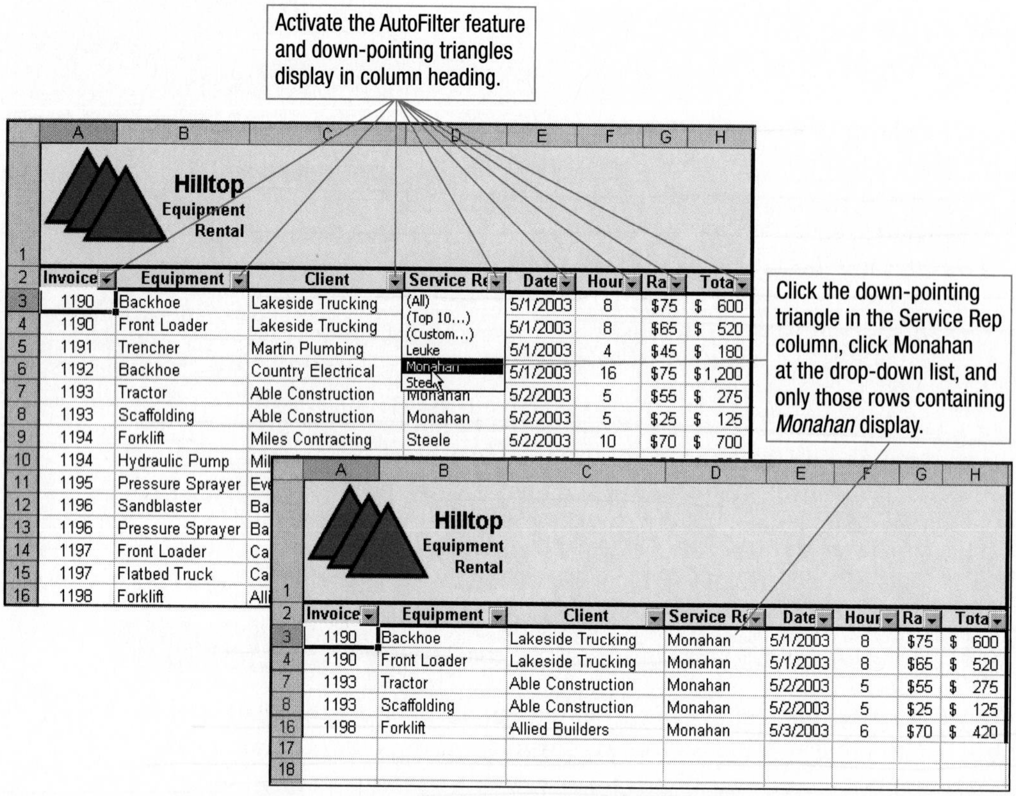

Activate the AutoFilter feature and down-pointing triangles display in column heading.

Click the down-pointing triangle in the Service Rep column, click Monahan at the drop-down list, and only those rows containing *Monahan* display.

4.15 *Top 10 AutoFilter Dialog Box*

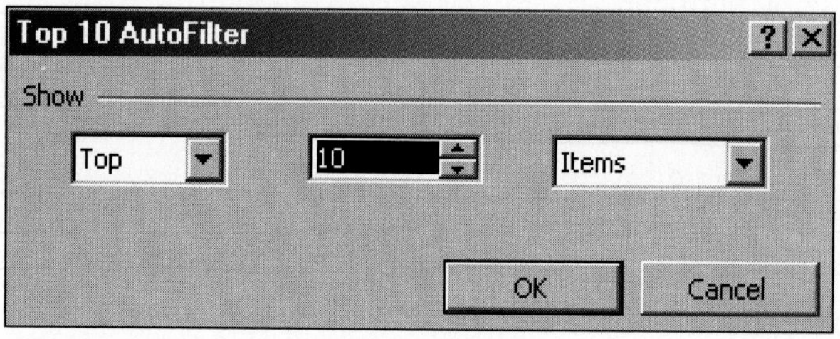

When you filter a list, the drop-down triangle in the column heading turns blue as well as the row number for the selected rows. This color indicates that rows in the worksheet have been filtered. To deactivate AutoFilter, click Data, point to Filter, and then click AutoFilter.

EXCEL

1. Open Excel Worksheet 26.
2. Save the worksheet with Save As and name it CExl C04 Ex16.
3. Apply the AutoFilter by clicking Data, pointing to Filter, and then clicking AutoFilter. (This causes down-pointing triangles to appear in heading cells.)
4. Filter and then print a list of rows containing companies renting a forklift by completing the following steps:
   a. Click the down-pointing triangle at the right side of the *Equipment* heading.
   b. Click *Forklift* at the drop-down list.
   c. Print the list by clicking the Print button on the Standard toolbar.
   d. Redisplay all cells containing data by clicking the down-pointing triangle at the right side of the *Equipment* heading and then clicking *(All)* at the drop-down list.
5. Filter and then print a list of rows containing equipment rented by the service representative Monahan by completing the following steps:
   a. Click the down-pointing triangle at the right side of the *Service Rep* heading.
   b. Click *Monahan* at the drop-down list.
   c. Click the Print button.
   d. Redisplay all cells containing data by clicking the down-pointing triangle at the right side of the *Service Rep* heading and then clicking *(All)* at the drop-down list.

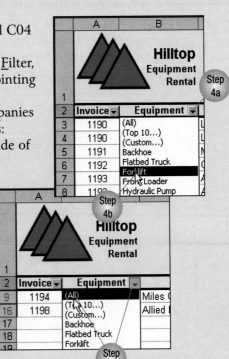

6. Filter and then print a list of rows containing only the client *Cascade Enterprises* by completing steps similar to those in steps 4 or 5. (Make sure you return the list to *(All)*.)
7. Display the top 3 highest totals by completing the following steps:
   a. Click the down-pointing triangle at the right side of the *Total* heading and then click *(Top 10...)* at the drop-down list.
   b. At the Top 10 AutoFilter dialog box, key **3** in the middle text box (automatically selected when the dialog box displays).
   c. Click OK.
   d. Click the Print button to print the list.
   e. Click the down-pointing triangle at the right side of the *Total* heading and then click *(All)* at the drop-down list.

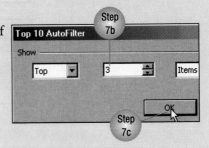

8. Deactivate AutoFilter by clicking Data, pointing to Filter, and then clicking AutoFilter.
9. Save, print, and then close CExl C04 Ex16.

Planning a Worksheet

The worksheets you have worked with so far basically have already been planned. If you need to plan a worksheet yourself, some steps you can follow are listed below. These are basic steps—you may think of additional steps or additional information to help you plan a worksheet.

- **Step 1: Identify the purpose of the worksheet.** The more definite you are about your purpose, the easier organizing your data into an effective worksheet will be. Consider things such as the purpose of the worksheet, the intended audience, the desired output or results, and the data required.
- **Step 2: Design the worksheet.** To do this, you need to determine how the data is to be organized, the titles of columns and rows, and how to emphasize important information. Designing the worksheet also includes determining any calculations that need to be performed.
- **Step 3: Create a sketch of the worksheet.** A diagram or sketch can help create a logical and well-ordered worksheet. With a sketch, you can experiment with alternative column and row configurations and titles and headings. When creating a sketch, start with the heading or title of the worksheet, which should provide a quick overview of what the data represents in the worksheet. Determine appropriate column and row titles that clearly identify the data.
- **Step 4: Enter the data in the worksheet.** Key the data in the worksheet, including the worksheet title, column titles, row titles, and data within cells. Enter any required formulas into the worksheet and then format the worksheet to make it appealing and easy to read.
- **Step 5: Test the worksheet data.** After preparing the worksheet and inserting any necessary formulas, check the data to be sure that the calculations are performed correctly. Consider verifying the formula results by completing the formula on a calculator.

✓ exercise 17

PLANNING AND CREATING A WORKSHEET

1. Look at the data shown in figure 4.16. (The first paragraph is simply a description of the data—do not include this in the worksheet.) After reviewing the data, complete the following steps:
   a. Create a sketch of how you think the worksheet should be organized.
   b. Create a worksheet from the sketch. (Be sure to include the necessary formula to calculate the total costs.)
   c. Apply formatting to enhance the appearance of the worksheet.
2. Save the worksheet and name it CExl C04 Ex17.
3. Print and then close CExl C04 Ex17.

FIGURE

4.16 *Exercise 17*

The following data itemizes budgeted direct labor hours and dollars by department for planning purposes. This data is prepared quarterly and sent to the plant manager and production manager.

DIRECT LABOR BUDGET

	Labor Rate	Total Hours	Total Costs
April			
Assembly	12.75	723	
Electronics	16.32	580	
Machining	27.34	442	
May			
Assembly	12.75	702	
Electronics	16.32	615	
Machining	27.34	428	
June			
Assembly	12.75	694	
Electronics	16.32	643	
Machining	27.34	389	

CHAPTER summary

➤ By default, a worksheet prints on the page in portrait orientation. This can be changed to landscape orientation at the Page Setup dialog box with the Page tab selected.

➤ Adjust the percentage size of data in a worksheet with options in the Scaling section of the Page Setup dialog box with the Page tab selected.

➤ Change the paper size with the Paper size option at the Page Setup dialog box with the Page tab selected.

➤ Create a header and/or footer for worksheet pages with options at the Page Setup dialog box with the Header/Footer tab selected.

➤ Change the beginning page number in a worksheet with the First page number option at the Page Setup dialog box with the Page tab selected.

➤ Excel uses 1-inch top and bottom margins and 0.75-inch left and right margins for a worksheet. Change these default margins at the Page Setup dialog box with the Margins tab selected.

➤ Center a worksheet horizontally and/or vertically on a page with options at the Page Setup dialog box with the Margins tab selected.

➤ Insert a page break in a worksheet with Insert and then Page Break.

➤ Print column and row titles on every page of a multiple-paged worksheet with options at the Page Setup dialog box with the Sheet tab selected.

➤ Print gridlines, column letters, and row numbers with options at the Page Setup dialog box with the Sheet tab selected.

➤ You can hide and unhide a worksheet in a workbook or columns or rows in a worksheet.

➤ Use the Print Area feature to select and print specific areas in a worksheet. Specify more than one print area in Page Break Preview.

➤ Change the print quality for most printers with options at the Properties dialog box. Print quality choices are available at the Page Setup dialog box with the Page tab selected.

➤ Use options at the Print dialog box to print a specific range of cells, selected cells, or multiple copies of a workbook.

➤ Complete a spelling check on a worksheet by clicking the Spelling button on the Standard toolbar or clicking Tools and then Spelling.

➤ Click the Undo button to reverse certain commands or delete the last data keyed in a cell. Click the Redo button to repeat the last command or action, if possible.

➤ Find data with options at the Find and Replace dialog box with the Find tab selected, and find and replace data in a worksheet with options at the Find and Replace dialog box with the Replace tab selected.

➤ Use options at the expanded Find and Replace dialog box to search for specific cell formatting and replace with other formatting.

➤ Sort the first column of selected cells with the Sort Ascending or Sort Descending buttons on the Standard toolbar.

➤ Use the Sort dialog box to sort in a column other than the first column, to maintain the relationship of the data, or to sort in more than one column.

➤ Use the AutoFilter feature to isolate temporarily a specific list. With the AutoFilter, you can filter all records in the list, display the top 10 records, create a custom filter, or select an entry that appears in one or more of the cells in the list.

➤ Plan a worksheet by completing these basic steps: identify the purpose of the worksheet, design the worksheet, create a sketch of the worksheet, enter the data in the worksheet, and test the worksheet data.

COMMANDS review

Command	Mouse/Keyboard
Display Page Setup dialog box	Click File, Page Setup
Insert a page break	Click Insert, Page Break
Hide columns	Select columns, click Format, point to Column, then click Hide
Hide rows	Select rows, click Format, point to Row, then click Hide
Unhide columns	Select column to left and right, click Format, point to Column, then click Unhide

EXCEL

Unhide rows	Select row above and below, click Format, point to Row, then click Unhide
Set a print area	Select cells, click File, point to Print Area, then click Set Print Area
Clear a print area	Select cells, click File, point to Print Area, then click Clear Print Area
Display Print dialog box	Click File, Print
Display Spelling dialog box	Click Spelling button on Standard toolbar or click Tools, Spelling
Display Find and Replace dialog box	Click Edit, Find, or click Edit, Replace
Sort first selected column in ascending order	Click Sort Ascending button on Standard toolbar
Sort first selected column in descending order	Click Sort Descending button on Standard toolbar
Display Sort dialog box	Click Data, Sort
Activate/Deactivate AutoFilter	Click Data, Filter, AutoFilter

CONCEPTS check

Completion: On a blank sheet of paper, indicate the correct term, symbol, or command for each item.

1. By default, a worksheet prints in this orientation on a page. *portrait*
2. Change the page orientation at the Page Setup dialog box with this tab selected. *Page*
3. This is the default paper size. *8.5" wide by 11" long*
4. This is the worksheet default top and bottom margin measurement. *1"*
5. This is the worksheet default left and right margin measurement. *0.75"*
6. A worksheet can be horizontally and/or vertically centered with options at the Page Setup dialog box with this tab selected. *Margins*
7. Click this to insert a page break in a worksheet. *Insert - Page Break*
8. Print gridlines with an option at the Page Setup dialog box with this tab selected. *Sheet*
9. To make a hidden column visible, select these columns, click Format, point to Column, and then click Unhide. ~~hidden columns~~ *columns to the left + right of the hidden column*
10. Use this feature to print specific areas in a worksheet. *Print Area*
11. To complete a spelling check on a worksheet, click this button on the Standard toolbar. *Spelling*
12. To display the Sort dialog box, click Sort from this drop-down menu. *Data*
13. Use this feature to temporarily remove from sight a specific list of rows in a worksheet containing related data. *AutoFilter* *Hide ✓*
14. List the steps you would complete to print column titles in a multiple-paged worksheet. *File - Page Setup - Sheet tab - Print section* *titles - key range in columns to ~~put work in rows~~ column left heading - OK*
15. List the steps you would complete to find all occurrences of *January* in a worksheet and replace with *July*.
Edit - Replace - Find what: January - Replace with: July - Options - ✓ in match entire cell contents - Replace All.

SKILLS check

✓
Assessment 1

1. Open Excel Worksheet 28.
2. Save the worksheet with Save As and name it CExl C04 SA01.
3. Make the following changes to the worksheet:
   a. Insert a formula in cell H3 that averages the amounts in cells B3 through G3.
   b. Copy the formula in cell H3 down to cells H4 through H8.
   c. Change the orientation of the worksheet to Landscape.
   d. Change the top margin to 3 inches and the left margin to 1.5 inches.
4. Save and then close CExl C04 SA01.

Assessment 2

1. Open Excel Worksheet 06.
2. Save the worksheet with Save As and name it CExl C04 SA02.
3. Make the following changes to the worksheet:
   a. Select the worksheet and then change the font to 11-point Garamond (or a similar serif typeface).
   b. Automatically adjust columns A through M.
   c. Delete row 2.
   d. Create the header *Excel Test Scores* that prints at the right margin on both pages.
   e. Create a footer that prints *Page x* (where *x* represents the correct page number) at the bottom center of the page.
4. Save the worksheet again with the same name (CExl C04 SA02).
5. Print the worksheet so the column titles (names) print on both pages.
6. Close CExl C04 SA02.

Assessment 3

1. Open Excel Worksheet 13.
2. Save the worksheet with Save As and name it CExl C04 SA03.
3. Make the following changes to the worksheet:
   a. Delete column H.
   b. Key **Total** in cell A9.
   c. Make cell B9 active and then use the AutoSum button to sum the amounts in B3 through B8.
   d. Copy the formula in cell B9 to cells C9 through G9.
4. Print the worksheet including gridlines and the row and column headings.
5. Save and then close CExl C04 SA03.

Assessment 4

1. Open Excel Worksheet 26.
2. Save the worksheet with Save As and name it CExl C04 SA04.
3. Make the following changes to the worksheet:
   a. Find all occurrences of cells containing *75* and replace with *90*.
   b. Find all occurrences of cells containing *20* and replace with *25*. (Make sure you insert a check mark in the *Match entire cell contents* check box.)
   c. Find all occurrences of *Barrier Concrete* and replace with *Lee Sand and Gravel*.

EXCEL

4. Save the worksheet again with the same name (CExl C04 SA04).
5. Print the worksheet horizontally and vertically centered on the page.
6. Close CExl C04 SA04.

Assessment 5

1. Open Excel Worksheet 27.
2. Save the worksheet with Save As and name it CExl C04 SA05.
3. Select cells A3 through F14 and then click the Sort Ascending button on the Standard toolbar.
4. Print the worksheet horizontally and vertically centered on the page. *(A)*
5. With the worksheet still open, select cells A3 through F14, and then sort the text in column B (Treatment) in ascending order (do this at the Sort dialog box).
6. Print the worksheet horizontally and vertically centered on the page. *(B)*
7. With the worksheet still open, select cells A3 through F14, and then sort by the *Client #* in ascending order and then by *Treatment* in ascending order. (This is one sort.)
8. Save the worksheet again with the same name (CExl C04 SA05). *(C)*
9. Print the worksheet horizontally and vertically centered on the page.
10. Close CExl C04 SA05.

Assessment 6

1. Open Excel Worksheet 06.
2. Print student names and scores for Test 12 on one page by completing the following steps:
    a. Hide columns B through L.
    b. Specify A1 through M20 as a print area.
    c. Print the print area. (Make sure the cells print on one page.)
    d. Clear the print area.
    e. Make columns B through L visible.
3. Close Excel Worksheet 06 without saving the changes.

Assessment 7

1. Open Excel Worksheet 23.
2. Save the worksheet with Save As and name it CExl C04 SA07.
3. Search for 11-point Arial formatting and replace with 11-point Garamond formatting (or another serif typeface such as Century Schoolbook or Times New Roman).
4. Search for 10-point Arial formatting and replace with 10-point Garamond formatting (or the typeface you chose in step 3) with a light yellow background color.
5. Save, print, and then close CExl C04 SA07. (This worksheet will contain blank cells in columns D and F.

Assessment 8

1. Open Excel Worksheet 27.
2. Save the worksheet with Save As and name it CExl C04 SA08.
3. Filter and then print a list of rows containing only the treatment *Physical Therapy*. (After printing, return the list to *(All)*.)
4. Filter and then print a list of rows containing only the client number *2085*. (After printing, return the list to *(All)*.)

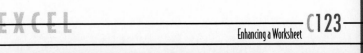

5. Filter and then print a list of rows containing the top 2 highest rates. (After printing, return the list to *(All)*.)
6. Save, print, and then close CExl C04 SA08.

Assessment 9

1. Using the Ask a Question button on the Menu bar, ask the question *What is Excel's default sorting order?*
2. Display information on default sort orders. After reading and printing the information presented, create a worksheet containing a summary of the information. Create the worksheet with the following features:
   a. Create a title for the worksheet.
   b. Set the data in cells in a serif typeface and change the data color.
   c. Add borders to the cells (you determine the border style).
   d. Add a color shading to cells (you determine the color—make it complementary to the data color).
3. Save the completed worksheet and name it CExl C04 SA09.
4. Print and then close CExl C04 SA09.

WORK IN Progress

Preparing and Formatting a Worksheet

ASSESSING proficiency

In this unit, you have learned to create, save, print, edit, and format Excel worksheets; create and insert formulas; and enhance worksheets with features such as headers and footers, page numbering, sorting, and filtering.

(Note: Before completing computer exercises, delete the Excel Chapter 04C *folder on your disk. Next, copy to your disk the* Excel Unit 01C *subfolder from the* Excel 2002 Core *folder on the CD that accompanies this textbook.)*

√Assessment 1

1. Create the Excel worksheet shown in figure U1.1. Format the cells as you see them in the figure. (Include a formula in cell D3 that subtracts the Quota sales from the Actual sales and then copy the formula down to cells D4 through D9.)
2. Save the completed worksheet and name it CExl U01 PA01.
3. Print the worksheet with gridlines and centered horizontally and vertically on the page.
4. Close CExl U01 PA01.

	A	B	C	D	E
1	SALES QUOTA REPORT				
2	Salesperson	Quota	Actual	Over/(Under)	
3	Chavis	$55,000	$63,450		
4	Hampton	$85,000	$74,000		
5	Martindale	$48,000	$51,250		
6	Enriquez	$93,000	$86,300		
7	Gorham	$45,000	$45,000		
8	Kline	$75,000	$78,560		
9	McGuinness	$65,000	$71,450		
10					

Figure U1.1 • Assessment 1

✓Assessment 2

1. Open CExl U01 PA01.
2. Save the worksheet with Save As and name it CExl U01 PA02.
3. Make the following changes to the worksheet:
   a. Add a row above row 7.
   b. Key the following data in the specified cells:

A7	=	**Dillinger**
B7	=	**95,000**
C7	=	**89,650**

   c. Make cell E2 the active cell and then key **% of Quota**.
   d. Insert a formula in cell E3 that divides the actual amount by the quota. Copy this formula down to the other cells. (The result will be a decimal point. Select the decimal numbers that are a result of the formula and then click the Percent Style button on the Formatting toolbar.)
   e. Select cells A1 through E10 and then apply an autoformat of your choosing.
4. Save, print, and then close CExl U01 PA02.

✓Assessment 3

1. Open CExl U01 PA01.
2. Save the worksheet with Save As and name it CExl U01 PA03.
3. Make the following changes to the worksheet:
   a. Key **Quota Met** in cell E2.
   b. Select cells A1 through E1 and then merge and center the cells. (To do this, click the Merge and Center button twice.)
   c. Increase the height of row 1 to 30.00.
   d. Increase the height of row 2 to 24.00.
   e. Vertically center the text in cell A1. *(Hint: To do this, make cell A1 active, click Format, and then click Cells. At the Format Cells dialog box, click the Alignment tab. Click the down-pointing triangle at the right of the Vertical option and then click Center at the drop-down list.)*
   f. Vertically center the text in cells A2 through E2.
   g. Change the width of column A to 16.00 and the width of columns B, C, D, and E to 14.00.
   h. Set the text in cell A1 in 14-point Arial bold.
   i. Set the text in cells A2 through E2 in 12-point Arial bold.
   j. Insert a formula in cell E3 that inserts the word *YES* if the quota is met and inserts *NO* if the quota is not met. *(Hint: Use the IF function to write the formula, which should look like this:* =IF(D3>=0,"YES",IF(D3<0,"NO")).)
   k. Copy the formula in cell E3 down to cells E4 through E9.
   l. Center align the text in cells E3 through E9.
   m. Select cells A1 through E9 and then apply an outline border to the selected cells.
   n. Select cells A2 through E2 and then apply to the cells a top and bottom border and light gray shading.
   o. Select cells A4 through E4 and then apply light yellow shading.
   p. Apply the light yellow shading to cells A6 through E6 and cells A8 through E8.

4. Hide column D and then print the worksheet.
5. Redisplay column D.
6. Create the footer *Annual Report* that prints at the bottom center of the page.
7. Print the worksheet horizontally and vertically on the page.
8. Save and then close CExl U01 PA03.

√Assessment 4

1. Open Excel Worksheet 30.
2. Save the worksheet with Save As and name it CExl U01 PA04.
3. The owner of Hilltop Equipment Rental is interested in purchasing a new tractor and needs to determine monthly payments on three different models. Insert a formula with the following specifications:
   a. Make cell E4 active.
   b. Use the Insert Function button on the Formula bar to insert a formula using the PMT function. At the formula palette, enter the following:

Rate	=	**C4/12**
Nper	=	**D4**
Pv	=	**-B4**

   c. Copy the formula in cell E4 down to cells E5 and E6.
4. Insert a formula in cell F4 that multiplies the amount in E4 by the amount in D4.
5. Copy the formula in cell F4 down to cells F5 and F6.
6. Insert a formula in cell G4 that subtracts the amount in B4 from the amount in F4. (The formula is =F4-B4.)
7. Copy the formula in cell G4 down to cells G5 and G6.
8. Save, print, and then close CExl U01 PA04.

√Assessment 5

1. Open Excel Worksheet 29.
2. Save the worksheet with Save As and name it CExl U01 PA05.
3. Using the DATE function, enter a formula in each of the specified cells that returns the serial number for the specified date:

C5	=	**February 6, 2003**
C6	=	**February 8, 2003**
C7	=	**March 2, 2003**
C8	=	**March 2, 2003**

4. Enter a formula in cell E5 that inserts the due date (date of service plus the number of days in the Terms column).
5. Copy the formula in cell E5 down to cells E6 through E8.
6. Make cell A10 active and then key your name.
7. Make cell A11 active and then use the NOW function to insert the current date as a serial number.
8. Save, print, and then close CExl U01 PA05.

✓ Assessment 6

1. Open CExl U01 PA02.
2. Save the worksheet with Save As and name it CExl U01 PA06.
3. Sort the names of the salespersons alphabetically in ascending order.
4. Save the worksheet again with the same name (CExl U01 PA06).
5. Print CExl U01 PA06, centered horizontally and vertically on the page. *step 5*
6. Sort the quota amounts in column B in descending order.
7. Save the worksheet again with the same name (CExl U01 PA06). *step 7*
8. Print CExl U01 PA06, centered horizontally and vertically on the page.
9. Close CExl U01 PA06.

✓ Assessment 7

1. Open Excel Worksheet 06.
2. Save the worksheet with Save As and name it CExl U01 PA07.
3. Make the following changes to the worksheet:
   a. Delete row 2.
   b. Insert a formula to average test scores for each student.
   c. Sort the data in the worksheet by the average test scores in *ascending* order.
   d. Select all cells in the worksheet and then change the font to 11-point Tahoma (or a similar sans serif typeface).
   e. Automatically adjust the widths of columns A through N.
   f. Add shading (you determine the color) to the first row.
   g. Create the header *Student Test Scores* that prints at the top center on both pages.
   h. Create a footer that prints *Page x* (where *x* represents the correct page number) at the bottom center on both pages.
4. Save the worksheet again with the same name (CExl U01 PA07).
5. Print the worksheet so the column titles (names) print on both pages.
6. Close CExl U01 PA07.

✓ Assessment 8

1. Open Excel Worksheet 31.
2. Save the worksheet with Save As and name it CExl U01 PA08.
3. Insert a formula in cell G5 that multiplies the amount in E5 by the percentage in F5 and then adds that total to the amount in E5. *(Hint: The formula should look like this: =(E5*F5)+E5.)*
4. Copy the formula in cell G5 down to cells G6 through G14.
5. Print CExl U01 PA08. *step 5*
6. Make the following changes to the worksheet:
   a. Find all occurrences of cells containing *11-279* and replace with *10-005*.
   b. Find all occurrences of cells containing *8.5* and replace with *9.0*.
   c. Search for 10-point Arial formatting and replace with 11-point Times New Roman formatting.
7. Filter and then print a list of rows containing only the client number *04-325*. (After printing, return the list to *(All)*.)
8. Filter and then print a list of rows containing only the service *Development*. (After printing, return the list to *(All)*.)

9. Filter and then print a list of rows containing the top 3 highest amounts due. (After printing, return the list to *(All)*.)

10. Save and then close CExl U01 PA08.

WRITING activities

The following activities give you the opportunity to practice your writing skills along with demonstrating an understanding of some important Excel features.

Activity 1

Plan and prepare a worksheet with the information shown below. Apply formatting of your choosing to the worksheet either with an autoformat or with formatting at the Format Cells dialog box. Save the completed worksheet and name it CExl U01 Act01. Print and then close CExl U01 Act01.

Prepare a weekly summary of orders taken that itemizes the product coming into the company and the average order size. The products and average order size include:

Black and gold wall clock—$2,450 worth of orders, average order size of $125
Traveling alarm clock—$1,358 worth of orders, average order size of $195
Water-proof watch—$890 worth of orders, average order size of $90
Dashboard clock—$2,135 worth of orders, average order size of $230
Pyramid clock—$3,050 worth of orders, average order size of $375
Gold chain watch—$755 worth of orders, average order size of $80

In the worksheet, total the amount ordered, and also calculate the average weekly order size. Sort the data in the worksheet by the order amount in descending order.

Activity 2

Assets within a company, such as equipment, can be depreciated over time. Several methods are available for determining the amount of depreciation such as the straight-line depreciation method, fixed-declining balance method, and the double-declining method. Use Excel's Help feature to learn about two depreciation methods—straight-line and double-declining depreciation. After reading about the two methods, create an Excel worksheet with the following information:

- An appropriate title
- A heading for straight-line depreciation
- The straight-line depreciation function
- The name and a description for each straight-line depreciation function argument category
- A heading for double-declining depreciation
- The double-declining depreciation function
- The name and a description for each double-declining depreciation function argument category

Apply formatting of your choosing to the worksheet. Save the completed worksheet and name it CExl U01 Act02. Print the worksheet horizontally and vertically centered on the page. Close CExl U01 Act02.

Open Excel Worksheet 32. Save the worksheet with Save As and name it CExl U01 SLN. Insert the function to determine straight-line depreciation in cell E3. Copy the formula down to cells E4 through E10. Apply formatting of your choosing to the worksheet. Print the worksheet horizontally and vertically centered on the page. Save and then close CExl U01 SLN.

INTERNET project

Make sure you are connected to the Internet. Use a search engine of your choosing to look for information on traveling to a specific country that interests you. Find sites that provide cost information for airlines, hotels, meals, entertainment, and car rentals. Create a travel planning worksheet for the country that includes the following:

- appropriate title
- appropriate headings
- airline costs
- hotel costs

- estimated meal costs
- entertainment costs
- car rental costs

Save the completed worksheet and name it CExl U01 Internet Act. Print and then close CExl U01 Internet Act.

JOB study

You are the owner of a small lawn mowing business. You need to prepare a budget with separate sections for income and expenses for April through November. Your worksheet will include these monthly expenses:

Gasoline (5-gallon container)—Each gallon will mow 8 yards. Create an absolute reference to figure the gas price. Use the current gas price in your area.

Mower (a new push mower with a bag attachment)—Select a model advertised in your local paper or go online to find the cost. Figure depreciation on the mower by taking the purchase price plus your local tax on the mower purchase price and dividing by 8 months.

Blade sharpening—$15 each month.

Figure your income based on the following parameters: 1) You will mow at least 15 yards per week. 2) You will provide services based on the following rates: mowing - $25.00 per yard; bagging grass - $10 extra per yard; and trimming and edging - $10.00 per yard.

Sort the expenses in ascending order. Then sort the income in ascending order. Create totals using formulas and functions. Determine the minimum, maximum, and average for each month's income and expenses sections. Apply formats where necessary (headers/footers, centering, shading, numeric formats, bolding, and so on). Save your worksheet as LAWN BUSINESS and print one copy.

EXCEL

CORE LEVEL UNIT 2: MAINTAINING AND ENHANCING WORKBOOKS

Moving Data within and between Workbooks

Maintaining Workbooks

Creating a Chart in Excel

Enhancing the Display of Workbooks

MICROSOFT® EXCEL 2002

CORE BENCHMARK MICROSOFT OFFICE SPECIALIST SKILLS-UNIT 2

Reference No.	Skill	Pages
Ex2002-1	**Working with Cells and Cell Data**	
Ex2002-1-1	Insert, delete and move cells	
	Move, copy, and paste selected cells	C133-C137
Ex2002-2	**Managing Workbooks**	
Ex2002-2-1	Manage workbook files and folders	
	Create a folder	C162-C163
	Select, delete, copy a workbook, move, and rename workbooks	C163-C169
	Send workbooks to a different drive or folder	C167-C168
	Open, close, and print workbooks	C169-C170
Ex2002-2-2	Create workbooks using templates	C185-C187
Ex2002-2-3	Save workbooks using different names and file formats	C173-C174
Ex2002-3	**Formatting and Printing Worksheets**	
Ex2002-3-2	Modify row and column settings	
	Freeze/unfreeze rows and columns	C140-C142
Ex2002-3-4	Apply styles	C175-C181
Ex2002-4	**Modifying Workbooks**	
Ex2002-4-1	Insert and delete worksheets	C137-C140
Ex2002-4-2	Modify worksheet names and positions	C139-C140, C170-C173
Ex2002-4-3	Use 3-D references	C151
Ex2002-5	**Creating and Revising Formulas**	
Ex2002-5-1	Create and revise formulas	
	Select and then name a range, use a range in a formula	C143-C144
Ex2002-6	**Creating and Modifying Graphics**	
Ex2002-6-1	Create, modify, position and print charts	
	Create, print, preview a chart	C193-C199
	Delete, size, and move a chart	C199-C200
	Change chart type	C200-C203
	Change data in cells; change data series	C203-C206
	Add and format chart elements	C206-C214
Ex2002-6-2	Create, modify, and position graphics	
	Insert, size, move, delete, and format images	C223-C228
	Create, size, move, and customize WordArt	C228-C235
	Draw and customize shapes, lines, and autoshapes	C235-C240
Ex2002-7	**Workgroup Collaboration**	
Ex2002-7-1	Convert worksheets into Web pages	
	Save a workbook as a Web page	C219-C223
	Preview a workbook in Web Page Preview	C220-C223
Ex2002-7-2	Create hyperlinks	
	Create and modify hyperlinks	C220-C223
Ex2002-7-3	View and edit comments	
	Insert and edit comments	C181-C183
	Create and respond to Web discussion comments	C183-C184

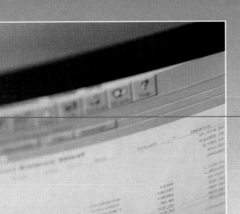

CHAPTER 5

MOVING DATA WITHIN AND BETWEEN WORKBOOKS

PERFORMANCE OBJECTIVES

Upon successful completion of chapter 5, you will be able to:
- Move, copy, and paste cells within a worksheet
- Create a workbook with multiple worksheets
- Split a worksheet into windows and freeze panes
- Name a range of cells and use a range in a formula
- Open and close workbooks
- Arrange, size, and move workbooks
- Copy and paste data between workbooks
- Link data between worksheets
- Link worksheets with a 3-D reference
- Copy and paste a worksheet between programs

Excel Chapter 05C

Moving and pasting or copying and pasting selected cells in different locations in a worksheet is useful for rearranging data in a worksheet or for saving time. Up to this point, the workbooks you have been working in have consisted of only one worksheet. In this chapter, you will learn to create a workbook with several worksheets and complete tasks such as copying and pasting data within and between worksheets. You will also work with multiple workbooks and complete tasks such as arranging, sizing, and moving workbooks, and opening and closing multiple workbooks.

Use styles to automate formatting in a large workbook containing multiple worksheets. A style is a predefined set of formatting attributes. In this chapter, you will learn to define, apply, modify, remove, delete, and copy styles.

Moving, Copying, and Pasting Cells

Situations may arise where you need to move cells to a different location within a worksheet; or, you may need to copy repetitive data in a worksheet. You can perform these actions by selecting cells and then using the Move, Copy, and/or Paste buttons on the Standard toolbar. You can also perform these actions with the mouse or with options from the Edit drop-down menu.

Cut

Paste

Moving Selected Cells

You can move selected cells and cell contents in a worksheet and between worksheets. Move selected cells with the Cut and Paste buttons on the Standard toolbar, by dragging with the mouse, or with options on the Edit drop-down menu.

To move selected cells with buttons on the Standard toolbar, select the cells, and then click the Cut button. This causes a moving dashed line to display around the selected cells. Click the cell where you want the first selected cell inserted and then click the Paste button on the Standard toolbar. If you change your mind and do not want to move the selected cells, press the Esc key to remove the moving dashed line or double-click in any cell.

To move selected cells with the mouse, select the cells, and then position the mouse pointer on any border of the selected cells until it turns into an arrow pointer. Hold down the left mouse button, drag the outline of the selected cells to the desired location, and then release the mouse button.

Selected cells can also be moved by selecting the cells, clicking Edit, and then clicking Cut. This causes a moving dashed line to display around the selected cells. Click the cell where you want the first selected cell inserted, click Edit, and then click Paste.

HINT

Ctrl + X is the keyboard command to cut selected data.

HINT

Ctrl + V is the keyboard command to paste data.

exercise 1

MOVING SELECTED CELLS IN A WORKSHEET

1. Open Excel Worksheet 02.
2. Save the worksheet with Save As and name it CExl C05 Ex01.
3. Make the following changes to the worksheet:
   a. Move cells in column D to column E by completing the following steps:
      1) Select cells D1 through D8.
      2) Click the Cut button on the Standard toolbar.
      3) Click cell E1 to make it active.
      4) Click the Paste button on the Standard toolbar.
   b. Move cells in column B to column D by completing the following steps:
      1) Select cells B1 through B8.
      2) Position the mouse pointer on any boundary of the selected cells until it turns into an arrow pointer.
      3) Hold down the left mouse button, drag the outline of the selected cells to column D, and then release the mouse button. (After the cells are moved, they should occupy cells D1 through D8.)

	A	B	C	D	E
1	Expense	Actual	Budget		Variance
2	Salaries	126000	126000		D1:D8 0
3	Commissions	58000	54500		-3500
4	Media space	8250	10100		1850
5	Travel expenses	6350	6000		-350
6	Dealer display	4140	4500		360
7	Payroll taxes	2430	2200		-230
8	Telephone	1450	1500		50

Step 3b1

Step 3b3

   c. Delete column B.
   d. Select cells A1 through D8 and then apply the Accounting 2 autoformat.
   e. Select row 1 and then turn on Bold and change the alignment to center.
4. Save, print, and then close CExl C05 Ex01.

EXCEL

Copying Selected Cells

Copying selected cells can be useful in worksheets that contain repetitive data. To copy cells, select the cells, and then click the Copy button on the Standard toolbar. Click the cell where you want the first selected cell copied and then click the Paste button on the Standard toolbar.

Selected cells can also be copied using the mouse and the Ctrl key. To do this, select the cells to be copied, and then position the mouse pointer on any border around the selected cells until it turns into an arrow pointer. Hold down the Ctrl key and the left mouse button, drag the outline of the selected cells to the desired location, release the left mouse button, and then release the Ctrl key.

You can also use the Copy and Paste options from the Edit drop-down menu to copy selected cells in a worksheet. To do this, select the cells, click Edit, and then click Copy. Click the cell where you want the first selected cell copied, click Edit, and then click Paste.

Copy

HINT

Ctrl + C is the keyboard command to copy selected data.

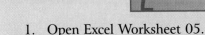

COPYING SELECTED CELLS IN A WORKSHEET

1. Open Excel Worksheet 05.
2. Save the worksheet with Save As and name it CExl C05 Ex02.
3. Make the following changes to the worksheet:
   a. Key **Total** in cell D2.
   b. Make cell D3 active and then insert a formula that multiplies the contents of cell C3 with the contents of cell B3.
   c. Copy the formula in cell D3 down to cells D4 through D8.
   d. Select cells A1 through D1.
   e. Click the Merge and Center button on the Formatting toolbar. (This splits the cells.)
   f. Click the Merge and Center button again. (This merges cells A1 through D1.)
   g. Copy and paste cells by completing the following steps:
      1) Select cells A1 through D8.
      2) Position the mouse pointer on any boundary of the selected cells until it turns into an arrow pointer.
      3) Hold down the Ctrl key and then the left mouse button.
      4) Drag the outline of the selected cells so the top left corner of the outline is positioned at the top of cell A10.
      5) Release the left mouse button and then the Ctrl key.

   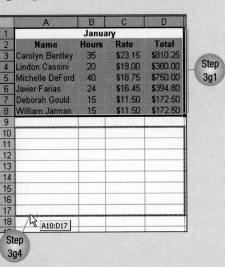

   Step 3g1

   Step 3g4

   h. Change the contents of the following cells to the specified data:
      A10: From *January* to *February*
      B12: From *35* to *40*
      B14: From *40* to *32*
      B16: From *15* to *30*
   i. Select cells A1 through D8 and then apply the Colorful 2 autoformat.
   j. Select cells A10 through D17 and then apply the Colorful 2 autoformat.
4. Save, print, and then close CExl C05 Ex02.

HINT

The Clipboard Task Pane holds up to 24 items. After that number, items are discarded beginning with the oldest item.

Using the Office Clipboard

Use the Office Clipboard to collect and paste multiple items. You can collect up to 24 different items and then paste them in various locations. To display the Clipboard Task Pane, click Edit on the Menu bar and then click Office Clipboard, or press Ctrl + C twice. You can also display the Clipboard Task Pane by clicking the Other Task Panes button (displays as a down-pointing triangle) located in the upper right corner of the task pane, and then clicking Clipboard at the drop-down menu. The Clipboard Task Pane displays at the right side of the screen in a manner similar to what you see in figure 5.1.

FIGURE 5.1 ***Office Clipboard Task Pane***

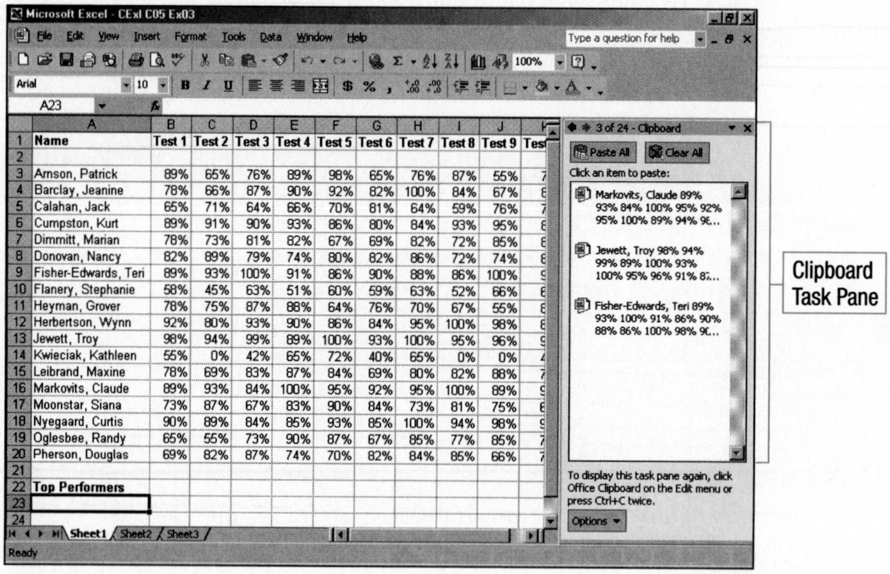

HINT

Click the Paste All button in the Clipboard Task Pane to paste all items at once.

Select data or an object you want to copy and then click the Copy button on the Standard toolbar. Continue selecting text or items and clicking the Copy button. To insert an item, position the insertion point in the desired location and then click the item in the Clipboard Task Pane. If the copied item is text, the first 50 characters display. When all desired items are inserted, click the Clear All button to remove any remaining items.

exercise 3

1. Open Excel Worksheet 06.
2. Save the worksheet with Save As and name it CExl C05 Ex03.
3. Make cell A22 the active cell, turn on bold, and then key **Top Performers**.
4. Display the Clipboard Task Pane by clicking Edit and then Office Clipboard.
5. Collect several rows of cells and then paste them by completing the following steps:
   a. Click the row header for row 9 (this selects the entire row).
   b. Click the Copy button on the Standard toolbar.
   c. Click the row header for row 13 and then click the Copy button on the Standard toolbar.
   d. Click the row header for row 16 and then click the Copy button on the Standard toolbar.
6. Paste the copied cells by completing the following steps:
   a. Make cell A23 active.
   b. Click the item in the Clipboard Task Pane representing row 13 (the row for Jewett).
   c. Make cell A24 active.
   d. Click the item in the Clipboard Task Pane representing row 16 (the row for Markovits).
   e. Make cell A25 active.
   f. Click the item in the Clipboard Task Pane representing row 9 (the row for Fisher-Edwards).
7. Click the Clear All button located toward the top of the Clipboard Task Pane.
8. Close the Clipboard Task Pane by clicking the Close button (contains an X) located in the upper right corner of the task pane.
9. Save, print, and then close CExl C05 Ex03.

Creating a Workbook with Multiple Worksheets

Up to this point, each workbook you have been creating has contained one worksheet. A workbook can contain several worksheets. You can create a variety of worksheets within a workbook for related data. For example, a workbook may contain a worksheet for the expenses for each salesperson in a company and another worksheet for the monthly payroll for each department within the company. Another example is recording sales statistics for each quarter in individual worksheets within a workbook.

The copy and paste features can be useful in creating more than one worksheet within a workbook. These features are helpful if some data within each worksheet is consistent. For example, you can create a worksheet containing

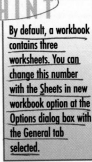

HINT

By default, a workbook contains three worksheets. You can change this number with the Sheets in new workbook option at the Options dialog box with the General tab selected.

information on a product and then copy this information to another worksheet where you would change data in specific cells.

To copy selected cells to a new worksheet, select the cells, click the Copy button on the Standard toolbar, click the worksheet tab (displayed immediately above the Status bar) representing the desired worksheet, and then click the Paste button.

Printing a Workbook Containing Multiple Worksheets

HINT

Print specific worksheets in a workbook by selecting the desired worksheet tabs.

In exercise 4, you will create a workbook that contains four worksheets. When printing this workbook, by default, Excel will print the worksheet currently displayed. If you want to print all worksheets in a workbook, display the Print dialog box by clicking File and then Print. At the Print dialog box, click Entire workbook in the Print what section, and then click OK.

Another method for printing specific worksheets within a workbook is to select the tabs of the worksheets you want to print. To do this, open the desired workbook, hold down the Ctrl key, and then click the desired tabs. If the tabs are adjacent, you can use the Shift key.

✓ exercise 4

COPYING CELLS TO DIFFERENT WORKSHEETS

1. Open Excel Worksheet 34.
2. Save the worksheet with Save As and name it CExl C05 Ex04.
3. Add a fourth worksheet by clicking Insert and then Worksheet. (This adds a *Sheet4* tab before the *Sheet1* tab.)
4. Click *Sheet1* to make worksheet 1 active and then make the following changes to the worksheet:
    a. Insert a formula in cell D3 that subtracts from the amount in B3 the amount in C3.
    b. Copy the formula in cell D3 down to cells D4 through D9.
5. Copy cells and paste them into worksheets 2, 3, and 4 by completing the following steps:
    a. Click the Select All button that displays immediately to the left of the column A header and immediately above the row 1 header.
    b. Click the Copy button on the Standard toolbar.
    c. Click the *Sheet2* tab that displays immediately above the Status bar.
    d. At worksheet 2, make sure cell A1 is the active cell, and then click the Paste button.
    e. Click the *Sheet3* tab that displays immediately above the Status bar.
    f. At worksheet 3, make sure cell A1 is the active cell, and then click the Paste button.
    g. Click the *Sheet4* tab.
    h. At worksheet 4, make sure cell A1 is the active cell, and then click the Paste button.

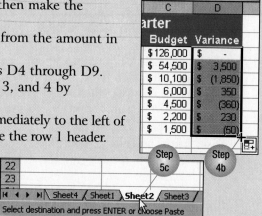

6. Click the *Sheet2* tab and then make the following changes to cell entries in worksheet 2:
    A1: From *First Quarter* to *Second Quarter*
    B4: From *58,000* to *60500*
    C4: From *54,500* to *58500*
    B8: From *2,430* to *2510*
    C8: From *2,200* to *2350*

EXCEL

7. Click the *Sheet3* tab and then make the following changes to cell entries in worksheet 3:
   A1: From *First Quarter* to *Third Quarter*
   B4: From *58,000* to *60200*
   C4: From *54,500* to *60500*
   B8: From *2,430* to *2500*
   C8: From *2,200* to *2550*
8. Click the *Sheet4* tab and then make the following changes to cell entries in worksheet 4:
   A1: From *First Quarter* to *Fourth Quarter*
   B4: From *58,000* to *61000*
   C4: From *54,500* to *60500*
   B8: From *2,430* to *2550*
   C8: From *2,200* to *2500*
9. Save the workbook again with the same name (CExl C05 Ex04).
10. Print all of the worksheets in the workbook by completing the following steps:
    a. Make sure there are no selected cells (just an active cell).
    b. Click <u>F</u>ile and then <u>P</u>rint.
    c. At the Print dialog box, click <u>E</u>ntire workbook in the Print what section.
    d. Click OK. (Each worksheet will print on a separate piece of paper.)
11. Close CExl C05 Ex04.

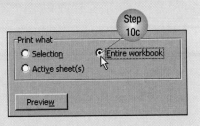

Step 10c

Managing Worksheets

Right-click a sheet tab and a shortcut menu displays with the options <u>I</u>nsert, <u>D</u>elete, <u>R</u>ename, <u>M</u>ove or Copy, and <u>S</u>elect All Sheets. Use these options to manage worksheets in a workbook. For example, remove a worksheet by clicking the <u>D</u>elete option. Move or copy a worksheet by clicking the <u>M</u>ove or Copy option. Clicking this option causes a Move or Copy dialog box to display where you specify before what sheet you want to move or copy the selected sheet. By default, Excel names worksheets in a workbook *Sheet1, Sheet2, Sheet3,* and so on. To rename a worksheet, click the <u>R</u>ename option (this selects the default sheet name), and then key the desired name.

You can manage more than one worksheet at a time by selecting the worksheets first. If the tabs are adjacent, click the first tab, hold down the Shift key, and then click the last tab. If the tabs are nonadjacent, click the first tab, hold down the Ctrl key, and then click any other tabs you want selected.

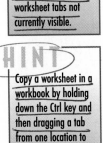

HINT
Use the tab scroll buttons, located to the left of the sheet tabs, to bring into view any worksheet tabs not currently visible.

HINT
Copy a worksheet in a workbook by holding down the Ctrl key and then dragging a tab from one location to another.

✓ exercise **5**

DELETING SELECTED WORKSHEETS

1. Open CExl C05 Ex04.
2. Save the workbook with Save As and name it CExl C05 Ex05.
3. Delete worksheets 3 and 4 by completing the following steps:
   a. Click the left mouse button on *Sheet3* that displays at the bottom of the workbook window.
   b. Hold down the Ctrl key, click *Sheet4*, and then release the Ctrl key.
   c. Position the arrow pointer on the *Sheet4* tab and then click the *right* mouse button.

d. At the pop-up menu that displays, click <u>D</u>elete.
e. At the message telling you that the selected sheets will be permanently deleted, click the Delete button.

4. Rename worksheets 1 and 2 by completing the following steps:
   a. Right-click the *Sheet1* tab and then click <u>R</u>ename.
   b. Key **First Quarter**.
   c. Right-click the *Sheet2* tab and then click <u>R</u>ename.
   d. Key **Second Quarter**.

5. Move the Second Quarter sheet tab by completing the following steps:
   a. Right-click the *Second Quarter* sheet tab and then click <u>M</u>ove or Copy at the shortcut menu.
   b. At the Move or Copy dialog box, make sure *First Quarter* is selected in the <u>B</u>efore sheet list box, and then click OK.

6. Save and then print the entire workbook (two worksheets).
7. Close CExl C05 Ex05.

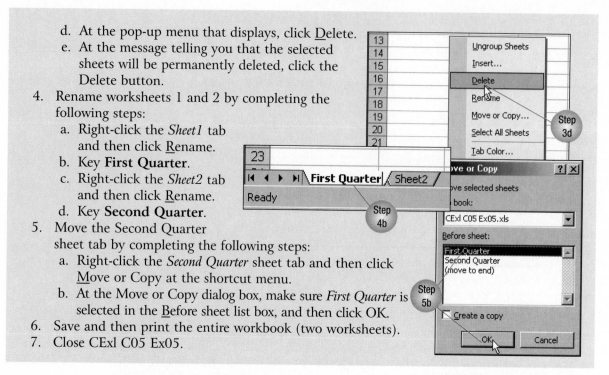

Splitting a Worksheet into Windows and Freezing and Unfreezing Panes

In some worksheets, not all cells display at one time in the worksheet area (such as Excel Worksheet 06). When working in worksheets with more cells than can display at one time, you may find splitting the worksheet window into panes helpful.

Split the worksheet window into panes with the <u>S</u>plit option from the <u>W</u>indow drop-down menu or use the split bars that display at the top of the vertical scroll bar and at the right side of the horizontal scroll bar. Figure 5.2 identifies these split bars.

F I G U R E

5.2 *Split Bars*

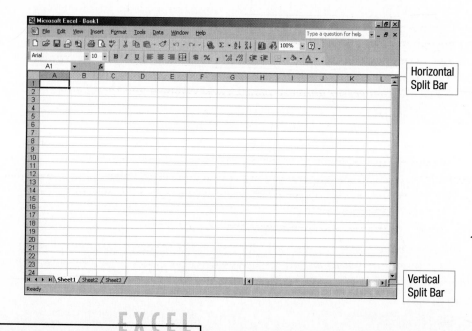

To split a window with the split bar located at the top of the vertical scroll bar, position the mouse pointer on the split bar until it turns into a double-headed arrow with a short double line in the middle. Hold down the left mouse button, drag down the thick gray line that displays until the pane is the desired size, and then release the mouse button. Split the window vertically with the split bar at the right side of the horizontal scroll bar.

To split a worksheet window with the Window drop-down menu, click Window and then Split. This causes the worksheet to split into four window panes as shown in figure 5.3. The windows are split by thick gray lines (with a three-dimensional look).

FIGURE

5.3 *Split Window*

A window pane will display the active cell. As the insertion point is moved through the pane, another active cell with a blue background may display. This additional active cell displays when the insertion point passes over one of the gray lines that creates the pane. As you move through a worksheet, you may see both active cells—one with a normal background and one with a blue background. If you make a change to the active cell, the change is made in both. If you want only one active cell to display, freeze the window panes by clicking Window and then Freeze Panes. With panes frozen, only the display of the pane with the active cell will change. To unfreeze panes, click Window and then Unfreeze Panes.

Using the mouse, you can move the thick gray lines that divide the window into panes. To do this, position the mouse pointer on the line until it turns into a double-headed arrow with a double line in the middle. Hold down the left mouse button, drag the outline of the gray line to the desired location, and then release the mouse button. If you want to move both the horizontal and vertical lines at the same time, position the mouse pointer on the intersection of the thick gray lines until it turns into a four-headed arrow. Hold down the left mouse button, drag the thick gray lines in the desired direction, and then release the mouse button.

By splitting a worksheet into windows, you can maintain the display of column headings while editing or keying text in cells. You can do the same for row headings. You will be doing this with a worksheet in exercise 6.

1. Open Excel Worksheet 06.
2. Save the worksheet with Save As and name it CExl C05 Ex06.
3. Select the entire worksheet and then change the font size to 11 points.
4. Automatically adjust the width of the columns.
5. Make cell A1 active and then split the window by completing the following steps:
   a. Click <u>W</u>indow and then <u>S</u>plit. (This causes the window to split into four panes.)
   b. Drag both the horizontal and vertical gray lines by completing the following steps:
      1) Position the mouse pointer on the intersection between the horizontal and vertical lines until it turns into a four-headed black arrow.
      2) Hold down the left mouse button, drag up and to the left until the horizontal gray line is immediately below the first row and the vertical gray line is immediately to the right of the first column, and then release the mouse button.
   c. Freeze the window panes by clicking <u>W</u>indow and then <u>F</u>reeze Panes.
   d. Add two rows by completing the following steps:
      1) Select rows 18 and 19.
      2) Click <u>I</u>nsert and then <u>R</u>ows.
   e. Key the following text in the specified cells:

A18	=	**Nauer, Sheryl**	A19	=	**Nunez, James**
B18	=	75	B19	=	98
C18	=	83	C19	=	96
D18	=	85	D19	=	100
E18	=	78	E19	=	90
F18	=	82	F19	=	95
G18	=	80	G19	=	93
H18	=	79	H19	=	88
I18	=	82	I19	=	91
J18	=	92	J19	=	89
K18	=	90	K19	=	100
L18	=	86	L19	=	96
M18	=	84	M19	=	98

   f. Edit the text in the following cells:
      D3: Change *76%* to *92%*
      K6: Change *81%* to *74%*
      E8: Change *74%* to *90%*
      M12: Change *89%* to *95%*
      C14: Change *0%* to *70%* (*Be sure to press Enter to change from the* Enter *mode to the* Ready *mode.*)
   g. Unfreeze the window panes by clicking <u>W</u>indow and then Unfreeze Panes.
   h. Remove the panes by clicking <u>W</u>indow and then Remove Split.
6. Save the worksheet and then print it in landscape orientation.
7. Close CExl C05 Ex06.

Step 5b2

Microsoft Excel - CExl C05 Ex06
File Edit View Insert Format Tools
Arial   11   B I U
A1   Name

	A	B	C
1	Name	Test 1	Test 2
2			
3	Arnson, Patrick	89%	65%
4	Barclay, Jeanine	78%	66%
5	Calahan, Jack	65%	71%
6	Cumpston, Kurt	89%	91%
7	Dimmitt, Marian	78%	73%
8	Donovan, N...	82%	89%

Working with Ranges

A selected group of cells is referred to as a *range*. A range of cells can be formatted, moved, copied, or deleted. You can also name a range of cells and then move the insertion point to the range or use a named range as part of a formula.

To name a range, select the cells, and then click in the Name Box button to the left of the Formula bar. Key a name for the range (do not use a space) and then press Enter. To move the insertion point to a specific range and select the range, click the down-pointing triangle at the right side of the Name Box button and then click the range name.

You can use a range name in a formula. For example, if a range is named *Profit* and you want to insert the average of all cells in the *Profit* range, you would make the desired cell active and then key **=AVERAGE(Profit)**. You can use a named range in the current worksheet or in another worksheet within the workbook.

exercise 7

NAMING A RANGE AND USING A RANGE IN A FORMULA

1. Open Excel Worksheet 09.
2. Save the worksheet with Save As and name it CExl C05 Ex07.
3. Click the *Sheet2* tab and then key the following text in the specified cell:

A1	=	**EQUIPMENT USAGE REPORT**
A2	=	**Yearly Hours**
A3	=	**Avoidable Delays**
A4	=	**Unavoidable Delays**
A5	=	**Total Delay Hours**
A6	=	(leave blank)
A7	=	**Repairs**
A8	=	**Servicing**
A9	=	**Total Repair/Servicing Hours**

4. Make the following formatting changes to the worksheet:
   a. Automatically adjust the width of column A.
   b. Center and bold the text in cells A1 and A2.
5. Select a range of cells in worksheet 1, name the range, and use it in a formula in worksheet 2 by completing the following steps:
   a. Make worksheet 1 active by clicking the *Sheet1* tab.
   b. Select cells B4 through M4.
   c. Click in the Name Box button to the left of the Formula bar.
   d. Key **adhours** (for Avoidable Delays Hours) and then press Enter.
   e. Click the *Sheet2* tab to make worksheet 2 active.
   f. Make cell B3 active.
   g. Key the equation **=SUM(adhours)** and then press Enter.
6. Make worksheet 1 active and then complete the following steps:

a. Select cells B5 through M5 and then name the range *udhours*.
b. Make worksheet 2 active, make cell B4 active, and then insert the equation **=SUM(udhours)**.
c. Make worksheet 1 active.
d. Select cells B6 through M6 and then name the range *rhours*.
e. Make worksheet 2 active, make cell B7 active, and then insert the equation **=SUM(rhours)**.
f. Make worksheet 1 active.
g. Select cells B7 through M7 and then name the range *shours*.
h. Make worksheet 2 active, make cell B8 active, and then insert the equation **=SUM(shours)**.

7. With worksheet 2 still active, make the following changes:
   a. Make cell B5 active.
   b. Click the AutoSum button on the Standard toolbar and then press Enter.
   c. Make cell B9 active.
   d. Double-click the AutoSum button on the Standard toolbar.

8. Save the workbook and then print worksheet 2.

9. Make worksheet 1 active and then move to the range *adhours* by clicking the down-pointing triangle at the right side of the Name Box button and then clicking *adhours* at the drop-down list.

10. Close CExl C05 Ex07.

Working with Windows

You can open multiple workbooks in Excel and arrange the open workbooks in the Excel window. With multiple workbooks open, you can cut and paste or copy and paste cell entries from one workbook to another using the same techniques discussed earlier in this chapter with the exception that you activate the destination workbook before executing the Paste command.

Opening Multiple Workbooks

With multiple workbooks open, you can move or copy information between workbooks or compare the contents of several workbooks. The maximum number of workbooks that you can have open at one time depends on the memory of your computer system and the amount of information in each workbook. When you open a new workbook, it is placed on top of the original workbook. Once multiple workbooks are opened, you can resize the workbooks to see all or a portion of them on the screen.

Open multiple workbooks at one time at the Open dialog box. If workbooks are adjacent, display the Open dialog box, click the first workbook name to be opened, hold down the Shift key, and then click the last workbook name to be opened. If the workbooks are nonadjacent, click the first workbook name to be opened, and then hold down the Ctrl key while clicking the remaining desired workbook names. Release the Shift key or the Ctrl key and then click the Open button.

To see what workbooks are currently open, click Window on the Menu bar. The names of the open workbooks display at the bottom of the drop-down menu. The workbook name with the check mark in front of it is the *active* workbook.

EXCEL

The active workbook is the workbook containing the active cell. To make one of the other workbooks active, click the desired workbook.

Closing Multiple Workbooks

Close all open workbooks at one time by holding down the Shift key, clicking File on the Menu bar, and then clicking Close All. The Close option becomes the Close All option when the Shift key is down.

exercise 8

OPENING AND CLOSING MULTIPLE WORKBOOKS

(Note: If you are using Excel on a network system that contains a virus checker, you may not be able to open multiple workbooks at one time.)

1. Open several workbooks at the same time by completing the following steps:
   a. Display the Open dialog box.
   b. Click the workbook named Excel Worksheet 02.
   c. Hold down the Ctrl key, click *Excel Worksheet 04,* and then click *Excel Worksheet 06.*
   d. Release the Ctrl key and then click the Open button in the dialog box.
2. Make Excel Worksheet 06 the active workbook by clicking Window and then 3.
3. Make Excel Worksheet 04 the active workbook by clicking Window and then 2.
4. Close all open workbooks by completing the following steps:
   a. Hold down the Shift key.
   b. Click File on the Menu bar.
   c. Click Close All.

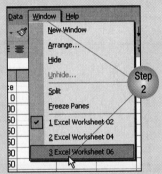

Arranging Workbooks

If you have more than one workbook open, you can arrange the workbooks at the Arrange Windows dialog box shown in figure 5.4. To display this dialog box, open several workbooks, click Window, and then click Arrange. At the Arrange Windows dialog box, click Tiled to display a portion of each open workbook. Figure 5.5 displays four tiled workbooks.

FIGURE

5.4 *Arrange Windows Dialog Box*

Use options at this dialog box to choose an arrange method.

5.5 Tiled Workbooks

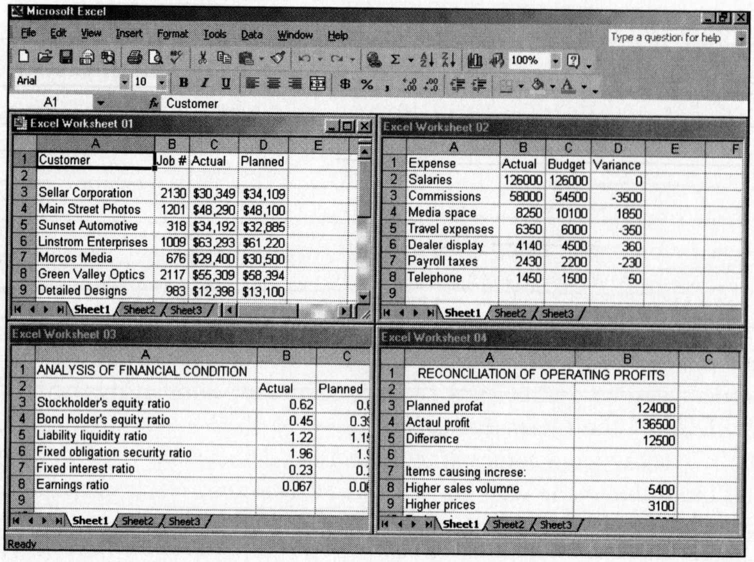

Choose the Horizontal option at the Arrange Windows dialog box and the open workbooks display across the screen. The Vertical option displays the open workbooks up and down the window. The last option, Cascade, displays the Title bar of each open workbook. Figure 5.6 shows four cascaded workbooks.

5.6 Cascaded Workbooks

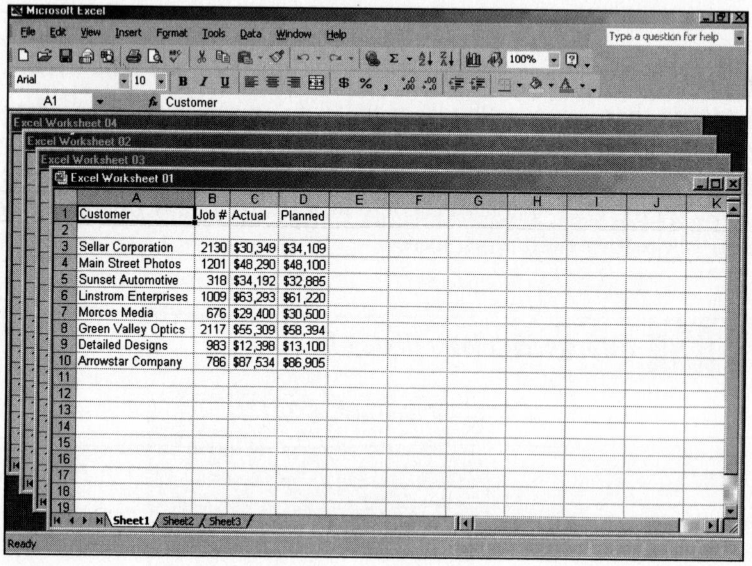

1. Open the following workbooks: Excel Worksheet 01, Excel Worksheet 02, Excel Worksheet 03, and Excel Worksheet 04.
2. Tile the workbooks by completing the following steps:
   a. Click Window and then Arrange.
   b. At the Arrange Windows dialog box, make sure Tiled is selected, and then click OK.
3. Tile the workbooks horizontally by completing the following steps:
   a. Click Window and then Arrange.
   b. At the Arrange Windows dialog box, click Horizontal.
   c. Click OK.
4. Cascade the workbooks by completing the following steps:
   a. Click Window and then Arrange.
   b. At the Arrange Windows dialog box, click Cascade.
   c. Click OK.
5. Close all of the open workbooks by holding down the Shift key, clicking File, and then clicking Close All.

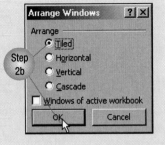

Step 2b

Sizing and Moving Workbooks

The Maximize and Minimize buttons in the upper right corner of the active workbook window can be used to change the size of the window. The Maximize button is the button in the upper right corner of the active workbook immediately to the left of the Close button. (The Close button is the button containing the *X*.) The Minimize button is located immediately to the left of the Maximize button.

If you arrange all open workbooks and then click the Maximize button in the active workbook, the active workbook expands to fill the screen. In addition, the Maximize button changes to the Restore button. To return the active workbook back to its size before it was maximized, click the Restore button.

Clicking the Minimize button causes the active workbook to be reduced and positioned as a button on the Taskbar. In addition, the Minimize button changes to the Restore button. To maximize a workbook that has been reduced, click the button on the Taskbar representing the workbook.

Maximize

Minimize

Close

Restore

1. Open Excel Worksheet 01.
2. Maximize Excel Worksheet 01 by clicking the Maximize button at the right side of the workbook Title bar. (The Maximize button is the button at the right side of the Title bar, immediately to the left of the Close button.)
3. Open Excel Worksheet 03 and Excel Worksheet 05.
4. Make the following changes to the open workbooks:

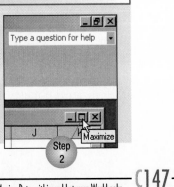

Step 2

a. Tile the workbooks.
b. Make Excel Worksheet 01 the active workbook (Title bar displays with a blue background [the background color may vary depending on how Windows is customized]).
c. Minimize Excel Worksheet 01 by clicking the Minimize button that displays at the right side of the Title bar.
d. Make Excel Worksheet 03 the active workbook and then minimize it.
e. Minimize Excel Worksheet 05.
5. Close all workbooks by holding down the Shift key, clicking File, and then clicking Close All.

Moving, Copying, and Pasting Data

With more than one workbook open, you can move, copy, and/or paste data from one workbook to another. To move, copy, and/or paste data between workbooks, use the cutting and pasting options you learned earlier in this chapter, together with the information about windows in this chapter.

exercise 11

COPYING SELECTED CELLS FROM ONE OPEN WORKSHEET TO ANOTHER

1. Open Excel Worksheet 35.
2. If you just completed exercise 10, click the Maximize button so the worksheet fills the entire worksheet window.
3. Save the worksheet and name it CExl C05 Ex11.
4. With CExl C05 Ex11 still open, open Excel Worksheet 01.
5. Select and then copy text from Excel Worksheet 01 to CExl C05 Ex11 by completing the following steps:
   a. With Excel Worksheet 01 the active workbook, select cells A5 through D10.
   b. Click the Copy button on the Standard toolbar.
   c. Click Window and then click 2 CExl C05 Ex11.
   d. Make cell A7 the active cell and then click the Paste button on the Standard toolbar.
6. Select cells A1 through D12 in CExl C05 Ex11 and then apply the Colorful 1 autoformat.
7. Save the worksheet again with the same name (CExl C05 Ex11).
8. Print CExl C05 Ex11 horizontally and vertically centered on the page.
9. Close CExl C05 Ex11.
10. Close Excel Worksheet 01.

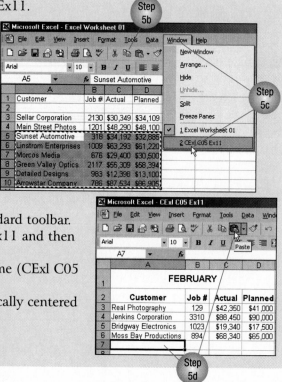

Linking Data between Worksheets

In workbooks containing multiple worksheets or between related workbooks, you may want to create a link between worksheets or workbooks with data in cells. When data is linked, a change made in a linked cell is automatically made to the other cells in the link. Links can be made with individual cells or with a range of cells.

Linking cells between worksheets creates what is called a *dynamic link*. Dynamic links are useful in worksheets or workbooks that need to maintain consistency and control over critical data. The worksheet that contains the original data is called the *source* worksheet and the worksheet relying on the source worksheet for the data in the link is called the *dependent* worksheet.

To create a link, make active the cell containing the data to be linked (or select the cells), and then click the Copy button on the Standard toolbar. Make active the worksheet where you want to paste the cell or cells, click Edit, and then click Paste Special. This displays the Paste Special dialog box as shown in figure 5.7.

FIGURE

5.7 *Paste Special Dialog Box*

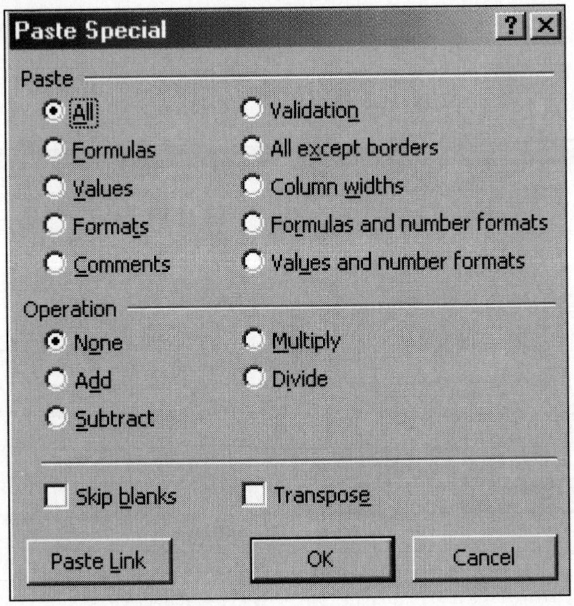

At the Paste Special dialog box, specify what in the cell you want to copy and what operators you want to include, and then click the Paste Link button. When a change is made to the cell or cells in the source worksheet, the change is automatically made to the linked cell or cells in the dependent worksheet.

1. Open Excel Worksheet 34.
2. Save the worksheet with Save As and name it CExl C05 Ex12.
3. Make the following changes to the worksheet:
   a. Change the text in cell A1 from *First Quarter* to *FIRST HALF, 2002*.
   b. Insert a formula in cell D3 that subtracts from the amount in B3 the amount in C3.
   c. Copy the formula in cell D3 down to cells D4 through D9.

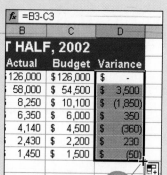

4. Copy data in the worksheet to *Sheet2* by completing the following steps:
   a. Select cells A1 through D9.
   b. Click the Copy button on the Standard toolbar.
   c. Click the *Sheet2* tab.
   d. With cell A1 the active cell, click the Paste button on the Standard toolbar.
   e. Automatically adjust the widths of the cells.
   f. Select cells C3 through C9 and then delete the cell data.
5. Link cells C3 through C9 from *Sheet1* to *Sheet2* by completing the following steps:
   a. Click the *Sheet1* tab.
   b. Select cells C3 through C9.
   c. Click the Copy button on the Standard toolbar.
   d. Click the *Sheet2* tab.
   e. Make cell C3 active.
   f. Click Edit and then Paste Special.
   g. At the Paste Special dialog box, make sure All is selected in the Paste section of the dialog box, and then click the Paste Link button.

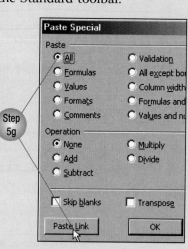

6. With *Sheet2* still the active worksheet, make the following changes to the specified cells:
   A1: Change *FIRST HALF, 2002* to *SECOND HALF, 2002*
   B3: Change *$126,000* to *123,500*
   B4: Change *$58,000* to *53,000*
   B6: Change *$6,350* to *6,125*
7. Make *Sheet1* the active worksheet and then make the following changes to some of the linked cells:
   C3: Change *$126,000* to *128,000*
   C4: Change *$54,500* to *56,000*
   C8: Change *$2,200* to *2,400*

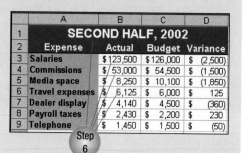

8. Click the *Sheet2* tab and notice that the values in cells C3, C4, and C8 automatically changed (because they are linked to *Sheet1*).
9. Save the worksheet with the same name (CExl C05 Ex12).
10. Print both worksheets in the workbook.
11. Close CExl C05 Ex12.

Linking Worksheets with a 3-D Reference

In multiple worksheet workbooks, you can use a 3-D reference to analyze data in the same cell or range of cells. A 3-D reference includes the cell or range of cells, preceded by a range of worksheet names. For example, you can add all of the values contained in cells in B2 through B5 in worksheets 1 and 2 in a workbook using a 3-D reference. To do this, you would complete these basic steps:

1. Make active the cell where you want to enter the function.
2. Key =SUM(and then click the *Sheet1* tab.
3. Hold down the Shift key and then click the *Sheet2* tab.
4. Select cells B2 through B5 in the worksheet.
5. Key) (this is the closing parenthesis that ends the formula) and then press Enter.

 exercise 13

| | LINKING WORKSHEETS WITH A 3-D REFERENCE |

1. Open Excel Worksheet 33.
2. Save the workbook with Save As and name it CExl C05 Ex13.
3. Make sure *Sheet1* is active.
4. Select columns B, C, and D and change the width to 14.00.
5. Make the following changes to worksheet 1:
   a. Make cell B10 active.
   b. Click the Center button and then the Bold button on the Formatting toolbar.
   c. Key **January Sales** and then press Alt + Enter.
   d. Key **1999-2001** and then press Enter.
6. Link worksheets 1, 2, and 3 with a 3-D reference by completing the following steps:
   a. With cell B11 active, key =SUM(.
   b. Hold down the Shift key and then click the *Sheet3* tab.
   c. Select cells B3 through B8.
   d. Key) and then press Enter.
   e. Make cell B11 active.
   f. Click the Currency Style button on the Formatting toolbar and then click twice on the Decrease Decimal button.

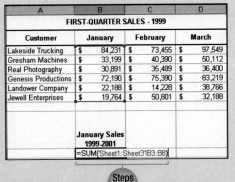

Steps 6a-6d

7. Complete steps similar to those in 5 to add February sales for 1999-2001 [on two lines] in cell C10 and complete steps similar to those in step 6 to insert the formula with the 3-D reference in cell C11.
8. Complete steps similar to those in step 5 to add March sales for 1999-2001 [on two lines] in cell D10 and complete steps similar to those in step 6 to insert the formula with the 3-D reference in cell D11.
9. Save the workbook again with the same name (CExl C05 Ex13).
10. Print worksheet 1 of the workbook.
11. Close CExl C05 Ex13.

Copying and Pasting a Worksheet between Programs

Microsoft Office is a suite that allows integration, which is the combining of data from two or more programs into one file. Integration can occur by copying and pasting data between programs. The program containing the data to be copied is called the *source* program and the program where the data is pasted is called the *destination* program. For example, you can create a worksheet in Excel and then copy it to a Word document. The steps to copy and paste between programs are basically the same as copying and pasting within the same program.

When copying data between worksheets or from one program to another, you can copy and paste, copy and link, or copy and embed the data. Consider the following when choosing a method for copying data:

Paste —
- Copy data in the source program and paste it in the destination program when the data will not need to be edited.

Link —
- Copy data in the source program and then link it in the destination program when the data is updated regularly in the source program and you want the update reflected in the destination program.

Embed —
- Copy data in the source program and then embed it in the destination program when the data will be edited in the destination program (with the tools of the source program).

Earlier in this chapter, you copied and pasted cells within and between worksheets and you also copied and linked cells between worksheets. You can also copy and link data between programs. Copy and embed data using options at the Paste Special dialog box. In exercise 14, you will copy cells in a worksheet and then embed the cells in a Word document. With the worksheet embedded in a Word document, double-click the worksheet and Excel tools display in the document for editing the worksheet.

INTEGRATED *exercise* 14

COPYING AND PASTING A WORKSHEET INTO A WORD DOCUMENT

1. Open the Word program and then open Word Letter 02.
2. Save the document and name it CExl Word C05 Ex14.
3. With CExl Word C05 Ex14 still open, make Excel the active program.
4. Open Excel Worksheet 03.
5. Save the worksheet with Save As and name it CExl C05 Ex14.
6. Make the following changes to the worksheet:
   a. Select cells B3 through D8 and then click the Percent Style button on the Formatting toolbar.
   b. Select cells A1 through D8 and then apply the Classic 2 autoformat.
7. Save the worksheet again with the same name (CExl C05 Ex14).
8. Copy the worksheet to the letter in CExl Word C05 Ex14 by completing the following steps:
   a. Select cells A1 through D8.
   b. Click the Copy button on the Standard toolbar.
   c. Click the button on the Taskbar representing the Word document CExl Word C05 Ex14.

EXCEL

d. Position the insertion point a double space below the first paragraph of text in the body of the letter.

e. Click Edit and then Paste Special.

f. At the Paste Special dialog box, click *Microsoft Excel Worksheet Object* in the As list box, and then click OK.

9. Edit a few of the cells in the worksheet by completing the following steps:

a. Double-click anywhere in the worksheet. (This displays the Excel toolbar for editing.)

b. Click in each of the following cells and make the change indicated:

  B6: Change *196%* to *110%*
  C6: Change *190%* to *104%*
  D6: Change *187%* to *101%*

c. Click outside the worksheet to remove the Excel tools (and deselect the worksheet).

10. Save, print, and then close CExl Word C05 Ex14.

11. Exit Word.

12. With Excel the active program, close CExl C05 Ex14.

Step 8d

Paste Special

Source: Microsoft Excel Worksheet Sheet1!R1C1:R8C4

As:

- Paste:
- Paste link:

Microsoft Excel Worksheet Object
Formatted Text (RTF)
Unformatted Text
Picture
Bitmap
Picture (Enhanced Metafile)
HTML Format

OK
Cancel

☐ Display as icon

Result — Inserts the contents of the Clipboard into your document so that you can edit it using Microsoft Excel Worksheet.

Step 8f

I rece... stocks and securities. The financial picture looks ... an return on investments. The following table displays ... tual, percentages.

	A	B	C	D
1	ANALYSIS OF FINANCIAL CONDITION			
2		Actual	Planned	Prior Year
3	Stockholder's equity ratio	62%	60%	57%
4	Bond holder's equity ratio	45%	39%	41%
5	Liability liquidity ratio	122%	115%	120%
6	Fixed obligation security ratio	110%	104%	101%
7	Fixed interest ratio	23%	20%	28%
8	Earnings ratio	7%	6%	6%

Sheet1 / Sheet2 / Sheet3

As you can see from the table, the highest increase of percenta obligation security ratio. If you have any ... ons about this

Step 9b

CHAPTER summary

➤ Move selected cells and cell contents in and between worksheets using the Cut, Copy, and Paste buttons on the Standard toolbar; dragging with the mouse; or with options from the Edit drop-down menu.

➤ Move selected cells with the mouse by dragging the outline of the selected cells to the desired position.

➤ Copy selected cells with the mouse by holding down the Ctrl key and the left mouse button, dragging the outline of the selected cells to the desired location, releasing the left mouse button, and then releasing the Ctrl key.

➤ Use the Office Clipboard to collect and paste up to 24 different items within and between worksheets and workbooks.

➤ A workbook can contain several worksheets. You can create a variety of worksheets for related data within a workbook.

➤ To print all worksheets in a workbook, click Entire workbook in the Print what section of the Print dialog box. You can also print specific worksheets by holding down the Ctrl key and then clicking the tabs of the worksheets you want printed.

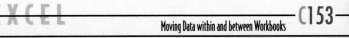

➤ Perform maintenance activities, such as deleting and renaming, on worksheets within a workbook by clicking the right mouse button on a sheet tab, and then clicking the desired option at the pop-up menu.

➤ Split the worksheet window into panes with the Split option from the Window drop-down menu or with the split bars on the horizontal and vertical scroll bars.

➤ Remove the split window by clicking Window and then Remove Split; or drag the split bars.

➤ Freeze window panes by clicking Window and then Freeze Panes. When panes are frozen, only the display of the pane with the active cell changes. Unfreeze window panes by clicking Window and then Unfreeze Panes.

➤ A selected group of cells is referred to as a range. A range can be named and used in a formula. Name a range by keying the name in the Name Box button to the left of the Formula bar.

➤ Open multiple workbooks that are adjacent by displaying the Open dialog box, clicking the first workbook to open, holding down the Shift key, and then clicking the last workbook. If workbooks are nonadjacent, click the first workbook, hold down the Ctrl key, and then click the desired workbook names.

➤ Click Window on the Menu bar to see a list of open workbooks.

➤ Close all open workbooks at one time by holding down the Shift key, clicking File, and then clicking Close All.

➤ Arrange multiple workbooks in a window with options from the Arrange Windows dialog box.

➤ Click the Maximize button located at the right side of the Title bar of the active workbook to make the workbook fill the entire window area. Click the Minimize button to shrink the active workbook to a button on the Taskbar. Click the Restore button to return the workbook back to its previous size.

➤ You can move, copy, and/or paste data between workbooks.

➤ Copy and then link data if you make changes in the source worksheet and you want the change reflected in the destination worksheet. The worksheet containing the original data is called the source worksheet and the worksheet relying on the source worksheet for data in the link is called the dependent worksheet.

➤ Copy and link data using the Paste Special dialog box.

➤ You can copy data from a document in one program (called the source program) and paste the data into a file in another program (called the destination program).

➤ Use a 3-D reference to analyze data in the same cell or range of cells.

➤ You can copy and then paste, link, or embed data between programs in the Office suite. Integrating is the combining of data from two or more programs in the Office suite.

COMMANDS review

Command	Mouse/Keyboard
Display Clipboard Task Pane	Click Edit, Office Clipboard; or press Ctrl + C twice
Split window into panes	Click Window, Split; or drag split bar
Freeze window panes	Click Window, Freeze Panes
Unfreeze window panes	Click Window, Unfreeze Panes
Remove window panes	Click Window, Remove Split
Display Arrange Windows dialog box	Click Window, Arrange
Display Paste Special dialog box	Click Edit, Paste Special

CONCEPTS check

Completion: On a blank sheet of paper, indicate the correct term, symbol, or command for each item.

1. To copy selected cells with the mouse, hold down this key while dragging the outline of the selected cells to the desired location. *Ctrl*
2. Press Ctrl + C twice and this task pane displays. *Office Clipboard*
3. Click this option at the Print dialog box to print all worksheets in the workbook. *Entire Workbook*
4. To split a window using a split bar, position the mouse pointer on the split bar until the mouse pointer turns into this. *double-headed arrow w/a double-line in the middle*
5. Clicking Window and then Split causes the active worksheet to be split into this number of windows. *four*
6. To see what workbooks are currently open, click this on the Menu bar. *Window*
7. To close all open workbooks at the same time, hold down this key while clicking File and then Close All. *Shift*
8. Arrange all open workbooks with options from this dialog box. *Arrange Windows*
9. Click this button to shrink the active workbook to a button on the Taskbar. *Minimize*
10. Click this button to return the workbook back to its original size. *Restore*
11. Click this button to make the active workbook fill the entire window area. *Maximize*
12. When copying and pasting data between programs, the program containing the original data is called this. *Source program*
13. List the steps you would complete to open all of the following workbooks at one time: Excel Worksheet 02, Excel Worksheet 03, and Excel Worksheet 05. *File-open-click on 02 - hold Ctrl while clicking on 03+05 -open*
14. List the steps you would complete to copy a range of cells from one workbook to another. *select range of cells - Click Copy on Standard toolbar — Window - put checkmark in workbook to be pasted in, making it the active workbook - put the insertion point (active cell) where you want to paste-Paste (standard toolbar)*

SKILLS check

✓**Assessment 1**

1. Open Excel Worksheet 34.
2. Save the worksheet with Save As and name it CExl C05 SA01.
3. Make the following changes to the worksheet:
   a. Insert a column between columns C and D. (The new column will be column D.)
   b. Move the content of cells B2 through B9 to D2 through D9.
   c. Delete the blank column B.
   d. Insert a formula in cell D3 that subtracts the Actual amount from the Budget amount.
   e. Copy the formula in cell D3 down to cells D4 through D9.
4. Save, print, and then close CExl C05 SA01.

✓**Assessment 2**

1. Open Excel Worksheet 05.
2. Save the worksheet with Save As and name it CExl C05 SA02.
3. Make the following changes:
   a. Copy cells A1 through C8 to *Sheet2*.
   b. With *Sheet2* active, make the following changes:
      A1: Change *January* to *February*
      B3: Change *35* to *40*
      B6: Change *24* to *20*
      B7: Change *15* to *20*
      C4: Change *$19.00* to *20.15*
      C6: Change *$16.45* to *17.45*
   c. Automatically adjust the width of column A.
   d. Copy cells A1 through C8 to *Sheet3*.
   e. With *Sheet3* active, make the following changes:
      A1: Change *February* to *March*
      B4: Change *20* to *35*
      B8: Change *15* to *20*
   f. Automatically adjust the width of column A.
4. Save the worksheets again and then print all worksheets in the CExl C05 SA02 workbook.
5. Close CExl C05 SA02.

✓**Assessment 3**

1. Open Excel Worksheet 09.
2. Save the worksheet with Save As and name it CExl C05 SA03.
3. Make the following changes to the worksheet:
   a. Split the window.
   b. Drag the intersection of the horizontal and vertical gray lines so that the horizontal gray line is immediately below row 9 and the vertical gray line is immediately to the right of column A.

EXCEL

c. Freeze the window panes.

d. Insert a new row 8 and then key the following in the specified cells:

A8	=	**Loaned Out**
B8	=	10
C8	=	0
D8	=	5
E8	=	0
F8	=	11
G8	=	3
H8	=	16
I8	=	0
J8	=	0
K8	=	5
L8	=	0
M8	=	0

e. Remove the split.

f. Select rows 1 through 10 and then change the row height to 18.00.

4. Save the worksheet again and then print the worksheet in landscape orientation (it will take two pages) so the row titles print on each page.

5. Close CExl C05 SA03.

✓ Assessment 4

1. Open Excel Worksheet 01.
2. Save the worksheet with Save As and name it CExl C05 SA04.
3. Make the following changes to the worksheet:
   a. Key **Difference** in cell E1.
   b. Insert the formula **=D3-C3** in cell E3 and then copy it down to E4 through E10.
   c. Select cells E3 through E10 and then name the range *Difference*.
   d. Key **Max Difference** in cell A13.
   e. Insert the formula **=MAX(Difference)** in cell B13.
   f. Key **Min Difference** in cell A14.
   g. Insert the formula **=MIN(Difference)** in cell B14.
   h. Key **Ave Difference** in cell A15.
   i. Insert the formula **=AVERAGE(Difference*)** in cell B15.
   j. Select cells B13 through B15 and then click the Currency Style button on the Formatting toolbar.
   k. With cells B13 through B15 selected, click twice the Decrease Decimal button.
   l. Automatically adjust column B.
   m. Bold and center the text in cells A1 through E1.
4. Save and then print CExl C05 SA04.A
5. Make the following changes to the worksheet:
   a. Change *63,293* in cell C6 to *55,500*.
   b. Change *12,398* in cell C9 to *13,450*.
   c. Create the header *Customer Jobs* that prints centered at the top of the page. *(Hint: Create this header at the Page Setup dialog box with the Header/Footer tab selected.)*
6. Save, print, and then close CExl C05 SA04.B

✓ Assessment 5

1. Create the worksheet shown in figure 5.8 (change the width of column A to 21.00).
2. Save the worksheet and name it CExl C05 SA05.
3. With CExl C05 SA05 still open, open Excel Worksheet 09.
4. Select and copy the following cells from Excel Worksheet 09 to CExl C05 SA05:
   a. Copy cells A3 through G3 in Excel Worksheet 09 and paste them into CExl C05 SA05 beginning with cell A12.
   b. Copy cells A9 through G9 in Excel Worksheet 09 and paste them into CExl C05 SA05 beginning with cell A13.
5. With CExl C05 SA05 the active worksheet, apply an autoformat of your choosing to cells A1 through G13.
6. Save the worksheet again and then print CExl C05 SA05 in landscape orientation and centered horizontally and vertically on the page.
7. Close CExl C05 SA05.
8. Close Excel Worksheet 09 without saving the changes.

FIGURE

5.8 *Assessment 5*

	A	B	C	D	E	F	G	H
1		EQUIPMENT USAGE REPORT						
2		January	February	March	April	May	June	
3	Machine #12							
4	Total Hours Available	2,300	2,430	2,530	2,400	2,440	2,240	
5	In Use	2,040	2,105	2,320	2,180	2,050	1,995	
6								
7	Machine #25							
8	Total Hours Available	2,100	2,240	2,450	2,105	2,390	1,950	
9	In Use	1,800	1,935	2,110	1,750	2,215	1,645	
10								
11	Machine #30							
12								

✓ Assessment 6

1. Open Excel Worksheet 33.
2. Save the workbook with Save As and name it CExl C05 SA06.
3. Make the following changes to the workbook:
   a. Select columns B, C, and D and then change the width to 15.00.
   b. Insert the heading **Average January Sales 1999-2001** (on multiple lines) in cell B10.
   c. Insert a formula in cell B11 with a 3-D reference that averages the total in cells B3 through B8 in *Sheet1*, *Sheet2*, and *Sheet3*.
   d. Make cell B11 active and then change to the Currency Style with zero decimal places.
   e. Insert the heading **Average February Sales 1999-2001** (on multiple lines) in cell C10.
   f. Insert a formula in cell C11 with a 3-D reference that averages the total in cells C3 through C8 in *Sheet1*, *Sheet2*, and *Sheet3*.
   g. Make cell C11 active and then change to the Currency Style with zero decimal places.
   h. Insert the heading **Average March Sales 1999-2001** (on multiple lines) in cell D10.

[handwritten note:] =AVERAGE(SUM('sheet1:Sheet3'! → B3:B8))

EXCEL

    i. Insert a formula in cell D11 with a 3-D reference that averages the total in cells D3 through D8 in *Sheet1*, *Sheet2*, and *Sheet3*.

    j. Make cell D11 active and then change to the Currency Style with zero decimal places.

  4. Save the workbook and then print page 1 of the workbook.

  5. Close CExl C05 SA06.

Assessment 7

1. Use Excel's Help feature to learn about linking data between programs.

2. After locating and reading the information on linking, complete the following steps:

    a. Open the Word program and then open Word Letter 02.

    b. Save the document and name it CExl Word C05 SA07.

    c. Make Excel the active program and then open Excel Worksheet 03.

    d. Save the worksheet with Save As and name it CExl C05 SA07.

    e. Make the following changes to the worksheet:

       1) Select cells B3 through D8 and then click the Percent Style button on the Formatting toolbar.

       2) Select cells A1 through D8 and then apply the Colorful 2 autoformat.

    f. Save and then print the worksheet. CExl C05 SA07 Step 2f

    g. Copy the worksheet and link it to CExl Word C05 SA07 (between the two paragraphs in the body of the letter).

    h. Save and then print CExl Word C05 SA07 A

    i. Click the button on the Taskbar representing the Excel worksheet CExl C05 SA07 and then make the following changes to data in cells:

       1) Change the title in cell A1 from *ANALYSIS OF FINANCIAL CONDITION* to *FINANCIAL ANALYSIS*.

       2) Change the content of cell B3 from *62%* to *80%*.

       3) Change the content of cell B4 from *45%* to *70%*.

    j. Save, print, and then close CExl C05 SA07. Step 2j

    k. Make active the Word document CExl Word C05 SA07.

    l. Save, print, and then close CExl Word C05 SA07 B

    m. Exit Word.

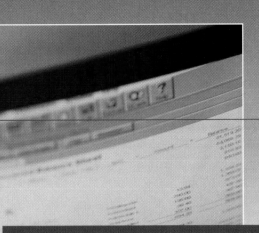

C H A P T E R 6

MAINTAINING WORKBOOKS

PERFORMANCE OBJECTIVES

Upon successful completion of chapter 6, you will be able to:
- **Create a folder**
- **Select multiple adjacent and nonadjacent workbooks**
- **Delete workbooks and folders**
- **Copy and move workbooks within and between folders**
- **Open, close, and print multiple workbooks**
- **Copy, move, and rename worksheets within a workbook**
- **Save a workbook in a different format**
- **Search for specific workbooks**
- **Maintain consistent formatting with styles**
- **Use comments for review and response**
- **Create financial forms using templates**

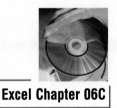

Excel Chapter 06C

Once you have been working with Excel for a period of time you will have accumulated several workbook files. Workbooks should be organized into folders to facilitate fast retrieval of information. Occasionally you should perform file maintenance activities such as copying, moving, renaming, and deleting workbooks to ensure the workbook list in your various folders is manageable.

Maintaining Workbooks

Many workbook management tasks can be completed at the Open and Save As dialog boxes. These tasks can include copying, moving, printing, and renaming workbooks; opening multiple workbooks; and creating a new folder. To display the Open dialog box, shown in figure 6.1, click the Open button on the Standard toolbar or click <u>F</u>ile and then <u>O</u>pen. To display the Save As dialog box, click <u>F</u>ile and then Save <u>A</u>s.

Open

Maintaining Workbooks C161

6.1 Open Dialog Box

Folder Icon

Current Folder

Workbook Icon

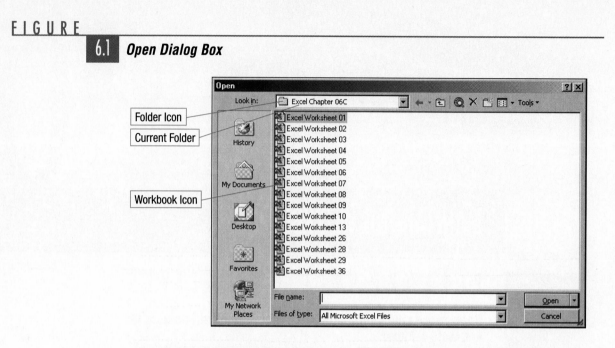

Some file maintenance tasks such as creating a folder and deleting files are performed by using buttons on the Open dialog box or Save As dialog box toolbar. Figure 6.2 displays the Open dialog box toolbar buttons.

6.2 Open Dialog Box Toolbar Buttons

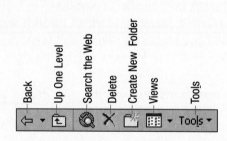

Creating a Folder

In Excel, workbooks should be grouped logically and stored in folders. For example, all of the workbooks related to one department could be stored in one folder with the department name being the folder name. A folder can be created within a folder (called a *subfolder*). If you create workbooks for a department by individual, each individual could have a subfolder name within the department folder. The main folder on a disk or drive is called the root folder. Additional folders are created as a branch of this root folder.

At the Open or Save As dialog boxes, workbook file names display in the list box preceded by a workbook icon and a folder name is preceded by a folder icon. The folder and workbook icons are identified in figure 6.1.

Create
New Folder

Create a new folder by clicking the Create New Folder button located on the dialog box toolbar at the Open dialog box or Save As dialog box. At the New Folder dialog box shown in figure 6.3, key a name for the folder in the Name text box, and then click OK or press Enter. The new folder becomes the active folder.

6.3 *New Folder Dialog Box*

New Folder

OK

Cancel

Name:

Key a name for the folder
in this text box.

If you want to make the previous folder the active folder, click the Up One
Level button on the dialog box toolbar. Clicking this button changes to the folder
that was up one level from the current folder. After clicking the Up One Level
button, the Back button becomes active. Click this button and the previously
active folder becomes active again.

A folder name can contain a maximum of 255 characters. Numbers, spaces,
and symbols can be used in the folder name, except those symbols explained in
chapter 1 in the "Saving a Workbook" section.

Up One
Level

Back

exercise

CREATING A FOLDER

1. Create a folder named *Finance* on your disk by completing the following steps:
   a. Display the Open dialog box and then double-click the *Excel Chapter 06C* folder name
      to make it the active folder.
   b. Click the Create New Folder button
      (located on the dialog box toolbar).
   c. At the New Folder dialog box, key
      Finance.
   d. Click OK or press Enter. (The
      Finance folder is now the active
      folder.)
   e. Change back to the *Excel Chapter
      06C* folder by clicking the Up One
      Level button on the dialog box
      toolbar.
2. Click the Cancel button to close the Open dialog box.

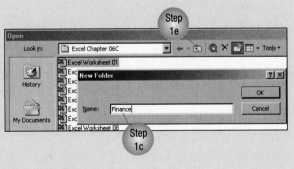

Step
1e

Step
1c

Selecting Workbooks

Workbook management tasks can be completed on one workbook or more than
one selected workbook. For example, you can move one workbook to a different
folder, or you can select several workbooks and move them all in one operation.
Selected workbooks can be opened, deleted, copied, moved, or printed.

To select one workbook, display the Open dialog box, and then click the
desired workbook in the file list. To select several adjacent workbooks (workbooks

opening mult. workbooks — *adjacent — Shift*
non-adjacent — Ctrl

HINT

Display all files in a folder by changing the Files of type option at the Open dialog box to *All Files*.

displayed next to each other), click the first workbook, hold down the Shift key, click the last workbook to be selected, and then release the Shift key.

You can also select workbooks that are not adjacent in the Open dialog box. To do this, click the first workbook, hold down the Ctrl key, click each additional workbook to be selected, and then release the Ctrl key.

Deleting Workbooks and Folders

At some point, you may want to delete certain workbooks from your data disk or any other disk or folder in which you may be working. If you use Excel on a regular basis, you should establish a periodic system for deleting workbooks that are no longer used. The system you choose depends on the work you are doing and the amount of folder or disk space available. To delete a workbook, display the Open or Save As dialog box, select the workbook, and then click the Delete button on the dialog box toolbar. At the dialog box asking you to confirm the deletion, click Yes.

You can also delete a workbook by displaying the Open dialog box, selecting the workbook to be deleted, clicking the Tools button on the dialog box toolbar, and then clicking Delete at the drop-down menu. Another method for deleting a workbook is to display the Open dialog box, right-click the workbook to be deleted, and then click Delete at the shortcut menu. Delete a folder and all of its contents in the same manner as deleting a workbook or selected workbooks.

X

Delete

Tools ▾

Tools

exercise 2

DELETING A WORKBOOK

1. Open Excel Worksheet 05.
2. Save the worksheet with Save As and name it CExl C06 Ex02.
3. Close CExl C06 Ex02.
4. Delete CExl C06 Ex02 by completing the following steps:
   a. Display the Open dialog box with the *Excel Chapter 06C* folder active.
   b. Click *CExl C06 Ex02* to select it.
   c. Click the Delete button on the dialog box toolbar.
   d. At the question asking if you are sure you want to delete the item, click Yes.
5. Close the Open dialog box.

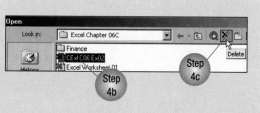

1. Delete selected workbooks by completing the following steps:
   a. Display the Open dialog box with the *Excel Chapter 06C* folder active.
   b. Click *Excel Worksheet 02.*
   c. Hold down the Shift key and then click *Excel Worksheet 04.*
   d. Position the mouse pointer on one of the selected workbooks and then click the right mouse button.
   e. At the shortcut menu that displays, click <u>D</u>elete.
   f. At the question asking if you are sure you want to delete the items, click <u>Y</u>es.
   g. At the message telling you that Excel Worksheet 02 is a read-only file and asking if you want to delete it, click the Yes to <u>A</u>ll button.
2. Close the Open dialog box.

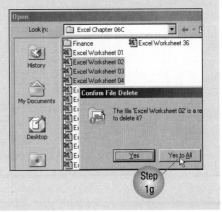

Step 1g

Deleting to the Recycle Bin

<u>Workbooks deleted from your data disk are deleted permanently.</u> (Recovery programs are available, however, that will help you recover deleted text. If you accidentally delete a workbook[s] from a disk, do not do anything more with the disk until you can run a recovery program.) <u>Workbooks deleted from the hard drive are automatically sent to the Windows Recycle Bin.</u> If you accidentally delete a workbook to the Recycle Bin, it can be easily restored. To free space on the drive, empty the Recycle Bin on a periodic basis. <u>Restoring a workbook from or emptying the contents of the Recycle Bin is done at the Windows desktop</u> (not in Excel).

To display the Recycle Bin, minimize the Excel window, and then double-click the *Recycle Bin* icon located on the Windows desktop. At the Recycle Bin, you can restore file(s) and empty the Recycle Bin.

Copying Files

In previous chapters, you opened a workbook from the data disk and saved it with a new name on the same disk. This process makes an exact copy of the workbook, leaving the original on the disk. You copied workbooks and saved the new workbook in the same folder as the original. You can also copy a workbook into another folder and use the workbook's original name or give it a different name, or select workbooks at the Open dialog box and copy them to the same folder or into a different folder. <u>To copy a workbook into another folder, open the workbook, display the Save As dialog box, change to the desired folder, and then click the <u>S</u>ave button.</u>

The Open and Save As dialog boxes contain an Up One Level button (located on the dialog box toolbar). Use this button if you want to change to the folder that is up one level from the current folder.

√exercise 4

1. Open Excel Worksheet 10.
2. Save the workbook with Save As and name it Quota&Bonus. (Make sure *Excel Chapter 06C* is the active folder.)
3. Save a copy of the Quota&Bonus workbook in the *Finance* folder created in exercise 1 by completing the following steps. (If you did not complete exercise 1, check with your instructor before continuing.)
    a. With Quota&Bonus still open, display the Save As dialog box.
    b. At the Save As dialog box, change to the *Finance* folder. To do this, double-click *Finance* at the beginning of the list box (folders are listed before workbooks).
    c. Click the <u>S</u>ave button located in the lower right corner of the dialog box.
4. Close Quota&Bonus.
5. Change back to the *Excel Chapter 06C* folder by completing the following steps:
    a. Display the Open dialog box.
    b. Click the Up One Level button located on the dialog box toolbar.
    c. Close the Open dialog box.

A workbook can be copied to another folder without opening the workbook first. To do this, use the <u>C</u>opy and <u>P</u>aste options from a shortcut menu at the Open (or Save As) dialog box.

√exercise 5

1. Copy Excel Worksheet 07 to the *Finance* folder by completing the following steps:
    a. Display the Open dialog box with the *Excel Chapter 06C* folder active.
    b. Position the arrow pointer on *Excel Worksheet 07,* click the right mouse button, and then click <u>C</u>opy at the shortcut menu.
    c. Change to the *Finance* folder by double-clicking *Finance* at the beginning of the list box.
    d. Position the arrow pointer in any white area (not on a workbook name) in the list box, click the right mouse button, and then click <u>P</u>aste at the shortcut menu.
2. Change back to the *Excel Chapter 06C* folder by clicking the Up One Level button located on the dialog box toolbar.
3. Close the Open dialog box.

A workbook or selected workbooks can be copied into the same folder. When you do this, Excel names the duplicated workbook(s) "Copy of xxx" (where *xxx* is the current workbook name). You can copy one workbook or selected workbooks into the same folder.

EXCEL

exercise 6

COPYING SELECTED WORKBOOKS INTO THE SAME FOLDER

1. Copy workbooks into the same folder by completing the following steps:
   a. Display the Open dialog box with *Excel Chapter 06C* the active folder.
   b. Select *Excel Worksheet 01, Excel Worksheet 07,* and *Excel Worksheet 09.* (To do this, hold down the Ctrl key while clicking each workbook name.)
   c. Position the arrow pointer on one of the selected workbooks, click the right mouse button, and then click Copy at the shortcut menu.
   d. Position the arrow pointer in any white area in the list box, click the right mouse button, and then click Paste at the shortcut menu. (In a few seconds, Excel will redisplay the Open dialog box with the following workbooks added: Copy of Excel Worksheet 01, Copy of Excel Worksheet 07, and Copy of Excel Worksheet 09.)
2. Close the Open dialog box.

exercise 7

COPYING SELECTED WORKBOOKS INTO A DIFFERENT FOLDER

1. Copy selected workbooks to the *Finance* folder by completing the following steps:
   a. Display the Open dialog box with *Excel Chapter 06C* the active folder.
   b. Select *Excel Worksheet 06, Excel Worksheet 08,* and *Excel Worksheet 10.*
   c. Position the arrow pointer on one of the selected workbooks, click the right mouse button, and then click Copy at the shortcut menu.
   d. Double-click the *Finance* folder.
   e. Position the arrow pointer in any white area in the list box, click the right mouse button, and then click Paste at the shortcut menu.
   f. Click the Up One Level button to change back to the *Excel Chapter 06C* folder.
2. Close the Open dialog box.

Sending Workbooks to a Different Drive or Folder

Copy workbooks to another folder or drive with the Copy and Paste options from the shortcut menu at the Open or Save As dialog box. With the Send To option, you can quickly send a copy of a workbook to another drive or folder. To use this option, position the arrow pointer on the workbook you want copied, click the right mouse button, point to Send To (this causes a side menu to display), and then click the desired drive or folder.

Cutting and Pasting a Workbook

You can remove a workbook from one folder or disk and insert it in another folder or on another disk using the Cut and Paste options from the shortcut menu at the Open dialog box. To do this, display the Open dialog box, position the arrow pointer on the workbook to be removed (cut), click the right mouse button, and then click Cut at the shortcut menu. Change to the desired folder or drive, position the arrow pointer in a white area in the list box, click the right mouse button, and then click Paste at the shortcut menu.

CUTTING AND PASTING A WORKBOOK

1. Move a workbook to a different folder by completing the following steps:
   a. Display the Open dialog box with the *Excel Chapter 06C* folder active.
   b. Position the arrow pointer on *Excel Worksheet 09,* click the right mouse button, and then click Cut at the shortcut menu.
   c. Double-click *Finance* to make it the active folder.
   d. Position the arrow pointer in the white area in the list box, click the right mouse button, and then click Paste at the shortcut menu.
   e. At the Confirm File Move dialog box asking if you are sure you want to move the file, click Yes. (This dialog box usually does not appear when you cut and paste. Since the files you copied from your student CD-ROM are read-only files, this warning message appears.)
   f. Click the Up One Level button to make the *Excel Chapter 06C* folder the active folder.

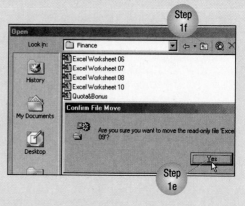

2. Close the Open dialog box.

Renaming Workbooks

At the Open dialog box, use the Rename option from the Tools drop-down menu or the shortcut menu to give a workbook a different name. The Rename option changes the name of the workbook and keeps it in the same folder. To use Rename, display the Open dialog box, click once on the workbook to be renamed, click the Tools button on the dialog box toolbar, and then click Rename. This causes a thin black border to surround the workbook name and the name to be selected. Key the new name and then press Enter.

You can also rename a workbook by right-clicking the workbook name at the Open dialog box and then clicking Rename at the shortcut menu. Key the new name for the workbook and then press the Enter key.

RENAMING A WORKBOOK

1. Rename a workbook located in the *Finance* folder by completing the following steps:
   a. Display the Open dialog box with *Excel Chapter 06C* the active folder.
   b. Double-click *Finance* to make it the active folder.
   c. Click once on *Excel Worksheet 07* to select it.
   d. Click the Tools button on the dialog box toolbar.
   e. At the drop-down menu that displays, click Rename.
   f. Key **Equipment** and then press the Enter key.

g. At the message asking if you are sure you want to change the name of the read-only file, click Yes.

h. Complete steps similar to those in 1c through 1g to rename Excel Worksheet 09 to **Equipment-Usage**.

i. Click the Up One Level button.

2. Close the Open dialog box.

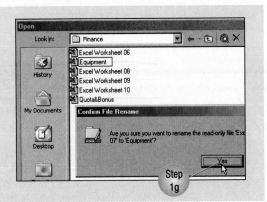

Step 1g

Deleting a Folder and Its Contents

As you learned earlier in this chapter, a workbook or selected workbooks can be deleted. In addition to workbooks, a folder (and all of its contents) can be deleted. Delete a folder in the same manner as a workbook is deleted.

exercise 10

DELETING A FOLDER AND ITS CONTENTS

1. Delete the *Finance* folder and its contents by completing the following steps:
   a. Display the Open dialog box with the *Excel Chapter 06C* folder active.
   b. Right-click on the *Finance* folder.
   c. Click Delete at the pop-up menu.
   d. At the Confirm Folder Delete dialog box, click Yes.
   e. At the Confirm File Delete dialog box, click the Yes to All button.
2. Close the Open dialog box.

Opening and Closing Workbooks

Previously you learned that to open multiple workbooks, select the desired workbooks, and then click the Open button. Hold down the Shift key to select adjacent workbooks; hold down the Ctrl key to select nonadjacent workbooks. All open workbooks can be closed at the same time. To do this, hold down the Shift key, click File and then Close All. Holding down the Shift key before clicking File causes the Close option to change to Close All.

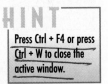

HINT
Press Ctrl + F4 or press Ctrl + W to close the active window.

exercise 11

OPENING AND CLOSING SEVERAL WORKBOOKS

1. Open several workbooks by completing the following steps:
   a. Display the Open dialog box with the *Excel Chapter 06C* folder active.
   b. Click *Excel Worksheet 06*, hold down the Shift key, and then click *Excel Worksheet 10*.
   c. Click the Open button.
2. Close the open workbooks by completing the following steps:
   a. Hold down the Shift key.
   b. Click File and then Close All.

Printing Workbooks

Up to this point, you have opened a workbook and then printed it. With the Print option from the Tools drop-down menu or the Print option from the shortcut menu at the Open dialog box, you can print a workbook or several workbooks without opening them.

✓ exercise 12

1. Display the Open dialog box with the *Excel Chapter 06C* folder active.
2. Select *Excel Worksheet 01* and *Excel Worksheet 08*.
3. Click the Tools button on the dialog box toolbar.
4. At the drop-down menu that displays, click Print.

Managing Worksheets

Individual worksheets within a workbook can be moved or copied within the same workbook or to another existing workbook. Exercise caution when moving sheets since calculations or charts based on data on a worksheet might become inaccurate if you move the worksheet.

Copying a Worksheet to Another Workbook

HINT

Make a duplicate of a worksheet in the same workbook by holding the Ctrl key and then dragging the worksheet tab to the desired position.

To copy a worksheet to another existing workbook, open both the source and the destination workbooks. Activate the sheet you want to copy in the source workbook, click Edit, and then click Move or Copy Sheet, or right-click the sheet tab located at the bottom of the screen just above the Status bar and then click Move or Copy at the shortcut menu. At the Move or Copy dialog box shown in figure 6.4, select the destination workbook name from the To book drop-down list, select the worksheet that you want the copied worksheet placed before in the Before sheet list box, click the Create a copy check box, and then click OK.

FIGURE

6.4 *Move or Copy Dialog Box*

EXCEL

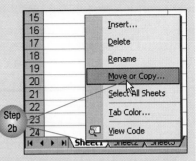

1. Open Excel Worksheet 26 and Copy of Excel Worksheet 09.

2. Copy the Equipment Usage Report Worksheet from the workbook named Copy of Excel Worksheet 09 to the Excel Worksheet 26 workbook by completing the following steps:

   a. Make sure Copy of Worksheet 09 is the active workbook.

   b. Right-click the *Sheet1* tab located at the bottom left of the screen just above the Status bar, and then click Move or Copy at the shortcut menu.

   c. Click the down-pointing triangle next to the To book option box and then click *Excel Worksheet 26.xls* at the drop-down list.

   d. Click *Sheet2* in the Before sheet list box.

   e. Click the Create a copy check box to insert a check mark.

   f. Click OK. (Excel switches to the workbook Excel Worksheet 26 and inserts the copied sheet with the sheet name *Sheet 1 (2)*.)

3. Save Excel Worksheet 26 with Save As and name it CExl C06 Ex13.

4. Print the entire CExl C06 Ex13 workbook by completing the following steps:

   a. Click File and then Print.

   b. Click Entire workbook in the Print what section

   c. Click OK.

5. Close CExl C06 Ex13.

6. Close Copy of Excel Worksheet 09.

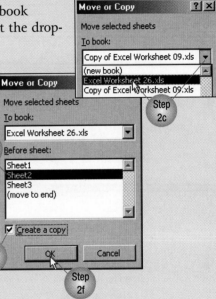

Moving a Worksheet to Another Workbook

To move a worksheet to another existing workbook, open both the source and the destination workbooks. Activate the sheet you want to move in the source workbook, click Edit, and then Move or Copy Sheet, or right-click the sheet tab located at the bottom of the screen just above the Status bar and click Move or Copy at the shortcut menu. At the Move or Copy dialog box shown in figure 6.4, select the destination workbook name from the To book drop-down list, select the worksheet that you want the worksheet placed before in the Before sheet list box, and then click OK.

HINT
To reposition a worksheet tab, drag the tab to the desired position.

Be careful when moving a worksheet to another workbook file. If formulas exist in the workbook that depend on the contents of the cells in the worksheet that is moved, they will no longer calculate properly.

MOVING A WORKSHEET TO ANOTHER WORKBOOK

1. Open Excel Worksheet 01.
2. Save the workbook with Save As and name it CExl C06 Ex14 W01.
3. Open Excel Worksheet 10.
4. Save the workbook with Save As and name it CExl C06 Ex14 W02.
5. Move *Sheet1* from CExl C06 Ex14 W02 to CExl C06 Ex14 W01 by completing the following steps:
   a. With CExl C06 Ex14 W02 the active workbook, click <u>E</u>dit on the Menu bar, and then click <u>M</u>ove or Copy Sheet at the drop-down menu.
   b. Click the down-pointing triangle next to the <u>T</u>o book option box and then click *CExl C06 Ex14 W01.xls* at the drop-down list.
   c. Click *Sheet2* in the <u>B</u>efore sheet list box.
   d. Click OK. (Excel switches to the workbook CExl C06 Ex14 W01 and inserts the moved sheet with the sheet name *Sheet 1 (2)*.)
6. Save the worksheet with the same name (CExl C06 Ex14 W01).
7. Print the entire CExl C06 Ex14 W01 workbook by completing the following steps:
   a. Click <u>F</u>ile and then <u>P</u>rint.
   b. Click <u>E</u>ntire workbook in the Print what section.
   c. Click OK.
8. Close CExl C06 Ex14 W01.
9. Close CExl C06 Ex14 W02 without saving changes.

Move or Copy ? X

Move selected sheets
<u>T</u>o book:

CExl C06 Ex14 W01.xls ▼

<u>B</u>efore sheet:

Sheet1
Sheet2
Sheet3
(move to end)

☐ <u>C</u>reate a copy

OK   Cancel

Step 5c

Step 5d

Renaming a Worksheet

The worksheets in exercises 13 and 14 that were moved or copied were assigned the name *Sheet 1 (2)* in the destination workbooks. This name, or for that matter, *Sheet1*, is not a very descriptive reference of the worksheet contents. When working with multiple worksheets in a workbook, changing the name of the worksheets to help identify the location of data is useful.

If a company was storing payroll for 12 months of the year in one workbook file with each month's payroll stored in an individual worksheet, the worksheets could be renamed January, February, March, and so on.

To rename a worksheet, right-click the sheet tab at the bottom left of the screen, and then click <u>R</u>ename at the shortcut menu. This selects the existing name. Key the new worksheet name and then press Enter. Another method for renaming the worksheet is to double-click the existing sheet name, key the new name, and then press Enter.

HINT

You can use up to 31 characters in a worksheet name.

exercise 15

1. Open CExl C06 Ex14 W01.
2. Save the workbook with Save As and name it CExl C06 Ex15.
3. Change the name of the two worksheets by completing the following steps:
   a. Right-click the sheet tab named *Sheet1 (2)* and then click <u>R</u>ename at the shortcut menu.
   b. Key **Sales by Salesperson** and then press Enter.
   c. Click the *Sheet1* tab to activate the Sheet1 worksheet.
   d. Double-click the sheet tab *Sheet1*.
   e. Key **Sales by Customer** and then press Enter.
4. Save and then close CExl C06 Ex15.

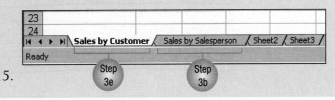

Step 3e

Step 3b

Saving a Workbook in a Different Format

When you save a workbook, it is automatically saved as an Excel workbook. If you need to share a workbook with someone who is using a different program or a different version of Excel, you can save the workbook in another format. A variety of formats is available for saving a workbook such as Web page, Web archive, XML Spreadsheet, Template, as well as previous versions of Excel and other spreadsheet programs such as Quattro Pro and dBASE. To save a workbook with a different format, display the Save As dialog box, click the down-pointing triangle at the right side of the Save as type option, and then click the desired format at the drop-down list.

By default, the Open dialog box displays Excel workbooks, which are files containing the .xls extension. If you want to display all files, display the Open dialog box, click the down-pointing triangle at the right side of the Files of <u>t</u>ype option, and then click *All Files* at the drop-down list.

exercise 16

1. Open Excel Worksheet 28.
2. Save the workbook as a Microsoft Excel 5.0 workbook (an older version of Excel) by completing the following steps:
   a. Click <u>F</u>ile and then Save <u>A</u>s.
   b. At the Save As dialog box, key **CExl C06 Ex16** in the File <u>n</u>ame text box.
   c. Click the down-pointing triangle at the right side of the Save as <u>t</u>ype option and then click *Microsoft Excel 5.0/95 Workbook* at the drop-down list. (You will need to scroll down the list to display this option.)
   d. Click the <u>S</u>ave button.

Step 2b

Step 2d

| File <u>n</u>ame: | CExl C06 Ex16 | | <u>S</u>ave |
| Save as <u>t</u>ype: | Microsoft Excel Workbook | | Cancel |

Unicode Text
Microsoft Excel 5.0/95 Workbook
Microsoft Excel 97-2002 & 5.0/95 Workbook
CSV (Comma delimited)
Microsoft Excel 4.0 Worksheet
Microsoft Excel 3.0 Worksheet

Step 2c

e. At the message telling you that some of the features are not compatible, click Yes.
3. Close CExl C06 Ex16.
4. Open CExl C06 Ex16 and notice that some of the formatting has been changed.
5. Close CExl C06 Ex16.

Searching for Specific Workbooks

Use options at the Basic Search Task Pane shown in figure 6.5 to search for specific workbooks. To display this task pane, click the Search button on the Standard toolbar. In the Search text text box, enter one or more words specific to the workbooks for which you are searching. The word or words can be contained in the workbook name, the text of the workbook, keywords assigned to the workbook, or in the workbook properties. After entering the search word or words, click the Search button and workbooks matching the search criteria display in the Search Results Task Pane.

FIGURE

6.5 **Basic Search Task Pane**

HINT
Click the *Advanced Search* hyperlink to display the Advanced Search Task Pane containing options for setting limits and conditions on the search.

Specify the locations to search with the Search in option. Click the down-pointing triangle at the right side of the Search in option box. This displays a drop-down list containing folders and network places. Click the plus symbol preceding a folder name to expand the display to include any subfolders. Insert a check mark in the check box next to any folders you want searched. Click a check box once and a check mark is inserted in the box and only that folder is searched. Click a check box a second time to specify that you want the folder and all subfolders searched. When you click the check box a second time, the check box changes to a cascading check box (check boxes overlapping). Click a check box a third time and the folder is deselected but all subfolders remain selected. Click a check box a fourth time and all subfolders are deselected.

Specify the types of files to search with the Results should be option. Click the down-pointing triangle at the right side of the Results should be option box and then, at the drop-down list that displays, insert a check mark in the check box before the types of files you want searched. For example, if you want only Excel files displayed, insert a check mark in the Excel Files check box.

EXCEL

1. At a blank Excel worksheet, click the Search button on the Standard toolbar.
2. Search for all Excel workbooks on your disk in drive A that contain the company name *Real Photography* by completing the following steps:
   a. Click in the Search text text box. (If text displays in the text box, select the text and then delete it.)
   b. Key **Real Photography** in the Search text text box.
   c. Click the down-pointing triangle at the right side of the Search in option box.
   d. Click the plus sign that precedes *My Computer*.
   e. Click twice in the 3½ Floppy (A:) check box to insert a check mark (and cascade the check box). (Make sure that it is the only check box containing a check mark.)
   f. Click in the task pane outside the Search in list box to remove the list.
   g. Click the down-pointing triangle at the right side of the Results should be option box.
   h. At the drop-down list, click in the Excel Files check box to insert a check mark. (Make sure that it is the only check box containing a check mark.)
   i. Click in the task pane outside the Results should be list box to remove the list.
   j. Click the Search button. (In a few moments, the Search Results Task Pane will display with workbook names containing *Real Photography*.)
   k. When the list of workbooks displays in the Search Results Task Pane, double-click *Excel Worksheet 07* in the task pane. (This opens the Excel Worksheet 07 workbook.)
   l. Close Excel Worksheet 07.
3. Close the Search Results Task Pane.

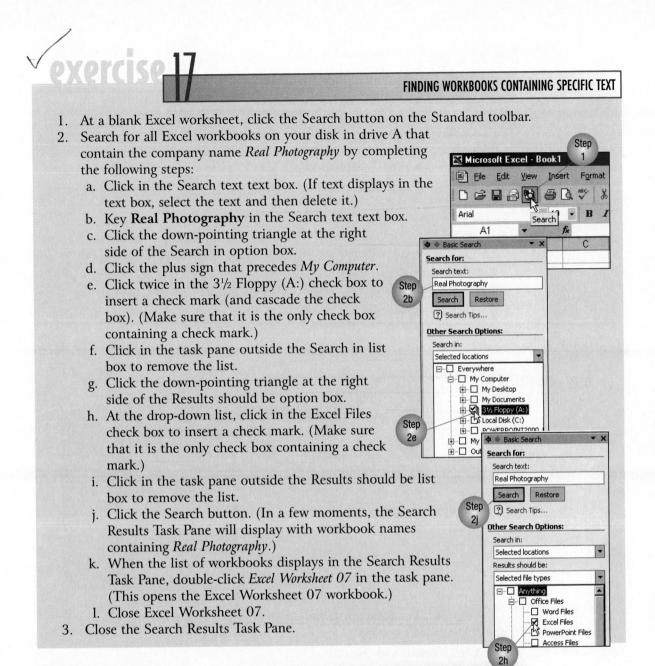

Formatting with Styles

To automate the formatting of cells in a workbook, consider defining and applying a style. A style, which is a predefined set of formatting attributes such as font, font size, alignment, borders, shading, and so forth, is particularly useful in large workbooks with data requiring a considerable amount of formatting.

Using a style to apply formatting has several advantages. A style helps to ensure consistent formatting from one worksheet to another. Once you define all attributes for a particular style, you do not have to redefine them again. If you need to change the formatting, change the style, and all cells formatted with that style automatically reflect the change.

Defining a Style

Excel contains some common number styles you can apply with buttons on the Formatting toolbar. For example, clicking the Currency Style button on the Formatting toolbar applies currency formatting to the cell or selected cells. The Percent Style and Comma Style buttons also apply styles to cells.

Two basic methods are available for defining your own style. You can define a style with formats already applied to a cell or you can display the Style dialog box, click the Modify button, and then choose formatting options at the Format Cells dialog box. Styles you create are only available in the workbook in which they are created.

To define a style with existing formatting, you would complete these steps:

1. Select the cell or cells containing the desired formatting.
2. Click Format and then Style.
3. At the Style dialog box, shown in figure 6.6, key a name for the new style in the Style name text box.
4. Click OK to close the dialog box.

FIGURE

6.6 *Style Dialog Box*

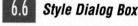

Check boxes identify formatting
options set by current style.

To define a new style without first applying the formatting, you would complete the following steps:

1. Click Format and then Style.
2. At the Style dialog box, key a name for the new style in the Style name text box.
3. Click the Modify button.
4. At the Format Cells dialog box, select the formats you want included in the style.
5. Click OK to close the Format Cells dialog box.
6. At the Style dialog box, remove the check mark from any formats that you do not want included in the style.
7. Click OK to define and apply the style to the selected cell. To define the style without applying it to the selected cell, click the Add button, and then click the Close button.

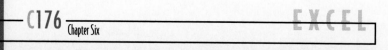

Applying a Style

To apply a style, select the cells you want to format, and then display the Style dialog box. At the Style dialog box, click the down-pointing triangle at the right side of the <u>S</u>tyle name text box, and then click the desired style name. Click OK to close the dialog box and apply the style.

exercise 18

1. Open Excel Worksheet 36.
2. Save the worksheet with Save As and name it CExl C06 Ex18.
3. Format a cell and then define a style with the formatting by completing the following steps:
   a. Make sure cell A1 is active.
   b. Change the font and apply a bottom border by completing the following steps:
      1) Click F<u>o</u>rmat and then C<u>e</u>lls.
      2) At the Format Cells dialog box, click the Font tab.
      3) At the Font tab, change the <u>F</u>ont to *Tahoma*, the <u>F</u>ont style to *Bold*, the <u>S</u>ize to *12*, and the <u>C</u>olor to *Indigo*. (Indigo is the second color from the *right* in the top row.)
      4) Click the Border tab.
      5) At the Format Cells dialog box with the Border tab selected, click the sixth Line Style option from the top in the second column.
      6) Click the down-pointing triangle at the right side of the <u>C</u>olor option and then click the Violet color at the color palette (seventh color from the left in the third row from the top).
      7) Click the bottom border of the preview cell in the dialog box.
      8) Click OK to close the Format Cells dialog box.
   c. With cell A1 still the active cell, define a style named Title with the formatting you just applied by completing the following steps:
      1) Click F<u>o</u>rmat and then <u>S</u>tyle.
      2) At the Style dialog box, key **Title** in the <u>S</u>tyle name text box.
      3) Click the <u>A</u>dd button.
      4) Click the Close button.

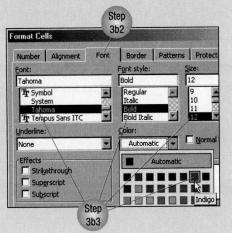

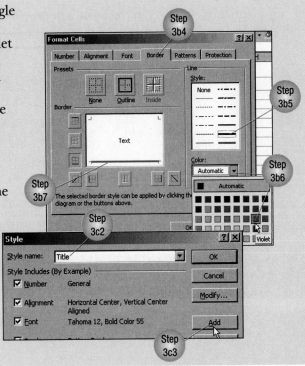

4. Apply the Title style to cell A1 by completing the following steps:
   a. Make sure cell A1 is the active cell. (Even though cell A1 is already formatted, the style has not been applied to it. Later, you will modify the style and the style must be applied to the cell for the change to affect it.)
   b. Click Format and then Style.
   c. At the Style dialog box, click the down-pointing triangle at the right side of the Style name text box, and then click *Title* at the drop-down list.
   d. Click OK to close the Style dialog box.

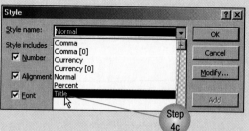
Step 4c

5. Apply the Title style to other cells by completing the following steps:
   a. Select cells A2 through D2.
   b. Click Format and then Style.
   c. At the Style dialog box, click the down-pointing triangle at the right side of the Style name text box, and then click *Title* at the drop-down list.
   d. Click OK to close the Style dialog box.
6. Define a new style named Font without first applying the formatting by completing the following steps:
   a. Click in any empty cell.
   b. Click Format and then Style.
   c. At the Style dialog box, key **Font** in the Style name text box.
   d. Click the Modify button.
   e. At the Format Cells dialog box, click the Font tab.
   f. At the Format Cells dialog box with the Font tab selected, change the Font to *Tahoma*, the Size to *12*, and the Color to *Indigo*.
   g. Click the Patterns tab.
   h. At the Format Cells dialog box with the Patterns tab selected, click a light blue color of your choosing in the color palette.
   i. Click OK to close the Format Cells dialog box.
   j. At the Style dialog box, click the Add button.
   k. Click the Close button. (Do not click the OK button.)
7. Apply the Font style by completing the following steps:
   a. Select cells A3 through D9.
   b. Click Format and then Style.
   c. At the Style dialog box, click the down-pointing triangle at the right side of the Style name text box, and then click *Font* at the drop-down list.
   d. Click OK to close the Style dialog box.
8. Make the following changes to the worksheet:
   a. Select cells B3 through D9.
   b. Click the Currency Style button on the Formatting toolbar.
   c. Click twice on the Decrease Decimal button on the Formatting toolbar.
   d. Automatically adjust columns A through D.
9. Save and then print CExl C06 Ex18.
10. With CExl C06 Ex18 still open, modify the Title style by completing the following steps:
    a. Click in any empty cell.
    b. Display the Style dialog box,
    c. Click the down-pointing triangle at the right side of the Style name text box and then click *Title* at the drop-down list.

d. Click the Modify button.
e. At the Format Cells dialog box, click the Alignment tab.
f. At the Format Cells dialog box with the Alignment tab selected, click the down-pointing triangle to the right of the Vertical option box, and then click *Center* at the drop-down list.
g. Click OK to close the Format Cells dialog box.
h. At the Style dialog box, click the Add button.
i. Click the Close button to close the Style dialog box.
11. Save, print, and then close CExl C06 Ex18.

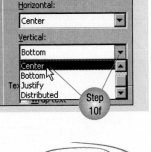

Copying Styles to Another Workbook

Styles you define are saved with the workbook in which they are created. You can, however, copy styles from one workbook to another. To do this, you would complete the following steps:

HINT
The Undo command will not reverse the effects of the Merge Style dialog box.

1. Open the workbook containing the styles you want to copy.
2. Open the workbook into which you want to copy the styles.
3. Display the Style dialog box.
4. At the Style dialog box, click the Merge button.
5. At the Merge Styles dialog box shown in figure 6.7, double-click the name of the workbook that contains the styles you want to copy.
6. Click OK to close the Style dialog box.

FIGURE

6.7 *Merge Styles Dialog Box*

Merge Styles

Merge styles from:

CExl C06 Ex 18.xls

OK   Cancel

Removing a Style

If you apply a style to text and then decide you do not want the formatting applied, remove the style. To do this, select the cells formatted with the style you want to remove and then display the Style dialog box. At the Style dialog box, click the down-pointing triangle at the right side of the Style name text box, and then click *Normal* at the drop-down list.

Deleting a Style

Delete a style at the Style dialog box. To do this, display the Style dialog box, click the down-pointing triangle at the right side of the Style name text box. At the drop-down list that displays, click the style you want deleted, and then click the Delete button.

exercise 19

1. Open CExl C06 Ex18.
2. Open Excel Worksheet 13.
3. Save the workbook with Save As and name it CExl C06 Ex19.
4. Delete column H.
5. Copy the styles in CExl C06 Ex18 into CExl C06 Ex19 by completing the following steps:
   a. Display the Style dialog box.
   b. At the Style dialog box, click the Merge button.
   c. At the Merge Styles dialog box, double-click *CExl C06 Ex18.xls* in the Merge styles from list box.
   d. Click OK to close the Style dialog box.

6. Modify the Font style by completing the following steps:
   a. Click in any empty cell.
   b. Display the Style dialog box.
   c. At the Style dialog box, click the down-pointing triangle at the right side of the Style name text box, and then click *Font*.
   d. Click the Modify button.
   e. At the Format Cells dialog box, click the Font tab.
   f. Change the Font to *Arial* and the Size to *10*.
   g. Click OK to close the Format Cells dialog box.
   h. At the Style dialog box, click the Add button.
   i. Click the Close button to close the Style dialog box.
7. Apply the following styles:
   a. Select cells A1 through G2 and then apply the Title style.
   b. Select cells A3 through G8 and then apply the Font style.
8. Remove the Font style from cells B3 through B8 by completing the following steps:
   a. Select cells B3 through B8.
   b. Display the Style dialog box.
   c. At the Style dialog box, click the down-pointing triangle at the right side of the Style name text box, and then click *Normal*.
   d. Click OK to close the dialog box.

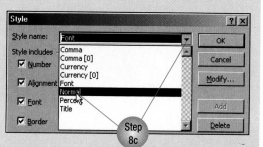

9. Select cells D3 through D8 and then press F4. (This repeats the last action, which was changing the style to *Normal*.)
10. Select cells F3 through F8 and then press F4.
11. Make the following changes to the workbook:
    a. Change the width of columns B through G to 11.00.

EXCEL

b. Select cells B3 through G8, click the Currency button on the Formatting toolbar, and then click twice on the Decrease Decimal button.

12. Save, print, and then close CExl C06 Ex19.

13. Close CExl C06 Ex18.

Inserting Comments

If you want to make comments in a worksheet, or if a reviewer wants to make comments in a worksheet prepared by someone else, insert a comment. A comment is useful for providing specific instructions, identifying critical information, or for multiple individuals reviewing the same worksheet to insert comments. Some employees in a company may be part of a *workgroup*, which is a networked collection of computers sharing files, printers, and other resources. In a workgroup, you may collaborate with coworkers on a specific workbook. Comments provide a method for reviewing the workbook and responding to others in the workgroup.

The Reviewing toolbar contains buttons for inserting and managing comments. Display this toolbar, shown in figure 6.8, by clicking View, pointing to Toolbars, and then clicking Reviewing.

FIGURE

6.8 *Reviewing Toolbar Buttons*

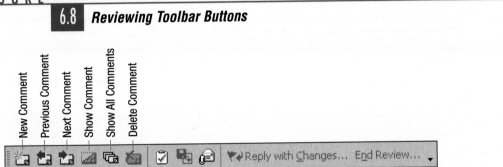

Inserting a Comment

Insert a comment by clicking the New Comment button on the Reviewing toolbar. This displays a yellow pop-up comment box with the user's name. Key the desired information or comment in this comment box. Click outside the comment box and the box is removed. A small, red triangle appears in the upper right corner of a cell containing a comment. You can also insert a comment by clicking Insert and then Comment, or by right-clicking a cell and then clicking Insert Comment at the shortcut menu.

New Comment

HINT

You can also display all comments by clicking View and then Comments.

Displaying a Comment

Hover the mouse over a cell containing a comment and the comment box displays. Turn on the display of all comments by clicking the Show All Comments button on the Reviewing toolbar. Turn on the display of an individual comment by making the cell active and then clicking the Show Comment button on the

Show All Comments

Show Comment

Next Comment

Previous Comment

Reviewing toolbar. Hide the display of an individual comment by making the cell active and then clicking the Hide Comment button on the Reviewing toolbar. (The Show Comment button becomes the Hide Comment button if the comment in the active cell is visible.) Move to comments in a worksheet by clicking the Next Comment or Previous Comment buttons on the Reviewing toolbar.

Printing a Comment

By default, comments do not print. If you want comments to print, display the Page Setup dialog box with the Sheet tab selected and then click the down-pointing triangle at the right side of the Comments option box. At the drop-down menu that displays, choose At end of sheet to print comments on the page after cell contents, or choose the As displayed on sheet option to print the comments in the comment box in the worksheet.

Editing and Deleting a Comment

Edit Comment

To edit a comment, click the cell containing the comment, and then click the Edit Comment button on the Reviewing toolbar. (The New Comment button changes to the Edit Comment button when the active cell contains a comment.) You can also edit a comment by right-clicking the cell containing the comment and then clicking Edit Comment at the shortcut menu.

Delete Comment

Cell comments exist in addition to data in a cell. Deleting data in a cell does not delete the comment. To delete a comment, click the cell containing the comment, and then click the Delete Comment button on the Reviewing toolbar. You can also delete a comment by clicking Edit, pointing to Clear, and then clicking Comments.

exercise 20

INSERTING, EDITING, AND PRINTING COMMENTS

1. Open Excel Worksheet 26.
2. Save the worksheet with Save As and name it CExl C06 Ex20.
3. Turn on the display of the Reviewing toolbar by clicking View, pointing to Toolbars, and then clicking Reviewing. (Skip this step if the Reviewing toolbar is already displayed.)
4. Insert a comment by completing the following steps:
   a. Click cell F3 to make it active.
   b. Click the New Comment button on the Reviewing toolbar.
   c. In the comment box, key **Bill Lakeside Trucking for only 7 hours for the backhoe and front loader on May 1.**
   d. Click outside the comment box.
5. Insert another comment by completing the following steps:
   a. Click cell C6 to make it active.
   b. Click the New Comment button on the Reviewing toolbar.

Date	Hours	
5/1/2003	8	Student Name:
5/1/2003	8	Bill Lakeside Trucking for
5/1/2003	4	only 7 hours for the
5/1/2003	16	backhoe and front loader on May 1.
5/2/2003	5	$55 $ 275

Step 4c

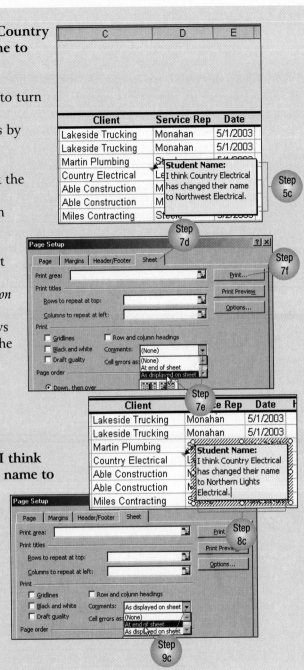

c. In the comment box, key **I think Country Electrical has changed their name to Northwest Electrical.**

d. Click outside the comment box.

6. Click the Show All Comments button to turn on the display of all comments.

7. Print the worksheet and the comments by completing the following steps:

   a. Click File and then Page Setup.

   b. At the Page Setup dialog box, click the Page tab.

   c. Click Landscape in the Orientation section.

   d. Click the Sheet tab.

   e. Click the down-pointing triangle at the right side of the Comments option and then click *As displayed on sheet*.

   f. Click the Print button that displays toward the upper right corner of the dialog box.

   g. At the Print dialog box, click OK.

8. Edit a comment by completing the following steps:

   a. Click cell C6 to make it active.

   b. Click the Edit Comment button.

   c. Edit the comment so it displays as **I think Country Electrical changed their name to Northern Lights Electrical.**

9. Save the worksheet again with the same name (CExl C06 Ex20).

10. Print the worksheet and the comments.

11. Click the Hide All Comments button (previously the Show All Comments button) to turn off the display of comments.

12. Close CExl C06 Ex20.

Creating and Responding to Discussion Comments

Microsoft Office XP includes the Web Discussions feature, which provides the ability for multiple users to open a Word document, an Excel workbook, or a PowerPoint presentation and attach comments to the file. The comments appear with the document but are stored on a Web server that has been configured as a *discussion server*. The comments are called *discussions* since each user can attach a response to any comment placed in the file. The comments appear in the file as *a thread*, which is the term used to describe the placement of the original comment and the attached responses grouped together in hierarchical order.

Note: Check with your instructor before completing this topic. You will need a discussion server address for your school's Web server, a username, and a password that have been configured for discussion permissions.

1. Open Excel Worksheet 37.
2. Save the workbook and name it CExl C06 Ex21.
3. Click Tools, point to Online Collaboration, and then click Web Discussions.
4. Click the Add button in the Discussion Options dialog box. (If the Discussion Options dialog box does not appear, click the Discussions button on the Web Discussions toolbar and then click Discussion Options.)
5. Key **http://***servername* (substitute *servername* with the address provided by your instructor) in the Type the name of the discussion server your administrator has provided text box of the Add or Edit Discussion Servers dialog box.
6. Click in the You can type any name you want to use as a friendly name for the discussion server text box, key **My Class Discussion Server**, and then click OK.
7. Key your username and password for the discussion server.
8. Click OK in the Discussion Options dialog box.
9. Click the Insert Discussion about the Workbook button on the Web Discussions toolbar located just above the Status bar.
10. With the insertion point positioned in the Discussion subject text box of the Enter Discussion Text dialog box, key **Cancun Package Price**.

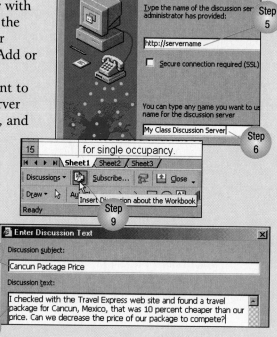

11. Click in the Discussion text text box and then key the following:
    I checked with the Travel Express Web site and found a travel package for Cancun, Mexico, that was 10 percent cheaper than our price. Can we decrease the price of our package to compete?
12. Click OK. (The Discussion comment is uploaded to a database file on the server and, in a few seconds, the Discussion pane will appear with the Discussion comment inserted.)
13. Click the Insert Discussion about the Workbook button on the Web Discussions toolbar and then create the following comment:
    Discussion subject   **Disneyland Package**
    Discussion text   **Laura is working on a travel package to Disneyland that should be available within two weeks.**
    In the next steps you will respond to the comment you created in steps 9-12. Normally, a reply would be posted by another user—you are replying to your own comment for practice to learn the steps.
14. Click the up scroll arrow in the Discussion pane to scroll to the end of the Cancun Package Price comment.

15. Click the Show a menu of actions button at the end of the comment and then click Reply.

16. With the insertion point positioned in the Discussion text text box, key the following:
    I checked with a Travel Express representative and discovered that their Cancun package includes lodging in a lower-grade hotel than our package.

17. Click OK.

18. Click the Discussions button on the Web Discussions toolbar and then click Print Discussions.

19. At the Print dialog box, click OK.

20. Click the Close button on the Web Discussion toolbar.

21. Close CExl C06 Ex21.

Using Excel Templates

Excel has included a number of *template* worksheet forms formatted for specific uses. For example, Excel has provided template forms for a balance sheet, expense statement, loan amortization, sales invoice, and timecard. To view the templates available with Excel, click the *General Templates* hyperlink in the New Workbook Task Pane. At the Templates dialog box, click the Spreadsheet Solutions tab and the template forms display as shown in figure 6.9.

HINT

If it fits your needs, consider using an Excel template worksheet form.

FIGURE

6.9   *Templates Dialog Box with Spreadsheet Solutions Tab Selected*

Entering Data in a Template

Templates contain unique areas where information is entered at the keyboard. For example, in the Sales Invoice template shown in figure 6.10, you enter information such as the customer name, address, and telephone number, and also the quantity, description, and unit price of products. To enter information in the appropriate location, position the mouse pointer (white plus sign) in the location where you want to key data, and then click the left mouse button. After keying the data, click the next location. You can also move the insertion point to another cell using the commands learned in chapter 1. For example, press the Tab key to make the next cell active, press Shift + Tab to make the previous cell active.

FIGURE

6.10 Sales Invoice Template

✓ exercise 22

PREPARING A SALES INVOICE USING A TEMPLATE

1. Click the _General Templates_ hyperlink in the New Workbook Task Pane. (If the task pane is not visible, display it by clicking View, Task Pane, and then clicking the Back button.)
2. At the Templates dialog box, click the Spreadsheet Solutions tab.
3. At the Templates dialog box with the Spreadsheet Solutions tab selected, double-click _Sales Invoice_.
4. Depending on your system, Microsoft may display a message box telling you that the workbook you are opening contains macros. Check with your instructor to make sure your system is secure and, if it is, click Enable Macros.
5. Key data in the invoice by completing the following steps:
   a. Key **IN-FLOW SYSTEMS** in the cell immediately right of _Name_. (This cell is automatically active when the sales invoice displays.)
   b. Press the Enter key. (This makes the cell immediately to the right of _Address_ active.)
   c. Key **320 Milander Way** and then press the Tab key twice. (This makes the cell immediately to the right of _City_ active.)
   d. Key **Boston** and then press the Tab key. (This makes the cell immediately to the right of _State_ active.)

EXCEL

e. Key **MA** and then press the Tab key. (This makes the cell immediately to the right of *ZIP* active.)

f. Key **02188** and then press the Tab key twice. (This makes the cell immediately to the right of *Phone* active.)

g. Key **(617) 555-3900**.

h. Position the mouse pointer (white plus sign) to the right of *Order No.* and then click the left mouse button.

i. Key **2388-348** and then press Enter. (This makes the cell immediately to the right of *Rep* active.)

j. Key **Jenkins** and then press Enter. (This makes the cell immediately to the right of *FOB* active.)

k. Key **Boston** and then press the Tab key.

l. Key the following data immediately *below* the specified heading (use the mouse, the Tab key, and/or the Enter key to make the desired cell active):

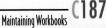

Qty.	=	**40**
Description	=	**Oscillator**
Unit Price	=	**340**
Qty.	=	**25**
Description	=	**Discriminator**
Unit Price	=	**570**
Qty.	=	**300**
Description	=	**Clamps**
Unit Price	=	**3.49**

6. Save the completed invoice and name it CExl C06 Ex22.

7. Print and then close CExl C06 Ex22.

CHAPTERsummary

➤ Perform file management tasks such as copying, moving, printing, and renaming workbooks; opening multiple workbooks; and creating a new folder at the Open or Save As dialog boxes.

➤ Workbooks should be grouped logically and stored in folders. A folder can be created within a folder. The main folder on a disk or drive is called the root folder. Additional folders are created as a branch of this root folder.

➤ Create a new folder by clicking the Create New Folder button located on the dialog box toolbar at the Open dialog box or Save As dialog box.

➤ A folder name can contain a maximum of 255 characters.

➤ Use the Shift key while selecting workbooks to select multiple workbooks that are adjacent.

➤ Use the Ctrl key while selecting workbooks to select multiple workbooks that are not adjacent.

➤ To delete a workbook, select the workbook, and then click the Delete button on the dialog box toolbar; click Tools, and then click Delete at the drop-down menu; or right-click the workbook to be deleted, and then click Delete at the shortcut menu.

➤ Workbooks deleted from your data disk are deleted permanently.

➤ Workbooks and/or folders deleted from the hard drive are automatically sent to the Windows Recycle Bin where they can be restored or permanently deleted.

➤ Create a copy of an existing workbook by opening the workbook and then using the Save As command to assign the workbook a different file name.

➤ Use the Copy and Paste options from the shortcut menu at the Open (or Save As) dialog box to copy a workbook from one folder to another folder or drive.

➤ When you copy a workbook into the same folder from which it originates, Excel names the duplicated workbook(s) "Copy of xxx" (where xx is the original workbook name).

➤ Use the Send To option from the shortcut menu to send a copy of a workbook to another drive or folder.

➤ Remove a workbook from a folder or disk and insert it in another folder or disk using the Cut and Paste options from the shortcut menu.

➤ Use the Rename option from the Tools drop-down menu or the shortcut menu to give a workbook a different name.

➤ Multiple workbooks can be opened, closed, or printed.

➤ To move or copy a worksheet to another existing workbook, open both the source and the destination workbook and then open the Move or Copy Sheet dialog box.

➤ Change the name of worksheets to help identify the data contained in them.

➤ Save a workbook in a different format with the Save as type option at the Save As dialog box. Click the down-pointing triangle at the right of the Save as type option and a drop-down list displays with the available formats.

➤ Use options at the Basic Search Task Pane to search for specific workbooks. Display this task pane by clicking the Search button on the Standard toolbar.

➤ Automate the formatting of cells in a workbook by defining and then applying styles. A style is a predefined set of formatting attributes.

➤ A style helps to ensure consistent formatting from one worksheet to another. All formatting attributes for a particular style are defined only once. Modify a style and all cells to which the style is applied automatically reflect the change.

➤ Define a style with formats already applied to a cell or display the Style dialog box, click the Modify button, and then choose formatting options at the Format Cells dialog box.

➤ Define, apply, modify, remove, and delete styles at the Style dialog box.

➤ Styles are saved in the workbook in which they are created. Styles can be copied, however, to another workbook. Do this with the Merge button at the Style dialog box.

➤ Insert comments in a worksheet to provide specific instructions, identify critical information, and review a workbook and respond to others in a workgroup about the workbook.

➤ Insert, display, edit, and delete comments using buttons on the Reviewing toolbar.

➤ By default, comments do not print. To print comments, display the Page Setup dialog box with the Sheet tab selected, and then choose the printing location with the Comments option.

➤ Excel provides preformatted templates for creating forms such as a balance sheet, expense statement, loan amortization, sales invoice, and timecard.

➤ Templates contain unique areas where information is entered at the keyboard. These areas vary depending on the template.

COMMANDS review

Command	Mouse/Keyboard
Display Open dialog box	Click File, then Open; or click Open button on the Standard toolbar
Display Save As dialog box	Click File, then Save As
Display New Folder dialog box	Click Create New Folder button on Open or Save As dialog box toolbar
Display Recycle Bin dialog box	Minimize Excel and then double-click *Recycle Bin* icon on the Windows desktop
Display Move or Copy Sheet dialog box	Click Edit, then click Move or Copy Sheet; or right-click sheet tab and then click Move or Copy
Close all open workbooks	Hold down Shift key, click File, and then click Close All
Display Basic Search Task Pane	Click Search button on Standard toolbar
Display Style dialog box	Click Format, Style
Display Merge Styles dialog box	At Style dialog box, click Merge button
Display Reviewing toolbar	Click View, point to Toolbars, then click Reviewing
Display Templates dialog box	Click *General Templates* hyperlink in the New Workbook Task Pane

CONCEPTS check

Completion: On a blank sheet of paper, indicate the correct term, symbol, or command for each item.

1. File management tasks such as copying, moving, or deleting workbooks can be performed at the Open dialog box or this dialog box. *Save As*
2. Select multiple adjacent workbooks by clicking the first workbook, holding down this key, and then clicking the last workbook. *Shift*
3. Click this button on the Open dialog box toolbar to display the folder that is up a level from the current folder. *Up One Level*
4. Select multiple nonadjacent workbooks by holding down this key while clicking each workbook name. *Ctrl*
5. Workbooks and/or folders deleted from the hard drive can be restored by opening this feature in Windows. *Recycling Bin*
6. Close multiple workbooks at the same time by holding down this key, clicking File, and then clicking Close All. *Shift*
7. Click the down-pointing triangle at the right side of this option at the Save As dialog box to display a list of available workbook formats. *Save as type*

8. Search for specific workbooks with options at this task pane. *Basic Search*
9. Click this button at the Style dialog box to display the Format Cells dialog box. *Modify*
10. In a cell containing a comment, this displays in the upper right corner of the cell. *small red triangle*
11. Print comments by choosing the desired printing location with the Comments option at the Page Setup dialog box with this tab selected. *Sheet*
12. Click this button on the Reviewing toolbar to display all comments in the worksheet. *Show all Comments*
13. Click this hyperlink in the New Workbook Task Pane to display the Templates dialog box. *General Templates*

SKILLS check

✓Assessment 1

1. Display the Open dialog box with *Excel Chapter 06C* the active folder.
2. Create a new folder named *Sales* in the *Excel Chapter 06C* folder.
3. Copy Excel Worksheet 01 and Excel Worksheet 10 to the *Sales* folder.
4. Rename Excel Worksheet 01 to Sales By Job in the *Sales* folder. (At the message asking if you are sure you want to rename the read-only file, click <u>Y</u>es.)
5. Rename Excel Worksheet 10 to Sales by Salesperson in the *Sales* folder. (At the message asking if you are sure you want to rename the read-only file, click <u>Y</u>es.)
6. Change the active folder back to *Excel Chapter 06C*.
7. Close the Open dialog box.

✓Assessment 2

1. Display the Open dialog box.
2. Delete all of the workbooks in the *Excel Chapter 06C* folder that begin with *Copy of*.
3. Move all of the workbooks that begin with *Excel Worksheet* to the *Sales* folder.
4. Change the active folder back to *Excel Chapter 06C*.
5. Close the Open dialog box.

✓Assessment 3

1. Display the Open dialog box.
2. Open all of the workbooks that begin with *CExl C06 Ex*.
3. Make CExl C06 Ex15 the active window.
4. Close CExl C06 Ex15.
5. Make CExl C06 Ex14 W01 the active window.
6. Close all of the open Excel Workbooks.

✓Assessment 4

1. Display the Open dialog box and make *Sales* the active folder.
2. Open Excel Worksheet 07 and Excel Worksheet 29.
3. Make Excel Worksheet 07 the active workbook and then copy *Sheet1* from Excel Worksheet 07 and position it before Sheet2 in Excel Worksheet 29.
4. With Excel Worksheet 29 the active workbook, rename *Sheet1* to Accounts.

5. With Excel Worksheet 29 the active workbook, rename *Sheet1 (2)* to Depreciation.
6. Save Excel Worksheet 29 with Save As and name it CExl C06 SA04.
7. Print and then close CExl C06 SA04.
8. Close Excel Worksheet 07.

Assessment 5

1. Use the Basic Search Task Pane to search for all workbooks on your disk containing the word *Equipment*. *Excel Worksheets: 07, 09, 26*
2. Search for all workbooks on your disk containing the words *Lakeside Trucking*.
Excel Worksheets: 13, 26, 28

Assessment 6

1. At a clear worksheet, define the following styles:
   a. Define a style named Heading that contains the following formatting:
      1) 14-point Times New Roman bold in Blue-Gray color
      2) Horizontal alignment of Center
      3) Double-line top and bottom border in Dark Red color
      4) Light purple shading
   b. Define a style named Column 01 that contains the following formatting:
      1) 12-point Times New Roman in Blue-Gray color
      2) Light purple shading
   c. Define a style named Column 02 that contains 12-point Times New Roman in Blue-Gray color
2. Save the worksheet and name it CExl C06 Style 01.
3. With CExl C06 Style 01 open, open Excel Worksheet 09.
4. Save the worksheet with Save As and name it CExl C06 SA06.
5. Copy the styles from CExl C06 Style 01 into CExl C06 SA06. *(Hint: Do this through the Style dialog box.)*
6. Select cells A1 through M1 and then click the Merge and Center button on the Formatting toolbar.
7. Apply the following styles:
   a. Select cells A1 through M2 and then apply the Heading style.
   b. Select cells A3 through A9 and then apply the Column 01 style.
   c. Select cells B3 through G9 and then apply the Column 02 style.
   d. Select cells H3 through M9 and then apply the Column 01 style.
8. Automatically adjust the widths of columns A through M.
9. Save the worksheet again and then print CExl C06 SA06 on one page in landscape orientation. (Make sure you choose the Fit to option at the Page Setup dialog box.) *CExl C06 SA06 step 9*
10. With CExl C06 SA06 still open, modify the following styles:
    a. Modify the Heading style so it changes the font color to Plum (instead of Blue-Gray) and inserts a solid, thick top and bottom border in Plum (instead of a double-line top and bottom border in Dark Red).
    b. Modify the Column 02 style so it adds a font style of Bold Italic (leave all of the other formatting attributes). Adjust column widths as needed.
11. Save the worksheet again and then print CExl C06 SA06 on one page and in landscape orientation. *Step 11*
12. Close CExl C06 SA06.
13. Close CExl C06 Style 01.

✓ Assessment 7

1. Open Excel Worksheet 37.
2. Save the worksheet with Save As and name it CExl C06 SA07.
3. Insert the following comments in the specified cells:
   B7   =   **Should we include Sun Valley, Idaho, as a destination?**
   B12   =   **Please include the current exchange rate.**
   G8   =   **What other airlines fly into Aspen, Colorado?**
4. Save CExl C06 SA07. step 4
5. Turn on the display of all comments.
6. Print the worksheet in landscape orientation with the comments as displayed on the worksheet.
7. Turn off the display of all comments.
8. Delete the comment in cell B12.
9. Print the worksheet again with the comments printed at the end of the worksheet. (The comments will print on a separate page from the worksheet.)
10. Save and then close CExl C06 SA07.

✓ Assessment 8

1. In this chapter, you learned about the styles feature, which automates formatting in a workbook. Another formatting feature is Conditional Formatting. Use Excel's Help feature to learn about Conditional Formatting.
2. Open Excel Worksheet 06.
3. Save the worksheet with Save As and name it CExl C06 SA08.
4. Select cells B3 through M20 and then use Conditional Formatting to display all percentages between 95% and 100% in red and with a red border.
5. Save, print (in landscape orientation), and then close CExl C06 SA08.

CHAPTER 7

CREATING A CHART IN EXCEL

PERFORMANCE OBJECTIVES

Upon successful completion of chapter 7, you will be able to:
- **Create a chart with data in an Excel worksheet**
- **Create a chart in a separate worksheet**
- **Print a selected chart and print a worksheet containing a chart**
- **Size, move, and delete a chart**
- **Change the type of chart**
- **Choose a custom chart type**
- **Change data in a chart**
- **Add, delete, and customize elements in a chart**

Excel Chapter 07C

In the previous Excel chapters, you learned to create data in worksheets. While a worksheet does an adequate job of representing data, you can present some data more visually by charting the data. A chart is sometimes referred to as a *graph* and is a picture of numeric data. In this chapter, you will learn to create and customize charts in Excel.

Creating a Chart

In Excel, create a chart by selecting cells containing the data you want to chart, and then clicking the Chart Wizard button on the Standard toolbar. Four steps are involved in creating a chart with the Chart Wizard. Suppose you wanted to create a chart with the worksheet shown in figure 7.1. To create the chart with the Chart Wizard, you would complete the following steps:

Chart
Wizard

1.   Select the cells containing data (in the worksheet in figure 7.1, this would be cells A1 through C4).
2.   Click the Chart Wizard button on the Standard toolbar.
3.   At the Chart Wizard - Step 1 of 4 - Chart Type dialog box shown in figure 7.2, choose the desired chart type and chart sub-type, and then click the Next button.
4.   At the Chart Wizard - Step 2 of 4 - Chart Source Data dialog box shown in figure 7.3, make sure the data range displays correctly (for the chart in figure 7.1, the range will display as =*Sheet1!$A$1:$C$4*), and then click the Next button.

Press F11 to create a
chart using the Chart
Wizard with all default
settings.

5. At the Chart Wizard - Step 3 of 4 - Chart Options dialog box shown in figure 7.4, make any changes to the chart, and then click the <u>N</u>ext button.

6. At the Chart Wizard - Step 4 of 4 - Chart Location dialog box shown in figure 7.5, specify where you want the chart inserted, and then click the <u>F</u>inish button.

If the chart was created with all of the default settings at the Chart Wizard dialog boxes, the chart would display below the cells containing data as shown in figure 7.6.

FIGURE

7.1 **Excel Worksheet**

	A	B	C	D
1	**Salesperson**	**June**	**July**	
2	Chaney	$34,239	$39,224	
3	Ferraro	$23,240	$28,985	
4	Jimenez	$56,892	$58,450	
5				

FIGURE

7.2 **Chart Wizard - Step 1 of 4 - Chart Type Dialog Box**

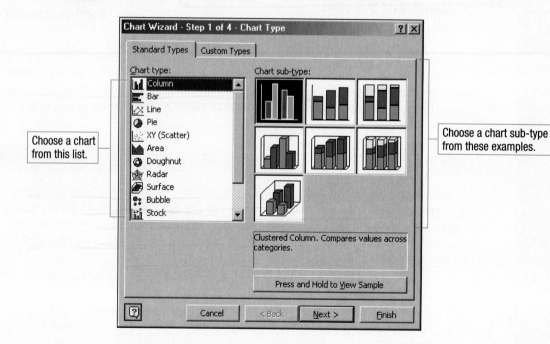

7.3 *Chart Wizard - Step 2 of 4 - Chart Source Data Dialog Box*

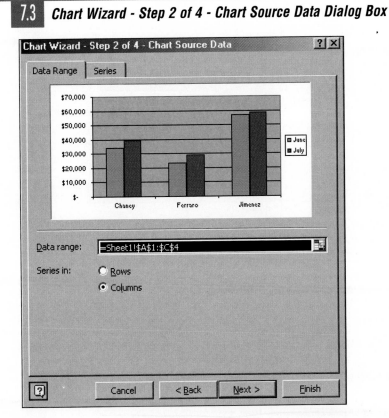

7.4 *Chart Wizard - Step 3 of 4 - Chart Options Dialog Box*

Add and/or format chart elements with options from this dialog box with various tabs selected.

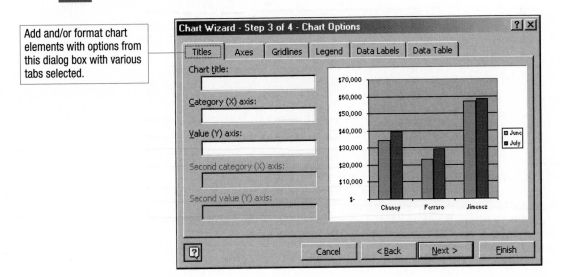

7.5 *Chart Wizard - Step 4 of 4 - Chart Location Dialog Box*

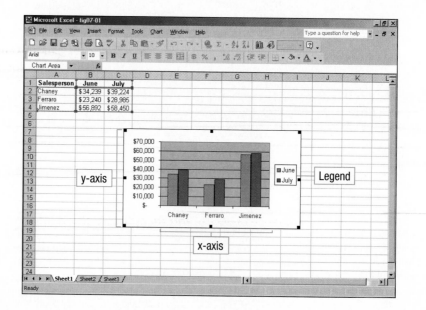

To insert the chart in the active worksheet, leave this at the default setting of As object in. Choose the As new sheet option to create the chart in a separate sheet.

7.6 *Chart Based on Excel Worksheet*

HINT

Preview the chart at step 1 of the Chart Wizard by positioning the arrow pointer on the Press and Hold to View Sample button and then holding down the left mouse button.

In the chart created in Excel, shown in figure 7.6, the left vertical side of the chart is referred to as the y-axis. The y-axis contains tick marks with amounts displaying the value at that particular point on the axis. The values in the chart in figure 7.6 are broken into tick marks by ten thousands beginning with zero and continuing to 70,000. The values for the y-axis will vary depending on the data in the table. The names in the first column are used for the x-axis, which runs along the bottom of the chart.

✓exercise 1

1. Open Excel and then open Excel Worksheet 15.
2. Save the worksheet with Save As and name it CExl C07 Ex01.
3. Create a chart using the Chart Wizard by completing the following steps:

    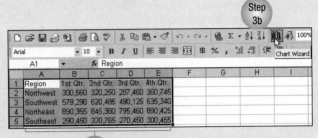

    a. Select cells A1 through E5.
    b. Click the Chart Wizard button on the Standard toolbar.
    c. At the Chart Wizard - Step 1 of 4 - Chart Type dialog box, click the <u>N</u>ext button.
    d. At the Chart Wizard - Step 2 of 4 - Chart Source Data dialog box, make sure the data range displays as *=Sheet1!$A$1:$E$5* and then click the <u>N</u>ext button.
    e. At the Chart Wizard - Step 3 of 4 - Chart Options dialog box, click the <u>N</u>ext button.
    f. At the Chart Wizard - Step 4 of 4 - Chart Location dialog box, make sure the As <u>o</u>bject in option is selected and that *Sheet1* displays in the text box, and then click the <u>F</u>inish button.
    g. Click outside the chart to deselect the chart.
    h. Change the page orientation to landscape.
4. Save, print, and then close CExl C07 Ex01.

Printing Only the Chart

In a worksheet containing data in cells as well as a chart, you can print only the chart. To do this, click the chart to select it and then display the Print dialog box. At the Print dialog box, *Selected Chart* will automatically be selected in the Print what section. Click OK to print only the selected chart.

Previewing a Chart

Preview a chart by clicking the Print Preview button on the Standard toolbar or by clicking <u>F</u>ile and then Print Pre<u>v</u>iew. This displays the worksheet containing the chart in Print Preview. After previewing the chart, click the <u>C</u>lose button, or print the worksheet by clicking the <u>P</u>rint button on the Print Preview toolbar and then clicking OK at the Print dialog box.

PREVIEWING AND THEN PRINTING ONLY THE CHART IN EXCEL

1. Open CExl C07 Ex01.
2. Preview the chart by completing the following steps:
   a. Click the Print Preview button on the Standard toolbar.
   b. In Print Preview, click the <u>Z</u>oom button to make the display of the worksheet bigger.
   c. Click the <u>Z</u>oom button again to return to the full-page view.
   d. Click the <u>C</u>lose button to close Print Preview.
3. Print only the chart by completing the following steps:
   a. Click the chart to select it.
   b. Click <u>F</u>ile and then <u>P</u>rint.
   c. At the Print dialog box, make sure *Selected Chart* is selected in the Print what section of the dialog box and then click OK.
4. Close CExl C07 Ex01.

```
                                      Step
                                       2b
  Microsoft Excel - Ch07Ex01
  [Next] [Previous] [Zoom] [Print...] [Setup...]


                              1,000,000
                                900,000
                                800,000
```

Creating a Chart in a Separate Worksheet

The chart you created in Excel in exercise 1 was inserted in the same worksheet as the cells containing data. You should not delete the data (displaying only the chart) because the data in the chart will also be deleted. If you want to create a chart in a worksheet by itself, click the As new <u>s</u>heet option at the Chart Wizard - Step 4 of 4 - Chart Location dialog box. When the chart is completed, it displays in a separate sheet and fills most of the page. The sheet containing the chart is labeled *Chart1*. This sheet label displays on a tab located toward the bottom of the screen. The worksheet containing the data is located in *Sheet 1*. You can move between the chart and the worksheet by clicking the desired tab.

CREATING A CHART IN A SEPARATE EXCEL WORKSHEET

1. Open Excel Worksheet 15.
2. Save the worksheet with Save As and name it CExl C07 Ex03.
3. Create a chart as a separate sheet using the Chart Wizard by completing the following steps:
   a. Select cells A1 through E5.
   b. Click the Chart Wizard button on the Standard toolbar.
   c. At the Chart Wizard - Step 1 of 4 - Chart Type dialog box, click the <u>N</u>ext button.
   d. At the Chart Wizard - Step 2 of 4 - Chart Source Data dialog box, make sure the data range displays as *=Sheet1!$A$1:$E$5*, and then click the <u>N</u>ext button.
   e. At the Chart Wizard - Step 3 of 4 - Chart Options dialog box, click the <u>N</u>ext > button.
   f. At the Chart Wizard - Step 4 of 4 - Chart Location dialog box, click As new <u>s</u>heet, and then click the <u>F</u>inish button.

```
  Chart Wizard - Step 4 of 4 - Chart Location          [?][X]
  Place chart:
            [▪▪]   ● As new sheet:    [Chart2          ]

            [▦]    ○ As object in:    [Sheet1        ▼]

  [?]          [Cancel] [< Back] [Next >] [Finish]
```

Step 3f

4. Save the workbook (two sheets) again and then print only the sheet containing the chart. (To do this, make sure the sheet containing the chart displays, and then click the Print button on the Standard toolbar.)
5. Close CExl C07 Ex03.

Deleting a Chart

Delete a chart created in Excel by clicking once in the chart to select it and then pressing the Delete key. If a chart created in a new worksheet is deleted, the chart is deleted but the worksheet is not. To delete the chart as well as the worksheet, position the mouse pointer on the *Chart1* tab, click the *right* mouse button, and then click Delete at the pop-up menu. At the message box telling you that selected sheets will be permanently deleted, click OK.

Sizing and Moving a Chart

You can change the size of a chart created in Excel in the same worksheet as the data containing cells. To do this, click the chart once to select it (this inserts black square sizing handles around the chart), and then drag the sizing handles in the desired direction.

A chart created with data in a worksheet can be moved by selecting the chart and then dragging it with the mouse. To move a chart, click once inside the chart to select it. Position the arrow pointer inside the chart, hold down the left mouse button, drag the outline of the chart to the desired location, and then release the button.

exercise 4

SIZING A CHART

1. Open CExl C07 Ex01.
2. Save the worksheet with Save As and name it CExl C07 Ex04.
3. Size the chart by completing the following steps:
   a. Select the chart by positioning the arrow pointer in the white portion of the chart just inside the chart border until a yellow box with the words *Chart Area* displays (takes approximately one second) next to the arrow pointer and then clicking the left mouse button. (Do not click on a chart element. This selects the element, not the entire chart.)
   b. Position the arrow pointer on the black, square sizing handle located in the middle of the bottom border until the arrow pointer turns into a double-headed arrow pointing up and down.
   c. Hold down the left mouse button, drag the outline of the bottom border of the chart down approximately five rows, and then release the mouse button.

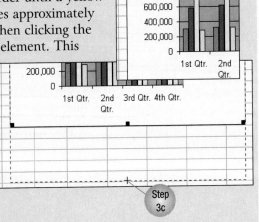

Step 3a

Step 3c

    d. Position the arrow pointer on the black square sizing handle located in the middle of the right border until the arrow pointer turns into a double-headed arrow pointer left and right.

    e. Hold down the left mouse button, drag the outline of the border to the right approximately two columns, and then release the mouse button.

    f. Deselect the chart. (To do this, click in an empty cell somewhere in the worksheet.)

4. Save the worksheet again with the same name (CExl C07 Ex04).

5. Print and close CExl C07 Ex04.

Changing the Chart Type

In exercises 1 and 3, you created a column chart, which is the default. The Chart Wizard offers 14 basic chart types along with built-in autoformats you can apply to save time to get the desired look for the chart. Figure 7.7 shows an illustration and explanation of the 14 chart types.

FIGURE

7.7 *Chart Types*

	Area	An Area chart emphasizes the magnitude of change, rather than time and the rate of change. It also shows the relationship of parts to a whole by displaying the sum of the plotted values.
	Bar	A Bar chart shows individual figures at a specific time or shows variations between components but not in relationship to the whole.
	Bubble	A Bubble chart compares sets of three values in a manner similar to a scatter chart with the third value displayed as the size of the bubble marker.
	Column	A Column chart compares separate (noncontinuous) items as they vary over time.
	Cone	A Cone chart displays columns with a conical shape.
	Cylinder	A Cylinder chart displays columns with a cylindrical shape.
	Doughnut	A Doughnut chart shows the relationship of parts to the whole.
	Line	A Line chart shows trends and change over time at even intervals. It emphasizes the rate of change over time rather than the magnitude of change.
	Pie	A Pie chart shows proportions and relationships of parts to the whole.

	Pyramid	A Pyramid chart displays columns with a pyramid shape.
	Radar	A Radar chart emphasizes differences and amounts of change over time and variations and trends. Each category has its own value axis radiating from the center point. Lines connect all values in the same series.
	Stock	A Stock chart shows four values for a stock—open, high, low, and close.
	Surface	A Surface chart shows trends in values across two dimensions in a continuous curve.
	XY (Scatter)	A Scatter chart shows either the relationships among numeric values in several data series or plots the interception points between x and y values. It shows uneven intervals of data and is commonly used in scientific data.

You can choose a chart type in step 1 of the Chart Wizard steps or change the chart type for an existing chart. When creating a chart with the Chart Wizard, choose the desired chart type and sub-type at the first Chart Wizard dialog box. To change the chart type for an existing chart, make sure the chart is active, click Chart, and then click Chart Type. This displays the Chart Type dialog box. Choose the desired chart type and chart sub-type at this dialog box and then click the OK button.

You can also change the chart type in an existing chart with a shortcut menu. To do this, position the arrow pointer in a white portion of the chart (inside the chart but outside any chart element), and then click the *right* mouse button. At the shortcut menu that displays, click Chart Type. This displays the Chart Type dialog box that contains the same options as the Chart Wizard - Step 1 of 4 - Chart Type dialog box.

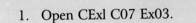

exercise 5

CHANGING CHART TYPE IN EXCEL

1. Open CExl C07 Ex03.
2. Save the workbook with Save As and name it CExl C07 Ex05.
3. Make sure the chart is displayed. If not, click the *Chart1* tab located at the bottom of the worksheet window.
4. Change the chart type to a Line chart by completing the following steps:
   a. Click Chart and then Chart Type.
   b. At the Chart Type dialog box, click *Line* in the Chart type list box.
   c. Change the chart sub-type by clicking the first chart in the second row in the Chart sub-type list box.

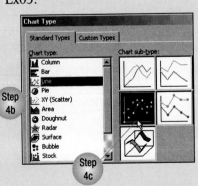

Step 4b

Step 4c

d. View a sample of how this sub-type chart will display by positioning the arrow pointer on the Press and Hold to View Sample button and then holding down the left mouse button. After viewing a sample of the selected Line chart, release the mouse button.

e. Click OK to close the dialog box.

5. Save the workbook again and then print only the sheet containing the chart. (To do this, make sure the sheet containing the chart is displayed, and then click the Print button on the Standard toolbar.)

6. With CExl C07 Ex05 still open, change the chart type to Bar by completing the following steps:

a. Click Chart and then Chart Type.

b. At the Chart Wizard dialog box, click *Bar* in the Chart type list box.

c. Change the chart sub-type by clicking the first chart in the second row in the Chart sub-type list box.

d. View a sample of how this sub-type chart will display by positioning the arrow pointer on the Press and Hold to View Sample button and then holding down the left mouse button. After viewing a sample of the selected Bar chart, release the mouse button.

e. Click OK to close the dialog box.

7. Save the workbook again and then print only the sheet containing the chart. (To do this, make sure the sheet containing the chart displays, and then click the Print button on the Standard toolbar.)

8. Close CExl C07 Ex05.

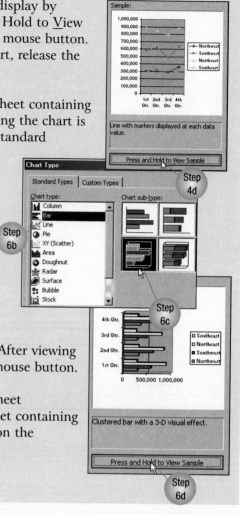

Choosing a Custom Chart Type

HINT

Preformatted custom charts are available. Use one of these custom charts if the formatting is appropriate.

The chart feature offers a variety of preformatted custom charts. A custom chart can be chosen in step 1 of the Chart Wizard steps or a custom chart type can be chosen for an existing chart. To choose a custom chart type while creating a chart, click the Custom Types tab at the Chart Wizard - Step 1 of 4 - Chart Type dialog box.

You can also choose a custom chart for an existing chart. To do this, click Chart and then Chart Type. At the Chart Type dialog box, click the Custom Types tab. This displays the Chart Type dialog box as shown in figure 7.8. You can also display the Chart Type dialog box by positioning the arrow pointer in the chart, clicking the *right* mouse button, and then clicking Chart Type at the shortcut menu. At the Chart Type dialog box with the Custom Types tab selected, click the desired custom chart type in the Chart type list box.

7.8 *Chart Type Dialog Box with Custom Types Tab Selected*

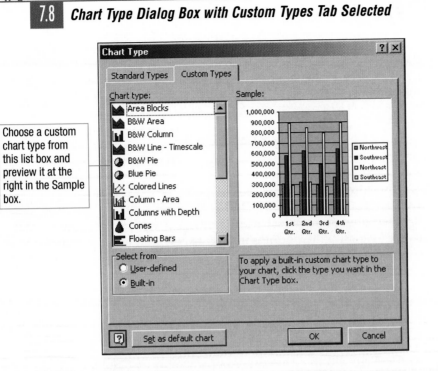

Choose a custom chart type from this list box and preview it at the right in the Sample box.

✓ exercise 6

CHOOSING A CUSTOM CHART TYPE

1. Open CExl C07 Ex03.
2. Save the workbook with Save As and name it CExl C07 Ex06.
3. Choose a custom chart type by completing the following steps:
   a. Click Chart and then Chart Type.
   b. At the Chart Type dialog box, click the Custom Types tab.
   c. At the Chart Type dialog box with the Custom Types tab selected, click *Columns with Depth* in the Chart type list box.
   d. Click OK to close the Chart Type dialog box.
4. Save the workbook again and then print only the sheet containing the chart.
5. Close CExl C07 Ex06.

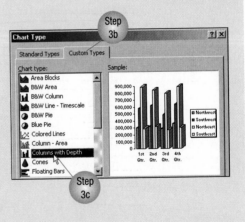

Changing Data in Cells

The Excel chart feature uses data in cells to create a chart. This data can be changed and the chart will reflect the changes. When a change is made to data in a worksheet, the change is also made to any chart created with the cells in the worksheet. The change is reflected in a chart whether it is located in the same worksheet as the changed cells or in a new sheet.

HINT

The chart is linked to the selected cells. If data is changed in a selected cell, the chart is automatically updated.

✓exercise 7

1. Open CExl C07 Ex03.
2. Save the workbook with Save As and name it CExl C07 Ex07.
3. Make the following changes to the data in cells in *Sheet1:*
   a. Make sure the worksheet containing the cells (not the chart) is active. If not, click the *Sheet1* tab located at the bottom of the worksheet window.
   b. Make the following changes to the specified cells:
      C2: Change *320,250* to *295,785*
      D3: Change *490,125* to *550,350*
      C5: Change *320,765* to *298,460*
      E5: Change *300,455* to *275,490*
4. Display the worksheet containing the chart *(Chart1).*
5. Save the workbook again and then print only the sheet containing the chart.
6. Close CExl C07 Ex07.

Changing the Data Series

HINT

A data series is information represented on the chart by bars, lines, columns, pie slices, and so on.

When a chart is created, the Chart Wizard uses the data in the first column (except the first cell) to create the x-axis (the information along the bottom of the chart) and uses the data in the first row (except the first cell) to create the legend. For example, in the chart in figure 7.6, the names (Chaney, Ferraro, and Jimenez) were used for the x-axis (along the bottom of the chart) and the months (June and July) were used for the legend.

When a chart is created, the option Rows is selected by default at the Chart Wizard - Step 2 of 4 - Chart Source Data dialog box. Change this to Columns and the data in the first column (except the first cell) will be used to create the x-axis and the data in the first row will be used to create the legend.

Change the data series in an existing chart by making the chart active, clicking Chart, and then clicking Source Data. This displays the Source Data dialog box shown in figure 7.9. Another method for displaying the Source Data dialog box is to position the arrow pointer in a white portion of the chart (inside the chart but outside any chart element) and then click the *right* mouse button. At the shortcut menu that displays, click Source Data. The Source Data dialog box contains the same options as the Chart Wizard - Step 2 of 4 - Chart Source Data dialog box.

7.9 Source Data Dialog Box

Source Data

Data Range | Series

Data range: =Sheet1!$A$1:$E$5

Series in: ⦿ Rows
            ○ Columns

Choose the Columns option to reverse the x-axis and the legend.

OK   Cancel

exercise 8

CHANGING DATA SERIES IN AN EXCEL CHART

1. Open CExl C07 Ex01.
2. Save the workbook with Save As and name it CExl C07 Ex08.
3. Change the data series by completing the following steps:
   a. Position the arrow pointer in a white portion of the chart (inside the chart but outside any chart element) and then click the *right* mouse button.
   b. At the shortcut menu that displays, click Source Data.
   c. At the Source Data dialog box, click the Columns option.
   d. Click OK to close the Source Data dialog box.
   e. Click outside the chart to deselect it.
4. Save, print, and then close CExl C07 Ex08.

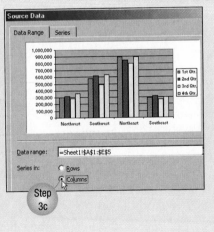

Step 3c

exercise 9

1. Open Excel Worksheet 16.
2. Save the worksheet with Save As and name it CExl C07 Ex09.
3. Create a pie chart by completing the following steps:
   a. Select cells A4 through B10.
   b. Click the Chart Wizard button on the Standard toolbar.
   c. At the Chart Wizard - Step 1 of 4 - Chart Type dialog box, click *Pie* in the Chart type list box, and then click the Next button.
   d. At the Chart Wizard - Step 2 of 4 - Chart Source Data dialog box, make sure the data range displays as =*Sheet1!$A$4:$B$10*. Click the Rows option to see what happens to the pie when the data series is changed, click Columns to return the data series back, and then click the Next button.
   e. At the Chart Wizard - Step 3 of 4 - Chart Options dialog box, click the Data Labels tab.
   f. At the dialog box with the Data Labels tab selected, click Percentage.
   g. Click the Next button.
   h. At the Chart Wizard - Step 4 of 4 - Chart Location dialog box, click As new sheet and then click the Finish button.
4. Save the workbook again and then print only the sheet containing the chart.
5. Close CExl C07 Ex09.

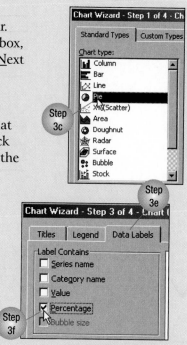

Adding Chart Elements

HINT

The legend identifies which data series is represented by which data marker.

Certain chart elements are automatically inserted in a chart created by the Chart Wizard including a chart legend and labels for the x-axis and y-axis. Add other chart elements such as a chart title and data labels at the Chart Wizard - Step 3 of 4 - Chart Options dialog box. Add chart elements to an existing chart by making the chart active, clicking Chart, and then clicking Chart Options. This displays the Chart Options dialog box shown in figure 7.10. Another method for displaying this dialog box is to position the arrow pointer in a white portion of the chart (inside the chart but outside any chart element), click the *right* mouse button, and then click Chart Options. The Chart Options dialog box contains the same options as the Chart Wizard - Step 3 of 4 - Chart Options dialog box.

EXCEL

7.10 **Chart Options Dialog Box with Titles Tab Selected**

Customize a chart with options at this dialog box with the various tabs selected.

Chart Options

| Titles | Axes | Gridlines | Legend | Data Labels | Data Table |

Chart title:

Category (X) axis:

Value (Y) axis:

Second category (X) axis:

Second value (Y) axis:

OK   Cancel

exercise 10

ADDING A TITLE TO A CHART AND CHANGING THE LEGEND LOCATION

1. Open CExl C07 Ex09.
2. Save the workbook with Save As and name it CExl C07 Ex10.
3. Add a title and data labels to the chart and change the location of the chart legend by completing the following steps:
   a. Make sure the sheet *(Chart1)* containing the pie chart displays.
   b. Click Chart and then Chart Options.
   c. At the Chart Options dialog box, click the Titles tab. (Skip this step if the Titles tab is already selected.)
   d. Click inside the Chart title text box and then key **DEPARTMENT EXPENSES BY PERCENTAGE**.
   e. Click the Data Labels tab.
   f. Click the Legend key option to insert a check box.
   g. Click the Legend tab.
   h. At the Chart Options dialog box with the Legend tab selected, click Left.
   i. Click the OK button to close the dialog box.
4. Save the workbook again and then print only the sheet containing the pie chart.
5. Close CExl C07 Ex10.

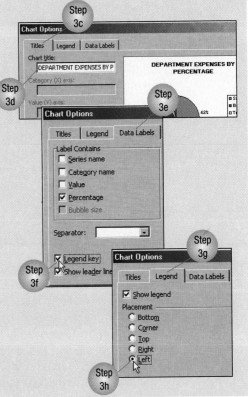

Step 3c

Step 3d

Step 3e

Step 3f

Step 3g

Step 3h

Moving/Sizing Chart Elements

When additional elements are added to a chart, the chart can become quite full and elements may overlap. If elements in a chart overlap, an element can be selected and then moved. To select an element, position the arrow pointer on a portion of the element, and then click the left mouse button. This causes sizing handles to display around the element. Position the mouse pointer toward the edge of the selected element until it turns into an arrow pointer, hold down the left mouse button, drag the element to the desired location, and then release the mouse button. To change the size of an element, drag the sizing handles in the desired direction.

Deleting/Removing Chart Elements

Chart elements can be selected by clicking the desired element. Once an element is selected, it can be moved and it can also be deleted. To delete a selected element, press the Delete key. If you delete a chart element in a chart and then decide you want it redisplayed in the chart, immediately click the Undo button on the Standard toolbar.

exercise 11

MOVING/SIZING/ADDING CHART ELEMENTS

1. Open CExl C07 Ex10.
2. Save the workbook with Save As and name it CExl C07 Ex11.
3. Move and size chart elements by completing the following steps:
   a. Move the legend to the right side of the chart by completing the following steps:
      1) Click the legend to select it.
      2) With the arrow pointer positioned in the legend, hold down the left mouse button, drag the outline of the legend to the right side of the chart, and then release the mouse button.
   b. Move the pie to the left by completing the following steps:
      1) Select the pie. To do this, position the arrow pointer in a white portion of the chart immediately outside the pie (a yellow box displays with *Plot Area* inside) and then click the left mouse button. (This should insert a square border around the pie. If not, try selecting the pie again.)

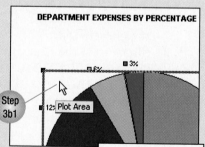

Step 3b1

      2) With the pie selected (square border around the pie), position the arrow pointer inside the square border that displays around the pie (not inside the pie), hold down the left mouse button, drag the outline of the pie to the left until it looks balanced with the legend, and then release the mouse button.

Step 3c2

   c. Increase the size of the legend by completing the following steps:
      1) Click the legend to select it.
      2) Use the sizing handles that display around the legend to increase the size. (You determine the direction to drag the sizing handles and the final size of the legend. Make sure the pie and legend are balanced.)

4. Save the workbook again and then print only the sheet containing the pie chart.
5. With CExl C07 Ex11 still open, remove the legend, change the data labels, and move the pie by completing the following steps:
   a. Delete the legend by completing the following steps:
      1) Click the legend to select it.
      2) Press the Delete key.
   b. Change the data labels by completing the following steps:

Step 5b3

Step 5b4

   1) Position the arrow pointer in a white portion of the chart (outside any chart element) and then click the *right* mouse button.
      2) At the shortcut menu that displays, click Chart Options.
      3) At the Chart Options dialog box, click the Data Labels tab.
      4) At the Chart Options dialog box with the Data Labels tab selected, click the Category name option to insert a check mark. (Make sure the Percentage option still contains a check mark.)
      5) Click OK to close the Chart Options dialog box.
   c. Move the pie by completing the following steps:
      1) Make sure the pie is selected. (If the pie is not selected, select it by positioning the arrow pointer in a white portion of the chart outside but immediately left or right at the top or bottom of the pie [a yellow box displays with *Plot Area* inside] and then clicking the left mouse button.)
      2) With the pie selected (square border around the pie), position the arrow pointer inside the square border that displays around the pie (not inside the pie), hold down the left mouse button, drag the outline of the pie until it looks centered between the left and right sides of the chart, and then release the mouse button.
6. Save the workbook again and then print only the sheet containing the pie chart.
7. Close CExl C07 Ex11.

Adding Gridlines

Gridlines can be added to a chart for the category, series, and value. Depending on the chart, some but not all of these options may be available. To add gridlines, display the Chart Options dialog box and then click the Gridlines tab. This displays the Chart Options dialog box with the Gridlines tab selected as shown in figure 7.11. At this dialog box, insert a check mark in those options for which you want gridlines.

7.11 *Chart Options Dialog Box with Gridlines Tab Selected*

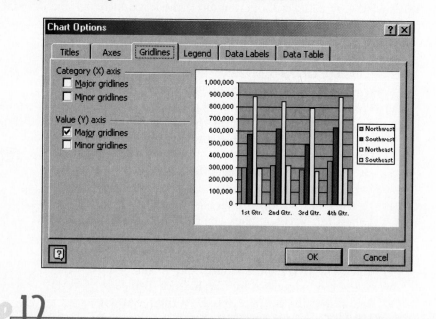

exercise 12

ADDING GRIDLINES TO A CHART

1. Open CExl C07 Ex03.
2. Save the workbook with Save As and name it CExl C07 Ex12.
3. Add gridlines to the chart by completing the following steps:
   a. Make sure the sheet containing the chart is displayed. (If not, click the *Chart1* tab located toward the bottom of the screen.)
   b. Click Chart and then Chart Options.
   c. At the Chart Options dialog box, click the Gridlines tab.
   d. At the Chart Options dialog box with the Gridlines tab selected, insert a check mark in the two options in the Category (X) axis section and also the two options in the Value (Y) axis section.
   e. Click OK to close the Chart Options dialog box.
4. Save the workbook again and then print only the sheet containing the chart.
5. Close CExl C07 Ex12.

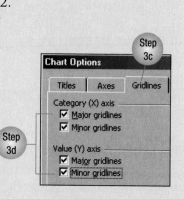

Formatting Chart Elements

A variety of formatting options are available for a chart or chart elements. Formatting can include adding a pattern, changing background and foreground colors of the selected element or chart, changing the font, and changing the alignment or placement. To customize a chart, double-click in the chart area (outside any chart element). This displays the Format Chart Area dialog box with the Patterns tab selected as shown in figure 7.12. You can also display this dialog box by clicking once in the chart area, clicking Format, and then clicking Selected Chart Area.

7.12 **Format Chart Area Dialog Box with Patterns Tab Selected**

Customize the chart area by adding a pattern and/or fill color and background at the Format Chart Area dialog box with the Patterns tab selected. Click the Font tab and options for changing the typeface, type style, and type size display.

The font and pattern of chart elements can also be customized along with additional formatting for specific elements. For example, if you double-click a chart title, the Format Chart Title dialog box displays. (You can also display this dialog box by clicking once on the title, clicking Format, and then clicking Selected Chart Title.) This dialog box contains three tabs—Patterns, Font, and Alignment. Clicking the Patterns or the Font tab displays the same options as those available at the Format Chart Area dialog box. Click the Alignment tab and options for changing the text alignment (horizontal or vertical) display along with options for the title orientation.

Double-click a chart legend and the Format Legend dialog box displays with three tabs—Patterns, Font, and Placement. (You can also display this dialog box by clicking once on the legend, clicking Format, and then clicking Selected Legend.) Clicking the Patterns or the Font tab displays the same options as those available at the Format Chart Area dialog box. Click the Placement tab to display options for specifying the location of the legend in relation to the chart.

Each chart element contains a formatting dialog box. To display this dialog box, double-click the desired chart element. For example, double-click text in either the x-axis or the y-axis and the Format Axis dialog box displays.

1. Open Excel Worksheet 25.
2. Save the worksheet with Save As and name it CExl C07 Ex13.
3. Create a Column chart with the data in the worksheet by completing the following steps:
   a. Select cells A4 through C7.
   b. Click the Chart Wizard button on the Standard toolbar.
   c. At the Chart Wizard - Step 1 of 4 - Chart Type dialog box, click the Next button.
   d. At the Chart Wizard - Step 2 of 4 - Chart Source Data dialog box, make sure the data range displays as =Sheet1!$A$4:$C$7 and then click the Next button.
   e. At the Chart Wizard - Step 3 of 4 - Chart Options dialog box, make the following changes:
      1) Click the Titles tab.
      2) Click inside the Chart title text box and then key **NORTHWEST REGION**.
      3) Click the Next button.
   f. At the Chart Wizard - Step 4 of 4 - Chart Location dialog box, click the As new sheet option, and then click the Finish button.
4. Change the font for the title and legend and add a border and shading by completing the following steps:
   a. Double-click the title *NORTHWEST REGION*.
   b. At the Format Chart Title dialog box, click the Font tab, and then change the font to 24-point Times New Roman bold (or a similar typeface).
   c. Click the Patterns tab.
   d. Click the white circle before Custom in the Border section of the dialog box.
   e. Click the down-pointing triangle to the right of the Weight text box. From the drop-down menu that displays, click the third option.
   f. Click the check box before the Shadow option.
   g. Add light green color by clicking the fourth color from the left in the fifth row.
   h. Click OK to close the Format Chart Title dialog box.

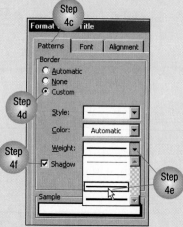

5. Format the legend with the same options as the title (complete steps similar to those in step 4, except change the font to 10-point Times New Roman bold instead of 24-point).
6. With the legend still selected, increase the width by dragging the left, middle sizing handle to the left so the legend slightly overlaps the chart. (Make sure *# of Computers* is completely visible in the legend.)
7. Save the workbook again and then print only the sheet containing the chart.
8. Close CExl C07 Ex13.

Changing Element Colors

Fill Color

A fill color can be added to a chart or a chart element with the Fill Color button on the Formatting toolbar. To add a fill color, select the chart or the chart element, and then click the down-pointing triangle at the right side of the Fill Color button on the Formatting toolbar. This displays a palette of color choices as shown in figure 7.13. Click the desired color on the palette.

FIGURE

7.13 *Fill Color Button Palette*

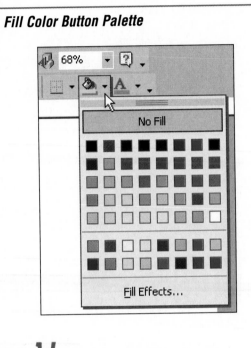

exercise 14

CHANGING ELEMENT COLORS IN A CHART

1. Open CExl C07 Ex09.
2. Save the workbook with Save As and name it CExl C07 Ex14.
3. Change the colors of the pieces of the pie by completing the following steps:
   a. Change the color of the piece of pie representing *Salaries* to red by completing the following steps:
      1) Position the arrow pointer on the *Salaries* piece of pie and then click the left mouse button. (Make sure the sizing handles surround only the *Salaries* piece of pie. You may need to experiment a few times to select the piece correctly.)
      2) Click the down-pointing triangle at the right of the Fill Color button on the Formatting toolbar.
      3) At the color palette, click the red color (first color in the third row).

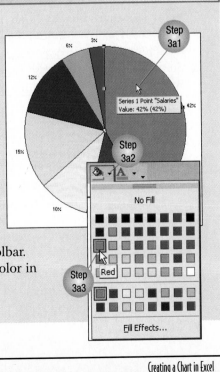

Step 3a1

Step 3a2

Step 3a3

b. Change the color of the *Miscellaneous* piece of pie to green by completing steps similar to those in step 3a. (You determine the shade of green.)

c. Change the color of the *Supplies* piece of pie to yellow by completing steps similar to those in step 3a. (You determine the shade of yellow.)

d. Change the color of the *Equipment* piece of pie to blue by completing steps similar to those in step 3a. (You determine the shade of blue.)

e. Change the color of the *Travel* piece of pie to violet by completing steps similar to those in step 3a.

f. Change the color of the *Training* piece of pie to light turquoise by completing steps similar to those in step 3a.

g. Change the color of the *Benefits* piece of pie to a color you have not used on the other pieces of pie by completing steps similar to those in step 3a.

4. Add a background color to the chart by completing the following steps:

a. Select the entire chart. (To do this, position the arrow pointer inside the chart window but outside the chart, and then click the left mouse button.)

b. Click the down-pointing triangle at the right of the Fill Color button on the Formatting toolbar.

c. From the color palette that displays, click a light blue color of your choosing.

5. Save the workbook again and then print only the sheet containing the pie chart.

6. Close CExl C07 Ex14.

CHAPTER summary

➤ Create a chart with data in an Excel worksheet. A chart is a visual presentation of data.

➤ Create a chart by selecting the cells containing the data to be charted and then clicking the Chart Wizard button on the Standard toolbar. Complete the four steps in the Chart Wizard.

➤ Insert a chart in the same worksheet as the cells containing data or in a separate sheet. If a chart is created in a separate sheet, the sheet is named *Chart1*.

➤ The left vertical side of a chart is referred to as the y-axis, and the bottom of the chart is referred to as the x-axis.

➤ In a worksheet containing cells of data as well as a chart, the chart can be printed (rather than all data in the worksheet) by selecting the chart first and then displaying the Print dialog box.

➤ To delete a chart in a worksheet, click the chart to select it, and then press the Delete key. To delete a chart created in a separate sheet, position the mouse pointer on the chart tab, click the right mouse button, and then click Delete.

➤ Change the size of a chart in an Excel worksheet by clicking the chart and then dragging the sizing handles in the desired direction. To move a chart, select the chart, position the arrow pointer inside the chart, hold down the left mouse button, drag the outline of the chart to the desired location, and then release the mouse button.

➤ Fourteen basic chart types are available and include Area, Bar, Bubble, Column, Cone, Cylinder, Doughnut, Line, Pie, Pyramid, Radar, Stock, Surface, and XY (scatter).

➤ The default chart type is a Column chart. Change this default type at the first Chart Wizard dialog box or at the Chart Type dialog box.

➤ A variety of custom charts is available at the Chart Type dialog box with the Custom Types tab selected.

➤ Change data in a cell used to create a chart and the data in the chart reflects the change.

➤ Add chart elements to a chart at the step 3 Chart Wizard dialog box or at the Chart Options dialog box.

➤ Move a chart element by selecting the element and then dragging the element to the desired location.

➤ Size a chart element by selecting the chart element and then dragging a sizing handle to the desired size.

➤ Delete a chart element by selecting the element and then pressing the Delete key.

➤ Customize the formatting of a chart element by double-clicking the element. This causes a formatting dialog box to display. The options at the dialog box will vary depending on the chart element.

➤ Add fill color to a chart or a chart element by selecting the chart or element and then clicking the Fill Color button on the Formatting toolbar. Click the desired color at the palette of color choices that displays.

COMMANDS review

Command	Mouse/Keyboard
Create a chart	Select the cells and then click the Chart Wizard button on the Standard toolbar. Complete steps 1 through 4 of the Chart Wizard.
Display Chart Type dialog box	Make chart active; click Chart, then Chart Type
Display Chart Source Data dialog box	Make chart active; click Chart, then Source Data
Display Chart Options dialog box	Make chart active; click Chart, then Chart Options
Display Format Chart Area dialog box	Double-click in chart area outside any chart element
Display Format Chart Title dialog box	Double-click chart title
Display Format Legend dialog box	Double-click chart legend

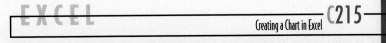

CONCEPTS check

Completion: On a blank sheet of paper, indicate the correct term, symbol, or command for each item.

1. Create a chart by selecting the cells containing data and then clicking this button on the Standard toolbar. *Chart Wizard*
2. To create a chart as a separate worksheet, click this option at the Chart Wizard - Step 4 of 4 - Chart Location dialog box. *As new sheet*
3. Change the size of a selected chart by dragging these. *black squares sizing handles*
4. This axis is located at the bottom of the chart. *x-axis*
5. Double-click a legend in a chart and this dialog box displays. *Format Legend*
6. Choose a custom chart type at the Chart Type dialog box with this tab selected. *Custom Types*
7. Double-click in a chart area and this dialog box displays. *Format Chart Area*
8. Add fill color to a chart element by selecting the element and then clicking this button on the Formatting toolbar. *Fill Color*
9. List the steps you would complete to create a default chart in Excel with cells A1 through D8 and insert the chart in a separate worksheet. *Select cells A1 through D8 – click Chart Wizard on Standard toolbar – Next for steps 1-3 – @ step four click in As new sheet option – Finish.*

SKILLS check

✓ Assessment 1

1. Open Excel Worksheet 01.
2. Save the worksheet with Save As and name it CExl C07 SA01.
3. Make the following changes to the worksheet:
   a. Delete column B.
   b. Delete row 2.
4. Select cells A1 through C9 and then create a chart in a separate sheet with the following specifications:
   a. At step 1 of the Chart Wizard, do not make any changes.
   b. At step 2, make sure the proper cell range displays.
   c. At step 3, add the title *COMPANY SALES*.
   d. At step 4, specify that the chart is to be created as a new sheet.
   e. After the chart is created, change the font size of the title to 24 points.
5. Save the workbook again and then print only the sheet containing the chart.
6. Close CExl C07 SA01.

✓ Assessment 2

1. Open Excel Worksheet 22.
2. Save the worksheet with Save As and name it CExl C07 SA02.
3. Select cells A1 through E3 and then create a chart in a new worksheet with the following specifications:

a. At step 1 of the Chart Wizard, choose the Line chart type.
b. At step 2, make sure the proper cell range displays.
c. At step 3, add the title *COMPANY SALES*.
d. At step 4, specify that the chart is to be created as a new sheet.
4. After creating the chart, make the following customizations:
   a. Add a light background color to the entire chart.
   b. Add a complementary light background color to the legend.
   c. Change the legend font to a serif typeface (you determine the typeface).
   d. Change the font for the title *COMPANY SALES* to the same serif typeface you chose for the legend and increase the font size.
   e. If some of the text in the legend is not visible, select the legend and then increase the size of the legend.
5. Save the workbook again and then print only the sheet containing the chart.
6. Close CExl C07 SA02.

Assessment 3

1. Open Excel Worksheet 03.
2. Save the worksheet with Save As and name it CExl C07 SA03.
3. Make the following changes to the worksheet:
   a. Delete column D.
   b. Select cells B3 through C8 and then click the Percent Style button on the Standard toolbar.
4. Select cells A2 through C8 and then create a chart in a new sheet with the default settings in Chart Wizard, except add the chart title *ANALYSIS OF FINANCIAL CONDITION*.
5. Make the following changes to the chart:
   a. Change the color of the bars in the chart (you determine the colors).
   b. Change the font of the title and add a border (you determine the font and border style).
   c. Change the background shading of the chart to light turquoise.
   d. Add the following gridlines: Major gridlines in Category (X) axis and Minor gridlines in Value (Y) axis.
6. Save the workbook again and then print only the sheet containing the chart.
7. Close CExl C07 SA03.

Assessment 4

1. At a clear worksheet window, create a worksheet with the following data:

Fund Allocations	
Fund	Percentage
Annuities	23%
Stocks	42%
Bonds	15%
Money Market	20%

2. Create a pie chart as a separate worksheet with the data with the following specifications:
   a. Create a title for the pie chart.
   b. Add data labels to the chart.

c. Add any other enhancements that will improve the visual presentation of the data.

3. Save the workbook and name it CExl C07 SA04.
4. Print only the sheet containing the chart.
5. Close CExl C07 SA04.

Assessment 5

1. Open CExl C07 SA04.
2. Save the workbook with Save As and name it CExl C07 SA05.
3. Choose a custom chart type at the Chart Type dialog box with the Custom Types tab selected. (Choose a custom pie chart.)
4. Save the workbook again and then print only the sheet containing the chart.
5. Close CExl C07 SA05.

Assessment 6

1. Open Excel Worksheet 18.
2. Save the workbook with Save As and name it CExl C07 SA06.
3. Look at the data in the worksheet and then create a chart to represent the data. Add a title to the chart and add any other enhancements to improve the visual display of the chart.
4. Save the workbook again and then print the chart.
5. Close CExl C07 SA06.

Assessment 7

1. Use Excel's Help feature to learn more about an XY (scatter) chart.
2. After reading the information presented by Help, create a worksheet with the data shown in figure 7.14. Create a scatter chart from the data in a separate sheet and create an appropriate title for the chart. (Excel will change the date *July 1* to *1-Jul* and change the other dates in the same manner. The XY scatter chart will display time in five-day intervals.)
3. Save the completed workbook and name it CExl C07 SA07.
4. Print both sheets of the workbook (the sheet containing the data in cells and the sheet containing the chart).
5. Close CExl C07 SA07.

FIGURE

7.14 *Assessment 7*

HIGHLAND PARK ATTENDANCE

Week	Projected	Actual
July 1	35,000	42,678
July 8	33,000	41,065
July 15	30,000	34,742
July 22	28,000	29,781
July 29	28,000	26,208

EXCEL

CHAPTER 8

ENHANCING THE DISPLAY OF WORKBOOKS

PERFORMANCE OBJECTIVES

Upon successful completion of chapter 8, you will be able to:
- Save an Excel workbook as a Web page
- Preview a Web page using Web Page Preview
- Create and modify a hyperlink
- Insert, size, move, and format a clip art image
- Create, size, move, and customize WordArt
- Draw and customize shapes, lines, and autoshapes using buttons on the Drawing toolbar

Excel Chapter 08C

You can save an Excel workbook as a Web page and then view it in Web Page Preview and in a Web browser. You can also insert hyperlinks in a workbook that connect to a Web site or to another workbook. Microsoft Excel contains a variety of features that help you enhance the visual appeal of a workbook. Some methods for adding visual appeal that you will learn in this chapter include inserting and modifying images, creating and customizing WordArt text, and drawing and aligning shapes.

Creating a Web Page

You can save an Excel workbook as a Web page. The Web page can be viewed in the default Web browser software, and hyperlinks can be inserted in the Web page to jump to other workbooks or sites on the Internet with additional information pertaining to the workbook content. In an organization, an Excel workbook can be saved as a Web page and posted on the company intranet as a timely method of distributing the workbook to the company employees.

> **HINT**
> Web pages are documents containing special formatting codes written in HTML (Hypertext Markup Language).

Saving a Workbook as a Web Page

Save a workbook as a Web page by opening the workbook, clicking File, and then clicking Save as Web Page. At the Save As dialog box shown in figure 8.1, key a name for the Web page in the File name text box if you want to save the Web page with a name that is different than the one provided, and then click the Save button.

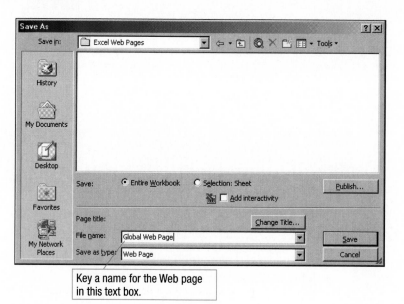

Key a name for the Web page
in this text box.

Previewing a Workbook in Web Page Preview

When creating a Web page, you may want to preview it in your default Web browser. Depending on the browser you are using, some of the formatting in a workbook may not display in the browser. To preview a workbook in your default Web browser, click File and then click Web Page Preview. This displays the currently open worksheet in the default Web browser and displays formatting supported by the browser. Close the Web browser window when you are finished previewing the page to return to Microsoft Excel.

Creating Hyperlinks

A hyperlink is text or an object that you click to go to a different file, an HTML page on the Internet, or an HTML page on an intranet. Create a hyperlink in an Excel worksheet by keying the address of an existing Web page such as www.emcp.com. By default, the automatic formatting of hyperlinks is turned on and the Web address is formatted as a hyperlink (text is underlined and the color changes to blue). (You can turn off the automatic formatting of hyperlinks. To do this, display the AutoCorrect dialog box by clicking Tools and then AutoCorrect Options. At the AutoCorrect dialog box, click the AutoFormat As You Type tab, and then remove the check mark from the Internet and network paths with hyperlinks check box.)

Insert
Hyperlink

You can also create a customized hyperlink by selecting text or an image in a workbook and then clicking the Insert Hyperlink button on the Standard toolbar. At the Insert Hyperlink dialog box shown in figure 8.2, key the file name or Web site address in the Address text box, and then click OK. You can also use the Look in option to browse to the desired folder and file and then double-click the file name. To link to the specified file or Web page, position the mouse pointer on the hyperlink, and then click the left mouse button.

8.2 *Insert Hyperlink Dialog Box*

```
Insert Hyperlink                                                    ? X
  Link to:    Text to display: American Airlines          ScreenTip...

   [icon]    Look in:  [] Excel Web Pages        [v] [↑] [Q] [→]
 Existing File or
   Web Page              [] Global Web Page _files    Bookmark...
            Current   [] Global Web Page
            Folder
   [icon]
 Place in This
 Document    Browsed
             Pages

   [icon]    Recent
 Create New  Files
 Document
            Address: http://www.aa.com               [v]
   [icon]
 E-mail Address                           [  OK  ]  [ Cancel ]
```

Key the Web address or specify the
file location in the Address text box.

✓ exercise

SAVING A WORKBOOK AS A WEB PAGE, PREVIEWING THE WEB PAGE, AND CREATING HYPERLINKS

1. Create a folder named *Excel Web Pages* within the *Excel Chapter 08C* folder on your disk.
2. Open Excel Worksheet 37.
3. Save the worksheet as a Web page in the *Excel Web Pages* folder by completing the following steps:
   a. Click File and then Save as Web Page.
   b. At the Save As dialog box, double-click *Excel Web Pages* in the list box.
   c. Select the text in the File name text box and then key **Global Web Page**.
   d. Click the Save button.

   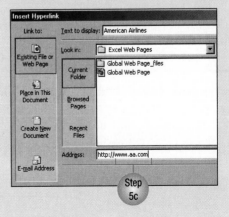

   Step 3c
   ```
   Page title:                              Change Title...
   File name:  Global Web Page          [v]     [ Save ]
   Save as type: Web Page               [v]     [ Cancel ]
   ```
   Step 3d

4. Preview the workbook in Web Page Preview by completing the following steps:
   a. Click File and then click Web Page Preview.
   b. If the viewing area in the browser is limited, click the Maximize button located in the upper right corner of the browser window.
   c. After viewing the worksheet in the Web browser, click File and then Close.
5. Create a hyperlink so that clicking *American Airlines* displays the American Airlines Web page by completing the following steps:
   a. Click cell G8 (this is the cell containing *American Airlines*).
   b. Click the Insert Hyperlink button on the Standard toolbar.
   c. At the Insert Hyperlink dialog box, key **www.aa.com** in the Address text box. (The *http://* is automatically inserted in the address.)
   d. Click OK. (This changes the color of the *American Airlines* text and also adds underlining to the text.)
   e. Repeat steps 5b to 5d in cell G11.

```
Insert Hyperlink
  Link to:    Text to display: American Airlines
   [icon]    Look in:  [] Excel Web Pages        [v]
 Existing File or
   Web Page              [] Global Web Page _files
            Current   [] Global Web Page
            Folder
   [icon]
 Place in This
 Document    Browsed
             Pages
   [icon]    Recent
 Create New  Files
 Document
            Address: http://www.aa.com
   [icon]
 E-mail Address
```
Step 5c

6. Complete steps similar to those in step 5 to create a hyperlink from *Northwest Airlines* to the URL *www.nwa.com* in cells G9 and G10.
7. Complete steps similar to those in step 5 to create a hyperlink from *Air Canada* to the URL *www.aircanada.ca* in cell G12.
8. Click the Save button on the Standard toolbar to save the Web page with the hyperlinks added.
9. Jump to the hyperlinked sites by completing the following steps:
   a. Make sure you are connected to the Internet.
   b. Click one of the <u>*American Airlines*</u> hyperlinks.
   c. When the American Airlines Web page displays, scroll through the page, and then click a hyperlink that interests you.
   d. After looking at this next page, click <u>F</u>ile and then <u>C</u>lose.
   e. At the Global Web Page workbook, click the <u>*Air Canada*</u> hyperlink.
   f. At the Air Canada Web page, click the hyperlink to see their site displayed in English.
   g. After viewing the Air Canada page, click <u>F</u>ile and then <u>C</u>lose.
   h. At the Global Web Page workbook, click one of the <u>*Northwest*</u> hyperlinks.
   i. At the Northwest Airlines Web page, click a link that interests you.
   j. After viewing the Northwest Airlines page, click <u>F</u>ile and then <u>C</u>lose.
10. Print and then close Global Web Page.

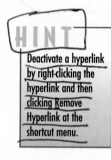

HINT

Deactivate a hyperlink by right-clicking the hyperlink and then clicking Remove Hyperlink at the shortcut menu.

In exercise 1, you created hyperlinks from an Excel workbook to sites on the Web. You can also insert hyperlinks in a workbook that link to other Excel workbooks or files in other programs in the Office suite. In exercise 2, you will create a hyperlink that, when clicked, displays another Excel workbook.

You can modify or change hyperlink text or the hyperlink destination. To do this, right-click the hyperlink, and then click Edit <u>H</u>yperlink. At the Edit Hyperlink dialog box, make any desired changes, and then close the dialog box. The Edit Hyperlink dialog box contains the same options as the Insert Hyperlink dialog box.

✓ *exercise 2*

CREATING AND MODIFYING A HYPERLINK TO AN EXCEL WORKSHEET

1. Open Excel Worksheet 33.
2. Save the workbook with Save As and name it CExl C08 Ex02.
3. Create a hyperlink that will display Excel Worksheet 28 by completing the following steps:
   a. Make cell A10 active.
   b. Key **Semiannual Sales** and then press Enter.
   c. Click cell A10 to make it the active cell.
   d. Click the Insert Hyperlink button on the Standard toolbar.
   e. At the Insert Hyperlink dialog box, click the down-pointing triangle at the right side of the <u>L</u>ook in option and then navigate to the *Excel Chapter 08C* folder on your disk.

f. Double-click *Excel Worksheet 28* in the *Excel Chapter 08C* folder on your disk. (This closes the Insert Hyperlink dialog box and displays the *Semiannual Sales* text as a hyperlink in the workbook.)

4. Display Excel Worksheet 28 by clicking the *Semiannual Sales* hyperlink.

5. Close Excel Worksheet 28.

6. Print CExl C08 Ex02.

7. Modify the hyperlink text in CExl C08 Ex02 by completing the following steps:

   a. Position the mouse pointer on the *Semiannual Sales* hyperlink, click the *right* button, and then click Edit <u>H</u>yperlink.

   b. At the Edit Hyperlink dialog box, select the text *Semiannual Sales* in the <u>T</u>ext to display text box and then key **Customer Sales Analysis**.

   c. Click OK.

8. Click the *Customer Sales Analysis* hyperlink.

9. Close Excel Worksheet 28.

10. Save, print, and then close CExl C08 Ex02.

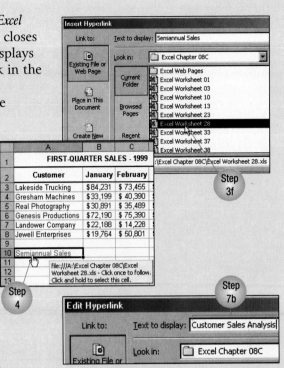

Step 3f

Step 4

Step 7b

Inserting Images in a Workbook

Microsoft Office includes a gallery of media images you can insert in a workbook such as clip art, photographs, and movie images, as well as sound clips. To insert an image in a workbook, click <u>I</u>nsert, point to <u>P</u>icture, and then click <u>C</u>lip Art. This displays the Insert Clip Art Task Pane at the right side of the screen as shown in figure 8.3. You can also display the Insert Clip Art Task Pane by clicking the Insert Clip Art button on the Drawing toolbar. (Display the Drawing toolbar by clicking the Drawing button on the Standard toolbar.)

Insert Clip Art

Drawing

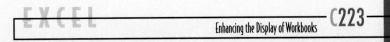

8.3 *Insert Clip Art Task Pane*

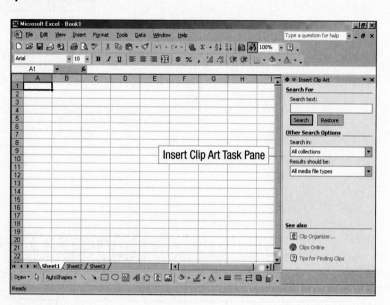

The first time you display the Insert Clip Art Task Pane, you may see a dialog box with a message telling you that the Media Gallery can catalog picture, sound, and motion files found on your hard disk(s) or in folders you specify and telling you to click Now to catalog all media file, click Later to postpone the task, or click Options to specify folders. At this message, click the Now button and Media Gallery will catalog all of your picture, sound, and motion files.

To view all picture, sound, and motion files, make sure no text displays in the Search text text box at the Insert Clip Art Task Pane and then click the Search button. Expand the viewing area of the task pane by clicking the button containing the left-pointing arrow that displays immediately below *Results*. Insert the image in your workbook by clicking the desired image.

Narrowing a Search

By default (unless it has been customized), the Insert Clip Art Task Pane looks for all media images and sound clips found in all locations. You can narrow the search to specific locations and to specific images. The Search in option at the Insert Clip Art Task Pane has a default setting of *All collections*. You can change this to *My Collections, Office Collections*, and *Web Collections*. The Results should be option has a default setting of *All media file types*. Click the down-pointing triangle at the right side of this option to display media types. To search for a specific media type, remove the check mark before all options at the drop-down list but the desired type. For example, if you are searching only for clip art images, remove the check mark before Photographs, Movies, and Sound.

If you are searching for specific images, click in the Search text text box, key the desired word, and then click the Search button. For example, if you want to find images related to computers, click in the Search text text box, key **computer**, and then click the Search button. To search for other images, click the Modify button. This redisplays the Search text text box. Click inside the text box and then key the desired word.

EXCEL

Sizing an Image

Size an image in a workbook using the sizing handles that display around a selected image. To change the size of an image, click in the image to select it, and then position the mouse pointer on a sizing handle until the pointer turns into a double-headed arrow. Hold down the left mouse button, drag the sizing handle in or out to decrease or increase the size of the image, and then release the mouse button.

Use the middle sizing handles at the left or right side of the image to make the image wider or thinner. Use the middle sizing handles at the top or bottom of the image to make the image taller or shorter. Use the sizing handles at the corners of the image to change both the width and height at the same time. When sizing an image, consider using the horizontal and vertical rulers that display in the Print Layout view. To deselect an image, click anywhere in the workbook outside the image.

HINT

Drag one of the corner sizing handles to maintain the original proportions of the image.

Moving and Deleting an Image

To move an image, select the image, and then position the mouse pointer inside the image until the pointer turns into a four-headed arrow. Hold down the left mouse button, drag the image to the desired position, and then release the mouse button. Rotate an image by positioning the mouse pointer on the green, round rotation handle until the pointer displays as a circular arrow. Hold down the left mouse button, drag in the desired direction, and then release the mouse button. Delete a clip art image by selecting the image and then pressing the Delete key.

HINT

You can use arrow keys on the keyboard to move a selected object.

✓ exercise 3

INSERTING AND SIZING A CLIP ART IMAGE IN A WORKSHEET

1. Open Excel Worksheet 03.
2. Save the worksheet with Save As and name it CExl C08 Ex03.
3. Make the following changes to the worksheet:
   a. Select the first four rows of the worksheet, then click Insert and then Rows. (This inserts four new rows at the beginning of the worksheet.)
   b. Click in cell A2, key **MYLAN COMPUTERS**, and then press Enter.
   c. Select cells A1 through D12 and then apply the Accounting 1 autoformat.
   d. Select cells B7 through D12 and then click the Percent Style button on the Formatting toolbar.
4. Insert an image in the worksheet by completing the following steps:
   a. Make cell B1 active.
   b. Click Insert, point to Picture, and then click Clip Art.
   c. At the Insert Clip Art Task Pane, click in the Search text text box.
   d. Key **computer** and then click the Search button.
   e. Click the computer image shown in the figure at the right. (If this computer clip art image is not available, click another image that interests you.)

f. Close the Insert Clip Art Task Pane.

g. With the computer image selected (white sizing handles display around the image), position the mouse pointer on the bottom right sizing handle until it turns into a diagonally pointing two-headed arrow.

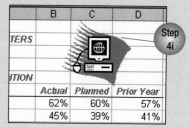

h. Hold down the left mouse button, drag into the image to decrease the size until the image is approximately the size shown at the right, and then release the mouse button.

i. If necessary, move the image so it is positioned as shown at the right.

j. Click outside the image to deselect it.

5. Save the worksheet again and then print the worksheet horizontally and vertically centered on the page.

6. Close CExl C08 Ex03.

Formatting Images with Buttons on the Picture Toolbar

You can format images in a variety of ways. Formatting might include adding fill color and border lines, increasing or decreasing the brightness or contrast, choosing a wrapping style, and cropping the image. Format an image with buttons on the Picture toolbar or options at the Format Picture dialog box. Display the Picture toolbar by clicking an image or by right-clicking an image and then clicking Show Picture Toolbar at the shortcut menu. Figure 8.4 identifies the buttons on the Picture toolbar.

F I G U R E

8.4 *Picture Toolbar Buttons*

Click this button	Named	To do this
	Insert Picture From File	Display the Insert Picture dialog box with a list of subfolders containing additional images.
	Color	Display a drop-down list with options for controlling how the image displays. Options include Automatic, Grayscale, Black & White, and Washout.
	More Contrast	Increase contrast of the image.
	Less Contrast	Decrease contrast of the image.
	More Brightness	Increase brightness of the image.
	Less Brightness	Decrease brightness of the image.

EXCEL

Icon	Name	Description
	Crop	Crop image so only a specific portion of the image is visible.
	Rotate Left	Rotate the image 90 degrees to the left.
	Line Style	Insert a border around the image and specify the border-line style.
	Compress Pictures	Reduce resolution or discard extra information to save room on the hard drive or to reduce download time.
	Format Picture	Display Format Picture dialog box with options for formatting the image. Tabs in the dialog box include Colors and Lines, Size, Position, Wrapping, and Picture.
	Set Transparent Color	This button is not active. (When an image contains a transparent area, the background color or texture of the page shows through the image. Set transparent color in Microsoft Photo Editor.)
	Reset Picture	Reset image to its original size, position, and color.

✓ exercise 4

INSERTING, MOVING, AND CUSTOMIZING AN IMAGE IN A WORKBOOK

1. Open Excel Worksheet 13.
2. Save the worksheet with Save As and name it CExl C08 Ex04.
3. Make the following changes to the worksheet:
   a. Delete column H.
   b. Insert a row at the beginning of the worksheet.
   c. Change the height of the new row to 99.00.
   d. Select cells A1 through G1 and then click the Merge and Center button on the Formatting toolbar.
   e. With cell A1 the active cell, make the following changes:
      1) Display the Format Cells dialog box. (To do this, click Format and then Cells.)
      2) At the Format Cells dialog box, click the Alignment tab.
      3) At the Format Cells dialog box with the Alignment tab selected, change the Horizontal option to *Right (Indent)* and the Vertical option to *Center*.
      4) Click the Font tab.
      5) At the Format Cells dialog box with the Font tab selected, change the font to 32-point Arial bold.

6) Click OK to close the dialog box.
   f. Key **Global Transport**.
4. Insert and format a clip art image by completing the following steps:

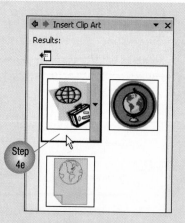

Step 4e

   a. Click outside cell A1 and then click cell A1 again.
   b. Display the Insert Clip Art Task Pane by clicking Insert, pointing to Picture, and then clicking Clip Art.
   c. Select the text in the Search text text box and then key **maps**.
   d. Click the Search button.
   e. Click the image shown at the right. (If this image is not available, choose another image related to maps.)
   f. Close the Insert Clip Art Task Pane.
   g. Change the size of the image by completing the following steps:
      1) With the clip art image selected, click the Format Picture button on the Picture toolbar. (If the Picture toolbar is not visible, click View, point to Toolbars, and then click Picture.)
      2) At the Format Picture dialog box, click the Size tab.
      3) Select the current measurement in the Height text box (in the Size and rotate section) and then key **1.5**.
      4) Click OK to close the dialog box.

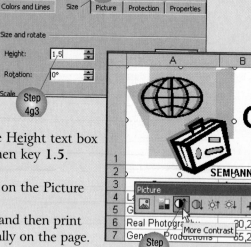

Step 4g2

Step 4g3

Step 4h

   h. Click Twice on the More Contrast button on the Picture toolbar.
5. Save the worksheet again with the same name and then print the worksheet centered horizontally and vertically on the page.
6. Close CExl C08 Ex04.

Downloading Images from the Microsoft Design Gallery Live Web Site

The Microsoft Design Gallery Live Web site offers a gallery with hundreds of images you can download. To display the Microsoft Design Gallery Live Web site, you must have access to the Internet. To download an image, display the Insert Clip Art Task Pane, and then click the *Clips Online* hyperlink located toward the bottom of the task pane. At the Microsoft Design Gallery Live Web site, click in the Search text box, key the desired category, and then click the Go button. Download the desired image by clicking the download button that displays below the image.

Creating WordArt

With the WordArt application, you can distort or modify text to conform to a variety of shapes. This is useful for creating company logos and headings. With WordArt, you can change the font, style, and alignment of text. You can also use different fill patterns and colors, customize border lines, and add shadow and three-dimensional effects.

EXCEL

To insert WordArt in an Excel workbook click Insert, point to Picture, and then click WordArt. This displays the WordArt Gallery shown in figure 8.5. You can also display the WordArt Gallery by clicking the Insert WordArt button on the WordArt toolbar or the Drawing toolbar. Display the WordArt or Drawing toolbar by right-clicking a visible toolbar, and then clicking *Drawing* or *WordArt* at the drop-down list.

Insert
WordArt

FIGURE

| 8.5 | *WordArt Gallery* |

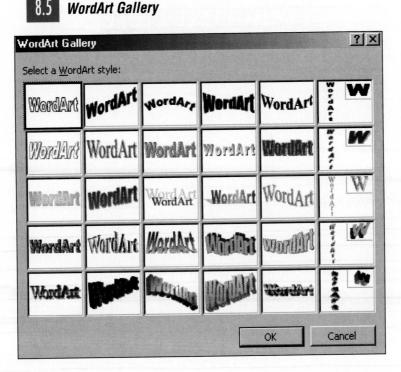

Entering Text

Double-click a WordArt choice at the WordArt Gallery and the Edit WordArt Text dialog box displays as shown in figure 8.6. At the Edit WordArt Text dialog box, key the WordArt text and then click the OK button. At the Edit WordArt Text dialog box, you can change the font and/or size of text and also apply bold or italic formatting.

8.6 *Edit WordArt Text Dialog Box*

Key WordArt text in this dialog box.

Sizing and Moving WordArt

WordArt text is inserted in the workbook with the formatting selected at the WordArt Gallery. The WordArt text is surrounded by white sizing handles and the WordArt toolbar displays near the text. Use the white sizing handles to change the height and width of the WordArt text. Use the yellow diamond located at the bottom of the WordArt text to change the slant of the WordArt text. To do this, position the arrow pointer on the yellow diamond, hold down the left mouse button, drag to the left or right, and then release the mouse button.

To move WordArt text, position the arrow pointer on any letter of the WordArt text until the arrow pointer displays with a four-headed arrow attached. Hold down the left mouse button, drag the outline of the WordArt text box to the desired position, and then release the mouse button.

HINT

Use the small, green circle that displays when an object, such as WordArt, is selected to rotate the object.

exercise 5

INSERTING WORDART IN A WORKSHEET

1. Open Excel Worksheet 01.
2. Save the worksheet with Save As and name it CExl C08 Ex05.
3. Select cells A1 through D10 and then apply the Classic 3 autoformat.
4. Insert the WordArt as shown in figure 8.7 by completing the following steps:
   a. Make cell E1 the active cell.
   b. Click Insert, point to Picture, and then click WordArt.
   c. At the WordArt Gallery, double-click the second option from the left in the second row.
   d. At the Edit WordArt Text dialog box, key **Cambridge** in the Text box and then press Enter.
   e. Key **Construction**.

Step 4c

f. Click the down-pointing triangle at the right side of the Font text box and then click *Tahoma*.

g. Click the OK button to close the Edit WordArt Text dialog box.

5. Change the location of the WordArt text by completing the following steps:

a. Position the arrow pointer on any letter in the WordArt text until the arrow pointer displays with a four-headed arrow attached.

b. Hold down the left mouse button, drag the outline of the WordArt text box so the upper left corner of the outline is located in cell E1, and then release the mouse button.

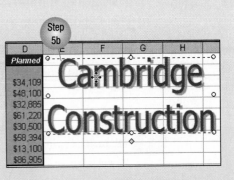

6. Change the size of the WordArt text by completing the following steps:

a. Position the arrow pointer on the middle white sizing handle located at the bottom of the WordArt text.

b. Hold down the left mouse button, drag down until the outline of the WordArt box is positioned at the bottom of row 10, and then release the mouse button.

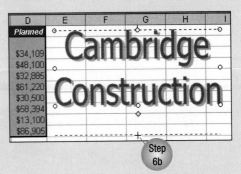

7. Click outside the WordArt text to deselect it.

8. Save the worksheet again with the same name (CExl C08 Ex05).

9. Print CExl C08 Ex05 in landscape orientation and horizontally and vertically centered on the page.

10. Close CExl C08 Ex05.

FIGURE

8.7 *Exercise 5*

	A	B	C	D	E	F	G	H	I
1	Customer	Job #	Actual	Planned					
2									
3	Sellar Corporation	2130	$30,349	$34,109					
4	Main Street Photos	1201	$48,290	$48,100					
5	Sunset Automotive	318	$34,192	$32,885					
6	Linstrom Enterprises	1009	$63,293	$61,220					
7	Morcos Media	676	$29,400	$30,500					
8	Green Valley Optics	2117	$55,309	$58,394					
9	Detailed Designs	983	$12,398	$13,100					
10	Arrowstar Company	786	$87,534	$86,905					
11									

Customizing WordArt

**WordArt
Gallery**

The WordArt toolbar, shown in figure 8.8, contains buttons for customizing the WordArt text. Click the Insert WordArt button and the WordArt Gallery shown in figure 8.5 displays. You can also display this gallery by clicking the WordArt Gallery button on the WordArt toolbar. Click the Edit Text button and the Edit WordArt Text dialog box displays.

Edit Te<u>x</u>t...

Edit Text

8.8   *WordArt Toolbar*

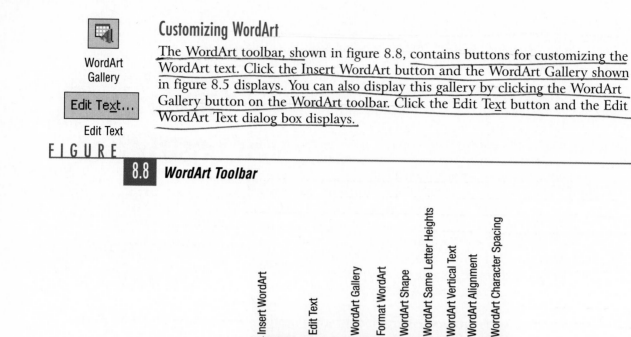

**Format
WordArt**

Customizing WordArt with Options at the Format WordArt Dialog Box

Customize WordArt text at the Format WordArt dialog box shown in figure 8.9. To display this dialog box, click the Format WordArt button on the WordArt toolbar.

8.9   *Format WordArt Dialog Box with the Colors and Lines Tab Selected*

Use options from this dialog box with the various tabs selected to customize WordArt text.

Change the color of the WordArt text and the line creating the text at the Format WordArt dialog box with the Colors and Lines tab selected. Click the Size tab and the dialog box displays with options for changing the size and rotation of the WordArt text as well as the scale of the text. At the Format WordArt dialog box with the Protection tab selected, you can specify if you want the WordArt text locked. You can only lock the WordArt text if the worksheet is protected. (Protect a worksheet with options at the Protect Sheet dialog box. Display this dialog box by clicking Tools, pointing to Protection, and then clicking Protect Sheet.)

Use options at the Format WordArt dialog box with the Properties tab selected to specify the positioning of the WordArt text. Choices include moving and sizing WordArt text with cells, moving but not sizing with cells, and not sizing or moving with cells. If you are going to post your worksheet on the Web, click the last tab, Web, and specify what text you want displayed while your WordArt text is being loaded.

Changing Shapes

The WordArt Gallery contains a variety of predesigned WordArt options. Formatting is already applied to these gallery choices. You can, however, customize the gallery choices with buttons on the WordArt toolbar. Use options from the WordArt Shape button to customize the shape of WordArt text. Click the WordArt Shape button on the WordArt toolbar and a palette of shape choices displays as shown in figure 8.10.

WordArt
Shape

FIGURE

8.10 **WordArt Shape Palette**

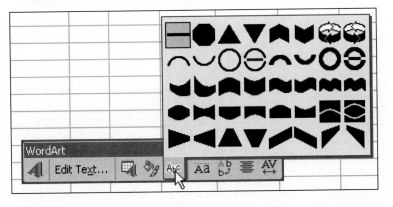

With the choices at the WordArt Shape palette, you can conform text to a variety of shapes. To select a shape, click the desired shape, and the WordArt text will conform to the selected shape. If you want to return text to the default shape, click the first shape in the first row.

exercise 6

1. Open Excel Worksheet 28.
2. Save the worksheet with Save As and name it CExl C08 Ex06.
3. Make the following changes to the worksheet:
   a. Insert a row at the beginning of the worksheet.
   b. Change the height of row 1 (the new row) to 90.00.
   c. Select cells A1 through H1 and then click the Merge and Center button.
   d. Insert a formula in cell H4 that averages the amounts in B4 through G4.
   e. Copy the formula in cell H4 down to cells H5 through H9.
4. Insert WordArt in the row 1, as shown in figure 8.11, by completing the following steps:
   a. Click Insert, point to Picture, and then click WordArt.
   b. In the Select a WordArt style section, double-click the first option from the left in the top row.
   c. At the Edit WordArt Text dialog box, key **Cascade Manufacturing**.
   d. Click the OK button.
   e. Change the shape of the WordArt text by clicking the WordArt Shape button on the WordArt toolbar and then clicking the first option from the left in the fourth row (Inflate).

   f. Change the size and color of the WordArt text by completing the following steps:
      1) Click the Format WordArt button on the WordArt toolbar.
      2) At the Format WordArt dialog box, click the Size tab.
      3) Select the current measurement in the Height text box and then key **1.4**.
      4) Select the current measurement in the Width text box and then key **6.8**.
      5) Click the Colors and Lines tab.
      6) At the Format WordArt dialog box with the Colors and Lines tab selected, click the down-pointing triangle at the right side of the Color option (in the Fill section) and then click the Tan color (second color from the left in the fifth row).
      7) Click OK to close the dialog box.

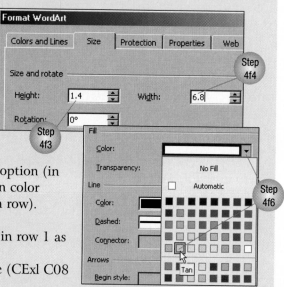

   g. Drag the WordArt text so it is positioned in row 1 as shown in figure 8.11.
5. Save the worksheet again with the same name (CExl C08 Ex06).
6. Print the worksheet in landscape orientation, horizontally and vertically centered on the page.
7. Close CExl C08 Ex06.

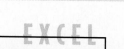

8.11 *Exercise 6*

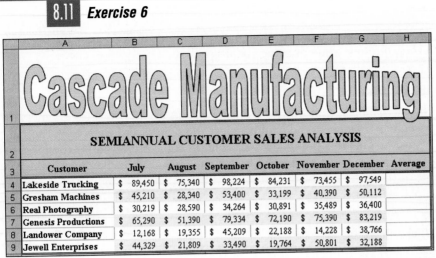

Customer	July	August	September	October	November	December	Average
Lakeside Trucking	$ 89,450	$ 75,340	$ 98,224	$ 84,231	$ 73,455	$ 97,549	
Gresham Machines	$ 45,210	$ 28,340	$ 53,400	$ 33,199	$ 40,390	$ 50,112	
Real Photography	$ 30,219	$ 28,590	$ 34,264	$ 30,891	$ 35,489	$ 36,400	
Genesis Productions	$ 65,290	$ 51,390	$ 79,334	$ 72,190	$ 75,390	$ 83,219	
Landower Company	$ 12,168	$ 19,355	$ 45,209	$ 22,188	$ 14,228	$ 38,766	
Jewell Enterprises	$ 44,329	$ 21,809	$ 33,490	$ 19,764	$ 50,801	$ 32,188	

Drawing Shapes, Lines, and Autoshapes

With buttons on the Drawing toolbar, you can draw a variety of shapes such as circles, squares, rectangles, ovals, straight lines, free-form lines, lines with arrowheads, and much more. To display the Drawing toolbar, shown in figure 8.12, click the Drawing button on the Standard toolbar.

Drawing

8.12 *Drawing Toolbar*

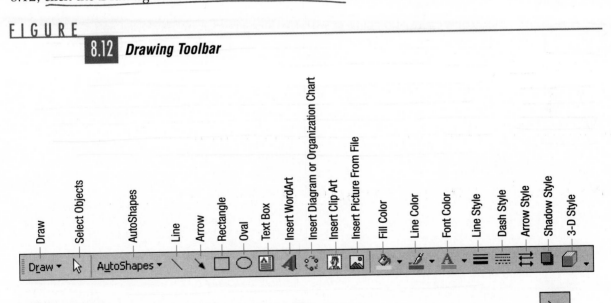

Drawing Shapes

With some of the buttons on the Drawing toolbar, you can draw a shape. If you draw a shape with the Line button or the Arrow button, the shape you draw is considered a *line drawing*. If you draw a shape with the Rectangle or Oval button, the shape you draw is considered an *enclosed object*. If you want to draw the same shape more than once, double-click the shape button on the Drawing toolbar. After drawing the shapes, click the button again to deactivate it.

Line

Arrow

Rectangle

Oval

Fill Color

Use the Rectangle button on the Drawing toolbar to draw a square or rectangle in a workbook. If you want to draw a square, hold down the Shift key while drawing the shape. The Shift key keeps all sides of the drawn object equal. Use the Oval button to draw a circle or an oval object. To draw a circle, hold down the Shift key while drawing the object.

Adding Fill Color

Use the Fill Color button on the Drawing toolbar to add color to an enclosed object such as a shape. To add color, select the object, and then click the Fill Color button. This fills the object with the fill color displayed on the Fill Color button. To choose a different color, select the object, click the down-pointing triangle at the right side of the Fill Color button, and then click the desired color at the palette that displays.

Line Color

Changing Line Color

Change the color of the line around a shape or a line drawn with the Arrow button with the Line Color button on the Drawing toolbar. To change the color, click the object, and then click the Line Color button. The line color of the selected object changes to the color displayed on the button. To change to a different color, click the down-pointing triangle at the right side of the button, and then click the desired color at the color palette.

Draw

Aligning Objects

Select Objects

Distribute and align objects with the Draw button on the Drawing toolbar. To align and distribute objects, select the objects, click the Draw button on the Drawing toolbar, and then point to Align or Distribute. Choose the desired alignment and distribution option from the side menu that displays.

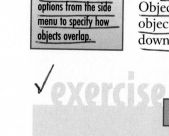

HINT
If objects overlap, click the Draw button, point to Order, and then use options from the side menu to specify how objects overlap.

To identify the objects you want to align and/or distribute, click the Select Objects button on the Drawing toolbar and then draw a border around the objects. Another method for selecting objects is to click the first object, hold down the Shift key, and then click any other objects you want aligned.

✓ exercise 7

DRAWING, CUSTOMIZING, AND COPYING CIRCLES

1. Open Excel Worksheet 38.
2. Save the worksheet with Save As and name it CExl C08 Ex07.
3. Click the Drawing button on the Standard toolbar to turn on the display of the Drawing toolbar. (The Drawing toolbar displays toward the bottom of the screen, above the Status bar.)
4. Draw a circle in cell A1 and then format the circle by completing the following steps:
   a. With cell A1 the active cell, click the Oval button on the Drawing toolbar.
   b. Hold down the Shift key and then use the mouse to draw a circle the approximate size of the circle shown in figure 8.13. After drawing the circle, release the mouse button.

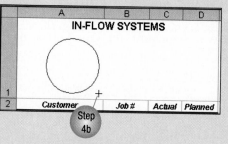

c. With the circle selected (small, white circles [sizing handles] display around the circle), click the down-pointing triangle at the right side of the Fill Color button on the Drawing toolbar, and then click the Blue color (sixth color from the left in the second row).

d. Click the down-pointing triangle at the right side of the Line Color button and then click the Black color (first color from the left in the top row).

e. Click the Line Style button and then click *2¼ pt* at the palette that displays.

5. With the circle selected, copy the circle three times by completing the following steps:

a. Position the mouse pointer on the circle and hold down the Ctrl key.

b. Hold down the left mouse button, drag to the right (refer to figure 8.13), and then release the mouse button.

c. With the Ctrl key down, drag the second circle to the right (refer to figure 8.13), and then release the mouse button.

d. With the Ctrl key down, drag the third circle to the right (refer to figure 8.13), and then release the mouse button.

6. Align and distribute the four circles by completing the following steps:

a. Click the Select Objects button on the Drawing toolbar.

b. Using the mouse, draw a box around the four circles. (When you release the mouse button, white sizing handles display around each of the circles.)

c. Click the Draw button on the Drawing toolbar, point to Align or Distribute, and then click Distribute Horizontally.

d. With the circles still selected, click the Draw button, point to Align or Distribute, and then click Align Bottom.

e. With the circles still selected, drag the circles so they are positioned in cell A1 as shown in figure 8.13.

7. Save the worksheet with the same name (CExl C08 Ex07).

8. Print the worksheet horizontally and vertically centered on the page.

9. Close CExl C08 Ex07.

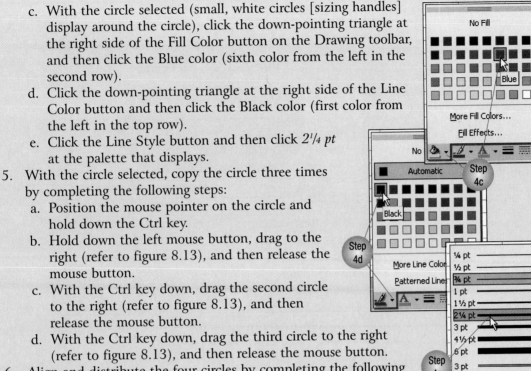

FIGURE

8.13 Exercise 7

	A	B	C	D
1	**IN-FLOW SYSTEMS**			
2	*Customer*	*Job #*	*Actual*	*Planned*
3	Sellar Corporation	$2,130.00	$30,349	$34,109
4	Main Street Photos	1,201.00	$48,290	$48,100
5	Sunset Automotive	318.00	$34,192	$32,885
6	Linstrom Enterprises	1,009.00	$63,293	$61,220
7	Morcos Media	676.00	$29,400	$30,500
8	Green Valley Optics	2,117.00	$55,309	$58,394
9	Detailed Designs	983.00	$12,398	$13,100
10	Arrowstar Company	786.00	$87,534	$86,905

Drawing Lines

To draw a line in a worksheet, click the Line button on the Drawing toolbar. Position the crosshairs where you want to begin the line, hold down the left mouse button, drag the line to the location where you want the line to end, and then release the mouse button. Customize a line by changing the line color, line style, or by applying an arrow style.

exercise 8

DRAWING AND CUSTOMIZING LINES

1. Open Excel Worksheet 10.
2. Save the worksheet with Save As and name it CExl C08 Ex08.
3. Delete column D (contains the heading *Bonus*).
4. Click in cell E1, turn on bold, key **Top Sales**, and then press Enter.
5. Click in cell A8.
6. Draw and customize two lines as shown in figure 8.14 by completing the following steps:
   a. Click the Arrow button on the Drawing toolbar.
   b. Position the crosshairs at the left side of the text *Top Sales* (located in cell E1).
   c. Hold down the left mouse button, drag down and to the left until the crosshairs are positioned near the contents of cell C4 (refer to figure 8.14), and then release the mouse button.

	C	D	E
	Actual Sales		**Top Sales**
	$ 103,295.00		
	$ 129,890.00		
	$ 133,255.00		
	$ 94,350.00		
	$ 167,410.00		
	$ 109,980.00	Step 6c	

d. With the line selected, click the down-pointing triangle at the right side of the Line Color button, and then click the Red color (first color from the left in the third row).

e. Click the Arrow button on the Drawing toolbar and then draw another arrow as shown in figure 8.14.

f. With the second arrow selected, click the Line Color button. (This changes the line to red since that was the last color selected.)

7. Save, print, and then close CExl C08 Ex08.

Step 6d

FIGURE

8.14 *Exercise 8*

	A	B	C	D	E	F
1	**Salesperson**	**Quota**	**Actual Sales**		**Top Sales**	
2	Allejandro	$ 95,500.00	$ 103,295.00			
3	Crispin	$ 137,000.00	$ 129,890.00			
4	Frankel	$ 124,000.00	$ 133,255.00			
5	Hiesmann	$ 85,500.00	$ 94,350.00			
6	Jarvis	$ 159,000.00	$ 167,410.00			
7	Littleman	$ 110,500.00	$ 109,980.00			
8						

Creating Autoshapes

Draw a variety of shapes with options from the AutoShapes button. Click the AutoShapes button, point to the desired menu option, and then click the desired shape. When you choose an autoshape, the mouse pointer turns into crosshairs. Position the crosshairs in the workbook, hold down the left mouse button, drag to create the shape, and then release the button.

AutoShapes ▼

AutoShapes

HINT

Choose an autoshape and then click in the worksheet and Excel will insert a standard-sized autoshape object.

Flipping and Rotating an Object

A selected object, such as a shape or line, can be rotated and flipped horizontally or vertically. To rotate or flip an object, select the object, click the Draw button on the Drawing toolbar, point to Rotate or Flip, and then click the desired rotation or flip option at the side menu that displays.

HINT

Display the AutoShapes toolbar by clicking Insert, pointing to Picture, and then clicking AutoShapes.

exercise 9

1. Open Excel Worksheet 23.
2. Save the worksheet with Save As and name it CExl C08 Ex09.
3. Increase the height of row 2 to 60.00.
4. Insert the autoshapes in cell B2 (refer to figure 8.15) by completing the following steps:
   a. Click the AutoShapes button on the Drawing toolbar, point to Block Arrows, and then click Striped Right Arrow (first shape from the left in the fifth row).
   b. Position the crosshairs at the left side of the text *Overdue Accounts*, hold down the Shift key, and then draw an arrow approximately the size of the arrow in figure 8.15.
   c. With the arrow selected, click the down-pointing triangle at the right side of the Fill Color button, and then click the light turquoise color (fifth color from the left in the bottom row).
   d. With the arrow selected, hold down the Ctrl key, drag the arrow to the right of the text *Overdue Accounts*, then release the mouse button and then the Ctrl key.
   e. Flip the arrow by clicking the Draw button, pointing to Rotate or Flip, and then clicking Flip Horizontal.
5. Save, print, and then close CExl C08 Ex09.

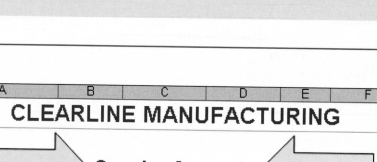

FIGURE

8.15 **Exercise 9**

	A	B	C	D	E	F
1	CLEARLINE MANUFACTURING					
2	Overdue Accounts					
3						
4	Customer	Account #	Amount Due	Purchase Date	Terms	Due Date
5	Archway Systems	9005	$ 5,250.00		30	
6	KM Construction	5042	$ 10,275.00		15	
7	Lowell-Briggs	6078	$ 3,920.00		15	
8	Everwear Products	7553	$ 20,775.00		30	

CHAPTER summary

➤ Save a workbook as a Web page by opening the workbook, clicking File, and then clicking Save as Web Page. Key the name of the Web page in the Save As dialog box and then click Save.

➤ To preview a workbook in your default Web browser, click File and then click Web Page Preview.

➤ To create a hyperlink in a workbook, select the text to which you want to attach the hyperlink, click the Insert Hyperlink button on the Standard toolbar, and then key the file name or Web site URL in the Address text box.

➤ To modify or edit a hyperlink, right-click the hyperlink and then click Edit Hyperlink at the shortcut menu.

➤ Insert an image in a workbook with options at the Insert Clip Art Task Pane.

➤ With options at the Insert Clip Art Task Pane, you can narrow the search for images to specific locations and to specific images.

➤ Size an image using the sizing handles that display around a selected image and move a selected image by dragging the image to the desired location using the mouse.

➤ Delete a selected image by pressing the Delete key.

➤ Format a clip art image with buttons on the Picture toolbar.

➤ If you are connected to the Internet, you can download images from the Microsoft Design Gallery Live Web site.

➤ Use WordArt to create, distort, modify, and/or conform text to a variety of shapes.

➤ The WordArt Gallery contains a variety of predesigned WordArt.

➤ Size WordArt using the sizing handles that display around selected WordArt text and move selected WordArt by dragging it to the desired location using the mouse.

➤ Customize WordArt text with buttons on the WordArt toolbar and/or with options at the Format WordArt dialog box.

➤ Customize the shape of WordArt text by clicking the WordArt Shape button on the WordArt toolbar and then clicking the desired shape at the palette that displays.

➤ Use buttons on the Drawing toolbar to draw and customize shapes, lines, and autoshapes.

➤ Display the Drawing toolbar by clicking the Drawing button on the Standard toolbar.

➤ Use options from the Draw button on the Drawing toolbar to align, distribute, rotate and/or flip selected objects.

COMMANDS review

Command	Mouse/Keyboard
Save a workbook as a Web page	File, Save as Web Page
Preview a workbook in Web Page Preview	File, Web Page Preview
Create a hyperlink	Select text, click Insert Hyperlink button; or click Insert, Hyperlink
Display Insert Clip Art Task Pane	Insert, Picture, Clip Art; or click Insert Clip Art button on Drawing toolbar
Display Microsoft Design Gallery Live Web site	Click the *Clips Online* hyperlink in the Insert Clip Art Task Pane
Display WordArt Gallery	Insert, Picture, WordArt; or click Insert WordArt button on Drawing or WordArt toolbar
Display Format WordArt dialog box	Click Format WordArt button on WordArt toolbar
Display Drawing toolbar	Click Drawing button on Standard toolbar

CONCEPTS check

Completion: On a blank sheet of paper, indicate the correct term, symbol, or command for each item.

1. If you want to view a workbook in a Web browser, save the workbook as this. *~~Microsoft~~ Web Page*
2. This term refers to text or an object you click to go to a different file or HTML page on the Internet. *hyperlink*
3. Insert an image in a workbook with options at this task pane. *Insert Clip Art*
4. Select a clip art image in a workbook and these display around the image. *white sizing handles*
5. Use buttons on this toolbar to format a selected image. *Picture*
6. Use this application to distort or modify text to conform to a variety of shapes. *WordArt*
7. Click this button on the WordArt toolbar to display a palette of shape options. *WordArt Shape*
8. Customize WordArt text with options at this dialog box. *Format WordArt*
9. To draw a circle, click the Oval button on the Drawing toolbar, hold down this key, and then use the mouse to draw the circle. *Shift*
10. Distribute and align objects with this button on the Drawing toolbar. *Draw - align & Distribute*
11. Draw a variety of shapes with options from this button on the Drawing toolbar. *Auto Shapes*
12. Write the steps you would complete to insert a clip art image related to summer in a workbook.

Position insertion point - Insert - Picture - ClipArt - @ ClipArt TaskPane, type Summer in the Search for: text box (& put a ✓ mark only in ClipArt in the Results should be :) — find one you like - double-click on image

EXCEL

SKILLS check

✓Assessment 1

1. Display the Open dialog box with *Chapter 08C* the active folder.
2. Open Excel Worksheet 39.
3. Save the workbook as a Web page in the *Excel Web Pages* folder on your disk (you created this folder in exercise 1) and name it Books Galore Web Page.
4. Preview the Web page in the default browser.
5. Close the browser application window.
6. Print Books Galore Web Page in landscape orientation.
7. Close Books Galore Web Page.

✓Assessment 2

1. Open Books Galore Web Page.
2. Select E12 and hyperlink it to www.microsoft.com.
3. Select E13 and hyperlink it to www.symantec.com.
4. Select E14 and hyperlink it to www.nasa.gov.
5. Select E15 and hyperlink it to www.cnn.com.
6. Make sure you are connected to the Internet and then click the hyperlink to NASA.
7. Jump to a link from the NASA Web page that interests you.
8. Print the page you viewed from NASA and then close the browser application window.
9. Jump to each of the remaining links in the Web page. At each Web page, jump to a link that interests you, print the page, and then close the browser application window.
10. Close Books Galore Web Page.

✓Assessment 3

1. Open Excel Worksheet 20.
2. Save the worksheet with Save As and name it CExl C08 SA03.
3. Make the following changes to the worksheet:
   a. Increase the height of row 1 to 75.00.
   b. Insert the clip art image shown in figure 8.16 (search for this clip art by keying **camera** in the Search text text box). If this clip art image is not available, choose another image related to *camera* or *photography*.
   c. Size and move the clip art image so it is positioned as shown in figure 8.16.
   d. Insert a formula in cell E7 using the PMT function that calculates monthly payments. *(Hint: Refer to chapter 3, exercise 9.)*
   e. Copy the formula in cell E7 down to cells E8 and E9.
   f. Insert a formula in cell F7 that calculates the total amount of the payments. *(Hint: Refer to chapter 3, exercise 9.)*
   g. Copy the formula in cell F7 down to cells F8 and F9.
   h. Insert a formula in cell G7 that calculates to the total amount of interest paid. *(Hint: Refer to chapter 3, exercise 9.)*
   i. Copy the formula in cell G7 down to cells G8 and G9.
4. Save the worksheet and then print the worksheet in landscape orientation.
5. Close CExl C08 SA03.

8.16 Assessment 3

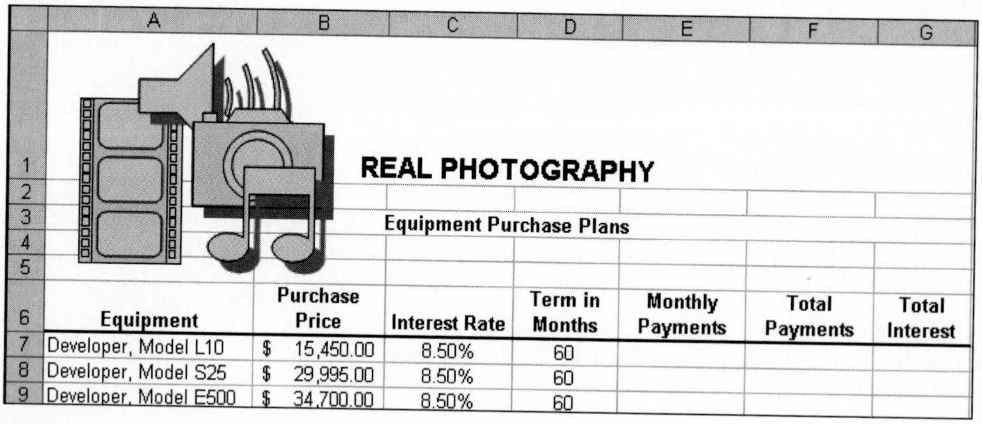

	A	B	C	D	E	F	G
1							
2			**REAL PHOTOGRAPHY**				
3			Equipment Purchase Plans				
4							
5							
6	Equipment	Purchase Price	Interest Rate	Term in Months	Monthly Payments	Total Payments	Total Interest
7	Developer, Model L10	$ 15,450.00	8.50%	60			
8	Developer, Model S25	$ 29,995.00	8.50%	60			
9	Developer, Model E500	$ 34,700.00	8.50%	60			

✓Assessment 4

1. Open Excel Worksheet 34.
2. Save the worksheet with Save As and name it CExl C08 SA04.
3. Make the following changes to the worksheet:
   a. Insert a new row at the beginning of the worksheet.
   b. Select cells A1 through D1 and then click the Merge and Center button.
   c. Increase the height of row 1 to 90.00.
   d. Insert a formula in cell D4 that subtracts the Actual amount from the Budget amount.
   e. Copy the formula in cell D4 down to cells D5 through D10.
   f. Insert the text **EZ Sports** as WordArt in cell A1. You determine the formatting and shape of the WordArt. Move and size the WordArt so it fits in cell A1.
4. Save, print, and then close CExl C08 SA04.

✓Assessment 5

1. Open Excel Worksheet 33.
2. Save the worksheet with Save As and name it CExl C08 SA05.
3. Make sure Sheet1 is the active tab. (This workbook contains three worksheets.)
4. Make the following changes to the worksheet:
   a. Insert a new row at the beginning of the worksheet.
   b. Select cells A1 through D1 and then click the Merge and Center button.
   c. Increase the height of row 1 to 75.00.
   d. In cell A1, key **Mountain**, press Alt + Enter, and then key **Systems**.
   e. Select *Mountain Systems* and then change the font to 18-point Arial bold.
   f. Change the horizontal alignment to left and the vertical alignment to center.
   g. Click outside cell A1.
   h. Use the Isosceles Triangle shape (to find it click AutoShapes, point to Basic Shapes, and then click Isosceles Triangle) to draw a triangle as shown in figure 8.17.
   i. Copy the triangle three times, add fill to the triangles, and position the triangles as shown in figure 8.17.
5. Save, print, and then close CExl C08 SA05.

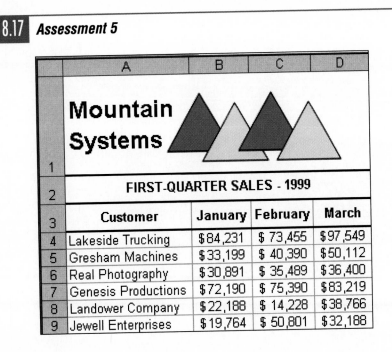

✓Assessment 6

1. Microsoft Excel contains a background feature that you can apply to a worksheet. Use the Help feature to learn how to apply a background to a worksheet. (A background does not print and is generally used for worksheets that are viewed in a Web browser.)
2. Open Global Web Page. (You created this Web page in exercise 1.)
3. Insert a sheet background of your choosing. If necessary, consider changing the font color to make the data in cells visible.
4. View Global Web Page in Web Page Preview.
5. Close your browser and then close Global Web Page.

WORKPLACE Ready

Maintaining and Enhancing Workbooks

ASSESSING proficiency

In this unit, you have learned how to work with multiple windows; move, copy, link and paste data between workbooks and applications; create and customize charts with data in a worksheet; save a workbook as a Web page; insert hyperlinks; and insert and customize clip art images, WordArt, and drawn objects.

(Note: Before completing computer exercises, delete the Excel Chapter 08C folder on your disk. Next, copy to your disk the Excel Unit 02C subfolder from the Excel 2002 Core folder on the CD that accompanies this textbook.)

✓ Assessment 1

1. Open Excel Worksheet 19.
2. Save the worksheet with Save As and name it CExl U02 PA01.
3. Make the following changes to the worksheet:
   a. Key **Ave.** in cell D2.
   b. Apply the same top and bottom border to cell D2 that is applied to cells A2 through C2.
   c. Merge and center cells A1 through D1.
   d. Delete row 14 (the row for Kwieciak, Kathleen).
   e. Insert a formula in cell D3 that averages the percentages in cells B3 and C3.
   f. Copy the formula in cell D3 down to cells D4 through D19.
   g. Make cell A21 active, turn on bold, and then key **Highest Averages**.
   h. Display the Clipboard Task Pane. (Make sure the Clipboard Task Pane is empty.)
   i. Select and then copy each of the following rows (individually): row 6, 9, 13, 15, and 17.
   j. Make cell A22 active and then paste row 13 (the row for Jewett, Troy).
   k. Make cell A23 active and then paste row 6 (the row for Cumpston, Kurt).
   l. Make cell A24 active and then paste row 9 (the row for Fisher-Edwards, Teri).
   m. Make cell A25 active and then paste row 15 (the row for Markovits, Claude).

n. Make cell A26 active and then paste row 17 (the row for Nyegaard, Curtis).

o. Click the Clear All button in the Clipboard Task Pane and then close the task pane.

4. Save, print, and then close CExl U02 PA01.

✓Assessment 2

1. Open Excel Worksheet 17.
2. Save the worksheet with Save As and name it CExl U02 PA02.
3. Complete the following steps:
   a. Select cells A1 through C11 and then copy the cells to *Sheet2*.
   b. With *Sheet2* displayed, make the following changes:
      1) Automatically adjust the width of columns A, B, and C.
      2) Delete the contents of cell B2.
      3) Change the contents of the following cells:
         A6: Change *January* to *July*
         A7: Change *February* to *August*
         A8: Change *March* to *September*
         A9: Change *April* to *October*
         A10: Change *May* to *November*
         A11: Change *June* to *December*
         B6: Change *8.30%* to *8.10%*
         B8: Change *9.30%* to *8.70%*
   c. Make *Sheet1* active and then copy cell B2 and paste link it to cell B2 in *Sheet2*.
   d. Make *Sheet1* active and then determine the effect on projected monthly earnings if the projected yearly income is increased by 10% by changing the number in cell B2 to *$1,480,380*.
4. Save the workbook (two worksheets) again and then print both worksheets of the workbook so they are horizontally and vertically centered on each page.
5. Determine the effect on projected monthly earnings if the projected yearly income is increased by 20% by changing the number in cell B2 to *$1,614,960*.
6. Save the workbook again and then print both worksheets of the workbook so they are horizontally and vertically centered on each page.
7. Close CExl U02 PA02.

✓Assessment 3

1. Open Excel Worksheet 41.
2. Save the workbook with Save As and name it CExl U02 PA03.
3. Make the following changes to the workbook:
   a. Insert the heading **Average Sales 2000-2002** (on multiple lines) in cell A13.
   b. Insert a formula in cell B13 with a 3-D reference that averages the total in cells B4 through B11 in *Sheet1*, *Sheet2*, and *Sheet3*.
   c. Make cell B13 active and then change to the Currency Style with zero decimal places.

d. Insert a formula in cell C13 with a 3-D reference that averages the total in cells C4 through C11 in *Sheet1*, *Sheet2*, and *Sheet3*.

e. Make cell C13 active and then change to the Currency Style with zero decimal places.

4. Rename *Sheet1* to *2000 Sales*, rename *Sheet2* to *2001 Sales*, and rename *Sheet3* to *2002 Sales*.

5. Save the workbook and then print the entire workbook.

6. Close CExl U02 PA03.

✓Assessment 4

1. Open Excel and then key the following information in a worksheet:

Country	Total Sales
Denmark	$85,345
Finland	$71,450
Norway	$135,230
Sweden	$118,895

2. Using the data just entered in the worksheet, create a column chart as a separate sheet.

3. Save the workbook (worksheet plus chart sheet) and name it CExl U02 PA04.

4. Print only the sheet containing the chart.

5. Change the column chart to a line chart of your choosing.

6. Save the worksheet (and chart) again with the same name (CExl U02 PA04).

7. Print only the sheet containing the chart.

8. Close CExl U02 PA04.

✓Assessment 5

1. Open Excel Worksheet 42.

2. Save the worksheet with Save As and name it CExl U02 PA05.

3. Create a pie chart as a separate sheet with the data in cells A3 through B10. You determine the type of pie. Include an appropriate title for the chart and include percentage labels.

4. Save the worksheet and chart with the same name (CExl U02 PA05).

5. Print only the sheet containing the chart.

6. Close CExl U02 PA05

✓Assessment 6

1. Create a new folder named *Travel Web Pages* in the Excel Unit 02C folder on your disk.

2. Open Excel Worksheet 40.

3. Save the worksheet as a Web page in the *Travel Web Pages* folder and name it Travel Advantage Web Page.

4. Preview the Web page in the default browser.

5. Make sure you are connected to the Internet and then search for sites that might be of interest to tourists for each of the cities in the Travel Advantage Web Page. Write down the URL for the best Web page you find for each city.

(handwritten notes in right margin)
assuming Maine
↓ -freeportusa.com
Freeport
Miami - destinations/location
www.flausa.com/ .php/location =ca-mi
Honolulu.com
aruba - visitaruba.com

6. Create a hyperlink in Travel Advantage Web page for each city to jump to the URL you wrote down in step 5.
7. Test the hyperlinks to make sure you entered the URLs correctly by clicking each hyperlink and then closing the Web browser.
8. Save, print, and then close Travel Advantage Web Page.

✓Assessment 7

1. Open Excel Worksheet 14.
2. Save the worksheet with Save As and name it CExl U02 PA07.
3. Make the following changes to the worksheet:
   a. Insert a formula in cell C3 using an absolute reference to determine the projected quotas at 10% of the current quotas.
   b. Copy the formula in cell C3 down to cells C4 through C12.
   c. Increase the height of row 1 (you determine the height) and then insert a clip art image in row 1 related to *money*. You determine the size and position of the clip art image.
4. Save, print, and then close CExl U02 PA07.

✓ Assessment 8

1. Open Excel Worksheet 33.
2. Save the worksheet with Save As and name it CExl U02 PA08.
3. Select and then delete the sheet tabs Sheet1 and Sheet2. At the message telling you that data may exist in the sheets selected for deletion, click the Delete button.
4. Make the following changes to the worksheet:
   a. Insert a new row at the beginning of the worksheet.
   b. Select and then merge cells A1 through D1.
   c. Increase the height of row 1 to approximately 100.00.
   d. Insert the text **Custom Interiors** as WordArt in cell A1. You determine the formatting and shape of the WordArt. Move and size the WordArt so it fits in cell A1.
   e. Insert the following comments in the specified cells:
      D4 = **Decrease amount to $100,000.**
      A5 = **Change the name to Gresham Technology.**
      A9 = **Decrease amounts for this company by 5%.**
5. Turn on the display of all comments.
6. Print the worksheet with the comments as displayed on the worksheet.
7. Turn off the display of all comments.
8. Delete the comment in A5.
9. Print the worksheet again with the comments printed at the end of the worksheet. (The comments will print on a separate page from the worksheet.)
10. Save and then close CExl U02 PA08.

✓Assessment 9

1. Open Excel Worksheet 03.
2. Save the worksheet with Save As and name it CExl U02 PA09.
3. Make the following changes to the worksheet so it displays as shown in figure U2.1:

EXCEL

a. Insert a new row at the beginning of the worksheet.
b. Select and then merge cells A1 through D1.
c. Select cells A2 through D9 and then apply the List 2 autoformat.
d. Select cells B4 through D9 and then click the Percent Style button.
e. Increase the height of row 1 to the approximate size shown in figure U2.1.
f. Insert the text **Solar Enterprises** in cell A1 set in 18-point Arial bold and center aligned.
g. Insert and fill the shapes using the AutoShapes button on the Drawing toolbar. (To find the Sun shape, click AutoShapes, point to Basic Shapes, and then click Sun.)

4. Save, print, and then close CExl U02 PA09.

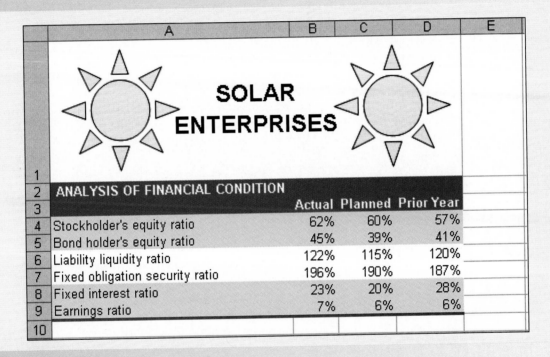

Figure U2.1 • Assessment 9

WRITING activities

The following activities give you the opportunity to practice your writing skills along with demonstrating an understanding of some of the important Excel features you have mastered in this unit. Use correct grammar, appropriate word choices, and clear sentence constructions.

Activity 1

Suppose that you are the accounting assistant in the financial department of McCormack Funds and you have been asked to prepare a yearly proposed department budget. The total amount for the department is $1,450,000. You are given the percentages for the proposed budget items, which are: Salaries, 45%; Benefits, 12%; Training, 14%; Administrative Costs, 10%; Equipment, 11%; and Supplies,

8%. Create a worksheet with this information that shows the projected yearly budget, the budget items in the department, the percentage of the budget, and the amount for each item. After the worksheet is completed, save it and name it CExl U01 Act01. Print and then close CExl U01 Act01.

Activity 2

Prepare a worksheet in Excel for Carefree Travels that includes the following information:

Scandinavian Tours

Country	Tours Booked
Norway	52
Sweden	62
Finland	29
Denmark	38

Use the information in the worksheet to create a bar chart as a separate worksheet. Save the workbook (worksheet and chart) and name it CExl U02 Act02. Print only the sheet containing the chart and then close CExl U02 Act02.

Activity 3

Prepare a worksheet for Carefree Travels that advertises a snow skiing trip. Include the following information in the announcement:

- At the beginning of the worksheet, create a company logo that includes the company name *Carefree Travels* and a clip art image related to travel.
- Include the heading *Whistler Ski Vacation Package* in the worksheet.
- Include the following below the heading:
  - Round-trip air transportation: $395
  - Seven nights' hotel accommodations: $1,550
  - Four all-day ski passes: $425
  - Compact rental car with unlimited mileage: $250
  - Total price of the ski package: (calculate the total price)

- Include the following information somewhere in the worksheet:
  - Book your vacation today at special discount prices
  - Two-for-one discount at many of the local ski resorts

Save the completed worksheet and name it CExl U02 Act03. Print and then close CExl U02 Act03.

INTERNET project

Make sure you are connected to the Internet. Locate two companies on the Internet that sell new books. At the first new book company site, locate three books on Microsoft Excel. Record the title, author, and price for each book. At the second new book company site, locate the same three books and record the prices. Create an Excel worksheet that includes the following information:

- Name of each new book company
- Title and author of the three books
- Prices for each book from the two book company sites

Create a hyperlink for each book company to the URL on the Internet. Then save the completed worksheet and name it CExl U02 Internet Act. Print and then close CExl U02 Internet Act.

JOB study

Create an invoice form in Excel for the customers of your lawn business from the Unit 1 Job Study. Design a logo that will go at the top left corner using the drawing tools. Use borders and shading to separate out various sections. You can use the Invoice template found within Excel as a sample. Save your template file as LAWN TEMPLATE. Print one copy. Be sure to copy your template file to the Microsoft template files folder found on your computer's hard drive. Print out a picture of the directory containing your new LAWN TEMPLATE fileand the other Excel templates.

Open the file LAWN BUSINESS you created in the Unit 1 Job Study and create three different chart types for the expenses section and three different chart types for the income section. You determine the options for each chart. Print each chart on a separate worksheet tab. Rename the worksheet tabs accordingly. You will incorporate these six charts into a presentation about your expansion project for the following year that you will give to a potential lender. Save your file as LAWN CHARTS.

INDEX

A

Absolute cell reference, 82–84
Accounting category, Format Cells dialog box, 42
Active cell, 6
Active workbook, 144–145
Adaptive menu, 8
Add interactivity checkbox, 220
Additions (+), 65
Add to Print Area command, 103
Advanced Search hyperlink, 174
Advanced Search Task Pane, 174
Alignment
    cell data, 43–46
    horizontal, 44
    vertical, 45
    WordArt, 233
Alignment tab, Format Cells dialog box, 44–46
Alignment tab, Format Chart Title dialog box, 211
Answer Wizard tab, Help window, 20
Argument
    definition, 70
    entering, 71
    Function Arguments palette, 71–72
    multiple, 71
Arrange Windows dialog box
    Cascade option, 146, 147
    Horizontal option, 146
    Tiled option, 145–146
    Vertical option, 146
AutoComplete feature, 12
AutoCorrect dialog box, 12–13, 220
AutoFill feature, 14–15
AutoFill fill handle, 66–67
AutoFilter feature, 115–117
AutoFormat As You Type tab, 220
AutoFormat feature, 17–18
AutoSum button, 63–64
AVERAGE function, 72–74

B

Before sheet list box, 170
Borders
    adding at Format Cells dialog box, 53–54
    adding with Borders button, 51–52
    color, 53, 54
    erasing, 51
    style, 53, 54
Borders toolbar
    display of, 52
    Erase button, 51
    Line Style button, 52
Brightness, 226

C

Cascaded workbooks, 146–147
Cell
    active, 6, 7, 10
    address, 6
    chart, changing data in, 203–204
    clearing data in, 50, 51
    copying selected, 135
    deleting, 50, 51
    editing data in, 10–11
    entering data in, 6–7
    formatting borders, 51–54, 55
    clearing, 50, 51
    finding and replacing, 110–112
    pattern, 53, 54, 56
    shading, 54–55, 56
    with styles, 175–181
    formatting data in, 39–47
    alignment, 43–46
    font, 46–47
    indentation, 43–45
    numbers, 39–43
    rotating, 45–46
    merging, 45
    moving selected, 134
    pointer, 7
    printing specific, 105
    range, 143–144

selecting data within cells, 17
    with keyboard, 17
    with mouse, 16–17
Cell reference, 6
    absolute, 82–84
    in formulas, 65–66, 82–85
    mixed, 82, 84–85
    relative, 65–66
Centering a worksheet, 97, 100
Chart, 193–215
    adding elements, 206–207
    creating, 193–199
    data in cells, changing, 203–204
    data series, changing, 204–205
    deleting, 199
    element color, 213–214
    elements, deleting/removing, 208, 209
    elements, moving, 208
    elements, sizing, 208
    formatting elements, 210–214
    gridlines, adding, 209–210
    legend, 204, 206, 207, 211
    moving, 199
    previewing, 196, 197–198
    sizing, 199–200
    title, adding, 207
    title, formatting, 211–212
    type, 200–203
    updating, automatic, 203
Chart Location dialog box, 194, 196, 198
    As new sheet option, 198
Chart Options dialog box, 193, 195, 206–207, 209–210
Chart Sources Data dialog box, 193, 195, 204–206
Chart Type dialog box, 193, 194, 201–203
    changing Chart type in, 201–202
Chart Wizard, 193
    Chart Location, 194, 196, 198
Choose Format From Cell option, 110
Clear command, 183
Clear Find Format option, 110
Clearing
    cell data, 50, 51
    cell formatting, 50, 51
Clear Print Area command, 103
Clear Replace Format option, 111
Clip Art, 223–228
Clipboard Task Pane, 136, 137
Clips Online hyperlink, 228
Close All command, 145, 169
    Close button, 8
    Borders toolbar, 52
    Print Preview toolbar, 30
    workbook window, 147
Closing
    workbooks, 8, 169
    worksheets, multiple, 145
Collate check box, 105
Color
    border, 53, 54
    chart element, 213–214
    fill, 54, 213–214, 236
    font, changing, 33
    line, 236
    WordArt, 233
Column
    boundary, 33–35
    deleting, 50, 51
    heading, printing, 102
    hiding and unhiding, 103
    inserting, 49
    labeling in worksheet, 5
    selecting with keyboard, 17
    selecting with mouse, 16
    sorting data in, 112–115
    title, printing, 100–101
    width
        changing with column boundaries, 33–35
        changing with Column width dialog box, 35–36

Column Width dialog box, 35–36
Comma (,), 39, 40
Comment
    deleting, 182, 183
    displaying, 181–182, 183
    editing, 182, 183
    inserting, 181, 182
    printing, 182, 183
Conditional function, 80
Confirm File Move dialog box, 168
Confirm Folder Delete dialog box, 169
Constant
    definition, 70
    entering, 71
Contents tab, Help window, 20
Contrast, 226
Copying
    cells, selected, 135
    data between applications, 152–153
    between workbooks, 148, 149, 150
    files, 165–167
    formula with fill handle, 66–67
    with relative cell references, 65–66
    styles to another workbook, 179, 180
    workbooks, 165–167
    worksheet, 139
    worksheet to another workbook, 170–171
COUNT function, 72, 75–76
Create a copy check box, 170
Currency category, Format Cells dialog box, 42
Custom category, Format Cells dialog box, 42
Customize dialog box, 3, 8
Custom Types tab, Chart Type dialog box, 202–203
Cutting data
    Cut button, 134
    keyboard command, 134
    workbooks, 167–168

D

Data menu
    Filter, 115
    Sort, 113
Data series, 204–205
Date category, Format Cells dialog box, 42
DATE function, 78–79
Date insertion, shortcut for, 76
Decrease Decimal button, 40
Decrease Indent button, 43, 44
Default file location text box, 9
Default folder, changing, 9
Degrees text box, 45
Delete dialog box, 50, 51
Delete option, Sheet tab, 139
Deleting
    cells, rows, or columns, 50, 51
    chart elements, 208, 209
    charts, 199
    comments, 183, 184
    folder, 164, 169
    images, 225
    to Recycle Bin, 165
    styles, 180
    workbooks, 164–165
    worksheets, selected, 139–140
Designing worksheet, 118–119
Divisions (/), 65
Docking, Task Pane, 15
Dollar sign ($), 39, 40, 82
Downloading images, 228
Draw Borders option, 52
Drawing
    lines, 238–239
    shapes, 235–236
Drawing toolbar, 223, 229, 235, 238
Drop-down menus, expanding, 8
Dynamic link, 149

E

Edit Hyperlink dialog box, 222

Editing
    cell data, 10–11
    comments, 183, 184
    hyperlink, 222, 223
Edit mode, 10
Edit WordArt Text dialog box, 229–230
Enter button, Formula bar, 10, 11, 64
Enter mode, 6
Equals (=) sign, 65
Excel icon, 8
Exiting Excel, 8
Exponentiations (^), 65
Extend mode, 17

F

File names, 7
Files of type option, Open dialog box, 164
Fill handle
    AutoFill, 14–15
    copying formulas, 66–67
Filtering lists, 115–117
Financial functions
    FV, 78
    PMT, 76–77
    writing formulas with, 76–78
Find and Replace dialog box, 108–112
    displaying, 108, 109
    expanded, 110–111
Find and Replace feature, 108–112
Find Format dialog box, 110–111
Find tab, Find and Replace dialog box, 108, 109
Fit to option, 92
Flipping an object, 239
Folder
    copying workbooks into, 167
    creating, 162–163
    cutting and pasting workbooks in, 167–168
    deleting, 164, 169
    sending workbooks to different, 167
Font button, Formatting toolbar, 32, 46
Font Color button
    Drawing toolbar, 235
    Formatting toolbar, 33
Font Size button, Formatting toolbar, 32, 46
Format Chart Legend dialog box, 211
Format Chart Title dialog box, 211
Footer
    deleting, 95
    inserting, 95
Footer dialog box, 93–94
Footer text box, 95
Format Axis dialog box, 211
Format button, Find and Replace dialog box, 110, 111
Format Cells dialog box
    Alignment tab, 44–46
    Borders tab, 53–54, 55
    displaying, 41
    Font tab, 46–47
    Number tab, 41–43
    Patterns tab, 53, 54–55, 56
    style application from, 176–179
Format Chart Area dialog box
    displaying, 210
    Patterns tab, 210–211
Format Chart Title dialog box, 211, 212
Format Legend dialog box, 211
Format Painter button, 46, 56–57
Format Picture dialog box, 226, 227, 228
Format symbol, 39
Formatting
    applying
        with Formatting toolbar buttons, 30–31
    with AutoFormat, 17–18
    borders, adding, 51–54, 55
    cell data, 39–47

alignment, 43–46
clearing, 50, 51
font, 46–47
indentation, 43–45
numbers, 39–43
rotating, 45–46
chart elements, 210–214
clearing, 50, 51
column width, 33–36
deleting cells, rows, and columns, 50, 51
font, 32, 46–47
font color, 33
with Format Painter, 46, 56–57
images, 226–227
inserting cells, rows, and columns, 48–49
patterns, 53, 54–55, 56
repeating last action, 55, 56
row height, 37–39
shading, 54–55, 56
Formatting toolbar, 4
alignment buttons, 43–44
Border button, 51–52
buttons, 30–31
Comma Style button, 176
Currency Style button, 176
display of, 4
Fill Color button, 54, 213–214
indentation buttons, 43–44
number formatting buttons on, 39–41
Percent Style button, 176
position of, 3
Formatting worksheet page, 91–104
centering, 97, 100
finding and replacing formatting, 110–112
headers/footers, 95–96
hiding and unhiding elements, 103
margins, 96–97
page breaks, 98–100
page layout, 92–95
page numbering, 93–95
printing column and row titles on multiple pages, 100–101
printing gridlines, 102
printing row and column headings, 102
printing specific areas, 103
print quality, changing, 103
Format WordArt dialog box, 232–234
Formula
AutoSum button and, 64
cell references
absolute, 82–84
mixed, 82, 84–85
relative, 65–66
copy
with fill handle, 66–67
with relative cell references, 65–66
display of common, 72
functions
date and time, 78–79
financial, 76–78
If, 80–82
Insert Function button, 70–72
statistical, 72–76
inserting, 63–86
with Insert Function button, 70–72
order of operations, 65
revising, 80
Trace Error button and, 68–70
writing
with functions, 72–82
with mathematical operators, 65
by pointing, 67–68, 69
Formula bar, 4
buttons, 10–11
Cancel button, 10, 11
display of formula in, 63
Enter button, 10, 11
entering formula into, 64
error editing, 68
Insert Function button, 70
Name box, 6
Fraction category, Format Cells dialog box, 42
Freeze panes command, 141, 142

Function
arguments, 70, 71
conditional, 80
definition, 70
nested, 70
range use in, 143–144
Function Arguments palette, 71–72
Future value of payment, finding, 78
FV function, 78

G
General tab, Options dialog box, 9–10
General Templates hyperlink, 185, 186
Go To dialog box, 103
displaying, 6
Reference text box, 6
Gridlines, 6
adding to chart, 209–210
printing, 102
Gridlines tab, Chart Options dialog box, 209–210

H
Header
deleting, 95
inserting, 95
Header/Footer, Page Setup dialog box, 93–96
Headings, printing row and column, 102
Help feature
Ask a Question button, 19
Help window
Answer Wizard tab, 20
buttons, 19–20
Contents tab, 20
displaying, 19
Expanded, 20–21
Index tab, 20–21
Office Assistant, 22
options, 20–21
Hide All (hyperlink), 21
Hide All Comments button, 183
Hide command, 103
Hide Comment button, 182
Hide the Office Assistant command, 22
Hiding workbook elements, 103
Horizontal alignment, 44
Horizontally option, Page Setup dialog box, 97
Horizontal option, Arrange Windows dialog box, 146
Horizontal page break, 98
HTML (Hypertext Markup Language), 219
Hyperlink
automatic formatting, 220
creating, 220–223
editing, 222, 223

I
IF function
logical test, 80
nested, 81–82
Images
deleting, 225
downloading, 228
formatting, 226–227
inserting, 223–224, 225
moving, 225
sizing, 225, 226
Increase Decimal button, 40
Increase Indent button, 43, 44
Index tab, Help window, 20–21
Insert Clip Art Task Pane, 223–224, 225, 228
Insert Diagram or Organization Chart button, Drawing toolbar, 235
Insert dialog box, 48–49
Insert Function dialog box, 70–71
Insert Hyperlink dialog box, 220–223
Inserting
columns, 49
formula, 63–86
images, 223–224, 225
page break, 98–100
rows, 48–49
WordArt, 229, 230
Insertion point
cell address display and, 6

moving, commands for, 6
Insert Picture dialog box, 226

K
Keyboard, selecting cells with the, 17

L
Landscape orientation, 92, 94
Layout, page, 92–95
Legend, 204, 206, 207
Lines, drawing, 238–239
Linking
data between worksheets, 149–150
worksheets with a 3-D reference, 151
Loans, finding periodic payments for, 76–77
Logical test, 80
Look in option box, 9

M
Managing worksheets, 139–140
Margins, changing worksheet, 96–97
Margins tab, Page Setup dialog box, 96–97
Match case option, 109
Match entire cell contents check box, 109
Mathematical operators, 65
MAX function, 72, 74–75
Media Gallery, 224
Menu bar, 4
Ask a Question button, 19
Excel icon, 8
Merge cells option, 45
Merge Styles dialog box, 179
Microsoft Design Gallery Live Web site, 228
Microsoft Excel Help. See Help feature
Microsoft Office, 152, 223
MIN function, 72, 74–75
Mixed cell reference, 82, 84–85
Mouse
column width, changing, 33
selecting with, 16–17
Move or Copy dialog box, 139, 140, 170–172
To book list, 170, 171
Before sheet list, 170
Moving
cells, selected, 134
chart elements, 208
charts, 199
data between workbooks, 148–153
images, 225
WordArt, 230, 231
worksheets, 139, 171–172
worksheet to another workbook, 171–172
Multiplications (*), 65

N
Name box, 4, 6
Name text, Print dialog box, 104
Naming a range of cells, 143
Nested functions, 70
New Folder dialog box, 162–163
New Workbook Task Pane, 185, 186
NOW function, 78–79
Number category, Format Cells dialog box, 42
Number of copies option, 105
Numbers
counting in a range, 75–76
default settings, 39
formatting, 39–43
Format Cells dialog box, 41–43
with format symbols, 39
Formatting toolbar buttons, 39–41
page numbering, 93–95
statistical functions, 72–76
Number symbols (###), 7
Number tab, Format Cells dialog box, 41–43

O
Office Assistant, 22
Office Clipboard, 136–137
Open dialog box, 7, 144, 169
copying a workbook at, 166–167

cutting and pasting a workbook at, 167–168
displaying, 161
Files of type option, 164
Look in option box, 9
Open button, 169
Print option, 170
Rename option, 168
selecting workbooks in, 163–164
toolbar buttons, 162–183
Opening
Excel, 3
workbooks, 7, 144, 169
Options dialog box, General tab, 9–10
Options tab, 3, 8
Order of operations, 65
Orientation of cell data, 45–46
Orientation section, Page Setup dialog box, 92

P
Page break, 98–100
displaying, 98, 99
inserting, 98–100
moving, 99
removing, 98
Page Break Preview, 98, 99, 100
Page numbering, 93–95
Page Setup dialog box, 30, 91
centering options, 97
Comments option box, 182
displaying, 92
Header/Footer tab, 93–96
Margins tab, 96–97
orientation, 91, 92, 94
Page tab, 92–95
print quality options, 103
scaling, 92
Sheet tab, 100–102, 182
Paper size drop-down menu, 92
Paste command, Edit menu, 134, 135
Paste Link button, 149, 150
Paste Special dialog box
displaying, 149
As list box, 153
Pasting data
between applications, 152–153
between workbooks, 148–150
with keyboard command, 134
from Office Clipboard, 136–137
Patterns tab
Format Cells dialog box, 53, 54–55
Format Chart Area dialog box, 210–211
Format Chart Legend dialog box, 211
Format Chart Title dialog box, 211
Percentage category, Format Cells dialog box, 42
Percent sign (%), 39, 40, 65
Periodic payment for a loan, 76–77
Picture toolbar, 226–227
Placement tab, Format Chart Legend dialog box, 211
Planning a worksheet, 118–119
Plus sign, white, 7
PMT function, 76–77
Pointing, creating a formula by, 67–68, 69
Point mode, 67
Portrait orientation, 91, 92
Position tab, Format WordArt dialog box, 233
PowerPoint, 233
Previewing
charts, 196, 197–198
Web page, 220, 221
workbook in Web Page Preview, 220
worksheet, 29–30, 32, 33
Print Area feature, 103
Print dialog box, 8
Active sheets option, 104
Copies section, 105
displaying, 104
Name text box, 104
Preview button, 29, 105
Print range section, 105
Print what section, 104, 138, 197

Printer, display of currently selected, 104
Printing
  cells in a worksheet, specific, 105
  chart only, 197
  collating copies, 105
  column and row titles on multiple pages, 100–101
  comments, 182, 183
  customizing print jobs, 104–105
  gridlines, 102
  headings, row and column, 102
  number of copies, 105
  from Open dialog box, 170
  range, 105
  specific area of a worksheet, 103
  workbooks, 8, 170
  with multiple worksheets, 138–139
Print Preview, 29–30
  page break display, 98
  Setup button, 92
Print Preview toolbar, 30
Print quality, changing, 103
Print quality text box, 92–93
Print what section, 138, 197
Pyramid chart, 201

R
Radar chart, 201
Range of cells, 143–144
Ready mode, 6, 10
Recycle Bin, 165
Relative cell reference, 65–66
Remove Page Break command, 98
Rename option
  Open dialog box, 168
  Sheet tab, 139
Renaming
  workbooks, 168–169
  worksheets, 139, 172–173
Repeat command, 55, 56
Replace tab, Find and Replace dialog box, 108, 109
Replace with text box, 108
Restore button, workbook window, 147
Results should be option, 174, 224
Returning the result, 70
Reviewing toolbar, 181–184
Rotating
  an image, 225, 227
  an object, 239
  cell data, 44, 45–46
Row
  boundary, 37–38
  deleting, 50, 51
  filtering lists, 115
  heading, printing, 102
  height
  changing with row boundaries, 37–38
  changing with Row Height dialog box, 38–39
  hiding and unhiding, 103
  inserting, 48–49
  labeling in worksheet, 5
  selecting with keyboard, 17
  selecting with mouse, 16
  title, printing, 100–101
Row Height dialog box, 38–39

S
Save As command, 161
Save As dialog box, 7
  Add interactivity checkbox, 220
  displaying, 161
  File name text box, 219
Save as type option, 173
  Up One Level button, 165, 166
Save As dialog box, 165, 166
  Standard toolbar, 7
Save in option, 7
Saving workbooks, 7
  in a different format, 173–174
  as Web pages, 219–220
Scientific category, Format Cells dialog box, 42
Scroll bars, 5, 7
Search for a function option, Insert Function dialog box, 71

Searching
  for clip art, 224
  workbooks, 174–175
Search in option, 174, 224
Search option, Find and Replace dialog box, 109
Search Results Task Pane, 174
Search text text box, 224
Select a function list box, Insert Function dialog box, 71
Select All Sheets option, 139
Selecting
  cells
  with keyboard, 17
  with mouse, 16–17
  workbooks, 163–164
Sending workbooks to different drive or folder, 167
Send To option, 167
Set Print Area command, 103
Shading, adding to cell, 54, 56
Sheets in new workbook option, 137
Sheet tab, Page Setup dialog box, 100–102
Sheet tabs, 5
Show All (hyperlink), 21
Show All Comments button, 181, 183
Show Picture Toolbar, 226
Show Standard and Formatting toolbars on two rows option, 3
Show the Office Assistant command, 22
Shrink to fit option, 45
Sizing
  chart elements, 208
  charts, 199–200
  images, 225, 226
  WordArt, 230–231
  workbooks, 147–148
Smart tag button, 68
Sort dialog box, 113–115
Sorting data
  columns, multiple, 114–115
  at Sort dialog box, 113–114
  with Standard toolbar buttons, 112–113
Source Data dialog box, 204–205
Special category, Format Cells dialog box, 42
Spell checking feature, 106, 107
Spelling dialog box, 106
Split bars, 140–141
Split option, Window menu, 140, 142
Splitting a worksheet into windows, 140–142
Spreadsheet Solutions tab, Templates dialog box, 185, 186
Standard toolbar, 4, 32, 33
  AutoSum button, 64
  Chart Wizard button, 193
  Copy button, 135, 136, 138, 148, 149, 150
  Cut button, 134
  display of, 4
  Drawing button, 223, 235
  Format Painter button, 46, 56–57
  Help button, 19
  Insert Hyperlink button, 220, 221
  Open button, 7, 144
  Paste button, 134, 135, 148
  position of, 3
  Print button, 8
  Print Preview button, 29, 33, 197, 198
  Redo button, 106
  Save button, 7
  Search button, 174, 175
  Sort Ascending button, 112–113
  Sort Descending button, 112–113
  Spelling button, 106, 107
  Undo button, 106
  Zoom button, 30, 32
Statistical functions
  AVERAGE, 72–74
  COUNT, 72, 75–76
  MAX, 72, 74–75
  MIN, 72, 74–75
  writing formulas with, 72–76
Status bar, 5
Point mode, 67

Ready/Enter mode display, 6, 10
Stock chart, 201
Storage of workbooks, 162–163
Style dialog box
  applying a style from, 177, 178–179
  Delete button, 180
  Merge button, 179, 180
  removing a style at, 179
Style name text box, 176, 177, 179, 180
Styles
  advantages of use, 175
  applying, 177–179
  copying to another workbook, 179, 180
  defining, 176, 177
  deleting, 180
  formatting with, 175–181
  removing, 179
Subfolder, 162
Subtractions (-), 65
Suggestions list box, 106
SUM function, 64, 70, 72
Symbols in file names, 7

T
Tab key for insertion point movement, 6
Task Pane, 5
  displaying, 15
  docking/undocking, 15
  maneuvering in, 15
Templates, 185–187
  data entry, 185–186
  sales invoice, 186–187
Templates dialog box, 185
Text category, Format Cells dialog box, 42
Thick Bottom Border option, 52
3-D reference, 151
Tiled workbooks, 145–146
Time category, Format Cells dialog box, 42
Time functions, 78–79
Title bar, 4
Titles, printing column and row, 100–101
Titles tab, Chart Options dialog box, 207
To book list box, 170, 171
Toolbar
  arrangement of, 3
  display of, 4
Tools menu
  AutoCorrect Options, 12, 220
  Customize, 3
  Options, 9
  Spelling, 106
Top 10 AutoFilter dialog box, 115–117
Trace Error button, 68–70
Typographical errors, correcting with AutoCorrect, 12–13

U
Unfreeze panes command, 141, 142
Unhide command, 103
Untile button, 19
Up One Level button
  Open dialog box, 162, 163, 165, 166
  Save As dialog box, 165, 166
Use the Office Assistant check box, 22

V
Vertical alignment, 45
Vertically option, Page Setup dialog box, 97
Vertical option, Arrange Windows dialog box, 146
Vertical page break, 98
View menu
  Comments, 181
  Normal, 99
  Page Break Preview, 99, 100
  Task Pane, 15
  Toolbars, 4, 181

W
Web Discussions feature, 183, 184
Web page
  hyperlink, creating, 220–223
  previewing, 220, 221
  saving a workbook as, 219–220
  static versus dynamic, 220
Windows
  arranging, 145–147
  freezing and unfreezing panes, 141–142
  splitting worksheet into, 140–142
Within option, 109
WordArt, 228–235
Word document, copying and pasting a worksheet into, 152–153
Workbook
  active, 144–145
  arranging, 145–147
  closing multiple, 145, 169
  copying, 165–167
  cutting and pasting, 167–168
  definition, 5
  deleting, 164–165
  formatting with styles, 175–181
  hiding and unhiding elements, 103
  images in, 223–228
  maintaining, 161–175
  with multiple worksheets, creating, 137–142
  opening, 7, 169
  opening multiple, 144–145
  printing, 8, 170
  renaming, 168–169
  saving, 7
  saving in different formats, 173–174
  searching for specific, 174–175
  selecting, 163–164
  sending to another drive or folder, 167
  sizing, 147–148
  storage of, 162–163
  as Web page, 219–223
Worksheet
  copying, 139
  to another workbook, 170–171
  between applications, 152–153
  deleting, 139–140
  elements of, 4–5
  insertion point movement, commands for, 6
  managing multiple, 139–140
  moving, 139, 171–172
  multiple, creating workbook with, 137–142
  planning, 118–119
  previewing, 29–30, 32, 33
  renaming, 139, 172–173
  splitting into windows, 140–142
Worksheet area, 5
Wrap text option, 45

X
.xls extension, 173
XY (Scatter) chart, 201

Z
Zoom button, 30, 32, 198